Treebanks

Text, Speech and Language Technology

VOLUME 20

The titles published in this series are listed at the end of this volume.

Treebanks

Building and Using Parsed Corpora

Edited by

Anne Abeillé
Universite Paris 7, Paris, France

KLUWER ACADEMIC PUBLISHERS
DORDRECHT / BOSTON / LONDON

A C.I.P. Catalogue record for this book is available from the Library of Congress.

ISBN 1-4020-1334-5

Published by Kluwer Academic Publishers,
P.O. Box 17, 3300 AA Dordrecht, The Netherlands.

Sold and distributed in North, Central and South America
by Kluwer Academic Publishers,
101 Philip Drive, Norwell, MA 02061, U.S.A.

In all other countries, sold and distributed
by Kluwer Academic Publishers,
P.O. Box 322, 3300 AH Dordrecht, The Netherlands.

Printed on acid-free paper

Printed in the Netherlands

Contents

Preface xi

Introduction xiii
Anne Abeillé
1 Building Treebanks xv
2 Using treebanks xix

Part I **Building treebanks**

ENGLISH TREEBANKS

Chapter 1
THE PENN TREEBANK: AN OVERVIEW 5
Ann Taylor, Mitchell Marcus, Beatrice Santorini
1 The annotation schemes 6
2 Methodology 16
3 Conclusions 20

Chapter 2
THOUGHTS ON TWO DECADES OF DRAWING TREES 23
Geoffrey Sampson
1 Historical background 23
2 Building treebanks 26
3 Exploiting the SUSANNE Treebank 29
4 Small is beautiful 33
5 Annotating a spoken corpus 35
6 Using the CHRISTINE Corpus 38
7 Conclusion 40

Chapter 3
BANK OF ENGLISH AND BEYOND 43
Timo Järvinen
1 Introduction 43
2 Annotating 200 million words 44
3 ENGCG Syntax 52
4 FDG parser 54
5 Conclusion 56

Chapter 4

COMPLETING PARSED CORPORA FROM CORRECTION TO EVOLUTION 61

Sean Wallis

1 Introduction 61
2 Conventional post-correction 63
3 A paradigm shift: transverse correction 65
4 Critique 68

GERMAN TREEBANKS

Chapter 5

SYNTACTIC ANNOTATION OF A GERMAN NEWSPAPER CORPUS 73

Thorsten Brants, Wojciech Skut, Hans Uszkoreit

1 Introduction 73
2 Treebank development 74
3 Corpus annotation 77
4 Applications 83
5 Conclusions 83
Appendix: Tagsets 87

Chapter 6

ANNOTATION OF ERROR TYPES FOR A GERMAN NEWSGROUP CORPUS 89

Markus Becker, Andrew Bredenkamp, Berthold Crysmann, Judith Klein

1 Introduction 89
2 Corpus Description 90
3 Annotation Strategy 91
4 Annotation Tools 93
5 Evaluation 96
6 First Results 98
7 Conclusion 99

SLAVIC TREEBANKS

Chapter 7

THE PDT: A 3-LEVEL ANNOTATION SCENARIO 103

Alena Böhmová, Jan Hajič, Eva Hajičová, Barbora Hladká

1 The Prague Dependency Treebank 103
2 Morphological Level 104
3 Analytical Level 106
4 Merging the Morphological and the Analytical Syntactic Level 114
5 Tectogrammatical Level 114
6 PDT versions 1.0 and 2.0 121
7 Conclusion 122
Appendix 126

Chapter 8

AN HPSG-ANNOTATED TEST SUITE FOR POLISH 129

Małgorzata Marciniak, Agnieszka Mykowiecka, Adam Przepiórkowski, Anna Kupść

1 Aims and design constraints 129
2 Correctness and complexity markers 130
3 Linguistic phenomena 131
4 Annotation schema 136
5 Implementation issues 137
6 Conclusion 143

TREEBANKS FOR ROMANCE LANGUAGES

Chapter 9

DEVELOPING A SPANISH TREEBANK 149

Antonio Moreno, Susana López, Fernando Sánchez, Ralph Grishman

1 Introduction 149
2 Data selection 150
3 Annotation scheme 151
4 Tools 157
5 Debugging and error statistics 158
6 Current state and future development 159
Appendix: Sample of trees 163

Chapter 10

BUILDING A TREEBANK FOR FRENCH 165

Anne Abeillé, Lionel Clément, Francois Toussenel

1 The tagging phase 166
2 The parsing phase 173
3 Current state and future work 180
4 Conclusion 181
Appendix 185

Chapter 11

BUILDING THE ITALIAN SYNTACTIC-SEMANTIC TREEBANK 189

Simonetta Montemagni, Francesco Barsotti, Marco Battista, Nicoletta Calzolari, Ornella Corazzari, Alessandro Lenci, Antonio Zampolli, Francesca Fanciulli, Maria Massetani, Remo Raffaelli, Roberto Basili, Maria Teresa Pazienza, Dario Saracino, Fabio Zanzotto, Nadia Mana, Fabio Pianesi, Rodolfo Delmonte

1 Introduction 190
2 ISST architecture 190
3 ISST corpus 191
4 ISST morpho-syntactic annotation 191
5 ISST syntactic annotation 192
6 ISST lexico-semantic annotation 196
7 The multi-level linguistic annotation tool 200
8 ISST evaluation 204
9 Conclusion 206
Appendix 209

Chapter 12

AUTOMATED CREATION OF A MEDIEVAL PORTUGUESE TREEBANK 211

Vitor Rocio, Mário Amado Alves, J. Gabriel Lopes, Maria Francisca Xavier, Gracia Vicente

1 Introduction 211
2 The parsed corpus of medieval portuguese texts 212
3 Tools and computational resources 215
4 Evaluation 222
5 Conclusion 224

TREEBANKS FOR OTHER LANGUAGES

Chapter 13

SINICA TREEBANK 231

Keh-Jiann Chen, Chi-Ching Luo, Ming-Chung Chang, Feng-Yi Chen, Chao-Jan Chen, Chu-Ren Huang, Zhao-Ming Gao

1 Introduction 231
2 Design criteria 232
3 Representation of lexico-grammatical information: ICG 233
4 Annotation guideline 235
5 Implementation 239
6 Representational issues: problematic cases and how they are solved 241
7 Current status of the sinica treebank and future work 243
Appendix: Syntactic Categories 248

Chapter 14

BUILDING A JAPANESE PARSED CORPUS 249

Sadao Kurohashi, Makoto Nagao

1 Introduction 249
2 Overview of the project 250
3 Morphological analyzer JUMAN 253
4 Dependency structure analyzer KNP 255
5 Conclusion 259

Chapter 15

BUILDING A TURKISH TREEBANK 261

Kemal Oflazer, Bilge Say, Dilek Zeynep Hakkani-Tür, Gökhan Tür

1 Turkish: Morphology and syntax 262
2 What information needs to be represented? 263
3 The annotation tool 270
4 Some difficult issues 272
5 Conclusions and future work 273
Appendix: Turkish Morphological Features 276

Part II **Using treebanks**

Chapter 16
ENCODING SYNTACTIC ANNOTATION 281
Nancy Ide, Laurent Romary
1 Introduction 281
2 XCES 283
3 Syntactic annotation: current practice 284
4 A model for syntactic annotation 286
5 Using the XCES scheme 291
6 Conclusion 293

EVALUATION WITH TREEBANKS

Chapter 17
PARSER EVALUATION 299
John Carroll, Guido Minnen, Ted Briscoe
1 Introduction 299
2 Grammatical relation annotation 302
3 Corpus annotation 308
4 Parser evaluation 309
5 Discussion 312
6 Summary 313

Chapter 18
DEPENDENCY-BASED EVALUATION OF MINIPAR 317
Dekang Lin
1 Introduction 317
2 Dependency-based parser evaluation 318
3 Evaluation of minipar with susanne corpus 320
4 Selective evaluation 323
5 Related work 326
6 Conclusions 328

GRAMMAR INDUCTION WITH TREEBANKS

Chapter 19
EXTRACTING STOCHASTIC GRAMMARS FROM TREEBANKS 333
Rens Bod
1 Introduction 333
2 Summary of data-oriented parsing 335
3 Simulating stochastic grammars by constraining the subtree set 337
4 Discussion and conclusion 344

Chapter 20

STOCHASTIC LEXICALIZED TREE GRAMMARS 351

Günter Neumann

1 Introduction 351
2 Related work 352
3 Grammar extraction 353
4 SLTG from treebanks 355
5 SLTG from HPSG 359
6 Future steps: towards merging SLTGs 362

Chapter 21

FROM TREEBANK RESOURCES TO LFG F-STRUCTURES 367

Anette Frank, Louisa Sadler, Josef van Genabith, Andy Way

1 Introduction 368
2 Methods for automatic f-structure annotation 370
3 Two Experiments 380
4 Discussion and Current Research 383
5 Summary 385

Appendix: Example of an Automatically Generated F-Structure (Susanne Corpus) 389

Contributing Authors 391

Index 398

Preface

The papers in this volume are either original or based on presentations at several workshops and conferences (LINC, LREC, EACL), in particular the ATALA workshop on treebanks (Paris, 1999). The papers have been greatly reworked, and I thank the authors for rewriting their own, and reviewing each other's papers. I also thank three anonymous Kluwer reviewers, as well as the series editors Nancy Ide and Jean Véronis for their helpful contribution.

The introduction is meant to give a brief overview on the work being done on parsed corpora (or treebanks) and is by no means an exhaustive state of the art. This field is moving very fast and one can only hope to point out basic motivation and methodology, as well as the results and open problems, common to the different projects presented.

I want to thank Nicolas Barrier for postediting, indexing and formatting, as well as Jesse Tseng for help with proofreading. I also thank University Paris 7 for material help support.

ANNE ABEILLE

Introduction

Anne Abeillé

It is now quite easy to have access to large corpora for both written and spoken language. Corpora have become popular resources for linguists and engineers developing applications in Natural Language Processing (NLP). Linguists typically look for various occurrences of specific words or patterns, engineers extract lexicons and language models (associating probabilities with sequences of words). This kind of research is not new but has produced new results with the availability of larger and larger corpora in electronic form, and with the growing memory of computers which can now easily handle texts of several million words.

Nethertheless, as observed for example by (Manning 2002), corpus-based linguistics has been largely limited to phenomena that can be accessed via searches on particular words. Inquiries about subject inversion or agentless passives are impossible to perform on commonly available corpora.

More generally, corpus-based research has faced two (related) kinds of problems:

- Results are necessarily limited as long as they are dealing with corpora with no linguistic annotations. Such corpora may have some metalinguistic annotations such as paragraph boundaries or italics but lack linguistic information such as parts of speech or clause boundaries. As ambiguity is pervasive in natural languages, most computations on such corpora are biased. To take just one example, from French, it is difficult to count how many words the following contains, or how many occurrences of the word "le" ?

  Paul ouvre le sac de pommes de terre et le pose sur la table.
  "Paul opens the bag of potatoes and puts it on the table"

  In this sentence, "pommes de terre" is in fact a compound word (meaning potato, literarily 'apple of earth') although no typographical sign sets

A. Abeillé (ed.), Treebanks: Building and Using Parsed Corpora, xiii–xxvi.

it apart from other word sequences. So the sentence has 12 words and not 14. In this sentence, the form "le" which occurs twice, corresponds in fact to two distinct words: the definite determiner (before the Noun "sac") and the accusative pronoun (before the Verb "pose"). So if one looks for other contexts of the same word, one must know whether one wants the determiner or the pronoun. This is why some linguistic annotations are needed, in order to make searches and computations more precise.

- Automatic tools for annotating corpora exist for many languages, but make mistakes. One could, in principle, run some automatic part of speech tagger or lemmatizer on a given corpus, and take the resulting annotation into account before searching it, but the quality of the resulting corpus is not guaranteed and the annotation choices are usually not documented (the parser designer may not have foreseen a lot of cases encountered in corpora). The quality of the search will be highly dependent on the particular choice of a particular tagger.

This is why people started to develop, in the late sixties, linguistically annotated corpora, to improve searches and computations. The idea is that these annotations are devised by experienced linguists or grammarians, fully documented for the end user, and fully checked to prevent remaining errors (introduced by a human annotator or by a machine). These constitute linguistically annotated reference corpora.

The first to be built were for English (the IBM/Lancaster treebank or the British National Corpus) and they have helped the development of both English NPL tools and English corpus linguistics. They emerged as the result of a convergence between computational linguistics and corpus linguistics. Computational linguists, once grammatical formalisms and parsing algorithms had been successfully developed, became aware that real texts usually contain lots of peculiarities overlooked in usual grammar books. Corpus linguists have always tended to emphasize minute descriptions of a given language over general theorizing.

A linguistically annotated reference corpus allows one to build (or improve) sizable linguistic resources (such as lexicons or grammars) and also to evaluate (or improve) most computational analyzers. One usually distinguishes tagged corpora (associating each token with a part of speech, and some morphological information) and parsed corpora (or treebanks) which provide, in addition to the category for each word, some of the following information:

- constituent boundaries (clause, NP...),
- grammatical function of words or constituents,

- dependencies between words or constituents.

This book gathers 21 papers on building and using such parsed corpora, raising among others the following questions:

- how does one choose the corpus to be annotated ?
- how does one choose the kind of annotation to be added ?
- is annotation best done manually or automatically ? with which tools ? with which formats ?
- how can one search such annotated corpora ?
- what kind of knowledge can be extracted (learned) out of them ? how is it better than extracting (or learning) from unannotated sources ?
- how can they be used to evaluate current NLP tools such as parsers or grammar checkers ?

The papers presented here deal with a variety of languages (Chinese, Czech, English, French, German, Italian, Japanese, Polish, Portuguese, Spanish, Turkish)[1]. The objective of this book is not to present a recipe for building your own treebank or using an existing one, but, in a more general perspective, to present an overview of the work being done in this area, the results achieved and the open questions. Unsurprisingly, many independent projects face some of the same issues, regarding corpus annotation or resource extraction.

1. BUILDING TREEBANKS

The main issues facing treebank designers are corpus choice, annotation choice, and annotation tools.

1.1 Motivation

The creation of syntactically annotated corpora started about thirty years ago, for English, with mostly manual methods. The goal then was to provide the most complete annotation scheme possible, on empirical grounds, and to test it on a small corpus (just large enough to train statistical annotation programs). The goal was to advocate linguistic empiricism against the linguistic theories of the time (cf Sampson, this volume).

In contrast, with the development of more mature linguistic models, the objective of some treebanks nowadays is to apply a given linguistic theory, such as a specific kind of dependency grammar for the Prague project (Bohmova et al. this volume), or HPSG for the Polish project (Marciniak et al. this volume).

But the most common goal, as naïve as it may seem, is to provide a new resource, not committed towards a particular linguistic theory, and convertible into different linguistic models.

Some projects also have a precise application in mind: The Bank of English (Järvinen this volume) was built to extract an enriched kind of dictionary (with observed constructions associated with the words). Other projects aim at training automatic tools or evaluating them, and this may affect their annotation choices (cf Becker et al. this volume). Corpora for evaluation allow for some remaining ambiguities but no errors, while the opposite may be true with corpora for training: the former may associate several plausible analyses with the same sentence, whereas the latter will try to always choose only one.

1.2 Corpus choice

The choice of the corpus depends on the objective. In most of the cases here, it consists of contemporary newspapers texts (Bohmova et al., Moreno, Lopez, Brants et al., Abeillé et al., Montemagni et al., Chen et al.). Some authors use medieval texts for diachronic studies (Rocio et al.), a sample of representative sentences for grammar evaluation (Marciniak et al.) or a corpus of mail messages for error annotation (Becker et al.). The corpus size can vary from a few hundred sentences (Turkish treebank) to hundreds of millions (Bank of English).

Some are balanced with extracts from different types of texts (literary, scientific etc), while others are not. As noted by Manning (2002), newspapers constitute in this respect a pseudo-genre, with texts from different domains, often written in different styles. Some projects now involve the syntactic annotation of speech corpora, such as the Christine Project mentioned by G. Sampson (this volume), or the Switchboard corpus mentioned by Taylor et al. (this volume) as a follow-up of the Penn treebank project. They involve transcription as their first annotation phase.

1.3 Annotation choice

The choice of annotation depends both on the availability of syntactic studies for a given language (formalized or not, theory oriented or not) and on the objective. Carroll et al. (this volume) show how difficult it is to choose a reasonable annotation scheme for parser evaluation, when a variety of parsing outputs have to be matched with the annotated corpus. Several annotation levels are usually distinguished, with morphosyntactic annotations such as parts of speech and syntactic annotations such as constituents or grammatical relations.

An ongoing debate, inspired by discussions in theoretical linguistics, is the choice between constituency and dependency annotation. As is well known, both annotations can be seen as equivalent, as long as each phrase is associated with a lexical head:

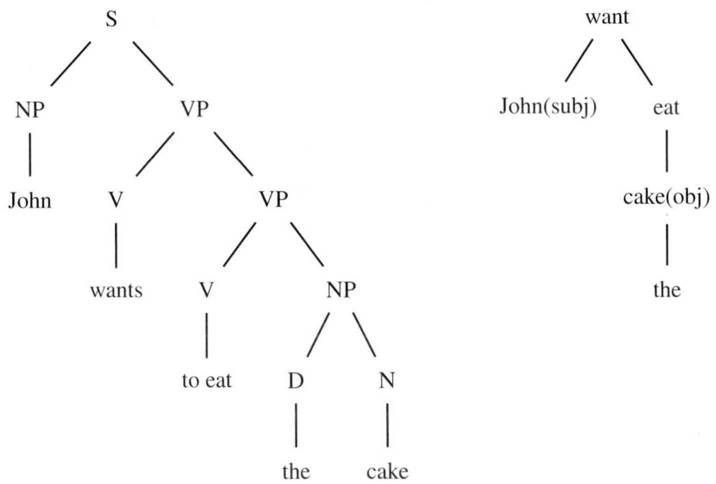

Figure I.1. Constituency and dependency trees for the same sentence

Another debate is between deep and shallow syntactic annotations: some projects limit themselves to overt elements, while others reconstruct empty subjects or elliptical material. In order to account for "deeper" information, in the tree above (figure 1), the complement of want would be an S with an empty subject coindexed with John; in the second tree, a link between John and eat would be added.

Both types of annotations have their advantages and their drawbacks: constituents are easy to read and correspond to common grammatical knowledge (for major phrases) but they may introduce arbitrary complexity (with more attachment nodes than needed and numerous unary phrases). Dependency links are more flexible and also correspond to common knowledge (the grammatical functions) but are less readable (word order is not necessarily preserved) and choosing one word as the head in any group may be arbitrary.

A hybrid solution, chosen by some of the projects, is to maintain some constituents with dependency relations between them (cf Negra corpus, Japanese, Chinese and Turkish treebanks). In this case, the constituents are usually minimal phrases, called chunks, bunsetsu or inflection groups.

Given the state of syntactic knowledge, some annotation choices may be arbitrary. What is most important is consistency (similar cases must be handled similarly) and expliciteness (a detailed documentation must accompany the annotated corpus). As noted by G. Sampson, for the Susanne Corpus, the size of the documentation can be bigger than the corpus itself.

The tagset (the list of symbols used for categories, phrases and functions) can vary from a dozen (Marcus et al. 1993) to several millions (Turkish project), with diverse possibilities in between (medium size for the French or Italian projects), large for the Prague treebank. They partly reflect the richness of the language's morphosyntax (with case or agreement systems yielding numerous features to be encoded).

Problematic cases are often the same across languages. Compounds or idioms are clustered as such (French and Turkish projects) or simply ignored (Penn Treebank, German or Portuguese treebanks). Discontinuities, null elements, and coordination are known to be debated in linguistics, and they are matter of debate for corpus annotation too. More specific to corpora are other problematic cases such as the annotation of titles, quotations, dates, and measure phrases.

1.4 Methodology

Corpus annotation was done entirely by humans in the first projects, for example in Sweden (Jäborg 1986) or for the Susanne corpus (Sampson 1995). It is now usually at least partially automated. Human post-checking is always necessary, be it systematic (as in the Penn Treebank or the Prague dependency treebank) or partial (as in the BNC). Ensuring coherence across several annotators is a crucial matter as pointed out by Wallis (this volume) for the ICE-GB project, or Brants et al. (this volume) for the Negra project.

Purely automatic annotation is only done by Rocio et al., and Jarvinen (this volume). Purely manual annotation is done by Marciniak et al., as a preliminary stage (this was also the case in the first phase of the Prague project).

Most projects involve a phase of automatic annotation followed by a phase of manual correction. Some check all annotation levels at the same time (Chinese treebank, Negra project), others check tagging and parsing information separately (Penn treebank, Prague treebank, French treebank).

Most treebanks presented here involve human validation, but in order to minimize time and cost, some new projects tend to favor merging different outputs of automatic annotation tools, such as tagging with different taggers and checking only the parts with conflicts in the French Multitag project (cf. Adda et al. 1999).

1.5 Annotation tools

Tools for annotation usually include tokenizers (for word boundaries and compounds), taggers (for part of speech annotation) and morphological analyzers, and parsers (for syntactic information).

They must be robust and minimize errors. Some projects prefer to build their own tools, in order to match their annotation choices better (French, Spanish,

Chinese, Turkish or Japanese treebanks). Others prefer to reuse existing ones, and some adaptation is often necessary : ICE-GB treebank reuses TOSCA tools, the Prague treebank reuses M. Collins' statistical parser originally developed for English, the medieval Portuguese treebank reuses a parser (and a grammar) originally developed for modern Portuguese. Some tools are rule-based, others are based on statistics, and sometimes trained on a subset of the corpus to be annotated. Usually, two annotation phases are distinguished, each with its own tool : a tagging phase, only dealing with morphosyntactic ambiguity (and part of speech annotation) and a parsing phase dealing with syntactic ambiguity per se and constituency (or dependency) annotations.

More specific tools are those for the annotators to check and correct the treebank. They are specifically developed in Wallis, Brants et al., Abeillé et al. (this volume). Sometimes, the tools for the annotators are the same as those for searching the annotated corpus.

Most corpora presented here are static resources. A recent line of research is to develop dynamic treebanks, which are parsed corpora distributed with all annotation tools, in order to be enlarged at will by the user (cf. Oepen et al. 2002).

2. Using treebanks

Treebanks allow for mutiple uses, by linguists, psycholinguists or computational linguists. Linguists may search for examples (or counter-examples) for a given theory or hypothesis. With the development of Optimality Theory (cf Dekkers et al. 2001), which relies on ranked and defeasible constraints, corpus-based research is now welcome in generative linguistics (cf Manning 2002)[2]. Psycholinguists are usually interested in computing frequencies, such as low or high attaching relative clauses, and comparing them with human preferences (cf Gibson and Schutze 1999). Sociolinguists, and those working on the history of language, have always worked with corpora and are starting to use treebanks (cf Kroch and Taylor 2000)

For simple linguistic queries, annotated texts enable a reduction of the noise usually associated with answers on raw texts, and also the formulation of new questions. When one is interested in French causatives, it is frustrating to list all the inflected forms of the verb *"faire"* in a simple query, and a lot of the answers are not relevant because they involve the homonymous noun *fait* (which is also part of a lot of compounds *en fait*, *de fait*, *du fait que* etc). Lemmatized tagged texts are thus helpful and, in a treebank, one can add the context of an infinitival verb in the same clause to be more precise.

New questions involve word order and complexity of various types of phrases. (Arnold et al. 2000) for example, have used the Penn treebank to determine which factors favor the non canonical V PP NP order in English.

One can also check psycholinguistic preferences, in the sense that a highly frequent construction can be claimed to be prefered over a less frequent one. For example, Pynte and Colonna (2000) have shown, on experimental reading tests, that given a sequence of two Nouns followed by a relative clause in French, the relative clause tends to attach to the first N if is long and to the second N if it is short. This claim can be easily checked on a treebank, where such a correlation can be measured (cf Abeillé et al. 2002).

Other applications include text classification, word sense disambiguation, multilingual text alignment and indexation. For text categorization, Biber (1988) works with richly annotated texts, and uses criteria such as the relative proportion of adjectives among categories (as a good discriminator for formal vs informal speech), and the relative proportion of pronominal subjects among all subjects (as a discrimator for speech vs written language). Such criteria are duplicated on other languages such as French by Malrieu and Rastier (2001).

For verb sense disambiguation, it is important to know the construction of each occurrence, since it is a good guide for semantic interpretation (can as a modal can be distinguished from can as a transitive verb etc). For automatic sense classification too, parsed texts are being used, for example by (Merlo & Stevenson 2001).

Bilingual text alignment is done automatically at the sentence level with good performance but the results are much poorer at the word level, because translations are not usually word by word and because of the pervasive ambiguity of word forms (homonymous forms etc). A more realistic perspective is to align clauses or major phrases such as NPs (cf. Sun et al. 2000).

For text indexing or terminology extraction, too, some syntactic structure is necessary, at least spotting the major noun phrases. Knowing that an NP is in argumental position (subject or object) may make it a better candidate for indexing than NPs only occurring in adjunct phrases.

On the other hand, treebanked texts are usually smaller than raw texts (usually available in quasi infinite quantity, especially via the various web sites in the world), especially for languages for which the annotation tools do not perform well enough to avoid human post-correction. Some searches for individual forms or patterns may yield poor results. Another obstacle si that treebanks are not readable as such and require specific search and viewing tools. This may be why they are still more used by computational linguists than by other linguists.

The papers gathered here all deal with applications in computational linguistics, such as lexicon induction (Järvinen), grammar induction (Frank et al., Bod), parser evaluation (Carroll et al.) or checker evaluation (Becker et al.). Some of the questions facing the treebanks' users are the following:

- what are the corpora most suited to her goal (domain, size...) ?

- are the linguistic annotations appropriate for the task ?
- is the tagset usable as such or does it have to be converted (reduced ? enlarged ?)
- in which format does the treebank come (and does it have to be converted) ?
- does the treebank come with appropriate tools (such as parameterized viewing tools or interactive search tools) ?

2.1 Exchange formats and search tools

For search tools or machine learning programs to be usable on different annotated corpora, one must define some kind of exchange format. Standards still have to be defined, and Ide and Romary (this volume) make a first step towards this goal, following the XCES (XML based corpus encoding standard).

Format standardization will promote the reuse of common search and viewing tools. One of the reasons for limited use of treebanks by everyday linguists is the lack of friendly search tools, a noticeable exception being the ICE-CUP query language associated with the ICE-GB corpus (Wallis this volume).

2.2 Resource induction

Different kinds of resources can be extracted from treebanks. The main motivation for the Bank of English project (Jarvinen this volume) was to extend the Collins COBUILD dictionary, with new examples and new constructions for most of the English verbs.

Another choice is grammar extraction or rule induction. The corpus-based grammar may be a traditional human-written grammar book such as (Biber et al. 2000). It can also be an online grammar, to be used by NLP programs. In this case, one has to choose a formal model of grammar, for example the simple context free rewriting rule type.

The papers included here in this domain involve several corpora (ATIS corpus, Penn treebank, Lancaster corpus), Dutch (Ovis) or German (Negra). Some papers (Neumann, Frank et al.) start with a richer model (LFG, HPSG or TAG) which guide the type of pattern (tree like or rule like) to be extracted.

Such corpus-based grammars are likely to perform better on similar corpora than grammars written independently (and likely to ignore phenomena not present in the training corpus). They can also associate with each rule its productivity or plausibility (given the number of times it is used in the corpus), and parsers using such grammars can easily decide in the case of several possible analyses (and avoid spurious ambiguities).

But a grammar is not just a list of independent rules, and some experiments also aim at capturing some generalizations, merging rules involving the same parts of speech for example, or ignoring rules with a very low number of application in the corpus.

A grammatical model (such as LFG) may also ask for information not present in the corpus (such as grammatical function) and part of the experiment is also to enrich the extracted rules in a semi automatic way (Frank et al.).

The result is usually far more rules than a parser can handle and still be efficient (cf Bod this volume). More experiments thus have to be done.

2.3 Training tools

Treebanks can be used to train different tools for automatic natural language processing: taggers, parsers, generators.

In the field of stochastic natural language processing (cf. Charniak 1993, Manning and Schutze 1999), corpora are the primary source of information for training such tools.

The first stochastic parsers were using unannotated texts (unsupervised learning) but new parsers now use richly annotated corpora and perform better. Bod (1998, this volume) proposes the Data-oriented Parsing (DOP) model as an alternative to classical parsers. His parsers are context-free parsers that use the subtrees of the learning corpus (the treebank) converted into rewriting rules and associated with probabilities. In essence, finding the correct analysis (the best parse) amounts to maximizing the probability of a derivation (the product of the probabilities of the rules being used). Such parsers are robust (they do not fail on real corpora) and deterministic (they always give one best result). In such experiments, one often divides the treebank in two parts: one for learning (called the training set) and one for evaluation (called the test set). It is natural that such parsers perform well on (unannotated) corpora similar to the original treebank; but it is an open question how well such parsers perfom on different corpora.

To train a parser that performs well, one has to find a balance between the size of the tagset (richness of information available in the annotated corpus) and the size of the corpus (number of word or sentences annotated). The better performances are obtained with a small tagset (less than 50 tags) and a large corpus (more than 1 million words). Srinivas and Joshi (1999), training a shallow parser (called a supertagger) on the PennTreebank (converted with 300 different tags), show how going from a training set of 8000 words to a training set of 1 Million words improve the parser's performance from 86% (of the words with the correct syntactic structure) to 92% (using a trigram model).

Srinivas and Rambow (2000) show how to train a generator on a treebank, favoring the choice for the most common constructions.

2.4 Evaluation with treebanks

Different resources and tools can be evaluated using a treebank.

One can evaluate available lexicons: their coverage, the precision of their valence information as noted in the reference lexicon compared to what is found in the treebank. An indirect result could be adding weights (or preferences) to category or valence information in existing dictionaries: from the treebank, one knows which categories or valence frames are more often used than others for a given verb.

One can also evaluate available grammars, to see how many of the treebank constructions they cover, and whether or not they provide the same analysis for similar phenomena. Xia et al. (2000), in order to evaluate an English handcrafted grammar based on the Tree Adjoining grammar formalism (XTAG), compare it with a grammar in the same format automatically extracted from the Penn Treebank[3]. As for lexicons, an indirect result can be adding weight to such a grammar, since one knows from the treebank which grammar rules are more often used than others.

In a larger sense, one also use treebanks to evaluate (and enrich) grammatical theories or formalisms. The construction of the Prague Dependency Treebank was part of a project to test whether the Functional Generative Description was appropriate for a rich collection of contemporary Czech texts. In a sense, the HPSG-based treebank for Polish, built by Marciniak et al. (this volume), is also a testing ground for Head-driven Phrase Structure Grammar, to see whether its description are broad or robust enough to account for samples of contemporary usage.

Different tools can be evaluated using a treebank. Part of speech taggers of course, but a (validated) tagged corpus is enough for that. More ambitious taggers assigning grammatical functions (such as Jarvinen's FDG parser) need more than tagged corpora to be evaluated.

As explained above, stochastic parsers are naturally evaluated with treebanks, but hand-crafted rule-based parsers can be also. Two papers (Caroll et al., Lin in this volume) present an exercise in parser evaluation using Susanne corpus. It is usually difficult to directly match the output of the tool to be evaluated (a tagger or a parser) and the treebank itself. Some conversions or transformations are usually necessary.

A common methodology, named Parseval, has been tested on the Penn treebank: in order not to penalize annotation choices diverging from the treebank, it only counts as erroneous crossing brackets and does not take the constituents' names into account. Still, this method (called Parseval) has been shown to be unfair to certain types of parsing schemes (Lin, Caroll et al. this volume) and a method evaluating grammatical functions is now often preferred.

Conclusion

The papers included in this volume deal with building and using parsed corpora for a variety of languages. As treebanks are still a new kind of resource, it is not surprising that more papers deal with building them than using them. Unsurprisingly, many projects dealing with different languages are faced with the same difficulties, regarding annotations of notoriously difficult constructions such as discontinuities, coordinations, parentheticals.

Most applications presented here belong to the field of computational linguistics, but treebanks are starting to be used in other fields of linguistics as well, and to renew traditional studies in corpus linguistics (which have long been limited to word level searches and computations). A goal for this book is precisely to encourage more treebank users and uses.

Obviously, treebanks are just one step towards richly annotated corpora. Future work involves adding semantic annotation such as in the Redwood treebank (Oepen et al. 2002), or adding pronoun-antecedent links as in (Tutin et al. 2000). Among projects not included in this book, one may cite ongoing treebank projects for languages such as Bulgarian (Simov et al. 2002), Dutch (van der Beek et al 2001) or modern Hebrew (Sima'an et al. 2001).

Notes

1. Some of these papers are revised versions of presentations at various workshops or conferences, among which the ATALA workshop on Treebanks held in Paris in June 1999 and the LINC conferences in Bergen 1999 and Saarbrücken 2000.

2. Optimality Theory proposes universal constraints which can be ranked differently among languages, but which are not weighted. More recently, some probabilistic versions of OT have been proposed (cf. Boerma & Hayes 2001).

3. The result is that more than half of the hand-crafted rules (elementary trees) are actually in the Treebank grammar, which cover more than 80% of the treebank sentences (and more than 90% once one eliminates errors in the Treebank and arbitrary differences in annotation choices between the grammarians and the treebanks annotators).

References

A. Abeillé, L. Clément, A. Kinyon, F. Toussenel 2002. " The Paris 7 annotated corpus for French : some experimental results " In *A Rainbow of corpora: Corpus linguistics and the languages of the world* , A. Wilson, P. Rayson and T. McEnery (eds.) Lincom Europa, Munich

G. Adda, J. Mariani, P. Paroubek, M. Rajman, J. Lecomte, 1999. L'action GRACE d'évaluation de l'assignation de parties du discours pour le français, *Langues*, 2-2, p. 119-129.

J. Arnold, T. Wasow, A. Losongco, R. Ginstrom. 2000. Heaviness vs. Newness: The effects of complexity and information structure on constituent ordering, *Language* 76, p. 28-55.

D. Biber 1988. *Variation accross speech and writing*, Cambridge: Cambridge University Press.

D. Biber, S. Johanson, G. Leech, S. Conrad, E. Finegan 2000 *The Longman grammar of spoken and written English*, London, Longman.

R. Bod 1998. *Beyond grammar. An experience-based theory of language*, CSLI, Stanford.

P. Boerma, B. Hayes 2001. Empirical tests for the graduallearning algorithm, *Linguistic Inquiry*, 32:1, p. 45-86.

E. Charniak, 1993. *Statistical language learning*, Cambridge, MIT Press.

E. Charniak, 1996. Treebank grammars, *Proceedings AAAI.*

J. Chen, K. Vijay-Shanker, 2000, Automated extraction of TAGs from the Penn Treebank, *Proceedings 6th International workshop on parsing technologies* (IWPT), Trento.

J. Dekkers, F. van der Leeuw, J. van de Wiejer (eds) 2000. *Optimality Theory: phonology, syntax and acquisition.* Oxford: Oxford University Press.

E. Gibson, C. Schutze, 1999. Disambiguation preferences in NP conjunction do not mirror corpus frequencies, *Journal of Memory and Language*, 40.

J. Jäborg 1986. Manual för syntaggning, Göteborg University, Institute för spräkvetenskaplig databehandling.

A Kroch, A Taylor, 2000. The Penn-Helsinki parsed corpus of middle English, Technical report, Linguistics Department, University of Pennsylvania.

F. Malrieu, F. Rastier, 2001. Genres et variations morphosyntaxiques, TAL, 42-1, p. 547-578.

C. Manning, H. Schütze, 1999. *Foundations of statistical natural language processing*, Cambridge, MIT Press.

C. Manning 2002. Probabilistic syntax, in Bod et al. (eds) *Probabilistic linguistics*, Cambridge, MIT Press.

M. Marcus, B. Santorini, M-A. Marcinkiewicz .1993. Building a large annotated corpus of English: the Penn Treebank, *Computational Linguistics*, 19:2, 313-330.

P Merlo, S. Stevenson. 2001. Automatic Verb Classification based on Statistical Distribution of Argument Structure, *Computational Linguistics*, 27:3, p. 373-408

S. Oepen, K. Toutanova, S. Shieber, C. Manning, D. Flickinger, T. Brants. 2002. The LinGO Redwood treebanks : motivation and preliminary application, *Proceedings COLING*, Taiwan.

J. Pynte, S. Colonna, 2000. Decoupling syntactic procesing from visual inspection; the case of relative clause attachment in French. In Kennedy, Raddach, Heller, & Pynte (Eds.). *Reading as a Perceptual Process*. Elsevier.

G. Sampson. 1995. *English for the Computer, The Susanne corpus*, Oxford, Oxford University Press.

K. Sima'an, A. Itai, Y. Winter, A. Altman, N. Nativ, 2001. Building a treebank for modern Hebrew text, *TAL*, 42-2, p. 347-380.

K. Simov et al. 2002. Building a linguistically interpreted corpus for Bulgarian: the Bultreebank project, *Proceedings LREC*, Canary islands.

B. Srinivas, A. Joshi, 1999. Supertagging: An approach to almost parsing, *Computational Linguistics*, 25-2: 237-266.

B. Srinivas, O. Rambow, 2000. Exploiting a probabilistic hierarchical model for generation, in *Proceedings COLING*, Sarrebrück.

L. Sun, Y. Jin, L. Du, Y. Sun, 2000. Word alignment of English-Chinese bilingual corpora based on chunks, *Proceedings Joint SIGDAT Conference on Empirical methods in NLP and very large corpora*, and 38th ACL Conference, Hong-Kong, 110-116.

A. Tutin, F. Trouilleux, C. Clouzot, E. Gaussier, 2000. Building a large corpus with anaphoric links in French: some methodological issues, *Proceedings Discourse anaphora and reference resolution Colloquium*, Lancaster.

L. van der Beek, G. Bouma, R. Malouf, G. van Noord, 2001. The Alpino Dependency treebank, *Proceedings LINC conference*, Saarbrücken.

H. van Halteren, N. Oostdijk. 1993. Towards a syntactic database: the TOSCA analysis system, in J. Aarts et al. (eds), *English Language corpora: design, analysis and exploitation*, Amsterdam, Rodopi. 145-162.

F. Xia, M. Palmer, A. Joshi 2000. A uniform method of grammar extraction and its application, *Proceedings Joint SIGDAT Conference on Empirical methods in NLP and very large corpora, and 38th ACL Conference*, Hong-Kong, 53:62.

I

BUILDING TREEBANKS

English treebanks

Chapter 1

THE PENN TREEBANK: AN OVERVIEW

Ann Taylor
University of York
Heslington, York, UK
at9@york.ac.uk

Mitchell Marcus, Beatrice Santorini
University of Pennsylvania
Philadelphia PA, USA
{mitch,beatrice}@linc.cis.upenn.edu

Abstract The Penn Treebank, in its eight years of operation (1989-1996), produced approximately 7 million words of part-of-speech tagged text, 3 million words of skeletally parsed text, over 2 million words of text parsed for predicate-argument structure, and 1.6 million words of transcribed spoken text annotated for speech disfluencies. This paper describes the design of the three annotation schemes used by the Treebank: POS tagging, syntactic bracketing, and disfluency annotation and the methodology employed in production. All available Penn Treebank materials are distributed by the Linguistic Data Consortium `http://www.ldc.upenn.edu`.

Keywords: English, Annotated Corpus, Part-of-speech Tagging, Treebank, Syntactic Bracketing, Parsing, Disfluencies

INTRODUCTION

The Penn Treebank, in its eight years of operation (1989-1996), produced approximately 7 million words of part-of-speech tagged text, 3 million words of skeletally parsed text, over 2 million words of text parsed for predicate-argument structure, and 1.6 million words of transcribed spoken text annotated for speech disfluencies. The material annotated includes such wide-ranging genres as IBM computer manuals, nursing notes, Wall Street Journal articles, and transcribed telephone conversations, among others. This pa-

A. Abeillé (ed.), Treebanks: Building and Using Parsed Corpora, 5–22.

per describes the design of the three annotation schemes used by the Treebank: POS tagging, syntactic bracketing, and disfluency annotation (section 1) and the methodology employed in production (section 2).[1] All available Penn Treebank materials are distributed by the Linguistic Data Consortium `http://www.ldc.upenn.edu`.

1. THE ANNOTATION SCHEMES

The majority of the output of the Penn Treebank consists of POS tagged and syntactically bracketed versions of written texts such as the Wall Street Journal and the Brown Corpus. In the early years of the project bracketing was done using a quite simple skeletal parse, while later phases made use of a richer predicate-argument bracketing schema. In the final phase of operation, we produced a tagged and parsed version of part of the Switchboard corpus of telephone conversations, as well as a version annotated for disfluencies. In the remainder of this section we discuss the design of the three annotation schemes.

1.1 Part-of-speech tagging

The part-of-speech (POS) tagsets used to annotate large corpora prior to the Penn Treebank were generally fairly extensive. The rationale behind developing such large, richly articulated tagsets was to approach "the ideal of providing distinct codings for all classes of words having distinct grammatical behaviour" (Garside, Leech, and Sampson 1987). The Penn Treebank tagset, like many others, is based on that of the Brown Corpus, but it differs from it in a number of important ways.

First, the stochastic orientation of the Penn Treebank and the resulting concern with sparse data led us to modify the Brown Corpus tagset (Francis, 1964; Francis and Kučera, 1982) by paring it down considerably. The key strategy in this reduction was to eliminate lexical and syntactic redundancy. Thus, whereas many POS tags in the Brown Corpus tagset are unique to a particular lexical item, the Penn Treebank tagset strives to eliminate such instances of lexical redundancy. For instance, the Brown Corpus distinguishes the forms of the verbs *have, be*, and *do* from other main verbs by different tags. By contrast, since the distinctions between the forms of these verbs is lexically recoverable, they are eliminated in the Penn Treebank and all main verbs receive the same set of tags. Distinctions recoverable with reference to syntactic structure were also eliminated. For instance, the Penn Treebank tagset does not distinguish subject pronouns from object pronouns even in cases where the distinction is not recoverable from the pronoun's form, as with *you*, since the distinction is recoverable on the basis of the pronoun's position in the parse tree in the parsed version of the corpus.

A second difference between the Penn Treebank and the Brown Corpus concerns the significance accorded to syntactic context. In the Brown Corpus, words tend to be tagged independently of their syntactic function. For instance, in the phrase *the one*, *one* is always tagged as CD (cardinal number), whereas in the corresponding plural phrase *the ones*, *ones* is always tagged as NNS (plural common noun), despite the parallel function of *one* and *ones* as heads of their noun phrase. By contrast, since one of the main roles of the tagged version of the Penn Treebank corpus is to serve as the basis for a bracketed version of the corpus, we encode a word's syntactic function in its POS tag whenever possible. Thus, *one* is tagged as NN (singular common noun) rather than as CD (cardinal number) when it is the head of a noun phrase.

Thirdly, since a major concern of the Treebank is to avoid requiring annotators to make arbitrary decisions, we allow words to be associated with more than one POS tag. Such multiple tagging indicates either that the word's part of speech simply cannot be decided or that the annotator is unsure which of the alternative tags is the correct one.

The Penn Treebank tagset is given in Table 1.1. It contains 36 POS tags and 12 other tags (for punctuation and currency symbols). A detailed description of the guidelines governing the use of the tagset can be found in Santorini (1990) or on the the Penn Treebank webpage[2].

1.2 Syntactic bracketing

Skeletal parsing. During the operation of the Penn Treebank, two styles of syntactic bracketing were employed. In the first phase of the project the annotation used was a skeletal context-free bracketing with limited empty categories and no indication of non-contiguous structures and dependencies.

```
( (S
   (NP Martin Marietta Corp.)
   was
   (VP given
       (NP a
           $ 29.9
           million Air Force contract
           (PP for
               (NP low-altitude navigation
                   and
                   targeting equipment)))))
  .)
```

The set of syntactic tags and null elements used in the skeletal bracketing are given in Table 1.2. More detailed information on the syntactic tagset and guide-

Table 1.1. The Penn Treebank POS tagset

CC	Coordinating conj.	TO	infinitival *to*
CD	Cardinal number	UH	Interjection
DT	Determiner	VB	Verb, base form
EX	Existential there	VBD	Verb, past tense
FW	Foreign word	VBG	Verb, gerund/present pple
IN	Preposition	VBN	Verb, past participle
JJ	Adjective	VBP	Verb, non-3rd ps. sg. present
JJR	Adjective, comparative	VBZ	Verb, 3rd ps. sg. present
JJS	Adjective, superlative	WDT	Wh-determiner
LS	List item marker	WP	Wh-pronoun
MD	Modal	WP$	Possessive *wh*-pronoun
NN	Noun, singular or mass	WRB	Wh-adverb
NNS	Noun, plural	#	Pound sign
NNP	Proper noun, singular	$	Dollar sign
NNPS	Proper noun, plural	.	Sentence-final punctuation
PDT	Predeterminer	,	Comma
POS	Possessive ending	:	Colon, semi-colon
PRP	Personal pronoun	(	Left bracket character
PP$	Possessive pronoun	)	Right bracket character
RB	Adverb	"	Straight double quote
RBR	Adverb, comparative	‘	Left open single quote
RBS	Adverb, superlative	“	Left open double quote
RP	Particle	’	Right close single quote
SYM	Symbol	”	Right close double quote

lines concerning its use are to be found in Santorini and Marcinkiewicz (1991) or on The Penn Treebank website[3].

Following the release of the first Penn Treebank CD-ROM, many users indicated that they wanted forms of annotation richer than those provided by the project's first phase, as well as an increase in the consistency of the preliminary corpus. Some also expressed an interest in a less skeletal form of annotation, expanding the essentially context-free analysis of the current treebank to indicate non-contiguous structures and dependencies. Most crucially, there was a strong sense that the Treebank could be of much more use if it explicitly provided some form of predicate-argument structure. The desired level of representation would make explicit at least the logical subject and logical object of the verb, and indicate, at least in clear cases, how subconstituents are semantically related to their predicates. Therefore in the second phase of the project a new style of annotation, Treebank II, was introduced.

Table 1.2. The Penn Treebank syntactic tagset

ADJP	Adjective phrase
ADVP	Adverb phrase
NP	Noun phrase
PP	Prepositional phrase
S	Simple declarative clause
SBAR	Subordinate clause
SBARQ	Direct question introduced by *wh*-element
SINV	Declarative sentence with subject-aux inversion
SQ	Yes/no questions and subconstituent of SBARQ excluding *wh*-element
VP	Verb phrase
WHADVP	Wh-adverb phrase
WHNP	Wh-noun phrase
WHPP	Wh-prepositional phrase
X	Constituent of unknown or uncertain category
*	"Understood" subject of infinitive or imperative
0	Zero variant of *that* in subordinate clauses
T	Trace of wh-Constituent

Predicate-argument structure. The new style of annotation provided three types of information not included in the first phase.

1 A clear, concise distinction between verb arguments and adjuncts where such distinctions are clear, with an easy-to-use notational device to indicate where such a distinction is somewhat murky.

2 A non-context free annotational mechanism to allow the structure of discontinuous constituents to be easily recovered.

3 A set of null elements in what can be thought of as "underlying" position for phenomena such as wh-movement, passive, and the subjects of infinitival constructions, co-indexed with the appropriate lexical material.

The goal of a well-developed predicate-argument scheme is to label each argument of the predicate with an appropriate semantic label to identify its role with respect to that predicate (subject, object, etc.), as well as distinguishing the arguments of the predicate, and adjuncts of the predication. Unfortunately, while it is easy to distinguish arguments and adjuncts in simple cases, it turns out to be very difficult to consistently distinguish these two categories for many verbs in actual contexts. It also turns out to be very difficult to determine a set of underlying semantic roles that holds up in the face of a few paragraphs of text. The Treebank II scheme is an attempt to come up with a middle ground which allows annotation of those distinctions that seem to hold up across a wide body of material. After many attempts to find a reliable test to distinguish between arguments and adjuncts, we abandoned structurally marking this difference. Instead, we decided to label a small set of clearly distinguishable roles, building upon syntactic distinctions only when the semantic intuitions were clear-cut. However, getting annotators to consistently apply even the small set of distinctions discussed here was fairly difficult.

In the skeletal parsing scheme discussed in section 1.2 we used only standard syntactic labels (e.g. NP, ADVP, PP, etc.) for our constituents (see Table 1.2) – in other words, every bracket had just one label. The limitations of this become apparent when a word belonging to one syntactic category is used for another function or when it plays a role which we want to be able to identify easily. In Treebank II style, each constituent has at least one label but as many as four tags, including numerical indices, taken from the set of functional tags given in Table 1.3. NPs and Ss which are clearly arguments of the verb are unmarked by any tag. An open class of other cases that individual annotators feel strongly should be part of the VP are tagged as *-CLR* (for CLosely Related); constituents marked *-CLR* typically correspond to the class of predication adjuncts proposed by (Quirk et al. 1985)[4]. In addition, a handful of semantic roles are distinguished: direction, location, manner, purpose, and time, as well as the syntactic roles of surface subject, logical subject, and (implicit in the syntactic structure) first and second verbal objects.

```
( (S (NP-SBJ-1 Jones)
     (VP followed
         (NP him)
         (PP-DIR into
                 (NP the front room))
         ,
         (S-ADV (NP-SBJ *-1)
                (VP closing
                    (NP the door)
                    (PP behind
                        (NP him)))))
     .))

( (S (ADVP-LOC Here)
     (NP-SBJ-1 he)
     (VP could
         n't
         (VP be
             (VP seen
                 (NP *-1)
                 (PP by
                     (NP-LGS (NP Blue Throat)
                             and
                             (NP his gang))))))
     .))
```

Treebank II style also adds null elements in a wide range of cases; these null elements are co-indexed with the lexical material for which the null element

Table 1.3. Functional Tags

Text Categories	
-HLN	headlines and datelines
-LST	list markers
-TTL	titles
Grammatical Functions	
-CLF	true clefts
-NOM	non NPs that function as NPs
-ADV	clausal and NP adverbials
-LGS	logical subjects in passives
-PRD	non VP predicates
-SBJ	surface subject
-TPC	topicalized and fronted constituents
-CLR	closely related - see text
Semantic Roles	
-VOC	vocatives
-DIR	direction & trajectory
-LOC	location
-MNR	manner
-PRP	purpose and reason
-TMP	temporal phrases

stands. The current scheme uses two symbols for null elements: **T**, which marks WH-movement and topicalization, and * which is used for all other null elements. Co-indexing of null elements is done by suffixing an integer to non-terminal categories (e.g. `NP-10, VP-25`). This integer serves as an id number for the constituent. A null element itself is followed by the id number of the constituent with which it is co-indexed. Crucially, the predicate-argument structure can be recovered by simply replacing the null element with the lexical material that it is co-indexed with.

```
(SBARQ (WHNP-1 What)
       (SQ is
           (NP-SBJ Tim)
           (VP eating
               (NP *T*-1)))
       ?)

Predicate Argument Structure:
eat(Tim, what)
```

```
(S (NP-SBJ-1 The ball)
   (VP was
       (VP thrown
           (NP *-1)
           (PP by
               (NP-LGS Chris)))))
```

```
Predicate Argument Structure:
throw(Chris, ball)
```

A null element is also used to indicate which lexical NP is to be interpreted as the null subject of an infinitive complement clause; it is co-indexed with the controlling NP, based upon the lexical properties of the verb.

```
(S (NP-SBJ-1 Chris)
   (VP wants
       (S (NP-SBJ *-1)
          (VP to
              (VP throw
                  (NP the ball))))))
```

```
Predicate Argument Structure:
wants(Chris, throw(Chris, ball))
```

Finally, we also use null elements to allow the interpretation of other grammatical structures where constituents do not appear in their default positions. Null elements are used in most cases to mark the fronting (or "topicalization" of any element of an S before the subject (except in subj-aux inversion). If an adjunct is topicalized, the fronted element does not leave a trace since the level of attachment is the same, only the word order is different. Topicalized arguments, on the other hand, always are marked by a null element:

```
(S (NP-TPC-5 This)
   (NP-SBJ every man)
   (VP contains
       (NP *T*-5)
       (PP-LOC within
               (NP him))))
```

Again, this makes predicate argument interpretation straightforward, if the null element is simply replaced by the constituent to which it is co-indexed.

With only a skeletal parse as used in the first phase of the Treebank project, many otherwise clear argument/adjunct relations cannot be recovered due to its essentially context-free representation. For example, there is no good representation for sentences in which constituents which serve as complements to the verb occur after a sentence-level adverb. Either the adverb is trapped within the VP, so that the complement can occur within the VP, where it belongs, or else the adverb is attached to the S, closing off the VP and forcing the complement to attach to the S. This "trapping" problem serves as a limitation when using skeletally parsed material to semi-automatically derive lexicons for particular applications.

"Trapping" problems and the annotation of non-contiguous structure can be handled by simple notational devices that use co-indexing to indicate discontinuous structures. Again, an index number added to the label of the original constituent is incorporated into the null element which shows where that constituent should be interpreted within the predicate argument structure. We use a variety of null elements to show how non-adjacent constituents are related; such constituents are referred to as "pseudo-attached". There are four different types of pseudo-attach, as shown in Table 1.4.

Table 1.4. The four types of pseudo-attachment

ICH	Interpret Constituent Here
PPA	Permanent Predictable Ambiguity
RNR	Right Node Raising
EXP	Expletive

The **ICH** pseudo-attach is used for simple extraposition, solving the most common case of "trapping":

```
(S (NP-SBJ Chris)
   (VP knew
       (SBAR *ICH*-1)
       (NP-TMP yesterday)
       (SBAR-1 that
               (S (NP-SBJ Terry)
                  (VP would
                      (VP catch
                          (NP the ball)))))))
```

Here, the clause *that Terry would catch the ball* is to be interpreted as an argument of *knew.*

The **RNR** tag is used for so-called "right-node raising" conjunctions, where the same constituent appears to have been shifted out of both conjuncts.

```
(S But
   (NP-SBJ-2 our outlook)
   (VP (VP has
           (VP been
               (ADJP *RNR*-1)))
       ,
       and
       (VP continues
           (S (NP-SBJ *-2)
              (VP to
                  (VP be
                      (ADJP *RNR*-1)))))
       ,
       (ADJP-1 defensive)))
```

In order that certain kinds of constructions can be found reliably within the corpus, we have adopted special marking of some special constructions. For example, extraposed sentences which leave behind a semantically null "it" are parsed as follows, using the **EXP** tag:

```
(S (NP-SBJ (NP It)
           (S *EXP*-1))
   (VP is
       (NP a pleasure))
   (S-1 (NP-SBJ *)
        (VP to
            (VP teach
                (NP her)))))

Predicate Argument Structure:
pleasure(teach(*someone*, her))
```

The **PPA** tag was introduced to indicate "permanent predictable ambiguity", those cases in which one cannot tell where a constituent should be attached, even given context. Here, annotators attach the constituent at the more likely site (or if that is impossible to determine, at the higher site) and pseudo-attach it at all other plausible sites using the **PPA** null element.[5]

```
(S (NP-SBJ I)
      (VP saw
          (NP (NP the man)
              (PP *PPA*-1))
          (PP-CLR-1 with
                    (NP the telescope))))
```

1.3 Disfluency annotation

The final project undertaken by the Treebank (1995-6) was to produce a tagged and parsed version of the Switchboard corpus of transcribed telephone conversations, along with a version which annotated the disfluencies common in speech (fragments of words, interruptions, incomplete sentences, fillers and discourse markers).

The disfluency annotation system (based on Shriberg (1994)) distinguishes complete utterances from incomplete ones, labels a range of non-sentence elements such as fillers, and annotates restarts.

Table 1.5. Disfluency Annotation

Utterances	
/	end of complete utterance
-/	end of incomplete utterance
Non-sentence elements	
F	fillers (*uh, um, huh, oh,* etc.)
E	explicit editing term (*I mean, sorry,* etc.)
D	discourse marker (*you know, well,* etc.)
C	coordinating conjunction (*and, and then, but,* etc.)
A	aside
Restarts	
[*RM* + *RR*]	restart with repair (see text)
[*RM*+]	restart without repair

Restarts have the following form:

```
Show me flights from Boston on  uh from Denver on Monday
               |-------RM-----|-IM------RR-------|
                              IP
  RM = reparandum
  IP = interruption point
  IM = interregnum (filled pause or editing terms)
  RR = repair
```

In the annotation, the entire restart with its repair is contained in square brackets. The IP is marked by a "+", and any IM material (filled pauses, etc.) follows the "+".

```
Show me flights
   [ from Boston on + {F uh } from Denver on ] Monday

   |-------RM-------|---IM---|-------RR------|
                    IP
```

A: he's pretty good. / He stays out of the street / {C and, } {F uh, } if I catch him I call him / {C and } he comes back. / {D So } [he, + he's] pretty good about taking to commands [and + –
B: {F Um. } /
A: – and] things. /
B: Did you bring him to a doggy obedience school or –
A: No – /
B: – just –
A: – we never did. /
B: – train him on your own / {C and, } -/
A: [I, + I] trained him on my own / {C and, } {F uh, } this is the first dog I've had all my own as an adult. /
B: Uh-huh. /

Figure 1.1. Sample disfluency annotation

A detailed account of the disfluency annotation can be found in Mateer and Taylor 1995 or on the Penn Treebank website `http://www.cis.upenn.edu/~treebank`.

2. METHODOLOGY

The three types of Treebank annotation, POS tagging, syntactic bracketing, and disfluency annotation, are all produced by the same two-step method, automatic annotation followed by manual correction. The correction of each type of annotation is done with the aid of a task-specific mouse-based package written in GNU Emacs Lisp, embedded in the GNU Emacs editor (Lewis and Laliberte 1990). POS tagging and disfluency annotation (when relevant) feed syntactic bracketing, but the first two are independent of each other and can be done in parallel, with the two output streams then being automatically merged, if desired.

2.1 Part-of-speech tagging

During the early stages of the Penn Treebank project, the initial automatic POS assignment was provided by PARTS (Church 1988), a stochastic algorithm developed at AT&T Bell Labs. PARTS uses a modified version of the Brown Corpus tagset close to our own and assigns POS tags with an error rate of 3–5%. The output of PARTS was automatically tokenized and the tags assigned by PARTS were automatically mapped onto the Penn Treebank tagset. This mapping introduced about 4% error, since the Penn Treebank tagset makes certain distinctions that the PARTS tagset does not. Later, the automatic POS assignment was provided by a cascade of stochastic and rule-driven taggers developed on the basis of our early experience. Since these taggers are based on the Penn Treebank tagset, the 4% error rate introduced as an artefact of mapping from the PARTS tagset to ours is eliminated, and we obtain error rates of 2–6%. Finally, during the Switchboard project we switched to the then recently released Brill tagger (Brill 1993).

The result of the first, automated stage of POS tagging is given to annotators to correct. The POS correction interface allows annotators to correct POS assignment errors by positioning the cursor on an incorrectly tagged word and then entering the desired correct tag (or sequence of multiple tags). The annotators' input is automatically checked against the list of legal tags and, if valid, appended to the original word-tag pair separated by an asterisk. Appending the new tag rather than replacing the old tag allows us to easily identify recurring errors at the automatic POS assignment stage. Finally, in the distribution version of the tagged corpus, any incorrect tags assigned at the first, automatic stage are removed.

2.2 Syntactic bracketing

The methodology for bracketing the corpus is completely parallel to that for tagging—hand correction of the output of an automatic process. Fidditch, a deterministic parser developed by Donald Hindle first at the University of Pennsylvania and subsequently at AT&T Bell Labs (Hindle 1988, Hindle 1989) is used to provide an initial parse of the material. Annotators then hand correct the parser's output using a task-specific mouse-based interface implemented in GNU Emacs Lisp. Fidditch has three properties that make it ideally suited to serve as a preprocessor to hand correction:

- It always provides exactly one analysis for any given sentence, so that annotators need not search through multiple analyses.
- It never attaches any constituent whose role in the larger structure it cannot determine with certainty. In cases of uncertainty, Fidditch chunks

Output of tagger

```
Battle-tested/NNP Japanese/NNP industrial/JJ managers/NNS
here/RB always/RB buck/VB up/IN nervous/JJ newcomers/NNS
with/IN the/DT tale/NN of/IN the/DT first/JJ of/IN
their/PP$ countrymen/NNS to/TO visit/VB Mexico/NNP ,/,
a/DT boatload/NN of/IN samurai/NNS warriors/NNS blown/VBN
ashore/RB 375/CD years/NNS ago/RB ./.
```

Hand-corrected by annotator

```
Battle-tested/NNP*/JJ Japanese/NNP*/JJ industrial/JJ
managers/NNS  here/RB always/RB buck/VB*/VBP up/IN*/RP
nervous/JJ newcomers/NNS  with/IN the/DT tale/NN of/IN
the/DT first/JJ of/IN their/PP$ countrymen/NNS to/TO
visit/VB Mexico/NNP ,/, a/DT boatload/NN of/IN
samurai/NNS*/FW  warriors/NNS blown/VBN ashore/RB 375/CD
years/NNS ago/RB ./.
```

Final version

```
Battle-tested/JJ Japanese/JJ industrial/JJ managers/NNS
here/RB always/RB buck/VBP up/RP nervous/JJ newcomers/NNS
with/IN the/DT tale/NN of/IN the/DT first/JJ of/IN
their/PP$ countrymen/NNS to/TO  visit/VB Mexico/NNP ,/,
a/DT boatload/NN  of/IN samurai/FW warriors/NNS  blown/VBN
ashore/RB 375/CD years/NNS ago/RB ./.
```

Figure 1.2. Part-of-speech tagging pipeline

the input into a string of trees, providing only a partial structure for each sentence.

- It has rather good grammatical coverage, so that the grammatical chunks that it does build are usually quite accurate.

The output of Fidditch, however, which is fairly complex, with word, X-bar, and phrase levels represented, was found to be too complicated for the annotators to handle at speed. They were therefore presented with a simplified parse containing only the phrase labels for correction. The simplified output of Fidditch is illustrated in Figure 2.2. In general, the annotators do not need to re-bracket much of the parser's output—a relatively time-consuming task. Rather, the annotators' main task is to "glue" together the syntactic chunks produced by the parser. Using a mouse-based interface, annotators move each unattached chunk of structure under the node to which it should be attached. Notational devices allow annotators to indicate uncertainty concerning constituent labels, and to indicate multiple attachment sites for ambiguous modifiers. Insertion and co-indexing of null elements is accomplished simply by dragging from the associated lexical material to the site of the null element.

```
( (S
        (NP Her eyes)
        (AUX were)
        (VP glazed))
    (?
        (PP as
            (NP (SBAR if
                    (S (NP she)
                        (AUX did)
                        (?
                            (NEG n't))
                        (VP hear))))))
    (? or)
    (? even)
    (?
        (S
            (VP see
                (NP him))))
    (? .))
```

Figure 1.3. Simplified output of Fidditch before correction

The bracketed text after correction is shown in Figure 1.3. The fragments are now connected together into one rooted tree structure, functional tags are added and null elements inserted and co-indexed.

Finally the POS tags can be automatically combined with the skeletal parse to produce a tree with both POS and syntactic information.

2.3 Disfluency annotation

As with POS tagging and syntactic bracketing, annotating disfluencies is done in two steps, although in this case the automated step is just a simple Perl script which attempts to identify and bracket the more common non-sentence elements, such as fillers. The correction interface for disfluencies allows easy

```
( (S (NP-SBJ-2 Her eyes)
     (VP were
         (VP glazed
             (NP *-2)
             (SBAR-ADV as if
                       (S (NP-SBJ she)
                          (VP did n't
                              (VP (VP hear
                                      (NP *RNR*-1))
                                  or
                                  (VP (ADVP even)
                                      see
                                      (NP *RNR*-1))
                                  (NP-1 him)))))))
     .))
```

Figure 1.4. Bracketed text after correction

input and manipulation of the annotations which mark restarts and repairs with the same sort of mouse-driven package used for correcting the syntactic parse.

2.4 Productivity

The learning curve for the POS tagging task takes under a month (at 15 hours a week), and annotation speeds after a month exceed 3,000 words per hour. The rate for disfluency annotation is similar. Not surprisingly, annotators take substantially longer to learn the more complicated bracketing task, with substantial increases in speed occurring even after two months of training. Even after extended training, performance varies markedly by annotator, however, with speeds on the task ranging from approx. 750 words per hour to well over 1,000 words per hour after three or four months experience.

3. CONCLUSIONS

Although the Penn Treebank is no longer in operation the large amount of data produced by the project continues to provide a valuable resource for computational linguists, natural language programmers, corpus linguists and others interested in empirical language studies. In addition, the tools and methodology developed by the Penn Treebank have been adopted with some revision by an ongoing project to create parsed corpora of all the historical stages of English, which is centred at the University of Pennsylvania and the University of York, with support from the University of Helsinki. The first corpus produced by the project, now in its second edition, the Penn-Helsinki Parsed Corpus of Middle English, Second Edition, (Kroch and Taylor 2000) (`http://www.ling.upenn.edu/mideng`), has been released and comparable corpora of Old and Early Modern English are in production .

Acknowledgments

The Penn Treebank has been supported by the Linguistic Data Consortium, by DARPA (grant No. N0014-85-K0018), by DARPA and AFOSR jointly (grant No. AFOSR-90-0066) and by ARO (grant No. DAAL 03-89-C0031 PRI). Seed money was provided by the General Electric Corporation (grant No. J01746000). The contribution of the staff of the Treebank, Grace Kim, Mary Ann Marcinkiewicz, Dagmar Sieglova (project administrators) Robert MacIntyre (data manager/programmer), and the many annotators who worked on the project over the years, Ann Bies, Constance Cooper, Leslie Dossey, Mark Ferguson, Robert Foye, Karen Katz, Shannon Keenan, Alison Littman James Reilly, Britta Schasberger, James Siegal, Kevin Stephens, and Victoria Tredinnick, is also gratefully acknowledged.

Notes

1. This paper is a revised and expanded version of two earlier papers: Marcus et al. (1993) "Building a large annotated corpus of English: the Penn Treebank," in *Computational Linguistics* 19(2):313-220, and Marcus et al. (1994) "The Penn Treebank: annotating predicate argument structure," in *ARPA Human Language Technology Workshop*.

2. `http://www.cis.upenn.edu/~treebank`

3. `http://www.cis.upenn.edu/~treebank`

4. This use of this tag was an experiment which was largely unsuccessful. Although some very experienced annotators were internally fairly consistent in their use of this tag, less experienced annotators had a hard time with it and consistency across annotators was not high. It was not used in the parsing of the Switchboard corpus.

5. The use of *PPA* was discontinued in the Switchboard phase, since annotators did not reliably detect these ambiguities.

References

Bies, Ann, Mark Ferguson, Karen Katz, and Robert MacIntyre. (1995). *Bracketing Guidelines for Treebank II Style.* Ms., Department of Computer and Information Science, University of Pennsylvania.

Brill, Eric. (1993). *A Corpus-based Approach to Language Learning*. PhD Dissertation, University of Pennsylvania.

Church, Kenneth W. (1980). *Memory Limitations in Natural Language Processing*, MIT LCS Technical Report 245. Master's thesis, Massachusetts Institute of Technology.

Church, Kenneth W. (1988). A stochastic parts program and noun phrase parser for unrestricted text. In *Proceedings of the Second Conference on Applied Natural Language Processing. 26th Annual Meeting of the Association for Computational Linguistics*, pages 136–143.

Francis, W. Nelson (1964). *A Standard Sample of Present-day English for Use with Digital Computers*. Report to the U.S Office of Education on Cooperative Research Project No. E–007. Brown University, Providence RI.

Francis, W. Nelson and Henry Kučera. (1982). *Frequency Analysis of English Usage. Lexicon and Grammar*. Houghton Mifflin, Boston.

Garside, Roger, Geoffrey Leech, and Geoffrey Sampson. (1987). *The Computational Analysis of English. A Corpus-based Approach*. Longman, London.

Hindle, Donald. (1983). *User Manual for Fidditch*. Technical memorandum 7590–142, Naval Research Laboratory.

Hindle, Donald. (1989). Acquiring disambiguation rules from text. In *Proceedings of the 27th Annual Meeting of the Association for Computational Linguistics*.

Kroch, Anthony S. and Ann Taylor. (2000). *The Penn-Helsinki Parsed Corpus of Middle English, Second Edition*. Department of Linguistics, University of Pennsylvania.

Lewis, Bil, Dan Laliberte, and the GNU Manual Group. (1990). *The GNU Emacs Lisp Reference Manual*. Free Software Foundation, Cambridge MA.

Marcus, Mitchell P., Beatrice Santorini, and Mary Ann Marcinkiewicz. (1993) Building a large annotated corpus of English: the Penn Treebank. *Computational Linguistics* 19(2):313-330.

Marcus, Mitchell P., Grace Kim, Mary Ann Marcinkiewicz, Robert MacIntyre, Ann Bies, Mark Ferguson, Karen Katz, and Britta Schasberger. (1994). The Penn Treebank: Annotating predicate-argument structure. In *ARPA Human Language Technology Workshop*.

Mateer, Marie, and Ann Taylor. (1995). *Disfluency Annotation Stylebook for the Switchboard Corpus*. Ms., Department of Computer and Information Science, University of Pennsylvania.

Quirk, R., S. Greenbaum, G. Leech, and J. Svartvik. (1985). *A Comprehensive Grammar of the English Language*, Longman, London.

Santorini, Beatrice. (1990). *Part-of-speech Tagging Guidelines for the Penn Treebank Project*. Technical report MS-CIS-90-47, Department of Computer and Information Science, University of Pennsylvania.

Santorini, Beatrice and Mary Ann Marcinkiewicz. (1991). *Bracketing Guidelines for the Penn Treebank Project*. Ms., Department of Computer and Information Science, University of Pennsylvania.

Shriberg, E.E. (1994). *Preliminaries to a Theory of Speech Disfluencies*. PhD Dissertation, University of California at Berkeley.

Chapter 2

THOUGHTS ON TWO DECADES OF DRAWING TREES

Geoffrey Sampson
School of Cognitive & Computing Sciences,
University of Sussex, Falmer, BRIGHTON BN1 9QH, ENGLAND
geoffs@cogs.susx.ac.uk

Abstract The task of producing consistent, comprehensive structural annotations for real-life written and spoken usage teaches lessons that run counter to some of the assumptions of recent linguistics. It is not easy to believe that a natural language is a well-defined system, or that questions about the analysis of particular turs of phrase always have "right answers". Computational linguistics has been at risk of repeating mistakes made by the general fiels of computing in the 1960s; we need to learn from the discipline of software engineering. On the other hand, annotated corpora of real-life usage are already yielding findings about human nature that were unsuspected before these resources become available.

Keywords: English, Treebank, Susanne Corpus, Christine Corpus

1. HISTORICAL BACKGROUND

If one lives in the English countryside, now and then an aeroplane flies over and photographs one's house, and then someone calls to sell the picture as a souvenir. On the wall of my study I have a picture taken from the air in the summer of 1983; if you look very closely you can see in the garden a white disc, with a much smaller pink disc adjacent to it. The pink disc is the top of my bald head, and the white disc is a garden table covered with papers, because the photographer happened to record one of the opening days of my career as a producer of natural-language parse trees. I was working then at Lancaster University, where my senior colleague, Geoffrey Leech, had a new research project concerned with statistics-based automatic parsing, and I had undertaken to parse manually a sample of written English to serve as a source of statistical data for the project. Glancing at the picture since, I have often

A. Abeillé (ed.), Treebanks: Building and Using Parsed Corpora, 23–41.

wondered how happy I would have felt about embarking on that task, if I had known how many years of my life I was destined to devote to it.

That original "treebank" - structurally analysed sample of natural language[1], – was for internal project use and was not published; but it led me on to develop the SUSANNE Corpus, another treebank of written English, which has been publicly available since 1992 and has established itself as a popular language-engineering research resource, and more recently the CHRISTINE treebank of spoken English, the first stage of which was circulated in summer 1999. Shortly before the Paris treebank conference, I was given the go-ahead for a new project, "LUCY", to create a treebank of written English with special relevance for the teaching of writing skills. When LUCY is completed, I shall have been working on English structural annotation, with the help of various researchers at different times, more or less continuously for the two decades of my title[2].

Before looking at details of this work, it is worth reminding ourselves of the flavour of computational linguistics as it was when I began drawing trees. In those days, most computational linguists did not work with real-life corpus data, and did not seem to want to. They made their data up out of their heads. By coincidence, 1983, the year when I began drawing trees, was also the year of the inaugural meeting of the recently-founded European Chapter of the Association for Computational Linguistics, and that conference (held at Pisa) was a good opportunity to take stock of the current state of play in the subject[3]. Here is a typical selection of example-sentences used by speakers at the Pisa meeting to illustrate the workings of their systems:

> *Whatever is linguistic is interesting.*
>
> *A ticket was bought by every man.*
>
> *The man with the telescope and the umbrella kicked the ball.*
>
> Hans bekommt von dieser Frau ein Buch.
>
> *John and Bill went to Pisa. They delivered a paper.*
>
> Maria é andata a Roma con Anna.
>
> *Are you going to travel this summer? Yes, to Sicily.*

By contrast, here is a sample of utterances from the CHRISTINE treebank, based on material representing spontaneous British speech of the 1990s collected in the British National Corpus:

> *well you want to nip over there and see what they come on on the roll*
>
> *can we put erm New Kids # no not New Kids Wall Of # you know*

well it was Gillian and # and # erm {pause} *and Ronald's sister erm* {pause} *and then er* {pause} *a week ago last night erm* {pause} *Jean and I went to the Lyceum together to see* Arsenic and Old Lace

lathered up, started to shave {unclear} {pause} *when I come to clean it there weren't a bloody blade in, the bastards had pinched it*

but er {pause} *I don't know how we got onto it* {pause} *er sh- # and I think she said something about oh she knew her tables and erm* {pause} *you know she'd come from Hampshire apparently and she #* {pause} *an- # an- yo- # you know er we got talking about ma- and she's taken her child away from* {pause} *the local school* {pause} *and sen- # is now going to a little private school up* {pause} *the Teign valley near Teigngrace apparently fra-*

It is hardly necessary to underline the differences between these data-samples, in terms of complexity and general "messiness". True, I have made the contrast particularly vivid by drawing my real-life examples from informal, spontaneous speech. But even written language which has undergone the disciplines of publication tends in practice to be much less predictable than the Pisa examples. Here are a few sentences drawn at random from the LOB Corpus of published British English:

Sing slightly flat.

Mr. Baring, who whispered and wore pince-nez, *was seventy if he was a day.*

Advice - Concentrate on the present.

Say the power-drill makers, 75 per cent of major breakdowns can be traced to neglect of the carbon-brush gear.

But he remained a stranger in a strange land.

In the first example we find a word in the form of an adjective, *flat*, functioning as an adverb. In the next example, the phrase *Mr. Baring* contains a word ending in full stop followed by a word beginning with a capital which, exceptionally, do not mark a sentence boundary. The third "sentence" links an isolated noun with an imperative construction in a logic that is difficult to pin down. In *Say the power-drill makers...*, verb precedes subject for no very clear reason. The last example is as straightforward as the examples from the Pisa meeting; but straightforward examples are not the norm.

Not surprisingly, then, the task of annotating the grammatical structure of real-life language samples turned out to be a good deal more complicated than I had anticipated.

It would be inappropriate, here, to give much detail about the structural annotation scheme we evolved. For the sake of concreteness, I shall briefly illustrate it with an extract from the CHRISTINE Corpus (see FIG. 2.1). In FIG. 2.1, the next to rightmost field contains the words of a speech turn uttered by the speaker whose CHRISTINE code name is Gemma006, and the rightmost field shows the tree structure in which the words occur, displayed on successive lines as segments of a labelled bracketing. Gemma's second word *you* is a noun phrase (`N`) functioning as subject (`:s`) of its clause, whose verb group (`V`) is the single word *want*. The object of *want* is an infinitival clause (`Ti:o`), whose understood logical subject is again *you*, hence a "ghost" element `s101` is inserted in the word stream with an index number, 101, which marks it as identical to the subject of the main clause – and so on. The field to the left of the words contains their "wordtags" – word classifications drawn from an alphabet of 350-odd structurally-distinct classes of word; Gemma's first word, *well*, is classified as one type of "discourse item" (a form, characteristic of speech, which does not usually constitute part of a wider grammatical structure).

```
T02_0120   -----     Gemma006
T02_0123   .....     00328
T02_0126   0051229 *   UW      well    .
T02_0129   0051241 |   PPY     you     [S[Ny:s101.Ny:s101]
T02_0132   0051252 |   VV0v    want    [V.V]
T02_0135   0000000 y   YG      s101    [Ti:o.
T02_0138   0051264 |   TO      to      [Vi.
T02_0141   0051274 |   VV0v    nip     .Vi]
T02_0144   0051285 |   RP      over    [R:q.
T02_0147   0051285 |   RLh     there   .R:q]
T02_0150   0051303 |   CC      and     [Ti+.
T02_0153   0000000 y   YG      s101    .
T02_0156   0051315 |   VV0v    see     [V.V]
T02_0159   0051326 |   DDQ     what    [Fn?:o[Dq:G103.Dq:G103]
T02_0162   0051338 |   PPHS2   they    [Nap:s.Nap:s]
T02_0165   0051350 |   VV0i    come    [V.V]
T02_0168   0051362 |   II      on      [P:p.
T02_0171   0000000 y   YG      103     .P:p]
T02_0174   0051372 |   II      on      [P:p.
T02_0177   0051382 |   AT      the     [Ns.
T02_0180   0051394 .   NN1c    roll    .Ns]P:p]Fn?:o]Ti+]Ti:o]S]
```

Figure 2.1. Extract from CHRISTINE corpus

2. BUILDING TREEBANKS

When I began drawing trees for Geoffrey Leech's project, he produced a 25-page typescript listing a set of grammatical category symbols which he suggested we use, with notes on how to apply them to debatable cases. I remember thinking that this seemed to cover every possible linguistic eventuality, so that all I needed to do was to apply Leech's guidelines more or less mechanically to a series of examples. I soon learned differently. Every second or third sentence seemed to present some new analytic problem, not covered in the existing body of guidelines. So I and the research team I was working with began making new decisions and cumulating the precedents we set into an ever-growing body of analytic rules. What grew out of a 25-page typescript was published in 1995 as a book of 500 large-format pages, *English for the Computer* (Sampson 1995). In the same year, an independently-developed but very comparable annotation scheme used for the University of Pennsylvania treebank was published via the Web, as Bies et al. (1995).

This great growth in annotation guidelines was caused partly by the fact that real-life language contains many significant items that are scarcely noticed by traditional linguistics. Personal names are multi-word phrases with their own characteristic internal structure, and so are such things as addresses, or references to weights, measures, and money sums; we need consistent rules for annotating the structures of all these forms, but they are too culture-bound to be paid much attention by the inherited school grammar tradition. In written language, punctuation marks are very significant structurally and must be fitted into parse trees in some predictable way, but syntactic analysis within theoretical linguistics ignored punctuation completely.

The more important factor underlying the complexity of our annotation rules, though, was the need to provide an explicit, predictable annotation for every turn of phrase that occurs in the language. As Jane Edwards has put it: "The single most important property of any data base for purposes of computer-assisted research is that similar instances be encoded in predictably similar ways" (Edwards 1992: 139).

For the theoretical linguists who set much of the tone of computational linguistics up till the 1980s, this kind of comprehensive explicitness was not a priority. Syntactic theorists commonly debated alternative analyses for a limited number of "core" constructions which were seen as having special theoretical importance, trying to establish which analysis of some construction is "psychologically real" for native speakers of the language in question. They saw no reason to take a view on the analysis of the many other constructions which happen not to be topics of theoretical controversy (and, because they invented their examples, they could leave most of those other constructions out of view). Language engineering based on real-life usage, on the other hand, cannot pick and choose the aspects of language structure on which it focuses – it has to deal with everything that comes along. For us the aim is not to ascertain what structural analysis corresponds to the way language is organized in speakers' minds – we have no way of knowing that; we just need some reliable, practical way of registering the full range of data in a consistent manner.

Often, so far as I can see, various different analyses of some usage would each be perfectly reasonable; our task is not to ask which analysis is "right", but to choose one of the analyses (at random, if necessary) and to make explicit that this is the analysis we have chosen, so that future examples of the same construction will be annotated in the same way, and statistics extracted from a treebank will not make the mistake of adding apples and pears. Consider, for example, the construction exemplified in *the more, the merrier* – the construction that translates into German with *je* and *desto*. Here are three ways of grouping a sentence using that construction into constituents:

[[the wider the wheelbase is], [the more satisfactory is the performance]]

[[the wider the wheelbase is], the more satisfactory is the performance]

[[[the wider the wheelbase is], the more satisfactory] is the performance]

The two clauses might be seen as co-ordinated (as in the first line), since both have the form of main clauses and neither of them contains an explicit subordinating element. Or the second clause might be seen as the main clause, with the first as an adverbial clause adjunct. Or the first clause might be seen as a modifier of the adjectival predicate within the second clause. There seems to be no strong reason to choose one of these analyses rather than another; what matters, if we are to produce meaningful statistics for use in language engineering, is to settle on one of the analyses and stick to it.

Theoretical linguists are sometimes inclined to look down their noses at this kind of taxonomic exercise as having little intellectual, scientific substance. Linguists of the Chomskyan, generative school have in the past been quite dismissive of taxonomic approaches[4]. But I do not see how the theoreticians can hope to make real progress in their own work, without a solid foundation of grammatical taxonomy to catalogue and classify the data which their theories ought to explain. In the comparable domain of natural history, it was two centuries after the taxonomic work of John Ray, and a century and a half after that of Linnaeus, before theoretical biology was able to develop as a substantial discipline in its own right in the late nineteenth century[5]. From a theoretical point of view the Linnaean system was somewhat "unnatural" (and was known from the start to be so), but it provided a practical, usable conspectus of an immensely complex world of data; without it, theoretical biology could not have got off the ground. The generative linguists' idea that they can move straight to theorizing, bypassing the painstaking work of taxonomy altogether, is one that I find baffling. In any case it is clear that language engineering, for which theories about psycholinguistic mechanisms are irrelevant, badly needs a comprehensive groundwork of data collection and classification.

One explanation for some linguists' lack of interest in the taxonomic approach may be their belief that natural-language structure is much simpler than it superficially appears to be. Underlying the diversity of observable linguistic "performance", it is suggested, there lurks a mental grammatical "competence" which is the proper object of scientific linguistic study, and which can be defined in terms of a limited number of rules, to a large extent genetically inherited and common to all natural languages. As "competence" systems, the grammars of natural languages such as English or Czech might be hardly more complex than those of programming languages such as Pascal or Java[6].

If that were so, one might well see little need for intensive data-systematizing activity. But the idea that a natural language is governed by a limited set of clear-cut grammatical rules does not survive the experience of structurally annotating real-life examples. One way I sometimes express this point is to say that if someone cares to identify a rule of English grammar which they regard as reliable, I would expect to be able to find in English corpus data an example that breaks the rule, not as a momentary error of "performance" but within wording that appears to be intended by the writer or speaker and which "works" as an act of communication.

Thus, one rule which grammarians of English might take to be as reliable as any is the rule that reflexive pronouns, being co-referential with earlier elements in the same clause, can never occur as clause subjects. Yet here is an example found in the LOB Corpus, taken originally from a published magazine article on the Cold War:

> *Each side proceeds on the assumption that itself loves peace, but the other side consists of warmongers.*

This use of *itself* is an absolutely direct violation of the rule; yet the sentence seems perfectly successful in making its point. In case anyone should suspect that the example was produced by a non-native speaker whose English was poor, the author was in fact Bertrand Russell, one of the leading English intellectuals of the twentieth century; and his very next sentence, not quoted here, has another example of the same construction, making it quite clear that this use of reflexive pronouns was no careless "performance error" but a studied effect.

The truth is that rules of natural-language grammar are not binding laws like the laws of physics or chemistry. They are flexible guidelines, to which users of a language tend to conform but which they are free to adapt or disregard. This makes the task of categorizing real-life usage much more challenging than it would be if natural languages were like programming languages with a few irregularities added, but it also means that the task cannot be bypassed via aprioristic theorizing.

3. EXPLOITING THE SUSANNE TREEBANK

Despite the low esteem in which theoretical linguists held taxonomic work, I soon found that even a small-scale English treebank yielded new scientific findings, sometimes findings that contradicted conventional linguistic wisdom. For instance, introductory textbooks of linguistics very commonly suggest that the two most basic English sentence types are the types "subject – transitive-verb – object", and "subject – intransitive-verb". Here, for instance, are the examples quoted by Victoria Fromkin and Robert Rodman in *An Introduction to Language* to illustrate the two first and simplest structures diagrammed in their section on sentence structure (Fromkin & Rodman 1983: 207-9):

the child found the puppy

the lazy child slept

Looking at statistics on clause structure in the treebank I developed at Lancaster, though, I found that this is misleading (Sampson 1987a: 90). "Subject – transitive verb – object" is a common sentence type, but sentences of the form "subject – intransitive-verb" are strikingly infrequent in English. If the sentence has no noun phrase object to follow the verb, it almost always includes some other constituent, for instance an adverbial element or a clause complement, in post-verb position. *The lazy child slept* may be acceptable in English, but it could be called a "basic" type of English sentence only in some very un-obvious sense of the word "basic".

Going a little deeper into technicalities, I was able to use the SUSANNE treebank to shed new light on an idea that has been known to most linguists since it was first discussed by Victor Yngve in 1960. Yngve argued that there is a constraint on the incidence of "left branching" in English parse trees[7]. Suppose, for instance, that we accept FIG. 2.2 (after Yngve 1960: 462) as an appropriate constituency diagram for the complex noun phrase *as good a young man for the job as you will ever find:* it is noticeable that the branches stretch down from the root much further in the "south-easterly" than the "south-westerly" direction. Yngve measured the left-branching factor of individual words numerically: for instance, *young* in FIG. 2.2 would be assigned the number three, because three of the four branches linking that word to the root are other than the rightmost branch below their respective mother nodes; and he suggested that there might be some fixed maximum, perhaps imposed by our mental language-processing machinery, such that grammatical structures are allowed to "grow" up to that maximum degree of left branching but not beyond it (whereas right branching is unlimited).

There is no doubt that Yngve was right to identify an asymmetry in English grammatical structure: the broadly N.W.-to-S.E. trend of parse trees is very noticeable in any English treebank. An investigation of the SUSANNE treebank, though, showed that the precise generalization was rather different from what Yngve supposed (Sampson 1997b). English does not have an absolute limit on the global left-branchingness of parse trees as wholes. It has a local and

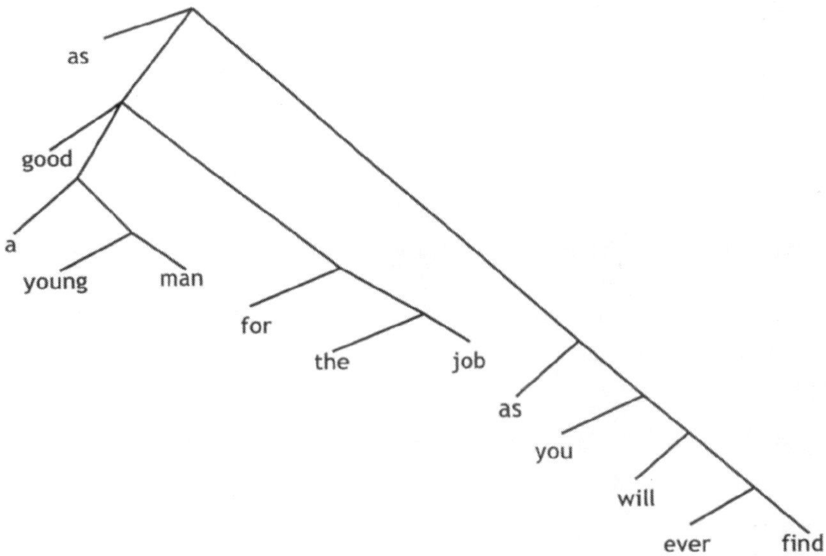

Figure 2.2. Tree for *"as good a young man for the job as you will ever find"*

statistical constraint on the left-branchingness of individual tree nodes: that is, there is a fixed probability for the expansion of any nonterminal symbol to contain another nonterminal symbol as other than the rightmost daughter, and, because this probability is low, in practice trees do not "grow" very far in the south-westerly direction. This was a rather pleasing finding: the fact that the constraint is local rather than global represents good news for computational tractability. Although Yngve's hypothesis had been a standard part of linguists' education for more than thirty years, there was no way of checking the facts before treebanks became available.

The statistics on left branching reveal a surprisingly precise kind of order underlying the diversity of natural-language constructions. Another kind of statistical investigation carried out on my original Lancaster treebank suggested a measure of precision in the extent of that diversity itself.

Richard Sharman (former Director of SRI Cambridge) has likened natural languages to fractal objects, which continue to display new detail no matter at what scale they are examined. An investigation I carried out on the frequencies of constructions in the Lancaster treebank made that analogy seem rather exact[8]. I took a high-frequency syntactic category, the noun phrase, and counted the frequencies of the various expansions of that category in the treebank – for instance, the commonest expansion of the category "noun phrase" (in terms of the coarse vocabulary of grammatical categories which I used for this purpose) was "determiner + singular noun", which accounted for about 14% of all noun phrases in the data. But there were more than 700 other noun-phrase types which occurred at lower frequencies – many types each occurred just once in the treebank. It turned out that there was a regular relationship between construction-frequencies, and the number of different constructions occurring at a given frequency. As one looks at lower and lower frequencies, more and more different constructions occur at those frequencies, with the consequence that quite large proportions of text include constructions which are individually rare. Specifically:

> if m is the frequency of the commonest single construction (in my data, m was about 28 per thousand words)
>
> and f is the relative frequency of some construction (fm is its absolute frequency)
>
> then the proportion of all construction-tokens which represent construction- types of relative frequency less than or equal to f is about $f^{0.4}$

This finding contradicts the picture of a natural language as containing a limited number of "competent" grammatical structures, which in practice are surrounded by a penumbra of more or less random, one-off "performance errors". If that picture were correct, one would expect to find construction frequencies distributed bimodally, with competent constructions occurring at reasonably high frequencies, individual performance errors each occurring at a low frequency, and not much in between. My data were not like that; constructions were distributed smoothly along the scale of frequencies, with no striking gaps[9].

Consider what the mathematical relationship I have quoted would mean, if it continued to hold true in much larger data sets that I was in a position to investigate. (I cannot know that it does, but as far as they went my data contained no suggestion that the relationship broke down at the lower frequencies.) If the relationship held true in larger bodies of data, then:

- one in every ten construction-tokens would represent a type which occurs at most once per 10,000 words
- one in every hundred construction-tokens would represent a type which occurs at most once per 3.5 million words

- one in every thousand construction-tokens would represent a type which occurs at most once per billion words

One per cent of all construction-tokens is surely far too high a proportion of language material for language engineering to wash its hands of as too unusual to deal with. One might feel that one in a thousand is still too high a proportion for that treatment. Yet, if we have to search millions, or even hundreds of millions, of words of text to find individual examples, we seem to be a long way away from the picture of natural language grammars as limited sets of rules. A fractal object can never be fully described – one has to be willing to ignore detail below some cut-off. But the degree of detail which computational linguistics ought to be taking into account extends well beyond the range of structures described in standard grammars of English.

These lessons which computational linguistics is beginning to learn about the need to come to grips with the tremendous detailed complexity of real-life data, and the inadequacy of approaches based on aprioristic ideas of language structure (such as the ideas which led to the invented example sentences I quoted from the Pisa conference), are parallel to lessons which the wider information-technology world learned twenty to thirty years earlier.

4. SMALL IS BEAUTIFUL

When increasing computer power first made it possible to attempt large-scale software projects in the late 1960s, software development hit a crisis (see e.g. Sommerville 1992: 3, Ghezzi et al. 1991: 4). Repeatedly, projects failed or massively overran their time and resource budgets, because the individualistic, "craftsman"-like style of programming which had worked well for small projects, where all the coding might be done by one person, could not be made to scale up for large industrial projects which are necessarily executed by teams, and which need to be robust under many variations of conditions over long periods. The supervisor of a programmer executing a one-man project could see the lines of code he wrote, but could not see the many factors the programmer was tacitly taking into consideration in deciding how to write the code (and hence did not grasp their significance); and those many factors were typically far fewer than *should* have been taken into consideration, if the software was to have a long life – with one-man programs it is cheaper to throw them away and write new ones if conditions change, but with large-scale projects one cannot do that. Large-scale software development requires all the real-life complications which software may face to be identified and made explicit among members of a team, before a line of code is written.

The IT response to the software crisis of the years around 1970 was to create the discipline of "software engineering", which nowadays trains computing professionals to resist the instinctive view that coding is their primary activity.

Software engineering teaches entrants to that profession to devote the bulk of their efforts to identifying and spelling out on paper, in increasing detail, the requirements and specifications for the software to be produced. Coding the software is the trivial stage at the end of the process; if the specifications have been made sufficiently explicit, translating them into code is an almost mechanical process.

The computational linguists of twenty years ago who developed language processing software on the basis of unnaturally simple invented examples were like the one-man programmers of the early 1960s who produced software that crashed when extraneous circumstances changed. Since about 1990, computational linguists have come to understand that invented examples cannot do justice to the reality of natural languages, and that there is no substitute for corpus data. The discipline has, one might say, learned part of the software engineering lesson. But it has not yet learned the whole. The discipline, as I see it, has not yet grasped that availability of real-life data is not enough: one must put time and effort into studying the detailed structure of the data, before one can develop language-processing systems which are responsive to that structure.

This partial vision is apparent in the widespread emphasis on size of language corpora. In the pre-software-engineering days, IT managers tended to evaluate their programmers in terms of lines of code written per week: the ultimate purpose of the job was to produce program code, so it seemed that someone who produced code faster must be a better worker. Nowadays, in that domain we understand that premature or too-rapid code production is not a virtue. But in corpus linguistics, whether we are talking about "raw", unannotated corpora or about structurally- annotated treebanks, too many people still seem to feel that the first or only desideratum is size[10].

Other things being equal, obviously more data are better than fewer data. If a corpus were entirely devoid of analytic mark-up, size might be the only consideration – though, now that (for the principal Western European languages, at least) virtually unlimited quantities of written material are freely available via the Internet, constructing a large but completely raw corpus would be an exercise of questionable value. Even relatively "raw" standard corpora such as Brown and LOB involved a great deal of effort put into ensuring that they were balanced and properly representative of a well-defined genre; this effort mattered, and to some extent it militated against large size (though the main size constraint on those early corpora derived from the technology of the time, which required the samples to be manually keyed in).

When we come to structurally annotated corpora, however, the picture is entirely different. The whole point of a treebank lies in the detail, consistency, and accuracy of its structural annotations, and, perhaps even more important, in the extent to which the scheme governing the annotations has been rendered explicit. All these things can be achieved only by methods which remain largely manual, so quality of annotation is a desirable feature which directly conflicts with quantity of annotated material. These features are both desirable, obviously; but one must be traded off against the other. At present, I sense a danger that computational linguists are much more aware of the quantity than of the quality factor (perhaps because quantity is more objective and easier to "sell" to research sponsors).

In the work of my group I have chosen the opposite priority: we treat detail, accuracy, and explicitness of annotation as more important than quantity of material annotated, with the inevitable consequence that our treebanks have to be relatively small. (The book which defines the SUSANNE annotation scheme contains quite a lot more wording than the SUSANNE treebank.) All agree that what is ultimately needed are very large quantities of very accurately annotated data. On the basis of the software engineering precedent, I would argue that we have a better chance of moving towards that ideal by taking care of analytic detail and accuracy first and worrying about quantity later, than the other way round. But alternative strategies may also be worth trying; my main point is that one should not be so dazzled by the quantity factor as to lose sight of the quality factor altogether.

5. ANNOTATING A SPOKEN CORPUS

Despite its small size, the SUSANNE treebank seems to have established itself over the seven years since its first release as a useful international research resource. I quite often encounter research based on it that was carried out by groups at distant sites of whom I had no prior knowledge. Now that my group has moved on, within the CHRISTINE project, to drawing trees for spoken language, many new analytic problems have been presenting themselves which again require detailed consideration, in order to develop consistent and logical annotation guidelines, and which in consequence again militate against corpus size.

How, for instance, are we to indicate what is going on in a "speech repair" – a passage in which a speaker corrects himself or changes tack in mid-utterance? FIG. 2.3 is an outline version (using spelled-out rather than coded grammatical category labels) of the CHRISTINE analysis of part of an utterance in which a speaker embarks on a relative clause modifying *any bonus* and then decides instead to use *anything* as the head of the phrase and to make *bonus* the predicate.

We use the # symbol to indicate the point where the speaker interrupts himself; but we need rules for deciding how to fit that symbol, and the words before and after it, into a coherent structure – do we, for instance, label what precedes the interruption point as a relative clause, even though only its first word, *that*,

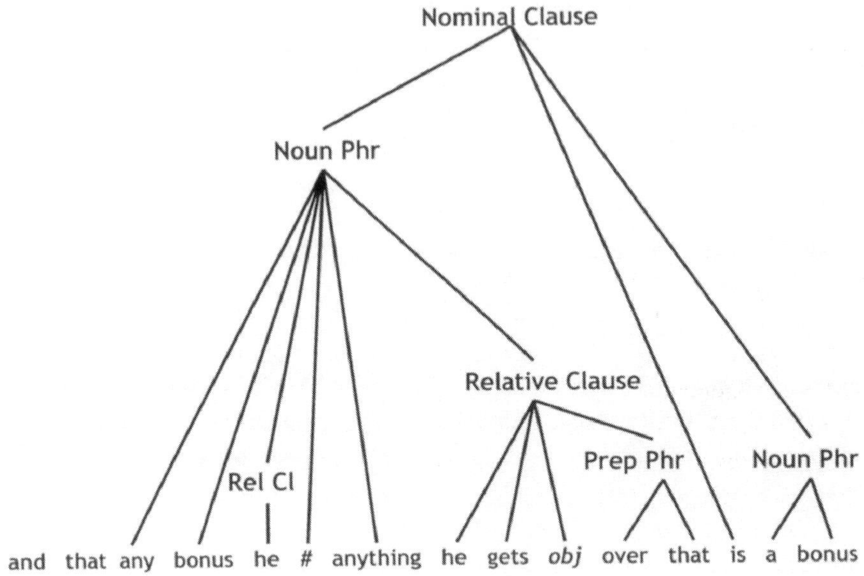

Figure 2.3. Tree from CHRISTINE Corpus

was actually uttered? Where in the tree do we attach the interruption symbol? The tree in FIG. 2.3 is based on explicit decisions about these and related questions, and the variety of speech management phenomena found in real-life spontaneous speech is such that these guidelines have had to grow quite complex; but only by virtue of them can thousands of individual speech repairs be annotated in a predictable, consistent fashion.

Structural annotation of spontaneous speech calls into question grammatical distinctions which, in writing, are fundamental. Written English takes pains to leave readers in no doubt about the distinction between direct and indirect speech, which is marked by punctuation even where the wording itself does not make the status of a particular quotation clear. Speech has no inverted commas, but commonly wording shows whether quotations are directly reported or paraphrased. For instance, in the following CHRISTINE example:

> *he said he hates drama because the teacher takes no notice, he said one week Stuart was hitting me with a stick and the teacher just said calm down you boys*

the words *he hates drama* (rather than *I hate ...*) show that the object of the first *he said* is indirect speech, whereas *hitting me* (rather than *hitting him*), and the imperative and second-person form in the quotation attributed to the teacher, show that the object of the second *he said* is a direct quotation which itself contains an internal direct quotation. But matters are not always so straightforward. Two more CHRISTINE examples run:

> *I said well that's his hard luck*

> *well Billy, Billy says well take that and then he'll come back*

The discourse item *well* at the beginning of *well that's his hard luck* usually marks the beginning of a direct quotation, but in context that would call for *your hard luck* rather than *his...* Again, following *Billy* the word *well* and the imperative *take* suggest direct speech, *he'll come* in place of *I'll come* suggests indirect speech. In spoken English it seems that directness of quotation is not an absolute property but a matter of gradience. Quotations may be reported more less directly, which creates a new challenge for an annotation scheme that was developed originally in connexion with written prose.

Indeed, the structures found in spontaneous speech sometimes call into question not merely the inherited range of grammatical-category distinctions but the very concept of grouping utterances into tree-shaped structures. It is no surprise to find that spontaneous utterances are sometimes too chaotic for any structure to be clearly assignable. More troubling are cases where the structure does seem clear, but it conflicts with the hierarchical assumption which is implicit in the use of tree diagrams or labelled bracketing. This applies to what I call "Markovian" utterances (which occur repeatedly in the CHRISTINE data), where a window of limited size moved through the wording would at each point contain a coherent, normal grammatical sequence, but the utterance as a whole cannot be assigned a single structure. Consider for instance the following, said by Anthony Wedgwood Benn, M.P., on a BBC radio programme:

> *and what is happening* {pause} *in Britain today* {pause} *is ay- demand for an entirely new foreign policy quite different from the Cold War policy* {pause} *is emerging from the Left*

The long noun phrase *an entirely new foreign policy quite different from the Cold War policy* seems to function, with respect to the words before it, as the complement of a prepositional phrase introduced by *for* which postmodifies *a demand*; yet, with respect to what follows it, the same phrase-token functions as subject of *is emerging*. Within the usual framework of grammatical analysis, one constituent cannot fill both of these roles simultaneously. Yet is it reasonable to abandon the concept of hierarchical grammatical structuring, which has been entrenched in Western linguistic thought for centuries, because of a limited number of "Markovian" examples which seem to conflict with it?

I have argued elsewhere (Rahman & Sampson 1999) that some of the difficulties in evolving well-defined guidelines for consistent structural annotation of spoken language may stem from the fact that our inherited grammatical tradition has evolved almost exclusively in connexion with written language. It may be that fully-adequate schemes for annotating speech treebanks will eventually need to adopt notational devices that depart further from traditional grammatical ideas that anything yet adopted in our CHRISTINE Corpus. These are problems with which we are only beginning to grapple.

6. USING THE CHRISTINE CORPUS

Already, though, our data on structures in spontaneous English speech are beginning to yield novel scientific findings that simply could not be addressed before speech treebanks were available. I used an early version of the CHRISTINE treebank, containing most but not all of the material now circulated as CHRISTINE/Stage I, to examine correlations between grammatical complexity and speakers' demographic characteristics (Sampson 2001, chapter 5). By "grammatical complexity" here I mean what traditional school grammar means when it calls some sentences "simple" and others "complex": a complex sentences is one that contains a subordinate clause. Informal speech cannot be divided straightforwardly into "sentences", but one can ask, for each successive word of a speaker's utterance, how many clause nodes occur on the path between that word and the root note of the largest structure within which the word occurs; that gives a complexity figure for individual words, and a speaker can be assigned a figure for the mean complexity of all his words.

The only earlier research on this issue of which I am aware is that of Basil Bernstein (e.g. 1971: chapters 5-6), who claimed to find a strong correlation between grammatical complexity and social class: middle-class speakers produced utterances of greater complexity than working-class speakers. (This was one of the research results on which Bernstein based his famous theory of "restricted" v. "elaborated" linguistic codes.) However, Bernstein's analysis was based on a small data-set which was gathered for the purpose in a rather artificial manner: it by no means represented a fair sample of spontaneous usage – no such samples were available to Bernstein.

My analysis of the CHRISTINE material – which, although it has its own shortcomings, can claim to be a genuine cross-section of spontaneous speech in the United Kingdom in the 1990s – did not show correlations between grammatical complexity and social class (though I would not want to rest much reliance on a negative finding – there may be such correlations which failed to show up in our material). However, the data did contain positive evidence of a different kind of grammatical/social relationship. There was a statistically significant correlation of grammatical complexity with age.

Of course, anyone would expect very young children to produce simpler utterances, on average, than mature speakers; but those who believe, with the generative linguists, in a "critical age" for language acquisition (e.g. Lenneberg 1967: 142ff., Pinker 1994: 290ff.) should predict that complexity will increase over the period until puberty, but will then flatten out as the innate biological clock closes the language acquisition machinery down and a speaker enters the period of his life during which he is a language-user but not a language-learner. Our figures were not like that. Complexity grew more slowly in adulthood than in childhood, but it continued to grow throughout life, so that, say, people in their fifties were producing slightly more complex utterances, on average, than people in their forties. This finding is, so far as I know, entirely novel, and is surely one of some human significance. (Having been born during the Second World War myself, I find it rather heartwarming.) It was only made possible by the creation of a speech treebank.

My new LUCY project, which will sample the writing of unskilled young adults as well as skilled producers of "model" documentation, will enable new kinds of question to be examined objectively for the first time, to my knowledge. Is the fumbling, imperfect writing of unskilled youngsters at the end of secondary schooling located (with respect to linguistic structure) on a direct route between the structure of spontaneous speech and that of model written prose, or does it have characteristics of its own, different from either of the latter? Is learning to be a skilled writer merely a matter of editing out features which are appropriate only to speech, or does it involve mastering structural techniques which are absent in spoken language?

People have ideas about these questions, but even the ideas of educated professionals in this domain are often based on guesswork which is sometimes demonstrably incorrect. That does not always mean that people overlook differences between spoken and written structure; sometimes, they see differences which do not exist. In the opening chapter of an influential book on this issue, Cheshire & Milroy (1993: 78) quote, as their paradigm example of a construction which is pervasive in spoken English but "avoided" or "unacceptab[le]" in the written language, what they call "dislocated" sentences, such as *These cats, they're hungry*. In reality, treebank data show that this construction is found in careful written English. Half the examples quoted when the construction is defined in the SUSANNE annotation scheme (Sampson 1995: §4.525) are taken from the highly literary genre called *belles lettres*. To date we know very little about structural differences between speech and writing, in the sense that our assertions are founded on objective, quantitative data.

7. CONCLUSION

We live surrounded by oceans of language; yet at the end of the twentieth century there are still vast areas of knowledge about language and its workings to be explored, which can only be approached through the painstaking work of developing structurally-annotated corpora of language samples. For those working on languages other than English, the existing resources are often less adequate than those with which we English linguists are blessed; but, by the same token, the range of virgin territory available for them to explore is all the greater. As a new century dawns, the future for treebank research looks bright indeed.

Notes

1. I believe the term "treebank", now in standard international use in this sense, was first coined by Geoffrey Leech in connexion with the project described here.

2. My home page, http://www.grsampson.net/, contains references to and locations of the treebank resources mentioned above. For the corpora mentioned below as providing language samples used in various treebanks, see http://nora.hd.uib.no/icame.html (Brown and LOB Corpora) and http://info.ox.ac.uk/bnc/ (British National Corpus).

3. I make no apology for repeating here examples which I used in order to make similar points in Sampson (1987a).

4. See, for instance, Chomsky's use of the term "taxonomic model" (1964: 11), or J.J. Katz's comments (1971) on linguistics as what he called "library science".

5. See, for instance, chapter 9 of Allen (1976).

6. For the doctrine of "competence" v. "performance", see Chomsky (1965: 4, 9, 15). Linguistic nativism is propounded in books such as *Reflections on Language* (Chomsky 1976) and *The Language Instinct* (Pinker 1994). I have pointed out the vacuousness of Chomsky's and Pinker's various arguments for linguistic nativism in my EDUCATING EVE (Sampson 1997a).

7. Others later suggested that the nature of the constraint may vary among different natural languages.

8. The analytic findings are presented in Sampson (1987b); see Sampson (1992: 440-5) for discussion of a critique of my conclusions by Briscoe and others.

9. It would in any case be surprising to find that "performance error" was an important factor in this treebank, which was based on published writing.

10. I have even heard a Swedish lady linguist comment, rather wickedly, that she realized that corpus linguistics was a male-dominated profession when she found that everyone with a new corpus wanted to tell her how big his was.

References

Allen, D.E. (1976). *The Naturalist in Britain: A Social History*. Penguin.

Bernstein, B. (1971). *Class, Codes and Control, vol. 1: Theoretical Studies Towards a Sociology of Language*. Routledge and Kegan Paul.

Bies, Ann, et al. (1995). *Bracketing Guidelines for Treebank II Style*. `http://www.cis.upenn.edu/~treebank/home.html`

Cheshire, Jenny, & J. Milroy (1993). Syntactic variation in non-standard dialects. In J. & Lesley Milroy, eds., *Real English: The Grammar of English Dialects in the British Isles*. Longman.

Chomsky, A.N. (1964). *Current Issues in Linguistic Theory*. Mouton.

Chomsky, A.N. (1965). *Aspects of the Theory of Syntax*. MIT Press (Cambridge, Mass.).

Chomsky, A.N. (1976). *Reflections on Language*. Temple Smith.

Edwards, Jane (1992). Design principles in the transcription of spoken discourse. In Svartvik 1992.

Fromkin, Victoria, & R. Rodman (1983). *An Introduction to Language* (3rd. ed.). Holt, Rinehart and Winston.

Ghezzi, C., et al. (1991). *Fundamentals of Software Engineering*. Prentice-Hall.

Katz, J.J. (1971). *The Underlying Reality of Language and Its Philosophical Import*. Harper & Row.

Lenneberg, E.H. (1967). *Biological Foundations of Language*. Wiley.

Pinker, S. (1994). *The Language Instinct: The New Science of Language and Mind*. William Morrow (New York). My page references are to the Penguin ed., 1995.

Rahman, Anna, & G.R. Sampson (1999). Extending grammar annotation standards to spontaneous speech. In J. Kirk, ed., *Corpora Galore*. Rodopi (Amsterdam).

Sampson, G.R. (1987a). Probabilistic models of analysis. In R.G. Garside et al., eds., *The Computational Analysis of English: A Corpus-Based Approach*. Longman.

Sampson, G.R. (1987b). Evidence against the 'grammatical'/'ungrammatical' distinction. In W. Meijs, ed., *Corpus Linguistics and Beyond*, Rodopi (Amsterdam). Reprinted in Sampson 2001.

Sampson, G.R. (1992). Probabilistic parsing. In Svartvik 1992.

Sampson, G.R. (1995). *English for the Computer: The SUSANNE Corpus and Analytic Scheme*. Clarendon Press (Oxford).

Sampson, G.R. (1997a). *Educating Eve*. Cassell. Revised paperback ed., Cassell, 1999.

Sampson, G.R. (1997b). Depth in English grammar. *Journal of Linguistics* 33.131-51.

Sampson, G.R. (2001). *Empirical Linguistics*. Continuum.

Sommerville, I. (1992). *Software Engineering* (4th ed.). Addison-Wesley (Wokingham, Berks.).

Svartvik, J., ed. (1992). *Directions in Corpus Linguistics: Proceedings of Nobel Symposium 82*. Mouton de Gruyter (Berlin).

Yngve, V. (1960). A model and an hypothesis for language structure. *Proceedings of the American Philosophical Society* 104.444-66.

Chapter 3

BANK OF ENGLISH AND BEYOND

Hand-crafted parsers for functional annotation

Timo Järvinen*

Conexor oy

Helsinki Science Park

Koetilantie 3, 00710 Helsinki, Finland

timo.jarvinen@conexor.fi

Abstract The 200 million word corpus of the Bank of English was annotated morphologically and syntactically using the English Constraint Grammar analyser, a rule-based shallow parser developed at the Research Unit for Computational Linguistics, University of Helsinki. We discuss the annotation system and methods used in the corpus work, as well as the theoretical assumptions of the Constraint Grammar syntax. Based on our experience in large-scale corpus work, we argue for a deeper and more explicit, dependency-based syntactic representation. We present a new practical parsing system, the Functional Dependency Grammar parser, developed from the Constraint Grammar system, and discuss its suitability for treebank annotation.

Keywords: Parsing, Tagging, Constraint Grammar, Functional Dependency Grammar, Bank of English

1. INTRODUCTION

The Bank of English is an international English language corpus project sponsored by Collins Publishers, Glasgow, and conducted by the COBUILD[1] team at the University of Birmingham, UK. A 200 million word portion of the corpus was annotated morphologically and syntactically from 1993 to 1995 at the Research Unit for Computational Linguistics (RUCL), University of Helsinki, using the English two-level morphological analyser, based on the

*The author was hired to conduct the annotation of the Bank of English data in Helsinki from February 1993 to January 1995.

A. Abeillé (ed.), Treebanks: Building and Using Parsed Corpora, 43–59.

model proposed by (Koskenniemi, 1983), and English Constraint Grammar (ENGCG) analyser, originally proposed by (Karlsson, 1990).

The ENGCG system was chosen for the project due to the very reliable morphological analyser. The main objective of the project was to provide annotated corpora for the lexicographers compiling the second edition of the Collins COBUILD Dictionary of the English language (Sinclair et al., 1995).

We present and discuss the methodology of the large-scale corpus work, first documented in (Järvinen, 1994). Finally, we focus on the issue of rule-based methods in functional syntactic annotation. Many of the later treebank projects use statistical methods for syntactic analysis. Probabilistic models are developed for dependency parsing, such as (Eisner, 1996) and (Collins, 1996). For instance, (Hajič, 1998), writes "It is a well known fact that hand-crafted rules work for restricted domains and vocabularies, whereas they generally fail for unrestricted text parsing". As some pending problems in the ENGCG-style analysis may provoke doubts concerning the feasibility of rule-based methods in general, another system, called the Functional Dependency Grammar (FDG) parser by (Tapanainen and Järvinen, 1997), is presented, with an illustrative comparison of these approaches to the corpus annotation task.

2. ANNOTATING 200 MILLION WORDS

2.1 Analysis System

The Constraint Grammar (CG) framework for the morphological and shallow syntactic parsing of natural languages, presented in detail in (Karlsson et al., 1995), consists of the following sequentially applied modules:

- pre-processing (segmentation and tokenisation)
- lexical analysis (POS assignment)
- morphological disambiguation (POS tagging)
- syntactic mapping and disambiguation (functional analysis)

The framework is supposed to be language independent, though (Karlsson et al., 1995) focus on the English Constraint Grammar, which is the earliest and probably the most mature system based on the Constraint grammar framework.[2]

Preprocessing. ENGCG system contains an effective pre-processing module which is able to detect sentence boundaries in the running text. The requirements for the input texts are very flexible. However, it is assumed that all sentence fragments are either markup coded or separated from the text passages e.g. by two or more blank lines.

The main component of the preprocessor is a rule-based tokeniser. It identifies punctuation marks and sentence boundaries, detects some 7,000 different multiword idioms (mainly complex prepositions and adverbs, e.g. *out of* and *more than*, respectively) and compounds (such as *United States*, *lost property*), and also splits enclitic forms (such as *I'll*, *it's*) into syntactically minimal tokens.

Lexical analysis. The lexical analysis is an integral part of the ENGCG analysis system. It uses the two-level (TWOL) morphological analyser by (Koskenniemi, 1983). The ENGTWOL master lexicon initially used in the Bank analyses contained approximately 55,000 entries. Morphological analysis caters for all inflected forms of the lexical items. Generally, the coverage of the lexicon is between 97% - 98% of all word-form tokens in running text. Words not known to the lexicon are assigned possible analysis by a separate heuristic morphological analyser by Voutilainen and Tapanainen, which is applied after ENGTWOL analysis. Given the heuristic component, there is strictly no need for updating the lexicon. During the Bank project, some 20,000 entries were added to the lexicon.

The lexical analysis assigns all possible readings to input tokens. On average, each input word-form token receives 1.7–2.2 alternative analyses, and 35–45% of the word-tokens in a running text are ambiguous in the ENGTWOL lexical analysis (Voutilainen, 1995).

ENGCG morphological disambiguation. In the ENGCG output, each input word is given in angle brackets followed by one or more morphological readings in indented lines. Each line contains the base form and morphosyntactic tags. The Figure 3.1 presents an ENGCG analysis of the sentence (1) below.

(1) *"Without a stable, sustainable housing system aimed at meeting need, the business performance of this country's biggest companies is compromised", said Shelter director Sheila McKechnie.*

There are 16 main part-of-speech categories in the ENGCG description, listed in Table 3.1. There is a large number of minor features used in combination with the main categories. In total, there are some 140 different morphological tags. For a comprehensive list, see (Voutilainen et al., 1992, pp. 17-21).

The ENGCG system is a very reliable morphological analyser. For example, the evaluation in (Voutilainen et al., 1992, pp. 11-12), shows that the ENGCG outperformed other statistical part-of-speech analysers, CLAWS (Garside et al., 1987) and PARTS (Church, 1988). The performance rates are *recall*, i.e., the ratio of assigned correct readings per all correct readings and *precision*, i.e., the ratio of assigned correct readings per all assigned readings.

Table 3.1. The ENGCG part- of- speech categories, adopted from (Voutilainen and Järvinen, 1996).

Feature	Description	Example
A	adjective	small
ABBR	abbreviation	Ltd.
ADV	adverb	soon
CC	coordinating conjunction	and
CS	subordinating conjunction	that
DET	determiner	any
INFMARK>	infinitive marker	to
INTERJ	interjection	hooray
N	noun	house
NEGPART	negative particle	not
NUM	numeral	two
PCP1	ing form	writing
PCP2	ed/en form	written
PREP	preposition	in
PRON	pronoun	this
V	verb	write

The lower precision of ENGCG is due to the fact that 3-6% of the tokens are assigned two or more readings. This means that some of the ambiguity has been left unresolved. For example, the word-form *aimed* in Figure 3.1 has two morphological readings after the ENGCG disambiguation: a past participle (PCP2) and a past tense (V PAST) form.

Table 3.2. Performance rates of part-of-speech taggers compared in (Voutilainen et al., 1992).

	CLAWS	**PARTS**	**ENGCG**
recall	96.95%	96.21%	99.77%
precision	96.95%	96.21%	95.54%

ENGCG syntactic mapping and disambiguation. The distinction between part-of-speech analysis (usually called morphological disambiguation in the context of CG literature) and syntactic analysis is notationally very clear. The syntactic labels are prefixed by the character '@' and they are assigned to the morphological readings. The assignment of all possible syntactic labels to each morphological reading is called mapping.

There are three syntactic readings in the word-form *aimed* in Figure 3.1: @APP, @<NOM-MAINV and @+FMAINV, for apposition, postmodifying

non-finite main verb and finite-main verb, respectively. The analysis is correct, because the contextually legitimate alternative, @<NOM-MAINV, is present in the analysis.

Note that in the ENGCG system, the syntactic analysis is not allowed to discard a morphological reading.

The syntactic part of the analyser was considerably less developed when the project commenced in February 1993. The original ENGCG syntax written by Arto Anttila comprised some 440 rules. During a two year period, the current author further expanded the existing syntactic description of ENGCG. The final version of the syntactic description comprised 1139 hand-written rules.

Based on a small sample of previously unseen text, the error rate achieved by the ENGCG syntactic analysis was approximately 2%, i.e., 2 words out of 100 did not get the correct syntactic code. Nevertheless, the ambiguity rate is still fairly high, 16.4% for a half-million word sample, which means that 16 words out of 100 still have more than one morphological or syntactic alternative. Much of the remaining ambiguity is of the prepositional attachment type, accounting for approximately 20% of all remaining ambiguity.

2.2 Methodology

The methodology used in the project differs from that used in many other corpus projects, e.g. Penn Treebank (Marcus et al., 1993) and Prague Dependency Treebank (Hajič, 1998), that rely on manual annotation and statistical models derived from the manually annotated corpora. A project with more similar aims and methodology was the contemporary annotation of the British National Corpus (Leech et al., 1994). First, the analysis system that was used in the Bank of English annotation existed prior to the project. Second, the size of the corpus to be annotated, 200 million words, in proportion to the two man-years of work allocated to the project sets very stricts limits on the manual corpus work. The major challenge of the Bank of English project was to apply and further develop the methods of updating the rule-based annotation system semi-manually.

The two man-years of work included everything that was done to the data in Helsinki. We received the data on tapes, uploaded it to the computer and started to process it. The annotated data was then saved to tapes, backups were made, and a copy was sent back to the COBUILD team. In all phases some random samples of the data were manually inspected and various automatic methods were developed to monitor the data. Some parts of the analysis system, especially the syntactic component, were continuously developed. However, to maintain the consistency of the analysis, it was decided that the morphological part of ENGCG should be frozen, as well as the set of labels used in the syntactic description.

The ENGCG analysis system relies on linguistic rules rather than statistical generalisations derived from corpora. The linguistic information possessed by a linguist is carefully hand-crafted in the parsing grammar.[3] Initially, there was no manually-checked syntactic corpus available, but it became evident that some amount of benchmarked data was necessary to monitor the quality of the analyser.

The data. Each month the COBUILD team from Birmingham University supplied an approximately 10 million word batch of markup coded running text, listed in Table 3.3, in ASCII format. Each batch consists of individual texts such as a book, magazine or radio program. The Bank of English corpus annotated in Helsinki comprises 26 different batches of data. The data includes all major variants; British English (BrE), American English (AmE) and Australian English. The last 30 million words were received in January 1995 and the annotation was completed in March 1995.

Table 3.3. The Bank of English data annotated by the Helsinki team.

data	**words**	**text type**
Today(1)	10,019,195	newspaper
Times	10,090,991	newspaper
BBC	18,076,124	broadcasting; BrE
Britcorp(1)	9,232,527	literature (scientific, popular); BrE
Britcorp(2)	13,925,852	literature (scientific, popular); BrE
Economist(1)	5,149,236	newspaper
WSJ	6,045,864	newspaper
Independent	4,915,838	newspaper
Magazines(1)	5,283,704	weekly magazines
Magazines(2)	10,365,173	weekly magazines
Ambooks(1)	10,532,267	literature (scientific, popular); AmE
Guardian	12,027,320	newspaper
NPR	21,396,415	broadcasting; AmE
Spoken(1)	8,423,078	spoken language
Ephemeral(1)	1,401,660	miscellaneous (ads, booklets etc)
Economist(2)	1,672,322	newspaper
New Scientist(1)	3,050,156	scientific magazine
Scbooks	3,873,478	literature (popular)
Magazines(3)	12,410,868	weekly magazines
Ambooks(2)	4,288,569	literature (scientific, popular); AmE
Economist(3)	1,638,116	newspaper
Ephemeral(2)	355,057	miscellaneous (ads, booklets etc)
New Scientist(2)	1,053,565	scientific magazine
Oz	9,977,125	newspapers, misc; Australian English
Spoken(2)	6,491,299	spoken language
Today(2)	7,483,020	newspaper
total	199,178,819	

Monitoring the input. Every new batch was first scanned using the ENGTWOL lexical and morphological analyser in a filtering mode for the purpose of detecting words not included in the lexicon.

Each batch of incoming data was inspected before annotation. During this phase, the pre-processing modules were updated. We developed rigorous procedures to filter the incoming data and update the lexicon of the parsing system. The syntactic description was developed and revised as part of the project.

Though the conversion from various formats into a markup-coded ASCII text was done by the COBUILD team, the incoming texts contained some variation with respect to the inventory and use of the markup code labels in different batches. The markup codes were retained in the output. Some information conveyed by the markup codes was utilised in the parsing process.

Lexical work. The practices of the lexical work in the Bank project differ somewhat from the principles obeyed in the compilation of the ENGTWOL master lexicon prior to the project. Among these principles were that no misspellings should be admitted and that domain-generic material should be preferred. Basically, it was assumed that the input should be error-free, fairly standard written English (Voutilainen and Heikkilä, 1995, pp. 92-96).

These assumptions did not hold very well with respect to a diverse range of texts in the Bank of English material. If our aim is to supply every word in running text with all proper morphological and syntactic readings, we should include all frequent non-standard words such as *larn*, *veggie*, *wanna* to the lexicon, because otherwise the whole sentence could be misanalysed.

An additional practical advantage of including all frequent tokens in the lexicon is that ENGTWOL filtering of incoming texts produces output that can be more reliably dealt with by automatic means. When all frequent non-standard and even foreign words are listed in the lexicon, the output can be used in a more straightforward way for generating new entries to be added to the lexicon.

In addition to various sub-standard forms, apparent misspellings should be accounted for. We decided to correct some of the most frequent misspellings such as the strings *ofthe* and *andthe*, for *of the* and *and the* already at the preprocessing stage, and a special code marking the correction was inserted into the text. It was considered crucial for the utilisation of the corpus in research purposes that no information is lost during possible standardisation in the analysis. Therefore, we aimed to mark all corrections made to the text.

We have also included highly domain-specific entries into the lexicon if they were frequent enough in certain types of data, especially when heuristics might produce erroneous or incomplete analyses for the word in question (e.g. the species of fish which have the same form in singular and plural: *brill*, *chub*, *garfish*).

We used the following procedure of adding new entries to the lexicon: first, all words are classified according to the part-of-speech they belong to. Second, new entries in the ENGTWOL format are generated automatically from these word-lists. Lists of new entries are carefully checked up and additional features (such as transitivity and complementation features for verbs) are supplied manually. In describing the items, we relied mainly on the Collins COBUILD Dictionary (Sinclair, 1987) and the Collins English Dictionary which were available to us in electronic form. But when the usage and distribution seemed to be unclear, we generated an on-line concordance directly from the corpus. Since only those word-forms that had a frequency of, say, at least ten tokens in the corpus, were taken into account, this method seems to be quite reliable.

Note that we have only very limited means of detecting errors and omissions in the lexicon during the initial filtering phase. Once a certain string has one entry in the lexicon, it is not present in the output of the filtering and other potential uses might not be added to the lexicon. However, frequent errors tend to get corrected since all incorrect analyses detected during the manual inspection were corrected in the lexicon.

Syntactic benchmark. Each rule or constraint in the parsing grammar contains a piece of linguistic information, and due to the large number of constraints that interact in a very complicated way in the disambiguation process, the consequences of adding or removing a constraint are not always easy to predict. To maintain the quality and consistency of the output when the grammar was constantly revised, we manually checked and corrected a small corpus according to the ENGCG annotation scheme.

In January 1995, the test corpus consists of 22 individual texts from the Bank of English data. This disambiguated corpus, consisting of some 43,000 words, makes it possible to test the rules automatically against representative language data. Texts were chosen to take variation in different text types into account.

Monitoring output. To meet the needs of the COBUILD team, two postprocessing modules were added to the system. First, all multiword compounds made by the ENGCG preprocessor were resolved after the syntactic analysis. This was considered necessary for the lexicographic work. Last, a simple program was added to check the output format of the analysed data.

Experiments with spoken data. The ENGCG system was developed mainly for the analysis of standard prose. Because the data included also a large spoken language sample (total 15 million words) which would have been poorly analysed by the standard version, I tested with a separate module which included a separate preprocessor and a separate lexicon. The additional pre-

```
"<'>"
"<*without>"
        "without" <*> PREP (@ADVL)
"<a>"
        "a" <INDEF> DET CENTRAL ART SG (@DN>)
"<stable>"
        "stable" N NOM SG (@<P)
        "stable" A ABS (@<P)
"<,>"
"<sustainable>"
        "sustainable" A ABS (@AN>)
"<housing>"
        "house" <SVO> <SV> PCP1 (@NN> @-FMAINV @AN>)
"<system>"
        "system" N NOM SG (@SUBJ @OBJ @NN>)
"<aimed>"
        "aim" <SVO> <SV> PCP2 (@APP @<NOM-FMAINV)
        "aim" <SVO> <SV> V PAST VFIN (@+FMAINV)
"<at>"
        "at" PREP (@ADVL)
"<meeting>"
        "meet" <SVO> <SV> PCP1 (@NN> @<P-FMAINV @AN>)
"<need>"
        "need" <SVO> <SV> V IMP VFIN (@+FMAINV)
        "need" N NOM SG (@OBJ)
"<,>"
"<the>"
        "the" <DEF> DET CENTRAL ART SG/PL (@DN>)
"<business>"
        "business" N NOM SG (@NN>)
"<performance>"
        "performance" N NOM SG (@OBJ @APP @<P)
"<of>"
        "of" PREP (@<NOM-OF)
"<this>"
        "this" DET CENTRAL DEM SG (@DN>)
"<country's>"
        "country" N GEN SG (@GN>)
        ...
```

Figure 3.1. A sample of the ENGCG annotation from the Bank of English.

processing includes e.g. the recognition of contracted verb forms. The main difference in the spoken language lexicon is that almost all abbreviations were removed, because no abbreviations were used in the transcripts. A number of entries which were apparent hesitations or false starts, such as *mm*, were added to the lexicon. Some new rules were added to the parsing grammar to cater for the syntactic cues provided by typical speech phenomena.

This adaptation of the ENGCG system took about one week of work: updating the lexicon (2 workdays), updating the pre- and postprocessors (2 workdays) and adaptation of syntax (1 workday). The results of the spoken language analysis were encouraging, e.g. the ambiguity rate at the syntactic level is considerably lower than in written texts, only about 10.5–11.0%.

3. ENGCG SYNTAX

Morphological syntax. The Constraint Grammar approach, as discussed in (Karlsson, 1995), relies on traditional grammar. However, the role of morphology is strongly emphasised. For example, (Karlsson, 1995, p. 37) writes: "the cornerstone of syntax is morphology, especially the language-particular systems of morphological features". The distinction between morphological disambiguation and syntactic analysis in the ENGCG system is linguistically less clear though they were conducted sequentially using distinct rule components, and there is a notational difference between morphological readings and syntactic functional labels in the output.

The output of the syntactic analysis did not contain any other structural information, but functional labels assigned to word-form tokens. Therefore, the ENGCG syntactic annotation is not a treebank, but rather a kind of "supertagging" where each token is assigned morphological and dependency-oriented syntactic information.

This is most undesirable, because syntactic functions are essentially relations between elements, not properties of a single element comparable to morphological features. Though a syntactic label in the ENGCG, such as @SUBJ for subject, correctly identifies the head of the noun phrase, it does not show which predicate is the head. The correct syntactic labels being masked by the spurious ambiguity makes the practical utilisation of the analysis very difficult.

Shallow syntax. (Karlsson, 1995, p. 33) maintains that "Constraint Grammar syntax is *surface syntax* rather than deep syntax because no syntactic structure is postulated or assigned that is not in direct correspondence with the word-form tokens that 'are there' in the sentence". This requirement results in an extremely shallow syntactic analysis. For example, as (Anttila, 1995) points out, the subject and complement functions are missing in the CG analysis of the sentences like *To be is to do*, the infinitives being analysed as non-finite main predicators.

In the original ENGCG syntactic grammar by (Anttila, 1995), infinitives received only verbal functions, but participles were assigned both nominal and verbal labels. The special treatment given to participles was due to the fact that the ambiguity between verbal and nominal usage was not introduced in the morphological description. For example, it was thought correct to analyse both *housing* and *meeting* simply as present participles (PCP1) in the ENGCG description, as Figure 3.1, shows though the former is apparently fully nominalised, i.e. *housing system*, whereas the latter is verbal in the context *aimed at meeting need.*

Because it is not possible to construct a parse tree mechanically on the basis of CG analysis as demonstrated in (Voutilainen and Järvinen, 1996), it is very difficult to test the formal consistency of the proposed analysis. For instance, even if a linguist wants to maintain that certain functions are unique, it is extremely difficult to formulate a practical grammar that uses such a principle consistently in a CG formalism (Tapanainen, 1999).

Ambiguity. Though the linguistic quality and merits of the ENGCG analysis are indisputable at the level of part-of-speech analysis, the output was not considered usable by the Birmingham/COBUILD team due to some pending problems. Since the distinction between the nominal and verbal usage of participles is crucial in the lexicographic work, the ENGCG morphological analysis alone is not suitable without the syntactic representation. However, there was only a limited number of digits to encode the POS information in the lookup program used by the lexicographers. Because every combination of tags requires one digit, due to the large number of different ambiguity classes in the ENGCG output, there were too many tag combinations to be accounted for.

The major problem in the Constraint Grammar systems seems to be the ambiguity that is left unresolved in the analysis. Given the amount of work dedicated to developing the syntactic grammar, the result obtained by English Constraint Grammar syntax was only moderate. Though some 97%–98% of the word-form tokens were assigned a correct syntactic label, the amount of ambiguity left pending was high: 14%–17% of word-forms retained two or more morphological or syntactic labels in the syntactic disambiguation. Comparable results were achieved by (Müürisep, 1998), using the Constraint Grammar approach to the surface syntactic description of Estonian. Therefore, it seems that it is very difficult to reduce the amount of syntactic ambiguity past a certain point in the Constraint Grammar framework without altering the accuracy of the analysis.

4. FDG PARSER

The system that Pasi Tapanainen and the current author started to build after the Bank of English project, in early 1995, was aimed to produce explicit syntactic representations for unrestricted text. In the first experiments with the new systems, the ENGCG syntactic grammar was used, but thanks to a new, more powerful rule formalism due to Tapanainen, a completely new grammar was written by Järvinen during the years 1995-96.

During the same period, the ENGCG morphological disambiguation grammar was rewritten by Atro Voutilainen. The most reliable parts of the new disambiguation grammar, EngCG-2, have been used as a preprocessor of the new syntactic grammar.[4]

Our early results showed that the new system, called the Functional Dependency Grammar (FDG) parser, was able to produce output that contained only a quarter of the ambiguity present in the ENGCG analysis (Tapanainen and Järvinen, 1997) without any rise in the error rate. Note that the amount of work being done in the FDG parsing is considerably greater than in the ENGCG analysis due to the fact that the morphological class of participles contains both nominal and verbal forms.

The new FDG grammar has wider coverage than the ENGCG grammar, and especially, it is able to take more complex phenomena into account, such as non-projective constructions, long-distance dependencies, elliptic constructions and gapping. For example, in Figure 3.1, the word *system* has lost the label @<P, though it is the prepositional complement, rather than the word *stable*. The analysis produced by the FDG is correct, as Figure 3.2 shows.

Our small-scale evaluation in (Tapanainen and Järvinen, 1997), suggested that the system was also clearly better than state-of-the-art statistical methods in the task of identifying heads. In the head-assigning task, the precision rate of FDG varied from 93%–96% in different types of texts, given the recall around 88%, whereas (Eisner, 1996), reports 79.2% precision/recall rate.

The FDG approach is applicable to different types of languages. In addition to English, broad coverage parsing descriptions exist for Spanish, Finnish and Swedish.[5]

Output formats. The FDG outputs a new layer of information that is not present in the ENGCG analysis. This layer consists of explicit functional dependencies between surface tokens. It can be best illustrated by a visual representation produced automatically by the parser, as in Figure 3.4. The linear order is also present in the visual output format, because the sentence reads from left-to-right.

The FDG textual output, seen in Figure 3.3 shows the dependency functional information, but it also contains information that is not displayed in the visual

0				
	‘			
2	Without	without	cla:>23	@ADVL PREP
3	a	a	det:>8	@DN> DET
4	stable	stable	cc:>6	@A> A
	,			
6	sustainable	sustainable	attr:>7	@A> A
7	housing	house	attr:>8	@A> N
8	system	system	pcomp:>2	@<P N
9	aimed	aim	mod:>8	@-FMAINV EN
10	at	at	tmp:>9	@ADVL PREP
11	meeting	meet	pcomp:>10	@<P-FMAINV ING
12	need	need	obj:>11	@OBJ N
	,			
14	the	the	det:>16	@DN> DET
15	business	business	attr:>16	@A> N
16	performance	performance	subj:>22	@SUBJ N
17	of	of	mod:>16	@<NOM-OF PREP
18	this	this	det:>21	@DN> DET
19	country's	country	attr:>20	@A> N
20	biggest	big	attr:>21	@A> A
21	companies	company	pcomp:>17	@<P N
22	is	be	v-ch:>23	@+FAUXV V
23	compromised	compromise	main:>0	@-FMAINV EN
	,			
	”			
26	said	say		@+FMAINV V
27	Shelter	shelter	attr:>28	@A> N
28	director	director	attr:>29	@A> N
29	Sheila	Sheila	attr:>30	@A> N
30	McKechnie	McKechnie	subj:>26	@SUBJ N
	.			

Figure 3.2. The FDG output for the sentence in 3.1. The columns from left to right are: running number, text token, base form, functional label, morpho-syntactic labels.

representation. The default output of the parser is the word-based format that presents the sentence in linear order though the linear order in the input tokens is presented by numbering. The third column presents the base form (lemma), the fifth column contains lexico-syntactic information (@-prefixed tags), and the leftmost column contains the categorial, i.e. morphological information.

The fourth column contains the functional information. The form of the functional information is [label:]>[Num]. The labels (suffixed by a colon) comprise some 30 different functions, listed in (Järvinen and Tapanainen, 1997, pp. 7-12). All labels contains a numerical index that points to the head. For example, in Figure 3.3 the gerundive *eating* has the functional label *subj:*, with a pointer to the word number four, the verb *nauseate*. The pointer for the main element of the sentence is zero.

There are lexico-syntactic labels attached to word-form tokens, comparable to the ENGCG syntactic level. The current set of FDG lexico-syntactic functions, listed in (Järvinen and Tapanainen, 1997, pp. 12-4), is slightly modified from the ENGCG syntactic tags, listed in (Voutilainen et al., 1992, p. 21-2). For example, @A> (nominal premodifier) replaces earlier distinctions between @AN> (adjective nominal premodifier), @GN> (genitive premodifier), @N (title), which are predictable on the basis of labels A, GEN and <Title>, respectively.

1	His	he	subj:>2	@A>	PRON GEN
2	eating	eat	subj:>4	@-FMAINV	ING
3	flesh	flesh	obj:>2	@OBJ	N
4	nauseates	nauseate	main:>0	@+FMAINV	V
5	her	she	obj:>4	@OBJ	PRON OBL

Figure 3.3. Text-based output of FDG for the sentence "His eating flesh nauseates her".

The dependency functional level makes the lexico-syntactic level mostly redundant, but it may be used to express some systemic relations that are not relevant to the dependency description. For example, one may argue that using a very shallow description, the genitive pronoun is a nominal premodifier in Figure 3.3 though functionally it is the subject of the following infinite clause.

5. CONCLUSION

We have discussed the methodology and the tools used in the Bank of English annotation work conducted by the Helsinki team in the years 1993-1995. The constraint grammar -based framework is demonstrably capable of a high-quality part-of-speech analysis, but its utilisation as a syntactic analysis tool

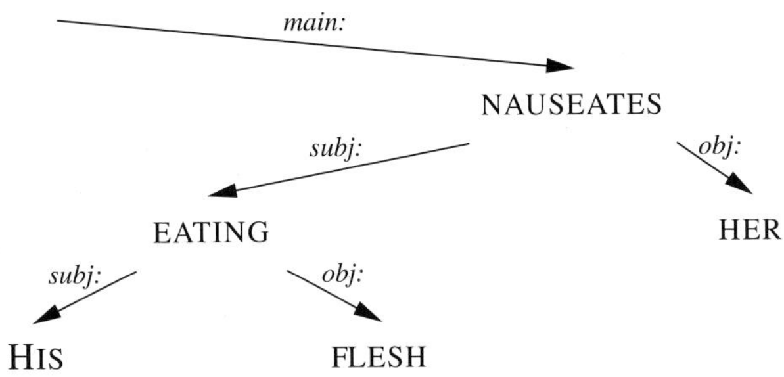

Figure 3.4. Dependency tree for the sentence in Fig. 3.3.

faces some problems due to the shallowness of the description and ambiguity left unresolved in the analysis. Therefore, a more powerful system, Functional Dependency Grammar, has been developed.

The FDG approach has a very practical orientation. For example, a concordance tool prototype has been built using the parser (Tapanainen and Järvinen, 1998). The idea is to use the dependency structure rather than word-form strings to make concordances. This is a practical aid for lexicographers that are interested in collocational information.

Notes

1. See http://titania.cobuild.collins.co.uk/boe_info.html

2. In addition, there are descriptions for at least Estonian (Müürisep, 1998), Finnish, Basque (Aduriz et al., 1996), German, Portuguese (Bick, 1997), Swahili (Hurskainen, 1996) and Swedish.

3. See (Voutilainen, 1999), for discussion.

4. The principal tagset of the EngCG-2 tagger corresponds to the ENGCG part-of-speech features. The main notational differences are that the labels 'ING' and 'EN' are used for 'PCP1' and 'PCP2', respectively.

5. See http://www.conexor.fi/parsers.html

References

Aduriz, I., Aldezabal, I., Alegria, I., Artola, X., Ezeiza, N., and Urizar, R. (1996). Euslem: A lemmatiser/tagger for Basque. In Gellerstam, M., Järborg, J., Malmgren, S.-G., Norén, K., Rogström, L., and Papmehl, C. R., (eds), *Papers submitted to the Seventh EURALEX International Congress on Lexicography*, p. 17–26, Göteborg. Göteborg University, Department of English.

Anttila, A. (1995). How to recognise Subjects in English. In (Karlsson et al., 1995), p. 315–358.

Bick, E. (1997). Dependensstrukturer i Constraint Grammar syntaks for portugisisk. In Bronsted, T. and Lytje, I., (eds), *Sprog og Multimedier*, p. 39–57. Universitetsforlag, Aalborg.

Church, K. (1988). A stochastic parts program and noun phrase parser for unrestricted text. In *Proceedings of the Second Conference on Applied Natural Language Processing*, p. 136–143, Austin, Texas.

COLING-96 (1996). *COLING-96. The 16th International Conference on Computational Linguistics*, Copenhagen, Denmark. Center for Sprogteknologi, COLING-96 Organizing Committee.

Collins, M. J. (1996). A new statistical parser based on bigram lexical dependencies. In *Proceedings of the 34th Annual Meeting of the Association for Computational Linguistics*, p. 184–191, Santa Cruz, USA. ACL.

Eisner, J. M. (1996). Three new probabilistic models for dependency parsing: An exploration. In (COLING-96, 1996), p. 340–345.

Garside, R., Leech, G., and Sampson, G. (1987). *The Computational Analysis of English. A Corpus-Based Approach.* Longman, London.

Hajič, J. (1998). Building a syntactically annotated corpus: The Prague Dependency Treebank. In Hajičová, E., (ed), *Issues of Valency and Meaning - Studies in Honour of Jarmila Panevova*, p. 106–132. Karolinum - Charles University Press, Prague.

Hurskainen, A. (1996). Disambiguation of morphological analysis in Bantu languages. In (COLING-96, 1996), p. 568–573.

Järvinen, T. (1994). Annotating 200 million words: The Bank of English Project. In *COLING 94. The 15th International Conference on Computational Linguistics Proceedings*, volume I, p. 565–568, Kyoto, Japan. International Committee on Computational Linguistics, COLING 94 Organizing Committee.

Järvinen, T. and Tapanainen, P. (1997). A dependency parser for English. Technical Report TR-1, Department of General Linguistics, University of Helsinki, Finland.

Karlsson, F. (1990). Constraint grammar as a framework for parsing running text. In Karlgren, H., (ed), *Papers presented to the 13th International Conference on Computational Linguistics, Vol. 3.*, p. 168–173. Helsinki.

Karlsson, F. (1995). Designing a parser for unrestricted text. In (Karlsson et al., 1995), p. 1–40.

Karlsson, F., Voutilainen, A., Heikkilä, J., and Anttila, A., (eds) (1995). *Constraint Grammar : a language-independent system for parsing unrestricted text*, volume 4 of *Natural Language Processing*. Mouton de Gruyter, Berlin and New York.

Koskenniemi, K. (1983). Two-level morphology: A general computational model for word-form recognition and production. Publications 11, Department Of General Linguistics, University of Helsinki, Finland.

Leech, G., Garside, R., and Bryant, M. (1994). CLAWS4: The tagging of the British National Corpus. In In *COLING 94. The 15th International Conference on Computational Linguistics Proceedings*, volume I, p. 622–628, Kyoto, Japan. International Committee on Computational Linguistics, COLING 94 Organizing Committee.

Marcus, M. P., Santorini, B., and Marcinkiewicz, M. A. (1993). Building a large annotated corpus of English: The Penn Treebank. *Computational Linguistics*, 19(2):313–330.

Müürisep, K. (1998). Eesti keele süntaksianalüsaatorist. *Keel ja Kirjandus*, XLI:47–56.

Sinclair, J. (1987). *Collins COBUILD English Language Dictionary*. (First Edition.) Collins, London.

Sinclair, J., Hanks, P., Fox, G., Moon, R., and Stock, P. (1995). *Collins COBUILD English Language Dictionary*. (Second Edition.) HarperCollins, London.

Sutcliffe, R. F., Koch, H.-D., and McElligott, A. (1996). *Industrial Parsing of Software Manuals*. Language and Computers: Studies In Practical Linguistics. Rodopi, Amsterdam.

Tapanainen, P. (1999). *Parsing in two frameworks: finite-state and functional dependency grammar*. PhD thesis, University of Helsinki.

Tapanainen, P. and Järvinen, T. (1997). A non-projective dependency parser. In *Proceedings of the 5th Conference on Applied Natural Language Processing, Washington, D.C*, p. 64–71, Washington, D.C. Association for Computational Linguistics.

Tapanainen, P. and Järvinen, T. (1998). Dependency concordances. *International Journal of Lexicography*, 11(3):187–203.

Voutilainen, A. (1995). Morphological disambiguation. In (Karlsson et al., 1995), chapter 6, p. 165–284.

Voutilainen, A. (1999). Hand-crafted rules. In van Halteren, H., (ed), *Syntactic Wordclass Tagging*, p. 217–246. Kluwer Academic Publishers, Dordrecht.

Voutilainen, A. and Heikkilä, J. (1995). Compiling and testing the lexicon. In (Karlsson et al., 1995), chapter 3, p. 89–102.

Voutilainen, A., Heikkilä, J., and Anttila, A. (1992). Constraint Grammar of English, a performance-oriented introduction. Publications 21, Department Of General Linguistics, University of Helsinki, Finland.

Voutilainen, A. and Järvinen, T. (1996). Using the English Constraint Grammar parser to analyse a software manual corpus. In (Sutcliffe et al., 1996).

Chapter 4

COMPLETING PARSED CORPORA

From correction to evolution

Sean Wallis
University College London
s.wallis@ucl.ac.uk

Abstract This paper describes the process of corpus annotation employed on ICE-GB, a one-million word parsed corpus of spoken and written English. Limitations of existing automatic annotation tools mean that, for the foreseeable future, completion of corpora will require manual intervention and correction. However, manual post-correction is labour-intensive and error-prone, requiring a very high degree of skill. In an earlier paper (Wallis and Nelson, 1997), we demonstrated that this problem far outweighs issues of tool design. We therefore proposed a paradigm shift from text-wise (longitudinal) to construction-based (transverse) correction. This permits the delicate problem of identifying and correcting errors in parses to be located within a context of similar problems across the corpus. Without removing the role of human judgment, we eased the difficulty level and increased the consistency of intervention. We discuss the technological requirements for this approach, its advantages and limitations.

Keywords: Corpus Annotation, Parsing, ICE, Corpus Correction, Tools, Fuzzy Tree Fragments.

1. INTRODUCTION

In 1998, the Survey of English Usage completed the *British Component* corpus of the *International Corpus of English* (ICE; Greenbaum, 1996a). ICE-GB (Nelson, et al., in press) is a one-million word parsed corpus (treebank) of spoken and written English[1]. All ICE corpora are sampled according to identical text categories. One of the main aims of ICE was to obtain samples covering a wide range of linguistic contexts in many varieties of English worldwide. Each corpus consists of 500 'texts' of 2,000 words. 60% of the corpus consists of transcribed speech. This material poses a particular challenge to parsing.

A. Abeillé (ed.), Treebanks: Building and Using Parsed Corpora, 61–71.

ICE-GB was collected, transcribed, divided into sentences and structurally annotated in SGML. It was then tagged with the TOSCA parser (Oostdijk, 1991). The tagged output was then prepared for parsing in two stages (Quinn and Porter, 1996). In the first, each text unit was standardised by a process of (a) 'commenting out' self-corrected words, as in Figure 4.1 (*...so it's [no] effortless for Canonbury*), and (b) introducing limited 'editor corrections', chiefly for spelling. In both cases, corrected words are 'removed' by marking them with an 'ignore' code. A second stage supported the TOSCA parser by manually introducing syntactic markers, e.g., to help the parser distinguish between NP postmodifiers (*He attacked* [NP *the man with the knife*]) and adverbials (*He attacked the man [A with the knife]*). Finally, certain compounds (e.g., nouns, *Margaret Thatcher*; intensifying adverbs, *sort of*) were linked.

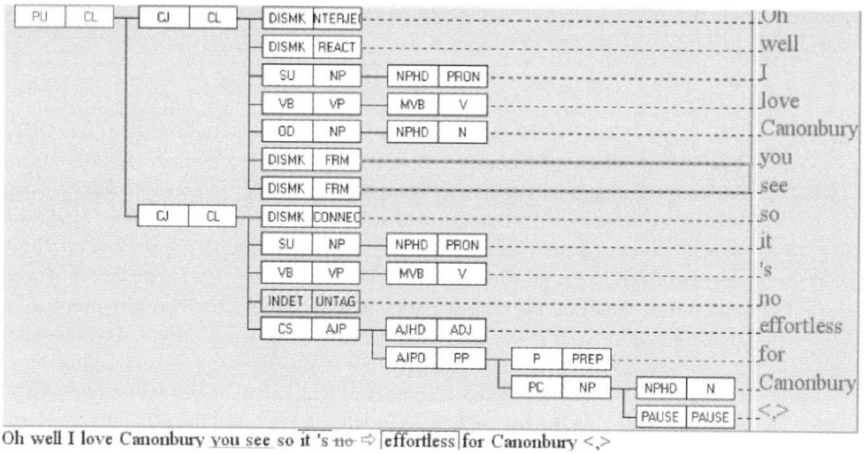

Figure 4.1. Sample tree from the ICE-GB corpus (text S1A-094, unit 38)[2]

The text was then parsed using a modified version of the TOSCA analysis (Oostdijk, 1991). This is a highly detailed surface grammar based on Quirk, et al. (1985), where constituents are labelled for *category, functional role*, and a large number of additional *features*, indicating, for example, transitivity, coordination and number (Nelson, et al., in press)[3]. Some of these features will 'percolate up' the tree. For example, *He attacked me* in text W2F-016, unit #147 (*'He attacked me' she'd said.*) is defined as a parataxis clause with the features main, monotransitive and past.

The aim was to develop a significant resource of spoken and written contemporary English containing a detailed grammar, which could be exploited by a wide variety of applications. To date, ICE-GB has been used for writing pedagogical grammars (Greenbaum, 1996b), interactive grammar teaching (Aarts et al., 1999), language research (Nelson et al., in press), training parsers (Fang, 1996) and expert-guided knowledge discovery (Wallis and Nelson, 2001).

The grammar was summarised in a stylebook of over 200 pages which was given to annotators. Automatic parsing was performed in two stages.

1 First, the TOSCA parser was employed. This top-down rule-based parser produces a number of alternative parses, which means that parsing must be followed by a (manual) disambiguation step. More seriously from the perspective of obtaining a complete parse, the TOSCA parser failed to produce an analysis for around 25% of text units.

2 The *Survey parser* (Fang, 1996) was developed to parse the remaining sentences. This is a probabilistic case-based parser, initially trained on sentences parsed and disambiguated in the first stage. It generates a single unambiguous parse. The results reflect the parser's probabilistic approach: simple phrases were identified effectively, but accuracy falls as one ascends the tree.

Clearly, using two parsers in this way increases the likelihood that the analysis in the corpus becomes inconsistent, and is obviously less than ideal. It increases the probability of error, and additionally necessitates manual intervention.

2. CONVENTIONAL POST-CORRECTION

Obtaining a clean parsed corpus is extremely labour intensive. Furthermore, the greater the detail required in parses, the more difficult the task. This difficulty can be summarised as having two aspects.

1 *The decision problem.* This is the task of obtaining a correct analysis for the sentence in question.

2 *The consistency problem.* This is the task of ensuring that this analysis is consistent with all other analyses in the corpus.

The significance of the consistency problem crucially depends on the complexity of the annotation scheme employed. Apart from keeping the analysis (or the decisions: Carter, 1997) simple, another common strategy is to develop extensive guidelines or 'stylebooks'. However, the question arises as to what happens in practice. Do the annotators keep to these guidelines or do they flexibly interpret them? (After all, if the guidelines are strictly deterministic, then surely they could be automated?)

For example, Treebank I was chosen for the UPenn corpus (Taylor, et al., this volume) on largely pragmatic grounds (Marcus, et al., 1993). Despite their use of a substantial stylebook, in 1994, the UPenn team comment that during the annotation of Treebank II they planned to overlap correction by 10% to check for inter-operator agreement (Marcus, et al., 1994). Our ICE scheme requires a complete analysis and is considerably more complex than either Treebank representation.

Sinclair (1992) argues against manual corpus correction on the grounds that annotators introduce errors and their efforts do not 'scale up'. In other words, if it takes ten person-years to correct a one million-word corpus, then it will take a hundred person-years to correct a ten million-word one. Given the demand for ever larger corpora, correction based on human intervention is doomed. The first argument against the first part of this position is the state of the art. Automatic parsers do not currently obtain wide coverage and disambiguation at an error rate (say, 5%) that would make human intervention unnecessary. Even if we suppose that this order of parsing accuracy might be achievable in restricted text types, in others, particularly natural spoken discourse, manual correction is likely to remain the only way of obtaining complete coverage.

A second argument is that corpus correction is a form of *situated knowledge acquisition*. In this view, the process of manually correcting a corpus is one that causes an expert to make a series of knowledge-intensive concrete human judgments about the grammar, and embeds these judgments in the corpus. The aim would be to generalise these concrete judgments post-hoc to aid future correction. This perspective permits the consideration of syntheses of computation and human intervention (from broad-brush search-and-replace to integrated learning parsers) that scale to larger corpora.

The most common method employed for correcting a corpus is what we might describe as 'longitudinal' correction, i.e., a corrector works through a text sentence-by-sentence until it is completed. Such correction may be performed in concert with a parser (Leech and Garside, 1991; Carter, 1997; Brants et al., this volume) or once the parsing process is completed, usually described as 'postchecking' (Taylor et al., this volume; Böhmová et al., this volume). These approaches can be complementary, depending on parser performance. The first supports disambiguation, whereas post-checking is necessary if the parser produces incomplete results.

In (Wallis and Nelson, 1997) we described the use of longitudinal post-checking to correct ICE-GB, and a study that we performed to examine our correctors' performance, using two different tree-editing tools to support the decision problem. These two tools were quite different in terms of their level of sophistication or robustness. ICE Tree I (Quinn and Porter, 1996) employed a 'grid' to which nodes were attached and then linked, resulting in a counter-intuitive interface. ICE Tree II (Wallis and Nelson, 1997) was more fluid, limited only by the constraints of the tree.

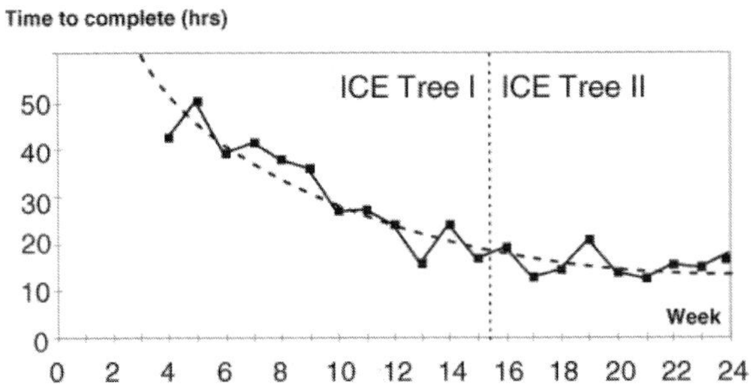

Figure 4.2. Learning curve in the correction of ICE-GB (simplified from Wallis and Nelson, 1997).

Figure 4.2 summarises the results of this experiment, plotting the estimated time to check and correct a standard text of 2,000 words, over a period of 24 weeks, during which annotators switched tools. As this was a case study of ongoing work, we did not randomise the order. Nevertheless, the results are clear. We found a learning curve that *dwarfed any difference between editing tools.* We discovered what our annotators already knew: the decision problem is very difficult. At this stage we were unable to tackle the consistency problem, or independently measure the error rate.

At the end of the post-checking process we had one million words with a detailed parse analysis but no real idea of how accurate the analysis was.

3. A PARADIGM SHIFT: TRANSVERSE CORRECTION

We realised that, in order to proceed further, the decision problem had to be tackled *from the perspective of the consistency problem.* We should correct *the corpus*, rather than a series of *trees*.

In longitudinal sentence-by-sentence, text-by-text correction, each text presents a wide variety of grammatical problems to the corrector (this is the case whether checking is performed during or after parsing). Moreover, these decisions are not placed alongside other comparable decisions in the corpus.

We proposed instead that, in the next phase, the corpus should be corrected on a *transverse* (cross-sectional) construction-by-construction basis. This would permit each corrector to concentrate on a particular grammatical construction in the corpus, examine, and potentially correct, each instance of the construction, and then move to the next. It would have two virtues: enforcing consistency and easing the decision problem. The slogan of this *evolutionary* perspective on corpus correction is:

If a decision can be made once, it can be made several times.

However, implementing transverse correction requires a far more sophisticated software infrastructure. Whereas longitudinal post-hoc correction may be performed on simple text files with isolated editors, transverse correction requires the instantiation of the corpus in a database. At the heart of this is a *corpus maintenance system* (CMS), which represents, cross-references and maintains the corpus, providing a platform into which tree editors and other tools may be integrated.

At the heart of a database platform is the *query*. Cross-sectional correction requires the reliable identification of all instances of a construction across the corpus. In our case this meant the development of an effective and intuitive search facility for grammatical queries.

We were developing the *Fuzzy Tree Fragment* (FTF: Aarts, Nelson and Wallis, 1998; Wallis and Nelson, 2000) system for corpus exploitation. This representation, and the CMS platform, is combined in our corpus exploration software. The *ICE Corpus Utility Program, ICECUP*, is available as a browser with the ICE-GB corpus[4]. The software has an editing option (disabled in the browsing version) that permits the correction of any sentence tree in the corpus. Moreover, the context of a matching case is readily retrievable.

The first application of FTFs, therefore, was to support the correction of ICEGB, identifying erroneous and suspect constructions in the corpus. The same system permits users to search and browse ICE-GB for linguistic queries.

Two example FTFs are given in Figure 4.3. Fuzzy Tree Fragments are approximate grammatical subtrees: models of general grammatical structures. They are 'fuzzy' in the sense that they may be inexactly specified, rather than that they are informally defined or statistically matched.

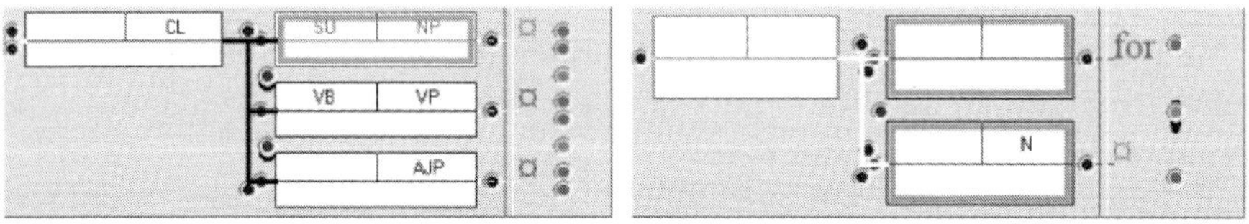

(a) Grammatical query for a clause containing a subject NP, a verb phrase and an adjective phrase, in that order.

(b) Textual query for a word + tag sequence: "for" followed by a noun. The node on the left will match only the root of the tree.

Figure 4.3. FTFs for grammatical and textual queries

FTFs reflect the tree/text dichotomy implicit in the language of 'treebanks' versus 'parsed corpora'. Thus elements may be related at the lexical level or via the tree.

When an FTF is applied to the corpus, ICECUP compiles an exhaustive list of matching cases and then visualises this index as a sequence of sentences or cases. It identifies *each independent matching configuration* in a tree view by highlighting the matched area of the sentence and the tree. In research, we use the same case identification principle to perform 'key construction in line' concordancing. Figure 4.4 shows how these FTFs match a text unit in ICE-GB. This tree viewer can be used to edit the tree. The tree editor from the earlier *ICETree 2* program (Wallis and Nelson, 1997) is included. A system of file locking prevents one tree being edited by two annotators simultaneously.

This raises the general problem of how to efficiently combine search and correction. The technical aspect of this problem concerns the computational efficiency of the process. It would be undesirable to search the entire corpus every time one wished to perform a query, so precompiled indices are used to reduce the set of candidates[5]. However, as we correct the corpus, these indices become out of date. How can this be resolved? One solution is to provide some kind of continuous indexing. In practice, however, we found that a far simpler strategy was to perform periodic reindexing from first principles, say, once a person-month, and to perform a double-check of previous searches to determine that each was effectively exhaustive. This has to be performed anyway, for the obvious reason that errors may be reintroduced. For the same reason we decided to gradually reduce the number of linguists working on the corpus from a maximum of eight during longitudinal postchecking to a single linguist at the tail end of cross-sectional correction.

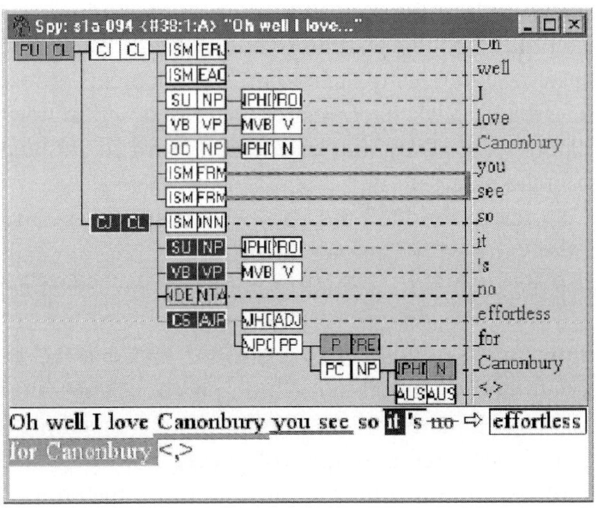

Figure 4.4. ICECUP tree viewer showing how the FTFs in Figure 4.3 match against the tree in Figure 4.1

Computing indices has one further advantage: index tables can be analysed. We were able to identify each low-frequency construction and single lexical item and examine them. Note that it is not possible to perform automatic 'search and replace': at each stage a human annotator must decide what the correct analysis should be. Finally, we can display the indices in a viewable form. Release 3.1 of the ICECUP software will support an integrated corpus-derived *lexicon* component that provides a summary of the corpus at lexical and tag level.

4. CRITIQUE

Both longitudinal and transverse correction have strengths and weaknesses. We have identified many of the weaknesses of longitudinal correction. Cross-sectional correction has some drawbacks, however.

Transverse correction is more difficult to implement, and the process is harder to manage[6]. Two correctors are given two different constructions, and correction proceeds independently. As a result, their correction effort may overlap. The problem of 'false negatives' means that search cannot be used to directly identify constituents that 'should form' a desired construction. As a corollary, it is difficult to ensure completeness. However, this is an advance on longitudinal correction where we merely *assume* that if correctors have checked all of the texts, the process may terminate.

Lest these comments appear too negative, we did find that transverse correction was much more effective in causing the number of obvious mistakes and inconsistencies to fall. We were able to gain confidence in the overall consistency of the corpus through searching, both for errors and – as we started to perform linguistic research using the corpus – for elements of research interest. We don't believe that transverse correction increased within-tree inconsistency because annotators were aware that an apparent error might be due to a problem elsewhere in the parse.

Transverse correction bridged the gap between per-text correction and research applications driven by queries. During this phase we also distributed beta-releases of the corpus to a small number of linguists for their own research.

One of our practical problems was due to the fact that the software development ran concurrently with the correction process. Thus, during the initial stage analysed in Wallis and Nelson (1997), there was simply no possibility of performing cross-sectional grammatical search. For this reason, we are very interested in exploiting the benefits of search earlier in the project lifecycle (see below). Secondly, as ICECUP was developed, new facilities tended to expose new errors – useful for the annotators, but a little galling in practice!

We were not able to perform the same kind of detailed quantitative analysis for transverse correction as for the longitudinal process. Each annotator was given a different problem to correct so we would need to measure the fall in the error rate, which cannot be independently assessed. Disambiguating the initial parse analysis took around four person-years, while post-checking required over ten person-years. Cross-checking the corpus, from this post-checked base, took under two.

Is a transverse correction phase necessary for any treebank and parsing scheme? Clearly, this will depend on corpus size, parse complexity and ultimate application. The greater the level of detail, the greater the possible inconsistency. Applications requiring clean examples rather than statistical summaries may require greater accuracy. Correction in general is necessary for corpus studies if we wish to learn how language varies rather than how a parser performs. Cross-sectional correction is necessary to ensure that our corrected analyses are consistent.

A more radical perspective would be to correct the entire corpus on a cross-sectional basis and only perform a longitudinal check for completeness at a pre-final stage. The idea would be to make broad-brush corrections of major errors first and then move towards finer distinctions. This process could be supported by tools permitting the enumeration of complete sets of existing atoms (a 'grammaticon' listing all nodes in the corpus and a lexicon) and user-specified structures (related FTFs).

In a new proposed project for rapid prototyping corpus parse annotation, we hope to exploit ICECUP's corpus maintenance system throughout the construction and correction process. Instead of employing an evolutionary perspective late in the day, we propose to evolve the corpus throughout the entire process, using ICE-GB as a model to correct further ICE corpora.

Acknowledgments

Thanks are due to Gerry Nelson for his many comments, our anonymous referees, and especially to the correctors of ICE-GB, for all their hard work.

Notes

1. For information on ICE-GB, availability and licensing, see http://www.ucl.ac.uk/english-usage/ice-gb/.

2. The main nodes are as follows. PU = parse unit (the whole tree), CL = clause, CJ = conjoin, VP = verb phrase, SU = subject, OD = direct object, VB = verbal, MVB = main verb. The sentence tail is analysed as an adjective phrase acting as a subject complement (labelled CS, AJP). The AJP consists of the adjective *effortless* and a postmodifying prepositional phrase (AJPO, PP). This consists of the preposition *for* and the complement noun phrase (PC, NP) *Canonbury*. Note that pauses, discourse markers (DISMK) and ignored material (grey hatched nodes) are included within the parse analysis.

3. The grammar is extremely detailed. For each word in the corpus, there are on average two tree analysis nodes. Each node must have one of 61 functions and one of 37 categories, subject to these pairs being compatible. Each category defines a set of permissible feature classes (some mandatory, some not) that group features into mutually exclusive alternatives (e.g., a verb may be transitive or copular, but not both). As a result, the 2 million+ nodes are to be found in over 7,500 grammatically distinct patterns. The full list of terms is at http://www.ucl.ac.uk/english-usage/ice-gb/grammar.htm.

4. ICECUP is available free, for non-commercial use, on-line from http://www.ucl.ac.uk/english-usage /ice-gb/sampler/. The download package includes a sample corpus of 20,000 words (ten texts) from ICE-GB and complete help files.

5. We obtain a set of candidates from the intersection between components of the FTF (Wallis and Nelson, 2000). As a result, we can identify that the FTF in Figure 4.3a may only match 30,694 candidates out of 88,357 text units; for the FTF in 3b, there are 7,117. The FTF is then matched against these candidate text units. In the case of simple FTFs (e.g., a single node or word without any structural restriction) retrieving the index may be sufficient.

6. For example, it is simple for longitudinal correction to be performed on more than one site. For part of the ICE-GB project one of our correctors worked at home and transferred files via disk as necessary. Cross-sectional correction is much more bandwidth-hungry, since any tree in the corpus may be retrieved, locked and edited at any point. An internet-based client-server CMS would be possible, however at present ICECUP combines client and server in one package and requires the corpus to be available on a local file system.

References

Aarts, Bas, Gerald Nelson, Sean Wallis (1998). Using fuzzy tree fragments to explore English grammar. *English Today*, 14.3: 52-56.

Aarts, Bas, Gerald Nelson, Sean Wallis (1999). Global resources for a global language: English language pedagogy in the modern age. In Claus Gnutzmann (ed.) *Teaching and Learning English as a Global Language: Native and Non-Native Perspectives*, Tübingen: Stauffenberg Verlag, p. 273-290.

Böhmová, Alena, J. Hajič, E. Hajičová, B. Hladká (2003), 'The Prague Dependency Treebank: a three-level annotation scenario'. This volume.

Carter, David (1997). The TreeBanker: a Tool for Supervised Training of Parsed Corpora. In *Proc. ACL Workshop on Computational Environments for Grammar Development and Linguistic Engineering, Madrid*. `http://www.cam.sri.com/tr/crc068/paper.ps.Z`

Fang, Alex Chengyu (1996a). The Survey Parser: Design and Development. In Sidney Greenbaum, p. 142-160.

Greenbaum, Sidney (ed) (1996a). *Comparing English Worldwide: The International Corpus of English*. Oxford: Clarendon.

Greenbaum, Sidney (ed) (1996b). *The Oxford English Grammar*. Oxford: OUP.

Leech, Geoffrey, Roger Garside (1991). Running a Grammar Factory: on the compilation of parsed corpora, or 'treebanks'. In Stig Johansson and Anna-Britte Stenstrm (eds), *English Computer Corpora: Selected Papers and Research Guide*. Berlin: Mouton de Gruyter. p. 15-32.

Nelson, Gerald, Sean Wallis, Bas Aarts. *Exploring Natural Language: Working with the British Component of the International Corpus of English*. Amsterdam: John Benjamins. In press.

Marcus, Mitchell P., Beatrice Santorini, Mary Ann Marcinkiewicz (1993). Building A Large Annotated Corpus of English: The Penn Treebank. *Computational Linguistics*, 19: 313-330.

Marcus, Mitchell P., Grace Kim, Mary Ann Marcinkiewicz, Robert MacIntyre, Ann Bies, Mark Ferguson, Karen Katz, Britte Schasberger (1994). The Penn Treebank: Annotating Predicate Argument Structure. *Proc. HLT Workshop.* San Francisco: Morgan Kaufmann.

Oostdijk, Nelleke (1991). *Corpus Linguistics and the Automatic Analysis of English.* Amsterdam: Rodopi.

Quinn, Akiva, Nick Porter (1996a). ICE Annotation Tools. In Sidney Greenbaum. p. 65-78.

Quirk, Randolph, Sidney Greenbaum, Geoffrey Leech, Jan Svartvik (1985). *A Comprehensive Grammar of the English Language*. London: Longman.

Sinclair, John (1992). The automatic analysis of corpora. In Jan Svartvik (ed) *Directions in Corpus Linguistics. Proceedings of Nobel Symposium 82.* Berlin: Mouton de Gruyter, p. 379-397.

Taylor, Ann, M. Marcus, B. Santorini (2003). 'The Penn treebank: an overview'. This volume.

Wallis, Sean, Gerald Nelson (1997). Syntactic parsing as a knowledge acquisition problem. In Enric Plaza and Richard Benjamins (eds.) *Knowledge Acquisition, Modeling and Management. Proceedings of 10th European Workshop, EKAW-97*, (Lecture Notes in AI 1319). Berlin: Springer Verlag. p. 285-300.

Wallis, Sean, Gerald Nelson (2000). Exploiting fuzzy tree fragments in the investigation of parsed corpora, *Literary and Linguistic Computing*, 15: 251-263.

Wallis, Sean, Gerald Nelson (2001). Knowledge discovery in grammatically analysed corpora, *Data Mining and Knowledge Discovery*.

GERMAN TREEBANKS

Chapter 5

SYNTACTIC ANNOTATION OF A GERMAN NEWSPAPER CORPUS

Thorsten Brants*, Wojciech Skut, Hans Uszkoreit
Saarland University,
FR 8.7 Computational Linguistics,
P.O.Box 171150,
D-66041 Saarbrücken, Germany
{brants,skut,uszkoreit}@coli.uni-sb.de

Abstract We report on the syntactic annotation of a German newspaper corpus. The annotations consist of context-free structures, additionally allowing crossing branches, with labeled nodes (phrases) and edges (grammatical functions). Furthermore, we present a new, interactive semi-automatic annotation process that allows efficient and reliable annotations. The annotation process is sped up by incrementally presenting structures and by automatically highlighting unreliable assignments.

Keywords: Corpus Annotation, German Newspaper Corpus, Annotation Tools

1. INTRODUCTION

Data-oriented and corpus-based methods have become one of the most important areas of applied as well as theoretical NLP. Currently, syntactic methods prevailingly belong to the *supervised learning* paradigm, i.e., they require as training material large corpora annotated with linguistic information. Since the preparation of such corpora usually involves manual human work, a lot of effort is put into the optimisation of the annotation process in order to make it less time-consuming and labour-intensive.

*The author's new affiliation is Xerox Parc, Palo, Alto, California
brants@parc.xerox.com

A. Abeillé (ed.), Treebanks: Building and Using Parsed Corpora, 73–87.

The amount of annotation work depends on how much information is associated with the raw language data. The present paper deals with the construction of a *treebank*, which is particularly labour-intensive. There are two main optimisation issues. Firstly, automatic processing methods can be used, so that the annotator only supervises, corrects and completes the analyses proposed by some tool. Secondly, the speed and consistency of annotation may depend on the annotation scheme employed.

Several annotation procedures are described in the literature. The Penn Treebank (Marcus et al., 1993) used the Fidditch parser (Hindle, 1983) for pre-processing. The structures were subsequently presented to human annotators and manually corrected. The Prague Dependency Treebank (Hajič, 1998; Böhmová et al., this volume) uses automatic initial category assignments and a subsequent manual correction step. A tree editor was developed for the annotation of the TOSCA corpus (Aarts et al., 1998), which is also used and further developed for the International Corpus of English (Greenbaum, 1996; Wallis, this volume). The *Treebanker* (Carter, 1997) is used for syntactical annotation in the ATIS (air travel information system) domain. It presents alternative readings in parallel and the annotator selects correct or rejects wrong readings. This mode of annotation requires a parser that generates the correct complete parse for most of the sentences. (Brants and Skut, 1998) present methods to automate the labeling of annotated structures as well as partial structures for NPs and PPs. Structures and labeling are generated incrementally.

In this paper, we present an interactive annotation mode that suggests new phrases to the annotator who can accept or reject the suggestion. Probabilities of suggested phrases are used to determine if confirmation by the annotator is necessary. It is also shown how to optimise the annotation scheme as far as the consistency and efficiency of annotation are concerned.

2. TREEBANK DEVELOPMENT

The NEGRA treebank has been under development since 1996 in the NEGRA project at the Saarland University in Saarbrücken. To our knowledge, it was the first project to build a large-scale corpus of German text at that time. The domain of the corpus is newspaper texts. We have chosen articles from the *Frankfurter Rundschau* of 1992, that are part of the *European Corpus Initiative Multilingual* CD I[1].

The publicly released treebank consists of a little more than 20,000 sentences (350,000 tokens) annotated with syntactic structures, syntactic categories and grammatical functions, including double annotation, comparison and correction. Currently corpus annotation is continued in the project TIGER funded by the Deutsche Forschungsgemeinschaft at the Universities of

Saarbrücken, Stuttgart and Potsdam[2]. In this project the annotation tools and methods described here are utilized for the production of a much larger treebank (> 50,000 sentences) with an extended annotation scheme and improved search facilities.

NEGRA was one of the first treebanks for languages other than English. The only documented large-scale treebanks available to us were the Penn Treebank (Marcus et al., 1993) and the Susanne corpus (Sampson, 1995), which were both based on context-free syntactic representations with additional trace-filler annotations for discontinuous constituents. This seemed very likely to become a standard in the corpora community, which led us to adopt this kind of annotation for our corpus.

On the other hand, it was clear from the beginning that the experience gained during the construction of English corpora would not always be useful in our case. In particular, we expected to encounter problems specific to the language type represented by German.

In fact, it turned out that the considerable degree of free word order exhibited by German makes context-free annotation of syntactic structures difficult. This is particularly due to the frequency of discontinuous constituents, which can be annotated by trace-filler coreferences, but only at the cost of lower transparency of annotations (the reader may imagine a sentence containing three non-local dependencies, each annotated by a separate coreference).

These considerations suggested that we should adopt a different representation format, preferably one specially developed for free word order languages. There is one such formalism, Dependency Grammar, which interprets natural language in terms of head-dependent relations (*dependencies*) between words. If the words are interpreted as tree nodes and the dependencies as branches connecting the words, the structure of a sentence can be drawn as a tree. In the original, non-projective version of Dependency Grammar, there are no restrictions on attaching words to each other. There may be crossing branches, which makes the formalism particularly suitable for free word order languages. The approach of Dependency Grammar annotations was chosen for the Prague Dependency Treebank (Hajič, 1998; Böhmová et al., this volume).

We used Dependency Grammar as the starting point for the development of our annotation scheme. It soon turned out that the sharp distinction between heads and modifiers stipulated by the formalism causes difficulties in practice. In particular, all kinds of constructions without a clear syntactic head are difficult to analyse: ellipses, sentences without a verb (e.g., copula-less predicatives), and coordinations.

Linguistic theories may well have solutions to these problems, but such solutions tend to be highly theory-specific, while our annotation effort aims at descriptive and theory-neutral annotation.

As a result, we abandoned the idea of pure dependency-based annotation scheme and adopted a hybrid framework that combines the advantages of phrase-structure and dependency grammars. We do employ phrasal nodes, but try to keep the structures flat: phrases typically have lexical heads, without any intermediate "X-bar" nodes. In other words, all modifiers and complements of a word are attached to its parent node.[3] No empty categories are added.

The best illustration of the advantages of this approach is our treatment of headedness, which is considered a grammatical function and expressed by labeling (edge label HD) rather than by the syntactic structure. As a result, it is no problem to have headless phrases, while the classical dependency grammar is forced to resort to quite disputable headedness assumptions (e.g., punctuation marks serving as syntactic heads of coordinated phrases without a conjunction in the Prague Treebank).

The branches of such a tree may cross, so there is no need for a special treatment of non-local dependencies, which occupy the same structural status as local ones. In addition to syntactic categories and structures proper, *grammatical functions* (subject, object, etc.) are annotated more explicitly than, e.g., in the Penn Treebank. This is no surprise since German does not express functional information by position as does English.

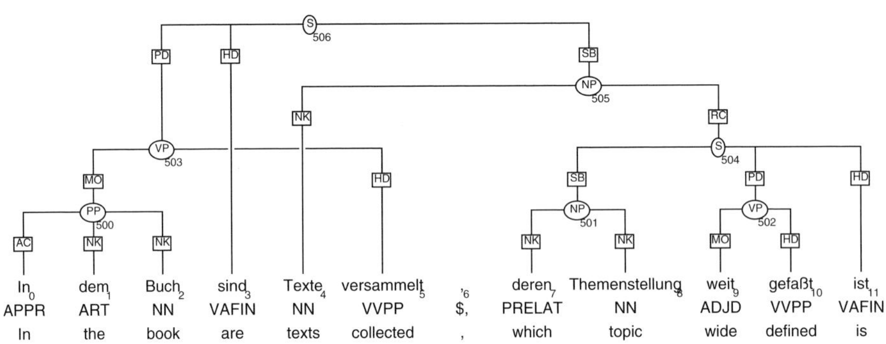

"The book collects texts with a wide range of topics"

Figure 5.1. Example sentence (#2412 in the corpus). It contains two crossing branches. One is caused by the PP in the Vorfeld (*In dem Buch*), the other one by the extraposed relative clause (*deren Themenstellung weit gefaßt ist*). Edges are labeled with grammatical functions.

The hybrid representation format adopted in NEGRA permits fast and consistent annotation. Consistency is supported by the following features:

- flat syntactic structures exhibit a low potential for attachment ambiguities;

- trees are mostly quite close to semantics (predicate-argument structures), and the annotators disambiguate sentences on the basis of our experience;
- remaining spurious ambiguities are dealt with by "default attachment" (e.g., always choose the highest possible attachment site);
- only clear-cut distinctions between grammatical functions are made, i.e., functions that can be ensured to have a high inter-annotator assignment agreement.

Figure 5.1 shows an example annotation. As was presented by (Skut et al., 1997), the crossing branches occurring in the annotations can be automatically converted to context-free structures with traces if required.

3. CORPUS ANNOTATION

We employ a new interactive annotation process for the annotation of our corpus data. The process incrementally guides a human annotator through the structure that is to be generated. The annotator can stop the process at any point and correct or alter the structure or the labeling manually. Furthermore, the automatic process includes a reliability measure. Using this automatic measure, the process classifies its decisions either as reliable or as unreliable. The latter require additional actions by the annotator in order to ensure a high accuracy of the annotated corpus. The process is integrated in a flexible graphical user interface.

3.1 Pre-Processing

Tokenisation and sentence boundary detection are done as part of the preprocessing of the corpus. Annotators can change both during the syntactic annotation if necessary. We leave spelling and grammatical errors in the corpus, but the annotators are advised to mark these with comments. A token is mainly defined as a sequence of non-blank characters between blanks, handling punctuation as separate tokens. Multi-token units, such as proper names or numbers, are marked at the structural level.

3.2 The Interactive Annotation Process

The annotation of our corpus includes part-of-speech tags, syntactic structures (including discontinuous constituents), and labeling of nodes and edges. A tagger and a parser are running in the background, the annotation is visualised with a graphical user interface (see next section).

The process is outlined in figure 5.2. Annotation starts with a raw sequence of words, separated into tokens and sentences. As a first step, the statistical tagger TnT (Brants, 2000b) is run on this sequence. The tagger implements

Step	Type	Description
1.	automatic	part-of-speech tagging
2.	automatic	determine reliable and unreliable tag assignments
3.	manual	confirm unreliable and alter wrong tags
4.	automatic	suggest new phrase that has highest probability
5.	manual	accept → step 7, retry → step 4, reject → step 6
6.	manual	insert or alter a phrase
7.	automatic	insert labels into new structure
8.	automatic	determine reliable and unrelibale label assignments
9.	manual	confirm unreliable and alter wrong labels
10.	manual	finished → end, continue → step 4

Figure 5.2. Processing steps during corpus annotation, which combine automatic processing and manual intervention/manual annotation based on the annotator's decisions.

second order Markov models, smoothed with linear interpolation. Unknown words are handled by suffix analysis (Samuelsson, 1993). The tagger yields state-of-the-art tagging results for German and several other languages.[4] A standard 90%/10% split and ten-fold cross-validation yields 96.7% accuracy for the NEGRA corpus. For its application in the annotation process, the tagger is trained on all previously annotated data. Therefore, the accuracy of TnT improves with the size of the corpus. (Brants, 2000b) presents an empirical analysis of the dependency between training size and tagging accuracy.

We not only exploit the tags that are assigned, but also their probabilities. We use the distance of the best and second best tags' probabilities, $P(t_{best})$ and $P(t_{second})$, expressed by their quotient. If their distance is large, the best tag is simply added to the annotation. If their distance is small, the annotator is asked to confirm the tag. So we choose a threshold θ and classify:

$$\text{reliable, if } \frac{P(t_{best})}{P(t_{second})} \geq \theta, \qquad \text{unreliable, if } \frac{P(t_{best})}{P(t_{second})} < \theta$$

Figure 5.3 shows an example part-of-speech annotation with $\theta = 100$. The tags and probabilities are automatically assigned. The tagset used here is the Stuttgart-Tübingen-Tagset, containing 54 tags (see appendix A for a partial description). Three of the words receive alternative readings with high probabilities (words *versammelt*, *deren*, and *weit*). Therefore, they are classified as unreliable. They are highlighted and a human annotator is asked for confirmation (or correction). The other words either receive unique tags, or the probabilities of the alternative tags are so small that they are ignored.

$\theta = 100$ was empirically chosen for the annotation of the entire corpus. The goal was an accuracy of at least 99%. A ten-fold cross-validation, using 90% of the corpus for training and 10% for testing yields the results shown in

In	dem	Buch	sind	Texte	**versammelt**	,
APPR	ART	NN	VAFIN	NN	**VVPP: 96.9%**	$,
(FM: 0.05%)	(PRELS: 0.2%)				**VVFIN: 3.1%**	
	(PDS: 0.003%)					

deren	Themenstellung	**weit**	gefaßt	ist
PRELAT: 93.5%	NN	**ADJD: 95.1%**	VVPP	VAFIN
PPOSAT: 3.3%		**ADV: 4.9%**		
PDAT: 3.1%				
(PDS: 0.08%)				

Figure 5.3. Automatic part-of-speech analysis of the example sentence ("*The book collects texts with a wide range of topics*"). Words for which alternative tags have high probability (greater than 1% of the best tag's probability) are **bold**. These are classified as unreliable and presented to a human annotator for confirmation. The other words are either unambiguous or their alternative readings receive low probabilities (shown in brackets), and are therefore classified as reliable.

		Fraction of words	Accuracy
reliable	$(p_{best} \geq \theta p_{second})$	84%	99.3%
unreliable	$(p_{best} < \theta p_{second})$	16%	82.7%
overall		100%	96.7%

Figure 5.4. Part-of-speech tagging accuracy when choosing $\theta = 100$. The corpus of 350,000 tokens was divided into 90% training and 10% test sets. The procedure was repeated 10 times, results are averaged.

table 5.4. Assignments that are classified as reliable are accurate in 99.3% of all cases. Unreliable assignments have an accuracy of only 82.7%. Thus, we indeed identify unreliable assignments with the proposed measure.

The procedure of highlighting unreliable assignments has an important impact on annotation speed. 84% of the assignments are classified as reliable, so they need almost no attention from the annotator. The annotator can concentrate on the 16% unreliable assignments. Annotation time is significantly reduced by investigating only this fraction of tags.

After part-of-speech tagging, the syntactic structure is built incrementally. The best phrase hypothesis given the current annotation is determined by Cascaded Markov models (Brants, 1999a; Brants, 1999b). Each layer of the structure is represented by a separate Markov Model, which assigns probabilities to each hypothetical phrase. The phrase with the highest probability is presented to the annotator, who can either accept or reject it. In the first case,

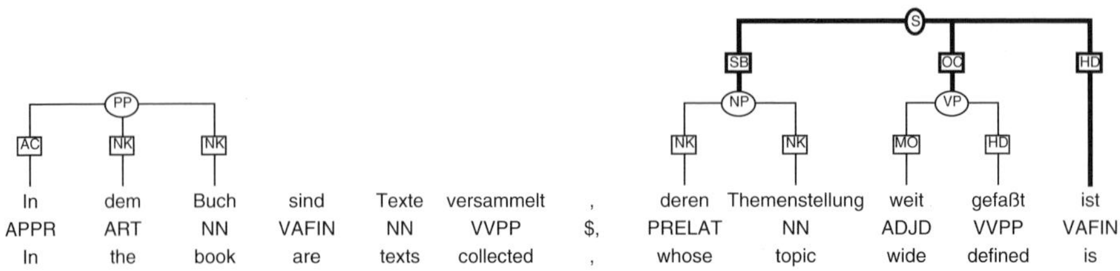

Figure 5.5. Annotation process of the example sentence. Given the previous annotation, the parser suggests a new phrase (highlighted). The human annotator can either accept, reject or manually alter the suggested phrase. Phrase categories (node labels) and grammatical functions (edge labels) are classified for reliability and handled accordingly.

annotation proceeds and the system builds the next phrase. In the latter case, the phrase is removed from the internal structures of the parser, probabilities are re-calculated, and the next-best phrase is presented. At any point, the annotator can manually change the structure if the suggested phrase needs a small change or if the parser is not able to generate the correct structure.

Figure 5.5 shows a stage during annotation of the example sentence. The structure is built bottom up. Three nodes (PP, NP, and VP shown with thin lines) are already generated. Now, the parser automatically suggests an S node for the relative clause (bold lines) which needs to be confirmed by the annotator. A ten-fold cross-validation of the parser shows that 71% of all suggested phrases are correct. A large number of errors stem from crossing edges which are allowed by the NEGRA annotation scheme. Due to the technique used, the parser has no chance of parsing these correctly. Even if a phrase suggested by the parser is not completely correct, it may be of use in the annotation process: it makes a difference whether only one constituent needs to be manually added/deleted or if the whole phrase needs to be re-built. Using a three-fold distinction, 71% of the phrases are correct, 17% need minor intervention (i.e., the addition or deletion of at most one constituent), and 12% need major intervention. A more detailed evaluation is presented in (Brants, 1999b, chapter 7).

If a structural element is confirmed, the parser tests the labels in the nodes and edges for reliability (as was done for the part-of-speech tags). Labeling is again performed with Markov models. The system highlights unreliable assignments and asks the annotator for confirmation. Thresholds are set to $\theta = 100$, such that reliable assignments have an accuracy above 99%. Nevertheless, annotators can change all labels if an error occurs, or change the structure at a later point. Accuracies for the automatic assignments are shown in table 5.6. Well above 80% of all cases are classified as reliable with an accuracy

	Grammatical functions (edge labels)		Phrase categories (node labels)	
	Fraction of edges	Accuracy	Fraction of nodes	Accuracy
reliable	88%	99.0%	83%	99.4%
unreliable	12%	76.5%	17%	87.8%
overall	100%	96.3%	100%	97.4%

Figure 5.6. Tagging accuracy for grammatical functions and phrase categories when choosing $\theta = 100$. The corpus of 350,000 tokens was divided into 90% training and 10% test sets. The procedure was repeated 10 times, results are averaged.

of over 99%. These need only minimal attention. The rest, 12% and 17%, are classified as unreliable. They are automatically highlighted and require the annotator's attention.

The tagger and parser need some minimum amount of annotated training data to enable automation. The exact amount depends on the language and the annotation scheme. It is typically around a few thousand tokens. Accuracy is lower with small amounts of training data, but the problem is alleviated by using the reliability measure.

3.3 Graphical User Interface

The process of selecting the best phrase hypothesis is integrated in a graphical user interface, which is shown in figure 5.7. The tool allows a variety of manual tree manipulations (grouping, ungrouping, re-attachment, labeling, etc.). It additionally runs taggers and parsers in the background. These are used for interactive annotation (Plaehn and Brants, 2000).

The tool can handle virtually any annotation scheme that is based on context-free structures (with crossing branches) and labelings of nodes and edges. For instance, it can be also used for the Penn Treebank and the Susanne corpus. The graphical user interface in combination with cascaded Markov models allows very efficient annotation. A trained annotator needs in average 50 seconds per sentence of newspaper text with an average sentence length of 17.5 tokens (approximately 1,300 tokens/hour). The annotation time was measured for two annotators during the normal annotation process and was averaged over 2,000 sentences. The annotation includes part-of-speech tagging, syntactic structure, and labeling of nodes and edges.

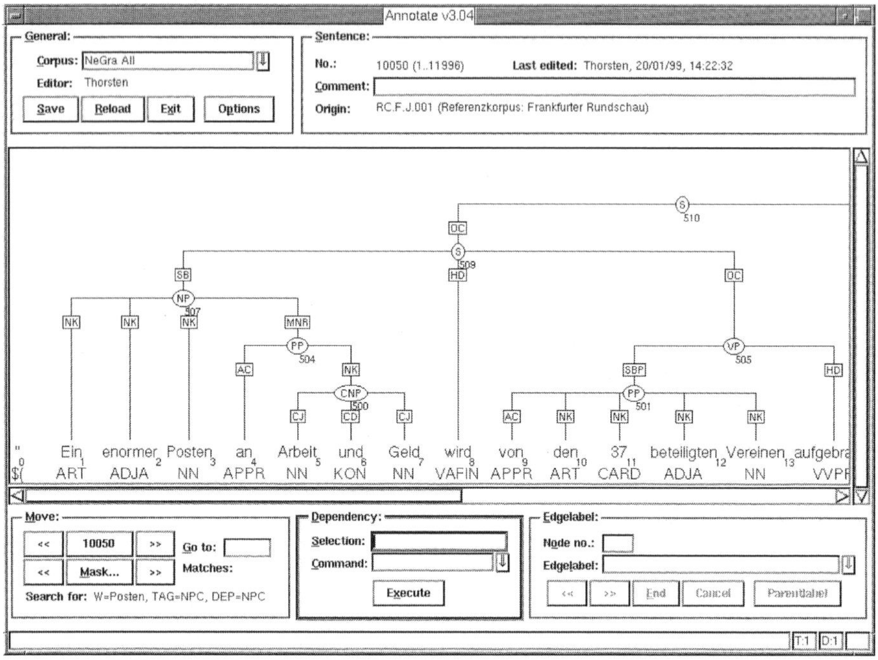

Figure 5.7. Graphical user interface for corpus annotation. The GUI uses an interface to cascaded Markov models that generate the next phrase hypothesis presented to the annotator. Additionally, all necessary manual tree manipulations are supported.

3.4 Comparison of Annotations

In order to ensure a high degree of accuracy, each sentence is independently annotated by two annotators. The annotations are compared. Differences in the structure and the labeling are automatically detected and presented to the annotators. Their task is to agree on one annotation. Before comparison, approximately 52% of all sentences receive the same annotation by both annotators, i.e., both sentences receive the same structure, same part-of-speech tags, same phrase categories and same grammatical functions. If only the structure is tested, 68% of all sentences are identical. This is equivalent to approx. 93% recall/precision. Annotators meet to discuss disagreements after correcting obvious errors. After discussions, differences remain in about 6% of the sentences, which is equivalent to 99% recall/precision. A more detailed analysis of the inter-annotator agreement is presented in (Brants, 2000a).

Our experience shows that the comparison phase needs much more time than the initial annotation. The overall time spent for the corpus amounts to approx. 10 minutes per sentence, including two initial annotations by two different annotators, correction of obvious errors after seeing an automatically generated list of differences, discussion of disagreements, and discussions of the annotation scheme, and including overhead caused by the training phases of the annotators, changes in the annotation scheme, and additional cleaning procedures.

All annotation rules are documented in the NEGRA annotation guidelines (Brants et al., 1999), enriched with a large number of examples. Comparison of annotations and subsequent discussions of disagreements played an important role in forming the annotation guidelines.

4. APPLICATIONS

The design of the corpus and its annotation scheme aims at re-usability for applications in language technology and for linguistic investigations. The corpus has been used to train part-of-speech taggers (Brants, 1999b) and chunkers (Skut and Brants, 1998; Brants, 1999a). It also has been used for an investigation on the extraposition of relative clauses (Uszkoreit et al., (1998)). The distribution of material between the NP and the relative clause exhibits length effects as proposed by Hawkins' principle of early immediate constituents (Hawkins, 1994), but it shows a systematic difference with respect to the results of a psycholinguistic experiment. The corpus provided data for an investigation on collocations (Krenn, 1998) and for an investigation on word order in the German Mittelfeld (Kurz, 2000). Furthermore, it was used to test incrementality properties of language in an investigation of (Sturt and Lombardo, 1999).

The corpus is freely available to non-profit organizations for research purposes[5]. This enables other investigations on rule-based and statistical processing as well as linguistic investigations, which have recently started. The corpus is distributed in an easy-to-process table based format. As part of the ongoing annotation in the TIGER project, an XML formatted version is being created (Mengel and Lezius, 2000).

5. CONCLUSIONS

The presented corpus is annotated with a hybrid scheme combining the advantages of phrase-structure and dependency grammars. In addition to context-free trees, crossing branches are allowed and predicate-argument information is encoded. This approach was motivated by free word order phenomena in German and by "incomplete" structures frequently found in corpora. The resulting flat structures are very well suited to human annotation.

We presented an efficient interactive annotation mode that guides the annotator through the annotation and asks for confirmation if the process detects unreliable assignments. Reliability is measured by probabilities which are assigned by the statistical tagger and parser. By highlighting unreliable assignments, the annotator can concentrate on these problematic cases.

The process is incremental, each increment consists of one new phrase. This is probably a point for further optimization. If the complete increment is classified as reliable, the process could enlarge the increment in order to speed up annotation. Currently, the NEGRA corpus consists of approx. 20,000 sentences (350,000 tokens).

Acknowledgments

This work was funded by the Deutsche Forschungsgemeinschaft in the Sonderforschungsbereich 378 "Resource-Adaptive Cognitive Processes" Project C3 "NEGRA".

We would like to thank the annotators of the NEGRA corpus for their combined efforts in finding the "correct" structures of naturally occurring sentences and for their constructive discussions on the annotation scheme.

Notes

1. The CD can be obtained from the European Language Resources Association ELRA and the Linguistic Data Consortium LDC.

2. `http://www.ims.uni-stuttgart.de/projekte/TIGER/`

3. An alternative approach was taken by Kurohashi and Nagao (Kurohashi:Nagao:00) who present the Kyoto japanese treebank with a similar methodology: minimal phrases (called bunsetsu) with dependency links between them.

4. For further information on the tagger and for information on availability, please check `http://www.coli.uni-sb.de/~thorsten/tnt/`.

5. See `http://www.coli.uni-sb.de/sfb378/negra-corpus/`

References

Aarts, J., H. van Halteren, N. Osstdijk (1998), The linguistic annotation of corpora: The TOSCA analysis system. *International Journal of Corpus Linguistics* **3(2)**, 1–22.

Böhmová, A., J. Hajič, E. Hajičová, B. Hladká (2003), The Prague Dependency Treebank: a three-level annotation scenario. This volume.

Brants, T. (1999a), Cascaded Markov Models. *Proceedings of 9th Conference of the European Chapter of the Association for Computational Linguistics EACL-99*. Bergen, Norway.

Brants, T. (1999b), *Tagging and Parsing with Cascaded Markov Models – Automation of Corpus Annotation*, Vol. 6 of *Saarbrücken Dissertations in Computational Linguistics and Language Technology*. Saarbrücken, Germany: German Research Center for Artificial Intelligence and Saarland University.

Brants, T. (2000a), Inter-Annotator Agreement for a German Newspaper Corpus. *Proceedings of the Second International Conference on Language Resources and Evaluation (LREC-2000)*. Athens, Greece.

Brants, T. (2000b), TnT – A Statistical Part-of-Speech Tagger. *Proceedings of the Sixth Conference on Applied Natural Language Processing ANLP-2000*. Seattle, WA.

Brants, T., R. Hendriks, S. Kramp, B. Krenn, C. Preis, W. Skut, H. Uszkoreit (1999), NEGRA Annotierschema. Technical report, Computational Linguistics, Sonderforschungsbereich 378, Universität des Saarlandes.

Brants, T., W. Skut (1998), Automation of Treebank Annotation. *Proceedings of New Methods in Language Processing NeMLaP-98*. Sydney, Australia.

Carter, D. (1997), The TreeBanker: a Tool for Supervised Training of Parsed Corpora. *ACL Workshop: Computational Environments for Grammar Development and Linguistic Engineering*. Madrid, Spain.

Greenbaum, S. (ed.) (1996), *Comparing English Worldwide: The International Corpus of English*. Oxford: Clarendon Press.

Hajic, J. (1998), Building a Syntactically Annotated Corpus: The Prague Dependency Treebank. *Issues of Valency and Meaning*. Praha: Karolinum.

Hawkins, J. A. (1994), *A performance theory of order and constituency*. Cambridge Studies in Linguistics 73: Cambridge Univ. Press.

Hindle, D. (1983), Deterministic Parsing of Syntactic Non-Fluencies. *Proceedings of the 21st Annual Meeting of the Association for Computational Linguistics ACL-83*. Cambridge, MA.

Krenn, B. (1998), A Competence-Performance Integrated Representation Model for Collocations. *Proceedings of AMLaP-98*. Freiburg.

Kurohashi, S., M. Nagao (2003), Building a Japanese parsed corpus while improving the parsing system. This volume.

Kurz, D. (2000), Wortstellungsphänomene im deutschen Mittelfeld. Masters thesis, Universität des Saarlandes, Computational Linguistics.

Marcus, M., B. Santorini, M. A. Marcinkiewicz (1993), Building a Large Annotated Corpus of English: The Penn Treebank. *Computational Linguistics* **19**(2), 313–330.

Mengel, A., W. Lezius (2000), An XML-based encoding format for syntactically annotated corpora. *Proceedings of the Second International Conference on Language Resources and Evaluation (LREC-2000)*. Athens, Greece, pp. 121–126.

Plaehn, O., T. Brants: 2000, Annotate - An Efficient Interactive Annotation Tool. *Proceedings of the Sixth Conference on Applied Natural Language Processing ANLP-2000*. Seattle, WA.

Sampson, G. (1995), *English for the Computer. The Susanne Corpus and Analytic Scheme*. Oxford: Oxford University Press.

Samuelsson, C. (1993), Morphological Tagging Based Entirely on Bayesian Inference. *9th Nordic Conference on Computational Linguistics NODALIDA-93*. Stockholm University, Stockholm, Sweden.

Skut, W., T. Brants (1998), A Maximum-Entropy Partial Parser for Unrestricted Text. *Sixth Workshop on Very Large Corpora*. Montreal, Canada, pp. 143–151.

Skut, W., T. Brants, B. Krenn, H. Uszkoreit (1997), Annotating Unrestricted German Text. *Fachtagung der Sektion Computerlinguistik der Deutschen Gesellschaft für Sprachwissenschaft*. Heidelberg, Germany.

Sturt, P., V. Lombardo (1999), Incrementality and Lexicalism: a Treebank Study. *Proceedings of Architectures and Mechanisms in Language Processing AMLaP-99*. Edinburgh.

Thielen, C., A. Schiller (1995), Ein kleines und erweitertes Tagset fürs Deutsche. *Tagungsberichte des Arbeitstreffens Lexikon + Text 17./18. Februar 1994, Schloß Hohentübingen. Lexicographica Series Maior*. Tübingen.

Uszkoreit, H., T. Brants, D. Duchier, B. Krenn, L. Konieczny, S. Oepen, W. Skut: 1998, Studien zur performanzorientierten Linguistik. Aspekte der Relativsatzextraposition im Deutschen. *Kognitionswissenschaft* **7**(3).

Wallis, S. (2003), Completing parsed corpora from correction to evolution. This volume.

Appendix: Tagsets

This section contains descriptions of tags used in this paper. These are *not* complete lists.

A.1 Part-of-Speech Tags

We use the Stuttgart-Tübingen-Tagset. The following list shows the tags used in this paper. The complete set, containing 54 tags, is described in (Thielen and Schiller, 1995).

ADJA	attributive adjective
ADJD	predicatively used adjective
ADV	adverb
APPR	preposition
ART	article
CARD	cardinal
FM	foreign material
KON	coordination
NE	proper noun
NN	common noun
PDAT	demonstr. pronoun, attributive
PDS	demonstr. pronoun, substituting
PPOSAT	possessive pronoun, attributive
PRELAT	relative pronoun, attributive
PRELS	relative pronoun, substituting
PROAV	pronominal adverb
VAFIN	finite auxiliary
VAINF	infinite auxiliary
VMFIN	finite modal verb
VVFIN	finite main verb
VVPP	past participle of main verb

A.2 Phrase Categories and Grammatical Functions

This list shows phrase categories and grammatical functions used in the examples of this paper. Complete lists showing all 25 phrase categories and 40 grammatical functions can be found at `http://www.coli.uni-sb.de/sfb378/negra-corpus/`.

CNP	coordinated noun phrase
NP	noun phrase
PP	prepositional phrase
S	sentence
VP	verb phrase
AC	adpositional case marker
CD	coordinator
CJ	conjunct
HD	head
MNR	post-nominal modifier
MO	modifier
NK	noun kernel
OC	clausal object
PD	predicative
RC	relative clause
SB	subject
SBP	passive subject

Chapter 6

ANNOTATION OF ERROR TYPES FOR GERMAN NEWSGROUP CORPUS

Markus Becker, Andrew Bredenkamp, Berthold Crysmann, Judith Klein
DFKI GmbH, Saarbrücken

Abstract This paper discusses the corpus annotation effort in the FLAG project and its application in the development of controlled language and grammar checking applications. A USENET corpus was collected and annotated using the error typology developed in the project. The DiET tool was used to support the automatic annotation effort, and to evaluate and validate the data. Finally, we report on some interesting aspects of the data which came out of our evaluation.

Keywords: German, Email Corpus, Error Annotation

1. INTRODUCTION

This paper will discuss the corpus annotation effort in the FLAG project and its application for assisting in the development of controlled language and grammar checking applications.

The main aim of the German government funded FLAG project[1] is to develop technologies for controlled language (CL) and grammar checking applications for German. The project work has therefore been divided into two separate but complementary streams of activity. Firstly, the aim was to develop a modular NLP software architecture for quickly building different kinds of CL and grammar checking applications. Secondly, to validate the first activity, it was seen as important to build up an empirical base for testing and formally evaluating checking components. Given the lack of existing annotated corpora of errors for German, the construction of such a corpus was a high priority task. This would enable us not only to perform quantitative tests, but also to derive an empirically based typology of errors which the project could use for orientation.

The corpus was particularly important given the approach which the FLAG project was taking to the task of grammar and controlled language checking,

A. Abeillé (ed.), Treebanks: Building and Using Parsed Corpora, 89–100.

which relies on a phenomenon-oriented approach to the problem of identifying errors, using shallow processing techniques. In order to fine-tune the heuristics which are central to such an approach, i.e. one based on identifying "candidate errors" of increasing probability, it is essential to have good test suites annotated with respect to the phenomena under investigation.

The annotation of the corpus was to be carried out in such a way that we could easily access and quantify snapshots of the data, for producing test suites for testing purposes and for producing statistics on the frequency of particular error types.

The research community not only lacked an annotated corpus of errors, there was no existing ontology of errors which could be easily translated into an annotation schema. The definition of such a schema based on traditional descriptions of errors (such as Luik, 1993a; Luik, 1993b) thus formed the first major workpackage. Fortunately, tools for the annotation of corpora, and the management thereof are becoming increasingly sophisticated; it was therefore necessary to evaluate a number of tools in light of our specific needs.

2. CORPUS DESCRIPTION

Given the use we intended to make of the language data, the corpus had to be carefully selected. The availability of unedited corpora with real errors proved to be somewhat problematic, since most available sources of texts, newspapers being a traditional source for such things, are rather heavily edited before they are made available. Our corpus needed the following characteristics:

- the texts should have a relatively high error density, i.e. as close to a real performance scenario as possible. It was important to avoid annotators having to annotate (or rather identify) too many grammatical sentences in building up a useable resource of ungrammatical ones.

- they should be easily accessible - the texts needed to be easily available in large quantities such that we could be assured of having a large quantity of errors for all error types.

- they should be electronically available - to facilitate the electronic manipulation (e.g. tokenization) and annotation of the corpus using the software tools, and for storing the results in a database to facilitate the querying of the data, for the production of test suites, etc.

The corpus selected was an archive of email messages posted to a number of internet USENET newsgroups. The initially selected corpus contained approximately 120,000 sentences, although additional text is added constantly to the archive and can be retrieved automatically as required. The corpus consists of email messages of various lengths and with varying degrees of register, although the tendency is clearly towards a rather colloquial style. The main benefit of the corpus is that it is largely unedited text with a relatively high proportion of grammatical errors, both performance errors and competence errors.[2]

3. ANNOTATION STRATEGY

The annotation proceeded in three main stages: the first stage was to develop a typology for grammatical errors for German. Subsequently, we undertook manual annotation on paper with a simplified error typology, the idea being that we could get a large set of sentences annotated quickly. This proceeded very rapidly and allowed us to focus on the annotation of ungrammatical sentences in the third stage, the annotation using computer tools.

3.1 Error Typology

The error typology took as its basis traditional grammar books and a collection of cases considered grammatically difficult, cf. “Stolpersteine” Luik, 1993a; Luik, 1993b. We produced a fine-grained error typology with various sub-classes for orthographic, morphological, morpho-syntactic, syntactic and syntactic-semantic errors (Crysmann, 1997). This typology was taken as the starting point for the annotation, with the intention that it would evolve in light of the experience gained from the detailed inspection of the corpus.

In order to support the integration of new error types derived in the course of the annotation effort, the initial error typology was designed as a type hierarchy, including some highly general supertypes in addition to the initial set of more specific error types.

In addition to the classification of error types, the typology also presents some preliminary ideas on error domains, in that it tries to define the relation between the affected words. This information could be of use in guiding checkers to detect errors, and could also help find the right correction/proposal on the basis of a diagnosis.

Finally, the typology also makes reference to the notion of “lexical anchors”, i.e. words which themselves are often the focus of a particular error type (cf. *Wissens* ‘knowledge’ in the contrast **meines Wissens nach* ‘my.GEN knowledge.GEN according’ vs. *meines Wissens* ‘as far as I know; lit.: my.GEN knowledge.GEN’ or *meinem Wissen nach* ‘as far as I know; lit.: my.DAT knowledge.DAT according’).

Given the time-consuming task of annotation a more coarse-grained version with 16 error types was used for the initial annotation task, as follows:

- one class for morphological errors e.g. derivation errors,

- syntax errors comprising word order, categorial, case, and three classes for agreement errors,
- one class for syntactic-semantic selection (such as for fixed verbal structures),
- four types of orthographic errors,
- one further general class for syntax errors which cannot be easily classified further.

(Subsequent classes which are less interesting for our immediate purposes are: a class for obvious tokenizer mistakes, one for typographical errors, e.g. repeated words, and one for competence errors which can't easily be reconstructed (corrected) to form grammatical sentences.)

3.2 Manual Annotation

When we started the annotation task in FLAG there were no customized annotation tools available. The sentences from the raw corpus were tokenized and presented in a format which facilitated the process of annotation, each sentence being printed with a number of boxes corresponding to the broad error categories we were using at this stage. The annotators had simply to identify the errors, mark the error position and check the appropriate error label box. For this task an average speed of 250 corrected sentences per hour was determined.

During this annotation phase, specific and very complex errors (and also ambiguities in analyzing/correcting the errors) occurred within the email sentences. Guidelines were established and the typology was further refined to help with consistent annotation.

The annotation group consisted of four people. Three of them were mainly responsible for manual and computer annotation. One person was responsible both for annotation and coordination of the group.

3.3 Computer Annotation

To best exploit the annotated news corpus, the email sentences needed to be electronically available and easily accessible. In the second phase of the annotation work, the manually annotated sentences were processed with the help of the two annotation tools. This computer annotation is being done by another annotator in order to validate the annotations and apply the latest version of the elaborated annotation guidelines.

This work serves also to help validate and customise the annotation tools themselves. On the basis of our experiences using two different tools, it was decided to focus the computer annotation effort on a single system, namely the

DiET tool (Klein et al., 1998b; Netter et al., 1998). The other tool evaluated, Annotate, whilst offering much more sophisticated annotation functionality for syntactic trees, was less well suited to dealing with the flexible ontology with which we were working.

As soon as all manually annotated email sentences are validated and recorded, new corpus data will directly be annotated with the DiET annotation tool. Even though the identification of errors on screen is slightly more error-prone than working on paper, the direct method is more economical.

Additionally, the search facility of DiET will be used to systematically check all annotations.

So far about 60,000 sentences have been annotated on paper, of which over 14,492 have now been recorded and checked in the DiET tool. Out of these, 6473 contain at least one error. More than 3900 sentences were annotated using the Annotate tool, which will be imported automatically into DiET.

4. ANNOTATION TOOLS

As mentioned above, two sophisticated annotation tools were evaluated: Annotate, the corpus annotation tool of the Negra project[3] (Skut et al., 1997; Brants et al., this volume) and DiET, the multi-purpose annotation tool developed within the DiET project[4]. The feedback we were able to provide has lead to a number of modifications and extensions in the tools.

Annotate is a Unix-based annotation tool which has been explicitly designed for the morpho-syntactic annotation of text corpora. It is equipped with a graphical user interface for efficient tree annotations and uses a relational database for storage and retrieval. In order to use the tree format for the error annotation Annotate has been customized such that the tree nodes provide the labels for the error types and the tree edges provide descriptive information on particular error types. The error position is indicated by the edges and nodes build upon the words. With Annotate we conducted some preliminary experiments for illustrating the error domains. The tree structure has been used in order to build the dependency relation between the words which are affected by the error.

While the tree format employed in Annotate provides for a rich representation of the structure of a particular error in terms of relations (cf. Figure 6.1), its major drawback lies in the fact that these representations have to be built up from bottom to top, with one of the most basic pieces of information, i.e. the error type, added last. Similarly, all dimensions of the annotation scheme, including locality, type, and domain, have to be entered in a single step, because integration of additional annotations at a later point cannot be performed without reconstructing major subparts of the annotation tree.

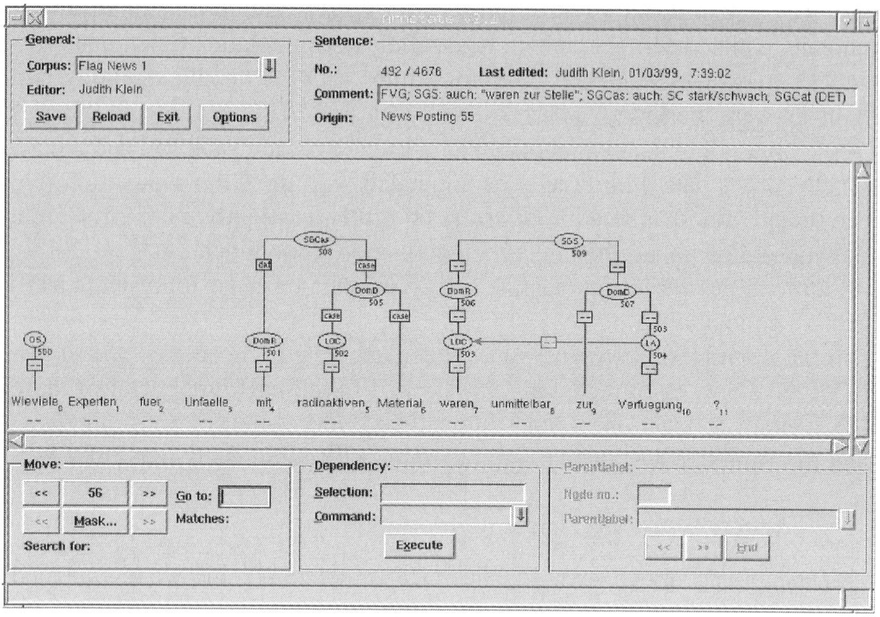

Figure 6.1. Error annotation in ANNOTATE

Furthermore, the tree-structural organization does not offer a convenient solution to the representation of overlapping errors.

DiET is a comprehensive software package for the construction, annotation, customization, and maintenance of structured reference data. The system is a Java application, implemented in a configurable, open client/server architecture with a central database system managing the data and a client integrating construction, annotation, and retrieval facilities. DiET allows the user to easily configure an annotation schema by specifying relevant annotation types (i.e. describing attributes for annotation) with adequate data types (numbers, strings, marking, trees, etc.). The marking mode is especially relevant for annotating the error site within the sentences.

As already mentioned, we decided to continue the computer annotation only on DiET which has substantially improved in the meantime. It now offers also a sophisticated tree grapher for illustrating the error dependencies within the error domains.

The FLAG annotation schema for error types contains the following information:

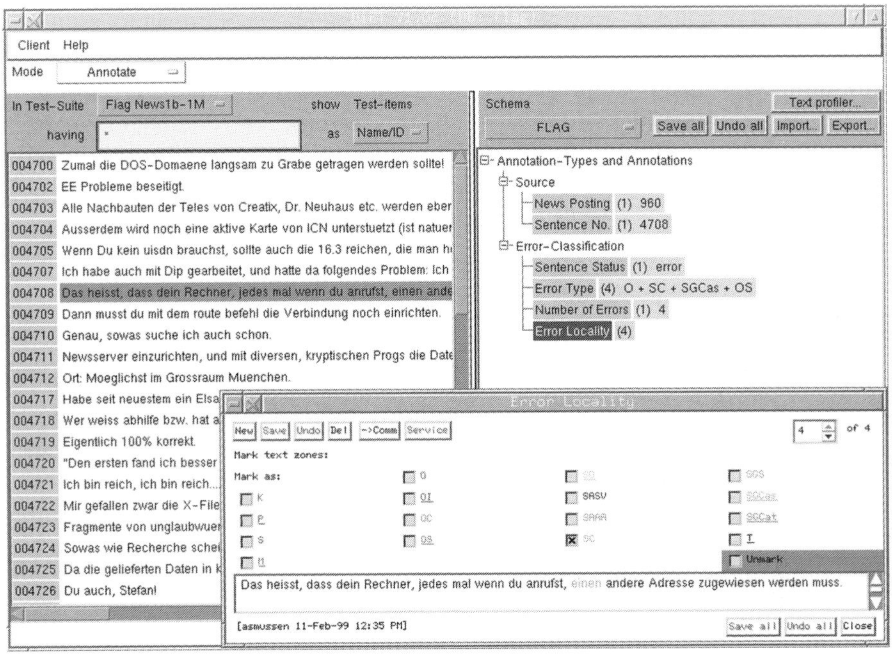

Figure 6.2. Error annotation in DIET

- email number and sentence number to identify the origin of the data,
- sentence status (grammatical, ungrammatical, colloquial),
- error type (orthography, subject-verb agreement, word order, etc.) ,
- number of errors per sentence,
- error localition (at what sentence position(s) the error occurs),
- error domain (dependency relation between the affected words).

The schema mainly reflects the manual annotation format and thus allows the annotators to easily transfer the manually annotated emails into the DiET database.

Although the tree grapher integrated in DiET provides a representation sligh-tly less expressive than the one in Annotate, most (if not all) aspects of the error annotation schema can be mimicked using DiET's concept of multiple annotation views. These views not only provide an elegant solution to the problem of overlap, they also support splitting up the entire annotation into several logical subtasks, e.g. localization and classification as basic annotations, which are then complemented by error domains at some later stage.

The retrieval facilities of DiET will be used in order to systematically check the annotations. With specific database queries it is possible, for instance, to check if there are entries where the sentence status is grammatical but there is also an entry for error type, or to search for sentences which have an entry for error type but no entry for number of errors per sentence.

5. EVALUATION

The original motivation for our annotation effort derived mainly from the need to verify the phenomenon-based error typology developed so far in the FLAG project. To process as much material as possible, annotators were given distinct subsets of the corpus for proof-reading and classification. However, when the results of the paper annotation were transferred into the DiET database, the classification was checked by a different annotator, thereby ensuring a certain level of precision and homogenity among the annotations.

In order to evaluate the usability of the corpus as a test suite, we conducted an experiment to measure the interjudge agreement, a valuable measure in the context of annotation tasks, on the basis of which recall and precision can be determined.[5] To achieve this, we handed out instances of the same subset of the corpus to our two main annotators. To get a realistic result, the annotators were given the directive to have no clarification dialogues during annotation. After the annotation, the two suite instances were frozen. A third instance of the same suite will be created as the result of a discussion of differently annotated items between the two annotators. At time of writing, we do not have this reference corpus, so we have to confine our discussion to the direct comparison of the two independently annotated corpora.

The annotation task consists of two different subtasks, namely error detection and error classification. Thus, in the absence of a reference corpus, we can still determine a preliminary measure of each annotator's recall, by comparing the error detection rates: to achieve this, we identified the total number of detectable errors as the set union of the errors found by the two annotators. Table 6.1 summarizes the results that were determined on a sentence by sentence basis, ignoring minor differences as to the exact position at which the error was identified.

The original subset of the corpus contained 745 sentences of which both annotators processed about 690 sentences. The remaining approximately 50 sentences were judged completely inacceptable and deleted, e.g. due to tokenization errors. Annotator A marked 727 errors, while 744 errors were found by annotator B. While the overall recall is above 80 % for both annotators,

Table 6.1. Error detection (Recall)

			Annotator A		*Annotator B*	
Error type	*Label*	*Total*	*Abs.*	*Rel.*	*Abs.*	*Rel.*
Syntax (general)	S	0	0	–	0	–
Subject-verb agreement	SASV	3	2	0.67	3	1.00
Antecedent-anaphor agreement	SAAA	0	0	–	0	–
Concord (NP agreement)	SC	16	12	0.75	12	0.75
Word order	SO	6	3	0.50	4	0.67
Valency (general)	SG	0	0	–	0	–
Case assignment	SGCas	10	7	0.70	6	0.60
Subcategorisation	SGCat	71	51	0.72	64	0.90
Semantic selection	SGS	34	25	0.74	24	0.71
Total Syntax		140	100	0.71	113	0.81
Orthography (general)	O	164	130	0.79	145	0.88
Punctuation	OI	193	173	0.90	169	0.88
One word vs. separate words	OS	116	85	0.73	84	0.72
Capital vs. small letters	OC	184	170	0.92	153	0.83
Morphology	M	17	8	0.47	15	0.88
Total Orthography		647	566	0.87	566	0.87
Performance	P	16	12	0.75	12	0.75
Tokeniser errors	T	60	49	0.82	51	0.85
All		890	727	0.82	744	0.84

annotator A has a slightly better recall with orthographical errors than with grammar errors, whereas no significant difference between these two major classes can be found for annotator B. Given that there is often no clearly defined boundary between stylistic and grammatical errors, it is hardly surprising that the class of syntax errors shows a higher degree of divergence than the class of orthographical errors.

In order to measure the degree of interjudge agreement concerning error classification, we compared the set of 478 errors which were marked at exactly identical positions within the 690 sentences. Of these, 454 errors were assigned the same error type. In other words, whenever two annotators find the same error they have a broadly similar intuition about the appropriate error type, i.e. we have a high precision rate of around 95%. The error types assigned to the remaining set of 24 errors were distributed quite equally across the different error categories, including orthographical and grammatical errors. We interpret the high level of interjudge agreement regarding the error classification as a confirmation of the error typology developed in FLAG.

6. FIRST RESULTS

So far, a subset of the corpus containing 14,492 sentences has been fully annotated using the DiET tool. Among these, 7392 sentences were well-formed, with another 627 sentences being considered badly tokenized. The remaining 6473 sentences thus contained at least one error. Table 6.2 gives a summary of the distribution of errors found in these sentences.

Table 6.2. Distribution of Error Types

Error type	*Label*	*Token*
Syntax (general)	S	3
Subject-verb agreement	SASV	63
Antecedent-anaphor agreement	SAAA	1
Concord (NP-internal agreement)	SC	180
Word order	SO	79
Valency (general)	SG	0
Subcategorisation	SGCat	854
Case assignment	SGCas	102
Semantic selection	SGS	265
Total Syntax		1547
Morphology	M	91
Othography (general)	O	2893
Punctuation	OI	1701
Capital vs. small letters	OC	2776
One word vs. separate words	OS	1100
Total Orthography		7561
All		9108

The first major result that can be derived from the inspection of Table 6.2 concerns the relative scarcity of true grammar errors. Even though the overall density of errors is comparatively high, mainly a result of the choice of corpus, affecting almost 50 % of all sentences, the vast majority (around 83%) are purely orthographical errors. Grammar errors, by contrast, amount to only around 16%.

If we take a closer look at the distribution within the class of syntax errors itself, we find that subcategorization errors make up the bulk of the grammatical errors found in the corpus (around 9.4%). Roughly two-thirds of these errors are target-deviant elisions (6.1%). Another major subclass of subcategorization errors involves the erroneous use of the complementizer *da* 'that' and the homophonous relative pronoun *das* 'which': in 49 cases the complementizer was used in place of a relative pronoun, while 103 times the relative pronoun was found instead of the complementizer, yielding a frequency of 1.7% for this specific error.

In contrast to subcategorization errors, all other syntax errors only display a frequency of 3% and below. Among these, there are classes which are practically unattested, e.g. antecedent-anaphor agreement (SAAA) with only a single occurrence in the entire set of 14,492 sentences. Results such as this are particularly useful in the design of error-checking applications, as they enable us to ignore very low frequency error types in case they would otherwise demand an inappropriately high level of processing.

The data extracted from the annotated test-suite can be useful inguiding not only the detection of errors, but also the direction in which errors should be corrected: subject-verb agreement, for example, involves the verb as the error site in 56 out of 63 cases.

The relative scarcity of grammar errors in general and their uneven distribution across the different subtypes of syntax errors appear to support the focused, phenomenon-based approach to error-checking adopted within the FLAG project, where inexpensive shallow processing technology is used to systematically identify error candidates, which are then subjected to more elaborate processing.

A final observation concerns the fact that annotators did not make much use of the more coarse-grained supertypes, such as S or SG. Along with the high precision rate in interjudge agreement discussed in the previous section, this fact appears to suggest that the error types identified in the FLAG annotation scheme are already sufficient to cover the relevant phenomena.

7. CONCLUSION

The corpus annotation effort in the FLAG project is a central part of the research effort, without the resources it provides it is not practically possible to optimize the software components under development. The methodology (fast paper annotation, followed by thorough evaluation in the course of computer annotation) is proving effective, and the "genuine" (i.e. corpus-derived) test-suites make for more realistic, but nevertheless focused testing.

Notes

1. The project is funded by the German Ministry for Education and Research (BMBF) Project number ITW 9700.

2. We regard grammar errors as all those errors whose detection involves grammatical knowledge beyond simple dictionary lookup. Performance errors, in this context, are typos, which give rise to existing, yet inappropriately used word forms. Competence errors, by contrast, typically involve larger linguistic units, e.g. phrases which are consistently used in an inappropriate way, e.g. featuring the wrong case specification.

3. `http://www.coli.uni-sb.de/cl/projects/negra.html`

4. `http://diet.dfki.de/`

5. Of course, the interjudge agreement so determined will also provide us with the upper bound in the context of evaluating the performance of automatic error checking components.

References

Brants, T., Skut, W., Uszkoreit, H. (2003). Syntactic annotation of a German newspaper corpus, This volume.

Crysmann, B. (1997). Fehlerannotation. Technical report, DFKI GmbH.

Klein, J., Lehmann, S., Netter, K., Wegst, T. (1998a). Construction and annotation of test-items in DiET. In *Proceedings of the ESSLLI Workshop on Recent Advances in Corpus Annotation*, Saarbrücken.

Klein, J., Lehmann, S., Netter, K., Wegst, T. (1998b). DiET in the context of MT evaluation. In Nübel, R. and Seewald-Heeg, U., editors, *Evaluation of the Linguistic Performance of Machine Translation System*, p. 107–126. Gardez! Verlag, St. Augustin.

Luik, G. (1993a). *Stolpersteine*, volume 1. Geiger Verlag, Wiesbaden.

Luik, G. (1993b). *Stolpersteine*, volume 2. Geiger Verlag, Wiesbaden.

Netter, K., Armstrong, S., Kiss, T., Klein, J., Lehmann, S., Milward, D., Regnier-Prost, S., Schäler, R., Wegst, T. (1998). DiET — diagnostic and evaluation tools for natural language processing applications. In *Proceedings of the First International Conference on Language Resources and Evaluation*, p. 573–579, Granada.

Skut, W., Krenn, B., Brants, T., Uszkoreit, H. (1997). An annotation scheme for free word order languages. In *Proceedings of ANLP*, p. 8–96, Washington.

SLAVIC TREEBANKS

Chapter 7

THE PRAGUE DEPENDENCY TREEBANK

A Three-Level Annotation Scenario

Alena Böhmová, Jan Hajič, Eva Hajičová, Barbora Hladká

Institute of Formal and Applied Linguistics

Faculty of Mathematics and Physics

Charles University

Malostranské nám. 25

CZ—118 00 Prague 1

{bohmova,hajic,hajicova,hladka}@ufal.mff.cuni.cz

Abstract The availability of annotated data (with as rich and "deep" annotation as possible) is desirable in any new developments. Textual data are being used for so-called training phase of various empirical methods solving various problems in the field of computational linguistics. While there are many methods that use texts in their plain (or raw) form (in most cases for so-called unsupervised training), more accurate results may be obtained if annotated corpora are available. The data annotation itself is a complex task. While morphologically annotated corpora (pioneered by Henry Kučera in the 60's) are now available for English and other languages, syntactically annotated corpora are rare. Inspired by the Penn Treebank, the most widely used syntactically annotated corpus of English, we decided to develop a similarly sized corpus of Czech with a rich annotation scheme.

Keywords: Corpora, Treebanks, Annotation Schema, Morphology, Syntax, Tectogrammatical Tree Structures, Czech

1. The Prague Dependency Treebank

The Prague Dependency Treebank (PDT) has a three-level structure. Full *morphological* annotation is done on the lowest level (Hajič, 1998; Hajič, in press). The middle level deals with superficial (surface) syntactic annotation (Bémová, et al., 1997) using dependency syntax; it is called the *analytical*

A. Abeillé (ed.), Treebanks: Building and Using Parsed Corpora, 103–127.

level, and it is conceptually close to the level of syntactic annotation used in the Penn Treebank (Marcus et al., 1993). The highest level of annotation is the *tectogrammatical* level, or the level of linguistic meaning (based on the framework of Functional Generative Description, Sgall et al., 1986).

The textual data used for the PDT task contain general newspaper articles (60%; including but not limited to politics, sports, culture, hobbies, etc.), economic news and analyses (20%), popular science magazines (20%), all selected from the Czech National Corpus (CNC, cnk). We annotate the same texts on all three levels, but the amount of annotated material decreases with the complexity of the levels[1], from about 1.8 mil. tokens on the morphological level to about 1 mil. tokens on the tectogrammatical level. SGML markup is used throughout as the data interchange format[2].

The PDT is a long-term project (1996-2000, now extended to 2004) with two major phases. In the first phase, now completed, the first two levels of annotation have been completed and made available; also the specification of the tectogrammatical level has been finished[3]. During the second phase, the tectogrammatical annotation will be completed and released.

2. MORPHOLOGICAL LEVEL

The morphological analysis of an isolated[4] word form produces a *lemma*[5] (or more in the case of a morphological ambiguity) and a combination of values of individual morphological categories. The combination of those values is called a morphological tag (*MTag*); in other words, the list of possible MTags together with corresponding lemmas represents the output of the morphological analysis of the input word form. In a given context, just one pair (MTag, lemma) "fits in"; the context-sensitive process of selecting the fitting pair is called morphological annotation (if it is done manually) or morphological tagging (if it is automatically). In order to use the tags effectively in applications, and for uniformity, we also follow the usual practice and assign "lemmas" and appropriate "morphological" tags to punctuation.

Thus on the morphological level of the PDT, a MTag and a lemma are assigned to each token in the input data. The morphological annotation of the PDT has been done semi-automatically. It is a two-step process: first, the input text (Figure 9.1) is processed automatically by the morphological analyzer (Hajič, in press), resulting in a list of possible (lemma, MTag) pairs for each input token (Fig 9.2, SGML markup `<MMl>, <MMt>`). Then, manual disambiguation yields the desired unique pair (Fig 7.3, SGML markup `<l>, <t>`). Currently, Czech MTags are defined as a concatenation of 15 morphological categories and each morphological category corresponds to precisely one position. For instance, the part of speech "sits" in the 1st position, gender in the 3rd, case in the 5th, etc. For example, the MTag `NNFS6-----A----` represents a singular (S) feminine (F) general (N) noun (N) in the locative case (6), without (negative) prefix (A)[6]. A detailed description of the positional MTag system is presented also in Hajič, in press.

```
<s id=''s/inf/j/1994/cmpr9410:001-p24s3''>   unique sentence ID
<f cap>Šance                                 word form token
<f>je                                        word form token
<f>přesto                                    word form token
<f>minimální                                 word form token
<d>.                                         punctuation token
```

Figure 7.1. The SGML format of CNC illustrated by the Czech sentence *Šance je přesto minimální* [lit. The chance is nevertheless minimal].

```
<s id=''s/inf/j/1994/cmpr9410:001-p24s3''>
<f cap>Šance<MMl>šance<MMt>NNFP1-----A----<MMt>NNFP4-----A-- --
   <MMt>NNFP5-----A----<MMt>NNFS1-----A- /---<MMt>NNFS2-----A----
   <MMt>NNFS5-----A----
<f>je<MMl>být<MMt>VB-S---3P-AA---<MMl>on <MMt>PPNS4--3-------
   <MMt>PPXP4--3-------
<f>přesto<MMl>přesto<MMt>Dg-------1A-- --
<f>minimální<MMl>minimální<MMt>AAFP1--- /-1A----
   <MMt>AAFP4----1A----<MMt>AAFP5----1A-- --<MMt>AAFS1----1A----
   <MMt>AAFS2----1A----<MMt>AAFS3----1A-- --<MMt>AAFS4----1A----
   <MMt>AAFS5----1A----<MMt>AAFS6----1A-- --<MMt>AAFS7----1A----
   <MMt>AAIP1----1A----<MMt>AAIP4----1A-- --<MMt>AAIP5----1A----
   <MMt>AAIS1----1A----<MMt>AAIS4----1A-- --<MMt>AAIS5----1A----
   <MMt>AAMP1----1A----<MMt>AAMP4----1A-- --<MMt>AAMP5----1A----
   <MMt>AAMS1----1A----<MMt>AAMS5----1A-- --<MMt>AANP1----1A----
   <MMt>AANP4----1A----<MMt>AANP5----1A-- --<MMt>AANS1----1A----
   <MMt>AANS4----1A----<MMt>AANS5----1A-- --
<d>.<MMl>.<MMt>Z:-------------
```

Figure 7.2. Input sentence (from Figure 1.1) after automatic morphological analysis

```
<s id=''s/inf/j/1994/cmpr9410:001-p24s3''>
<f cap>Šance<l>šance<t>NNFS1-----A----
<f>je<l>být<t>VB-S---3P-AA---
<f>přesto<l>přesto<t>Dg-------1A--- /-
<f>minimální<l>minimální<t>AAFS1----1A ----
<d>.<l>.<t>Z:-------------
```

Figure 7.3. Annotated input sentence (from Figure 1.2), after manual disambiguation

```
<s id=''s/inf/j/1994/cmpr9410:001-p24s3''>
<f cap>Šance<MDl>šance<MDt>NNFS1-----A----
<f>je<MDl>být<MDt>VB-S---3P-AA---
<f>přesto<MDl>přesto<MDt>Dg-------1A-- --
<f>minimální<MDl>minimální<MDt>AANS1--- -1A----
<d>.<MDl>.<MDt>Z:-------------
```

Figure 7.4. Tagged input sentence (from Figure 1.1), with "automatic" tags

A morphologically annotated corpus can then be used to train a tagger based on a probabilistic model (or another type of automatic tagger) which in turn can be used to automatically annotate large amounts of previously unseen (new) texts. Similar SGML markup is used there (Figure 7.4, SGML markup `<MDl>`, `<MDt>`).

2.1 Annotation

The morphological level has been annotated by a separate team of annotators. The group (seven undergraduate students with either a computer science or linguistics background) proceeded in two separate phases. During the first phase - for each text to be annotated - two annotators independently chose the (lemma, MTag) pair from the list suggested by the morphological analyzer. The two versions of the same text were compared to each other, and then in the second phase another annotator resolved the differences between them. Six of the seven students were the "first phase" annotators and only one was the "second phase" annotator-arbiter, with the hope of consistent tag assignment throughout the corpus.

In order to make the annotation of texts more human-friendly (and less error-prone), a special purpose tool has been developed. The tool was first implemented under Linux and then reimplemented for the MS Windows platform.

The input text contained about 56% ambiguous tokens at the time of the annotation[7]. In line with the observations of others (most notably, Marcus et al., 1994), we have found that about 4.9% of the input tokens were annotated differently by the two "first phase" annotators. Almost all the differences are caused by performance errors.

3. ANALYTICAL LEVEL

The analytical (syntactic) level of annotation(Bémová, et al., 1997) is the second (middle) level of the overall annotation scheme. We have chosen the dependency structure to represent the (surface) syntactic relations within a sentence; no "phrase labels" are used. The dependency structure is based on a dependency relation (often referred to as the relation of determination, or mother/daughter, or head/modifier relation) between a governor and its dependent node (labeled by words) in a dependency tree.

The basic design principles of the analytical level (or ATS, for Analytical Tree Structures) are:

(1) each word and each punctuation mark is represented by exactly one node,

(2) no nodes are added (with the exception of a special "technical" auxiliary root node of the tree),

(3) non-projectivity (i.e. crossing of edges) is allowed,

(4) the result is a dependency tree, in which the edges (links) are explicitly labeled analytical (syntactic) tags (*STags*),

(5) each node of the resulting analytical tree consists of three parts:

  (a) the original word form,

  (b) the morphological tag and lemma (which come from the morphological level, unchanged),

  (c) the syntactic tag (STag as a label of the dependency link).

All possible values (STags) of the analytical function attribute (*afun*) are described in Table 7.A.1 in Appendix.

The annotation rules (Bémová, et al., 1997) follow the traditional grammar books whenever possible, but are both extended (where no guidance has been found in such books) and modified (where the current grammars are inconsistent, for example).

Figure 9.2 gives an example of the analytical-level annotation[8] of the sentence

(1) Do 15. května budou cestující platit dosud platným způsobem.
Until May 15, passengers will pay using the current scheme.

The original word forms as well as the STags assigned to the analytical function node attributs are displayed. This example illustrates:

- the extra root node of the tree, with the number of the sentence within the file;
- the handling of an analytical verb form (`AuxV` *budou* + infinitive *platit*);

- the fact that the verb is the governing node of the whole sentence (or of every clause in compound sentences), as opposed to the complex subject–complex predicate distinction made even in the otherwise dependency-oriented traditional grammars of Czech, such as (Šmilauer, 1969);
- an attachment of a manner-type adverbial to an analytical verb form;
- the handling of a date;
- prepositional phrase structure (preposition as the governor);

and, of course, all the analytical functions at these nodes.

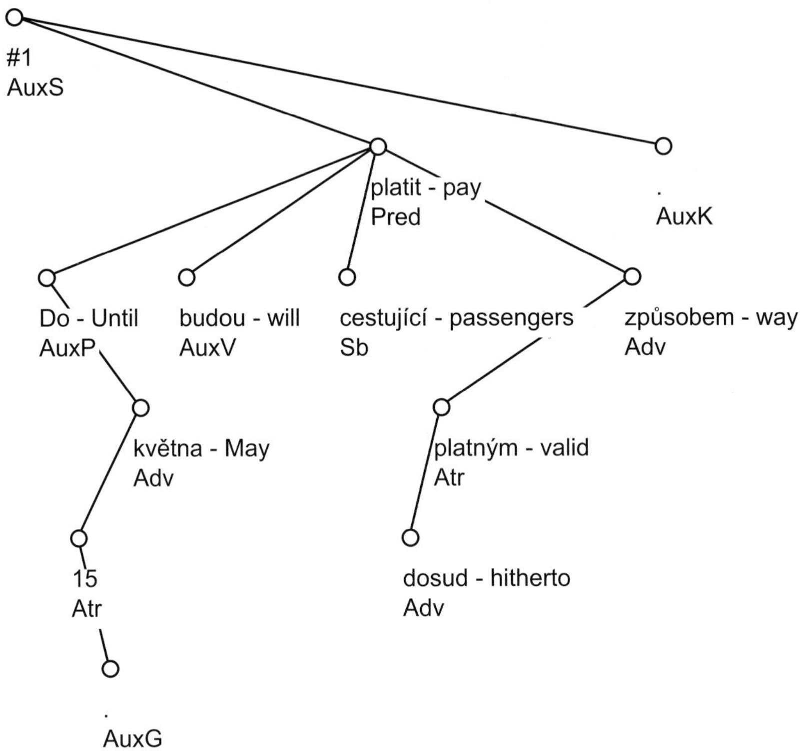

Figure 7.5. Analytical level annotation of sentence (1)

Figure 7.6 illustrates the SGML format of the PDT with both the morphological and analytical levels marked. The morphological level markup `<l>`,

```
<f cap>Do<l>do<t>RR--2----------<A>AuxP<r>1<g>7
<f num>15<l>15<t>C=-------------<A>Atr <r>2<g>4
<d>.<l>.<t>Z:-------------<A>AuxG<r>3<g>2
<f>května<l>květen<t>NNIS2-----A----<A>Adv<r>4<g>1
<f>budou<l>být<t>VB-P---3F-AA---<A>AuxV<r>5<g>7
<f>cestující<l>cestující<t>NNMP1---- -A----<A>Sb <r>6<g>7
<f>platit<l>platit<t>Vf--------A----<A >Pred<r>7<g>0
<f>dosud<l>dosud<t>Db-------------<A >Adv<r>8<g>9
<f>platným<l>platný<t>AAIS7----1A----< A>Atr<r>9<g>10
<f>způsobem<l>způsob<t>NNIS7-----A----<A>Adv<r>10<g>7
<d>.<l>.<t>Z:-------------<A>AuxK<r>11<g>0
```

Figure 7.6. The SGML format of the morphologically and analytically annotated input sentence

<t> is described above in Sect. 2; the analytical level markup <A>, <r> and <g> denotes the Stag (analytical function), the token numerical ID (based on the surface word order within the sentence) and the numerical ID of its governing token, respectively.

The annotation process was viewed as (an interative) process where the rules for annotation were constructed based on the evidence found in the data. Thus before the manual annotation began[9], we explained the basic principles of annotation to the annotators, and asked them to use existing grammar books, most notably (Šmilauer, 1969), an old, but still the most suitable and authoritative description of Czech syntax. It is based on a dependency framework, although there are some (easily identifiable and replaceable) deviations. We were aware of the fact that there are many gaps in such a traditional grammar from the point of view of an explicit annotation: mainly, the requirement to have each input word represented by a node in the tree (a demand quite natural from the computational point of view) is largely not reflected in any human-oriented grammar description.

3.1 Treatment of special phenomena

We believe that the dependency structure we use is a very good formal representation for the central notion of a dependency theory, i.e. the determination relation. However, it is not simple to represent syntactic relations of another type (non-determinative, such as coordination and apposition) in a plain two-dimensional graph; therefore we have introduced some special conventions for that purpose. Figure 9.3 illustrates a coordination of two members of a sentence (attributes in this case):

(2) V roce 1994 dochází k mírnému oživení světové ekonomiky a světového obchodu.

A weak rebound of the world's economy and world trade occurred in 1994.

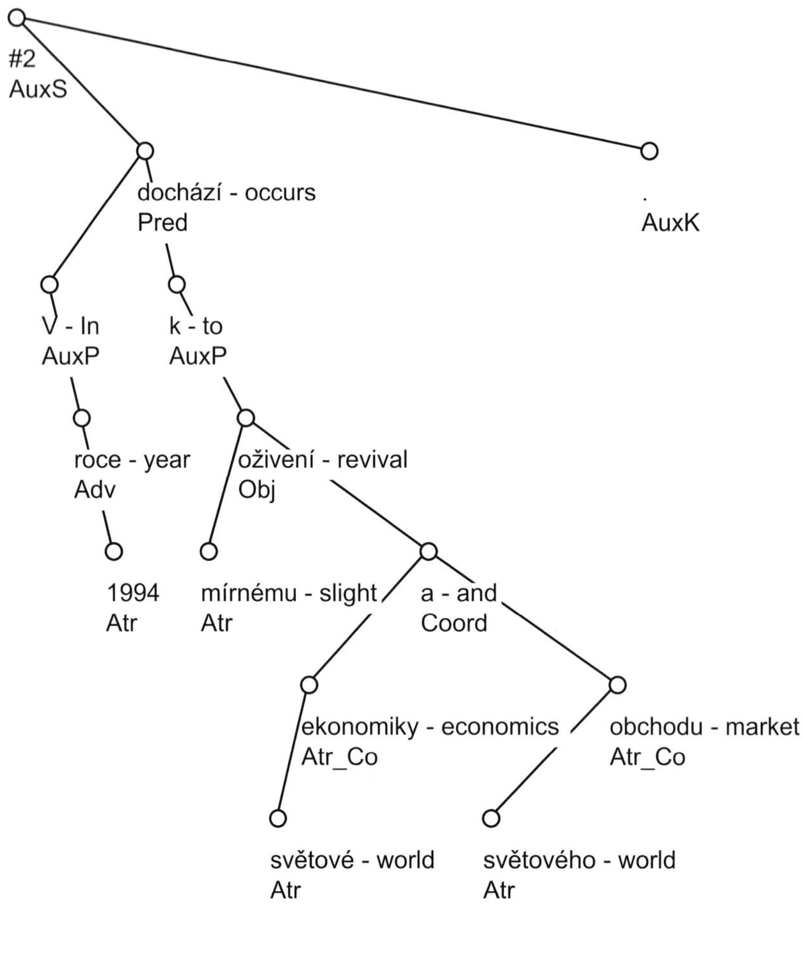

Figure 7.7. Example of coordination - sentence (2); lit. word translation used

The analytical function at the coordinated nodes now contains an Stag bearing a suffix `_Co`, which denotes coordinated nodes while still keeping the information about the true original Stag. As an additional rule, we have stated that all coordinated nodes must contain the same Stag (with the exception of elliptical constructions).

When a syntactically ambiguous sentence is being analyzed and the annotator is not able to decide on the preferred type of dependency (either an adverbial dependency, where a verb is a head, or an adnominal dependency with a noun as the head), and *both readings are in fact plausible*[10], "double" analytical functions (`ObjAtr, AdvAtr`) are used, see Examples (3) and (4):

(3) Moderní teorie o bytí říká, že bytí...

Modern theory of human beings says that human beings ...

(4) Napsal referát do vědeckého časopisu.

He has written a paper for a scientific journal.

In (3) either the dependency pair *říká* 'says' (as a mother node) and *o bytí* 'of human being' (daughter node with `Obj`(ect) function), or the pair *teorie* 'theory' (mother) and *o bytí* 'of human being' (daughter with `Attr`(ibute) function) is present): here the "double" function `ObjAtr`[11] is applied. In Ex. (4) the same phenomenon occurs with the prepositional case *do časopisu* 'for a scientific journal', which will be labeled by the `AdvAtr` function.

The sentence

(5) Maďarsko a Slovensko očekává stagnaci HDP, Polsko pokračující růst.

Hungary and Slovakia expect the GDP to stay flat while Poland expects its continued growth.

and its analytical tree structure in Figure 9.1 illustrate a situation when no token can be found in the sentence to be the governor of 'Poland' and 'growth' (i.e. the governor is deleted in the surface structure); in such a case we use the label `ExD` (extra dependency, denoting that the governor is actually missing) and point the dependency link towards a node that would normally govern the missing one. Even though in many sentences the missing node could easily be identified, we have decided not to add it at this level of annotation (thus sticking with the first and second basic principles of analytical level annotation) and deal with the problem properly at the third, tectogrammatical level.

A detailed description of the conventions used can be found in (Bémová, et al., 1997).

3.2 Two Modes of Annotation

At the beginning of the annotation effort the annotators were constructing the syntactic structure and deciding on the analytical functions at the tree nodes purely manually with only the help of "user-friendly" software with a graphical interface (Křen, 1996; see also Sect. 4). The only information they had at this stage was the textual form of the sentence itself, and a morphological analysis of each token (not disambiguated, however).

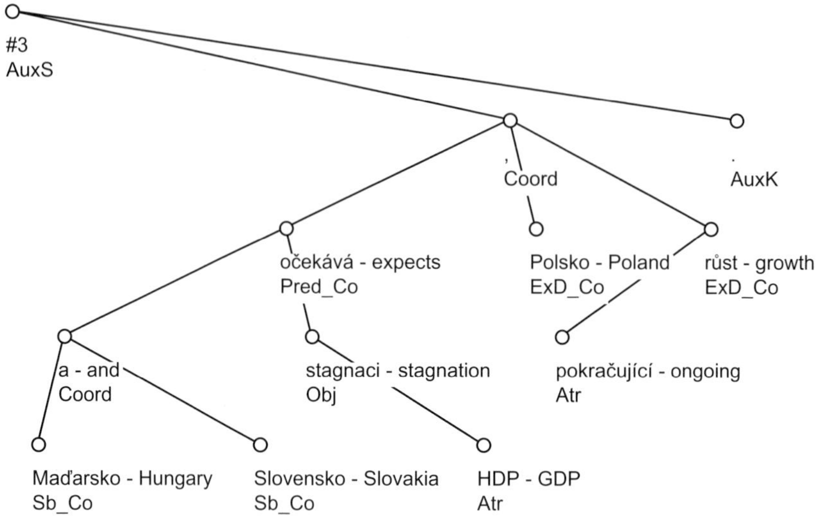

Figure 7.8. Example of ellipsis handling - sentence (5); lit. word translation used

Later, after macro programming capabilities had been added to the annotation software, a set of (manually written) rules was used to pre-assign the analytical functions (STags) to a completed tree. The annotators first had to manually build the tree structure, then - at a press of a button - the rules applied and populated the tree with possible STags achieving about 80% precision[12]. The annotators then reviewed, inserted, selected and/or corrected the resulting STags.

Once enough data had been annotated, even more preprocessing was introduced. Collins' lexicalized stochastic parser (Collins, 1997) was adapted to suit the data structure and format and trained on 19126 analytically annotated Czech sentences, assigning 80% of dependencies correctly. Our adaptation (Hajič et al., 1998; Collins, 1999) consists mainly of determining the phrase structure from the dependency structure[13] and the phrase labels from morphology[14], since Collins' parser works with labeled parse trees.

Using the parsing results in the later stages of the annotation effort, the annotators' task had changed: instead of building the tree structure from scratch, they were instructed to review the structure created by the parser, and correct it if necessary. The rest of the task remained unchanged; the analytical functions[15] were assigned by the manually written rules and checked by the annotators.

Figure 9.4 presents the analytic tree structure for the sentence

(6) Ve svobodných celních zónách dnes pracují po celém světě čtyři miliony lidí.

Today, four million people work off-shore all over the world.

which has been parsed correctly by the parser. At this sentence size, the parser's output is almost error-free. However, complicated, incomplete, coordinated, and/or partially ungrammatical sentences are unfortunately quite common in the treebank and are rarely parsed without an error. We have analyzed parsing results obtained on a randomly chosen set of 50 sentences, and found that 19 sentences were correctly assigned all the dependency links, 7 sentences contained one wrong dependency, and the rest required more than one intervention by the annotator.

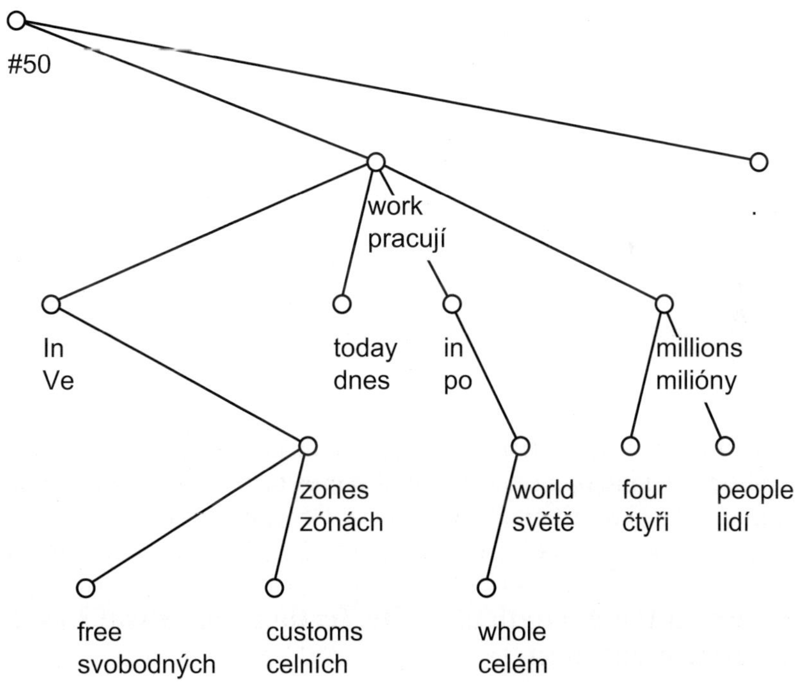

Figure 7.9. Sentence (6) correctly parsed by Collins' statistical parser

It is interesting to note than the Collins' statistical parser makes "human-like" errors[16] in most cases, as exemplified in the sentence (7):

(7) Uvádí se v analýze Komerční banky, kterou jsme dostali minulý týden.
It is presented in the Komerční bank's analysis, which we obtained last week.

The relative clause was (semantically) incorrectly determined to be a modifier of the noun *banka* 'bank' (instead of *analýza* 'analysis') because the morphological tags of both *banka* 'bank' and *analýza* 'analysis' are possible antecedents for the relative pronoun *kterou* 'which' (based on number and gender agreement).

We can also examine the nature of the errors the parser makes outside the project to obtain very important material for the study of syntactic irregularities and idiosyncrasies.

4. Merging the Morphological and the Analytical Syntactic Level

As has already been mentioned, the texts used for PDT come from the Czech National Corpus. They are reasonably but not 100% clean[17] and already have an SGML markup (Figure 9.1). These texts are then morphologically analyzed, and after that, they are annotated simultaneously on both the morphological as well as the analytical levels (see Figure 7.10 for a general scheme)[18]. The separately produced annotations must be then merged into a single resource. Due to the less than perfect state of the input texts, some manual corrections (such as adding or deleting a wrongly introduced sentence boundary) are done to the original markup, making the merging task nontrivial. The merging procedure is a semi-automatic process; any discrepancies must be resolved manually.

5. Tectogrammatical Level

The third level of annotation, the tectogrammatical level, aims to describe the linguistic meaning of a sentence. It also uses the dependency framework; in fact, it is at this level where the Functional Generative Perspective (Sgall et al., 1986) is followed most closely (and for the first time applied to real data).

5.1 From the Analytical to the Tectogrammatical Level of Representation

In comparison to the analytic tree structures (ATS), the tectogrammatical tree structures (TGTS) have the following characteristics:

(a) only autosemantic (lexical) words have a node of their own, while the correlates of function words (auxiliaries, prepositions etc.) are attached as

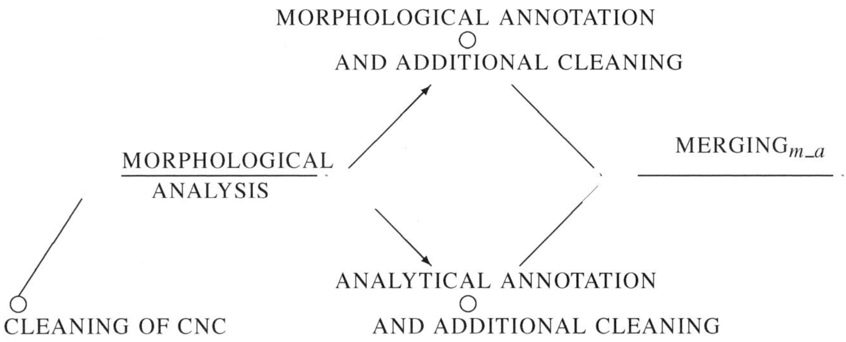

Figure 7.10. The scheme of merging the morphological and the analytical levels

indices to the autosemantic words to which they "belong" (auxiliaries and conjunctions to lexical verbs, prepositions to nouns, etc.);

(b) nodes are added in case of clearly specified deletions on the surface level;

(c) non-projectivity (i.e., crossing of edges with each other or with perpendiculars incident to nodes) is not allowed; the relevant nodes are rearranged so that the condition of projectivity is met in the TGTS; the rearrangement is not arbitrary, though: it follows from the information structure of the sentence (see also (e) below);

(d) analytic functions are substituted by tectogrammatical functions (such as Actor/Bearer, Patient, Addressee, Origin, Effect, different kinds of Circumstantials);

(e) basic features of the information structure of the sentences (Topic-Focus Articulation) are added.

5.2 Tectogrammatical Level of Representation

A detailed, though still tentative description of the attributes and their values assigned to nodes of the TGTS is given in Hajičová, 1998. For the purpose of perspicuity we give here a brief overview of the character of the labels; Table 7.A.2 in Appendix contains a list of all the attributes as prepared for the annotators (at this stage of the project).

Each label consists basically of three sets of attributes: the lexical value of the word (in the present phase, this value consists of the lemma attribute: *tr-lemma*), the so-called (morphosyntactic) grammatemes, reflecting the meaning of morphological categories, and the so-called functors, corresponding to syntactic functions (for the difference between grammatemes and functors, cf. the writings of the Functional Generative Description, esp. Sgall, 1967; Panevová, 1980; Sgall et al., 1986). In addition to these three parts, there is an attribute *tfa* attached to each node, capturing the basic features of the topic-focus articulation of the sentence; the three values of this attribute are T(opic), F(ocus) and C(ontrast).

Among the (morphosyntactic) grammatemes there are attributes for three kinds of modality (sentential, verbal, and that expressed by modal verbs: *sent-mod, verbmod, deontmod*), *tense, aspect, iterativeness, number, gender*, and degrees of comparison (*degcmp*).

About 40 functors (*func*) are distinguished, such as actor/bearer, addressee, patient, origin, effect, cause, regard, concession, aim, manner, extent, substitution, accompaniment, locative, means, temporal, attitude, cause, regard, directional, benefactive, comparison; there are also specific functors for dependents on nouns, as e.g. material, appurtenance, restrictive and descriptive adjunct, the relation of identity (see Table 7.A.2 in Appendix; compare also a similar scenario based on an assignment of 'cases' as presented in (Chen et al., this volume), or the assignment of predicate-argument structure as suggested by (Marcus et al., 1994) and performed by (Palmer et al., 2000). In addition to the above functors, we work with a more subtle differentiation of syntactic relations by means of the so-called syntactic grammatemes (in the present scheme, there are 12 syntactic grammatemes, attribute *gram*). The temporal relation can be supplemented by one of the grammatemes 'before', 'after', and 'on', accompaniment, regard and benefactive are accompanied by a positive or a negative grammateme (with/without, for/against). The possibility to express an uncertainty of the annotator is ensured (either by means of an assignment of a second functor or by adding a special mark denoting that the assignment of the value of the functor is doubted). There are no remaining "double" functors anymore (cf. Sect. 3.1). The node attributes listed in Table 7.A.2 in Appendix are reserved for future annotation efforts, e.g. marking the coreference relation, or some technical purpose (marking of deleted/inserted nodes.)

In order to preserve the form of a tree for the TGTS, we work with a special node of coordination, with values such as conjunction, disjunction, gradation, adversative relation, consequence, reason and apposition.

5.3 Automatic and Manual Processing

The transduction of the analytic trees to the tectogrammatical ones is conceived of in two phases:

(a) an automatic tree 'pruning' and transformation,

(b) a manual procedure (with the help of specifically designed software tools).

In the following sections we focus on the first of the two procedures, namely on the automatic procedure translating analytic tree structures to tectogrammatical tree structures. More detailed rules for building the final TGTS manually can be found in (Hajičová, 2000) and (Hajičová, 1998).

5.4 Automatic Preprocessing

The input to the automatic procedure are the analytic trees. The main task of the procedure is to reduce the number of nodes in the tree by creating complex labels of the nodes that represent more than one word (as a result of the attachment of synsemantic words to the autosemantic ones, see point 5.1 (a)) and to translate the values of synsemantic words into the attributes of autosemantic words. The nodes in the pre-processed tree keep the values of all the analytical attributes and newly created attributes are added for the description of the properties of the TGTS briefly characterized in Section 5.2. The nodes deleted in the automatic procedure are in fact only marked as hidden (and are not considered to be part of the TGTS nor are they displayed on the screen), but they remain in the tree structure and can be examined if needed. Thus no information gets lost for later research and analysis.

5.5 Tools

The same macro programming language on the analytical level has been taken advantage of within the tree structure editor, since it is a powerful tool for handling tree structures. The following operations are available:

(i) get a value of a given attribute of a given node,

(ii) assign an attribute a value,

(iii) find parent of a node,

(iv) find the left or right brother of a node,

(v) cut and paste a subtree.

The macros work either in an interactive mode, so that they can be run in the editor for the displayed tree, or in a batch mode, for pre-processing all the trees in a file.

Automatic Tree Structure Modifications. The following tree modifications are performed fully automatically in a batch mode, before the annotators get the data for manual work.

(i) Merge the verb with its auxiliary nodes (having the category `AuxV` or `AuxT` as their analytical function in ATS) and assign the values of the grammatemes of tense and verb modality to the respective verb on the basis of the lexical values of these auxiliary nodes. The lemmas of the merged nodes are concatenated into the trlema attribute of the verb. The original auxiliary nodes are deleted.

(ii) Merge the modal verb with the autosemantic verb that depends on it in the ATS. This procedure works in three steps: the tree is rearranged so that the modal verb depends on the autosemantic verb, the value for the attribute deontmod of the latter verb is assigned according to the lexical value of the modal verb, and the modal verb node is deleted.

(iii) Merge the nodes of complex prepositions and complex conjunctive expressions into a single node.

(iv) Delete the nodes for prepositions; the lexical values of the prepositions are temporarily 'preserved' as values of the attribute fw (function word) of the respective governing noun and wait for further (manual) treatment. In case of coordination the prepositions are added to all coordinated nodes.

(v) Delete the nodes representing subordinating conjunctions; the lemma of a conjunction is again 'preserved' as a value of the 'fw' attribute of the dependent verb and thus prepared for further (manual) treatment. In case of coordination the conjunction is added to all coordinated nodes.

(vi) Switch the direction of dependency for certain numerals and counted nouns (the numeral governs the noun in some cases on the analytical level, while in the tectogrammatical representation the noun should always be the governing node).

(vii) Change the governor of the predicative complement; the complement in the TGTS depends on the verb (while in the ATS the dependency relation on the verb was only implicit, with the explicit relation to the respective noun or adjective). Assign the number of the original governor to the cornum attribute of the complement (thus marking a trace where the complement was moved from).

(viii) Delete all auxiliary nodes with the analytic function `AuxX`.

(ix) Fill the unresolved attribute values by one of the following special values: `'???'` indicates that the value needs to be processed manually, the value `NIL` is temporarily assigned to the attributes for which this value is expected to apply in most cases (e.g. attribute antec), and the value `NA` is assigned to the nodes where the given attribute is not applicable (e.g. tense for nouns).

Procedures that can be called manually for selected subtrees. In addition to the procedures that are invoked automatically (i.e. in the batch mode before the manual annotation starts), the tree editor offers a possibility for the human annotators to invoke certain procedures in case they need to carry out some rather complex modification of the tree structure. The following tasks can be performed by using a single keystroke:

(i) Merge the current node with its mother into a single complex node.

(ii) Merge the current node as a function word with its mother. This procedure is called for prepositions or conjunctions not annotated in the ATS as such, and therefore not touched automatically.

(iii) Delete (hide) or undelete (restore) a subtree.

(iv) Add a node for an Actor of the given verb. This procedure is called when the subject of the verb is missing in the ATS (due to the pro-drop character of Czech). The new node is added as the daughter of the verb that is immediately "before" it. Mark the node by adding the value ELID in the attribute elided. Similar procedures can be used for other cases of adding nodes.

(v) Add a node for a missing verb.

(vi) Add a node as a daughter of the selected node. This procedure is used for adding the missing complements of the governor.

5.6 Illustration

In order to illustrate the differences between the ATS and the TGTS and the transformation described above, we show here the two tree structures for the Czech sentence

(8) Kdo chce investovat dvě stě tisíc korun do nového automobilu, nelekne se, že benzín byl změnou zákona trochu zdražen.

He who wants to invest two hundred thousand crowns into a new car does not get frightened by the fact that gas was made a little bit more expensive due to a law change.

Figure 7.11 is an ATS of the sentence (8), in which each word (as well as each punctuation mark) has a node of its own; only the lexical tags and the analytic functions are displayed.

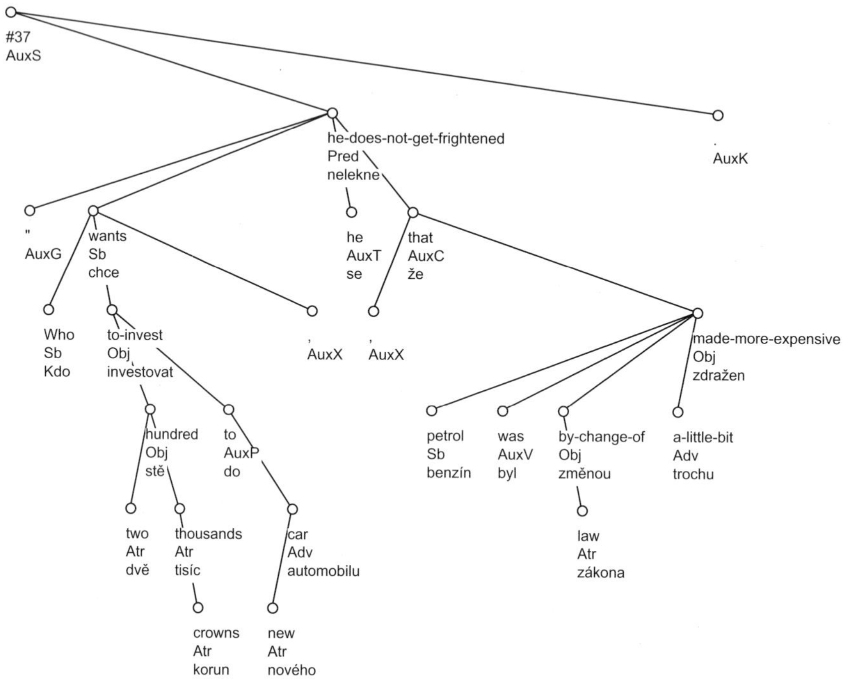

Figure 7.11. A Simplified ATS of sentence (8)

In a (dramatically) simplified TGTS of the same sentence (Figure 7.12) the tags written in lowercase letters denote the lexical values of the nodes; the uppercased tags are values of the dependency relations (attribute *func*) together with some of the grammatemes (*deontmod*, *func* and the *tfa* attribute). The value `DSPP` at the main verb of the sentence denotes that the given sentence is a part of a direct speech. For the purpose of perspicuity of the trees, morphological grammatemes other than those transformed from the function words occurring in the ATS are not displayed in our illustrative example. The tags T and F are the values of the attribute *tfa* capturing the backbone of the topic-focus articulation (information structure) of the sentence.

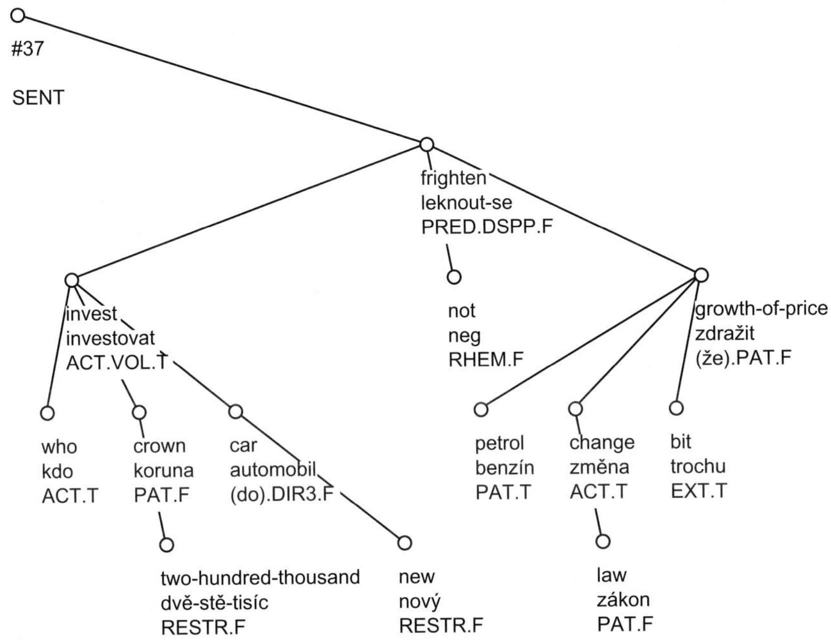

Figure 7.12. A Simplified TGTS of sentence (8)

6. PDT VERSIONS 1.0 AND 2.0

The PDT version 1.0 is the full version of the PDT, containing about three times more tokens and sentences than the PDT version 0.5[19].

The PDT version 1.0 contains complete manual annotation on the morphological and analytical levels. The volume on the morphological level is slightly higher (about 1.8M tokens), because a separate set of training data is needed to train taggers that might be used in the traditional serial[20] approach to statistical parsing. On the analytical level, about 1.3M tokens in about 90k sentences are annotated.

The annotation effort resulting in PDT version 1.0, including a preparation phase and a checking phase, took five years. A total of 22 people have been involved in one phase of the project or another, with about 17 simultaneously at the peak time. The total cost of the project can be determined only roughly, given the various funding sources and schemes; it is estimated at about $600,000 over the five-year period.

The PDT version 2.0 will add the final third level of annotation (tectogrammatical annotation) to PDT version 1.0. It will be available with a reduced amount of data as preliminary "version 1.5" during 2002, and the final data volume will be reached at the end of 2004. The current plan is to annotate the tectogrammatical structure (deleting and adding nodes, changing the "deep" word order etc.) first, and then annotate the rest, adding values to attributes one by one or in small groups. We do not expect all the attributes described in Table 7.A.1 in Appendix to be present[21] in either version, but an example file will be provided with all of them, in as high volume as possible. After 2004, the remaining attributes will continue to be filled in by manual and enhanced semi-automatic procedures.

The total effort resulting eventually in PDT version 2.0 will take roughly the same resources as version 1.0 did (slightly less people but somewhat higher total estimated expenses). Also, errors encountered at the lower two levels of annotation will be continuously corrected during this phase, and re-released in version 2.0.

7. CONCLUSION

Everybody certainly agrees that building a treebank is a difficult task. Our belief is, however, that all the hard work will pay off in that not only we who are building it, but all computational linguists interested in morphology and syntax of natural languages in general, and of Czech and other inflectional and free word order languages in particular, will benefit from its existence. The building of the treebank has been very fruitful even now, two-thirds of the way through the whole treebank annotation.

Acknowledgments

The project was started by the support from the grant GAČR (Formal specification of language structures) No. 405/96/0198, and the annotation process has been made possible by the grant GAČR No. 405/96/K214, by the project of the Ministry of Education of the Czech Republic No. VS96151, and by the NSF grant #IIS-9732388 through Johns Hopkins University, Baltimore. The development of some software tools used in this project has been supported by the grant GAČR No. 405/95/0190 and by an individual grant OSF RSS/HESP 1996/195. This contribution is an updated version of two papers presented at the ATALA treebanks workshop in Paris, June 18-19, 1999. Section 5 was in a preliminary form published in Prague Bulletin of Mathematical Linguistics No. 71, p. 5-12.

We would like to thank all those involved in the project, specifically Petr Sgall, and all the annotators who manually processed the large volume of text. We would also like to thank those who created the indispensable software tools used throughout the project, most notably Michal Křen and Petr Pajas, and Michael Collins for providing us with his parser adapted for Czech. The authors of the present paper gratefully acknowledge the valuable share of the co-authors of one of the original papers in the research that has led to the results reported here.

Notes

1. The decrease in the volume of the annotated material is dictated mostly by the technical considerations related to intended applications and current evaluation metrics.

2. Some annotation and processing tools do use a different format internally.

3. To the extent possible without the feedback of large scale annotation.

4. I.e., regardless of context.

5. A lemma is an identifier of the underlying lexical unit, and it is usually represented by a word (string of characters) corresponding to a usual dictionary headword for readability (possibly complemented by a distinguishing number for homonymous or polysemous words).

6. All other categories, such as person or tense, are irrelevant and denoted by a hyphen (-).

7. The ambiguity level is largely determined by the morphological analyzer. As new words are being added to its dictionary, more ambiguity is introduced.

8. Please note that for technical reasons, analytical functions are part of the dependent node label, even though they refer to the dependency link as a whole.

9. The manual annotation proper was started in November 1996 and finished in December 1999.

10. As opposed to the case when simply there is not enough context to decide, or the annotator's "world knowledge" is insufficient to separate the two incompatible readings; in such a case, someone eventually has to decide just one of them.

11. The order of the simple STags within the "double" Stag is not important.

12. About 10% of nodes have been left without any Stag, and about 5% of nodes got more than one Stag.

13. Which is a non-trivial task since the dependency-to-bracketing mapping is one-to-many.

14. This is also a non-trivial task given the rich inflectional morphology Czech enjoys, leading to data sparseness problems.

15. Analytical functions are not used nor produced by the adapted Collins' parser.

16. Of a semantically slightly challenged human, that is; purely syntactic errors are truly rare.

17. Duplicates are removed, numbers normalized and marked, sentence breaks identified, etc.

18. Obviously, we would have more (pre)processing options if we could do the morphological annotation first in full and the analytical level afterwards; unfortunately, various organizational, human resource, and funding constraints prevented that from happening.

19. Version 0.5 ("halfway through", rather optimistically) released in 1998 (http://ufal.ms.mff.cuni.cz/pdt/pdt.html) contains 26610 sentences and 456705 tokens.

20. If automatic tagging and parsing of a new text is done in this order, it is better to train the parser on an automatically tagged training corpus using an identical tagger (cf. also Figure 7.4). The tagger must obviously be trained on different training data to achieve realistic results.

21. Currently, a high-volume annotation effort has started for the attributes *func* and *tfa*. Also, many morphosyntactic attributes, such as *number*, *tense* and many others can be and will be filled in automatically.

References

Bémová Alla, Buráňová Eva, Hajič Jan, Kárník Jiří, Pajas Petr, Panevová Jarmila, Urešová Zdeňka, Jan Štěpánek. (1997). *Anotace na analytické rovině - příručka pro anotátory* [Annotation on the Analytical Level - Annotator's Guidelines], Technical Report #4 (draft), ÚFAL MFF UK, Prague, Czech Republic (in Czech).

Chen Keh-Jiann et al. (2003). Sinica Treebank, this volume.

Collins, Michael. (1997). Statistical Parser Based on Bigram Lexical Dependencies. In *Proceedings of the 35th Annual Meeting of the ACL/EACL'97*, p. 16-23, Madrid, Spain.

Collins, Michael, Hajič Jan, Brill Eric, Ramshaw Lance, Christopher Tillmann. (1999). A Statistical Parser of Czech. In *Proceedings of 37th ACL'99*, p. 505-512, University of Maryland, College Park, June 22-25.

Czech National Corpus (CNC). `http://ucnk.ff.cuni.cz`.

Hajič, Jan. (1998). Building a Syntactically Annotated Corpus: The Prague Dependency Treebank. In *Issues of Valency and Meaning. Studies in Honor of Jarmila Panevová*, ed. Eva Hajičová, p. 106-132, Karolinum, Charles University Press, Prague, Czech Republic.

Hajič, Jan. (in press). *Disambiguation of Rich Inflection (Computational Morphology of Czech).* Charles University Press - Karolinum.

Hajič, Jan, Brill Eric, Collins Michael, Hladká Barbora, Jones Douglas, Kuo Cynthia, Ramshaw Lance, Schwartz Oren, Tillmann Christopher, Daniel Zeman. (1998). Core Natural Language Processing Technology Applicable to Multiple Languages: *Workshop98 Final Report for the 1998 Language Engineering Workshop for Students and Professionals: Integrating Research and Education*, Center for Language and Speech Processing, Johns Hopkins University, Baltimore, MD, Research Note 37.

Hajič, Jan, Eva Hajičová. (1997). Syntactic Tagging in the Prague Tree Bank. In *Proceedings of the Second European Seminar "Language Applications for a Multilingual Europe"* (ed. by R. Marcinkeviciene and N. Volz), p. 55-68, Kaunas.

Hajič, Jan, Barbora Hladká. (1997). Probabilistic and Rule-Based Tagger of an Inflective Language - a Comparison. In *Proceedings of the 5th Conference on Applied Natural Language Processing*, p. 111-118, Washington, USA.

Hajič, Jan, Barbora Hladká. (1998). Tagging Inflective Languages: Prediction of Morphological Categories for a Rich, Structured Tagset. In *Proceedings of COLING-ACL Conference*, p. 483-490, Montreal, Canada.

Hajičová, Eva. (2000). Dependency-Based Underlying-Structure Tagging of a Very Large Corpus, TAL, 41-1, p. 47-66.

Hajičová, Eva, Panevová Jarmila, Petr Sgall. (1998). Language Resources Need Annotations To Make Them Really Reusable: The Prague Dependency Treebank. In *Proceedings of the First International Conference on Language Resources & Evaluation.* Granada, Spain, p. 713-718.

Křen, Michal. (1996). *GRAPH editor.* MSc. Thesis, Institute of Formal and Applied Linguistics, Charles University, Prague, Czech Republic

Marcus M. P., Kim G., Marcinkiewicz M. A. et al. (1994). The Penn Treebank: Annotating Predicate Argument Structure. In *Proceedings of the ARPA Human Language Technology Workshop.* San Francisco: Morgan Kaufmann.

Marcus M. P., Santorini Beatrice, Marcinkiewicz M. A. (1993). Building a large annotated corpus of English: the Penn Treebank. *Computational Linguistics, 19(2)*, 313-330.

Palmer, M., Dang, H.T., J. Rosenzweig. (2000). Sense Tagging the Penn Treebank. In: *Proceedings of LREC'00*, Athens, Greece.

Panevová, Jarmila. (1980). Formy a funkce ve stavbě české věty [Forms and functions in the structure of the Czech sentence], Prague:Academia.

Prague Dependency Treebank (PDT). `http://ufal.ms.mff.cuni.cz/pdt/pdt.html.`

Sgall, Petr. (1967). *Generativní popis jazyka a česká deklinace.* Academia, Prague, Czech Republic.

Sgall, Petr, Hajičová Eva, Jarmila Panevová. (1986) *The Meaning of the Sentence and Its Semantic and Pragmatic Aspects.* Reidel Publishing Company, Dordrecht, Netherlands, Academia, Prague, Czech Republic.

Šmilauer, Vladimír. (1969). *Novočeská skladba* [Syntax of Contemporary Czech], 3rd ed., SPN, Prague, Czech Republic.

Appendix

Table 7.A.1. Values of the analytical function attribute (STags)

afun	*Description*
`Pred`	Predicate if it depends on the added root node (main predicate)
`Sb`	Subject
`Obj`	Object
`Adv`	Adverbial (without a detailed type distinction)
`Atv`	Complement; technically depends on its non-verbal governor
`AtvV`	Complement; if only one governor is present (the verb)
`Atr`	Attribute
`Pnom`	Nominal predicate's nominal part, depends on the copula "to be"
`AuxV`	Auxiliary Verb "to be" (být)
`Coord`	Coordination node
`Apos`	Apposition node
`AuxT`	Reflexive particle *se*, lexically bound to its verb
`AuxR`	Reflexive particle *se*, which is neither `Obj` nor `AuxT` (passive)
`AuxP`	Preposition, or a part of compound preposition
`AuxC`	Conjunction (subordinate)
`AuxO`	(Superfluously) referring particle or emotional particle
`AuxZ`	Rhematizer or other mode acting to stress another constituent
`AuxX`	Comma (but not the main coordinating comma)
`AuxG`	Other graphical symbols not classified as AuxK
`AuxY`	Other words, such as particles without specific
	(syntactic) function, parts of lexical idioms, etc.
`AuxS`	The (artificially created) root of the tree (#)
`AuxK`	Punctuation at the end of sentence or direct speech or citation clause
`ExD`	Ellipsis handling (Ex-Dependency): function for nodes which "pseudo-depend" on a mode on which they would not if there were no ellipsis
`AtrAtr` `AdvAtr` `ObjAtr`	A node (analytical function: an attribute) which could depend also on its governor's governor (and have the appropriate other function). There must be no semantic or situational difference between the two cases (or more, in case of several attributes depending on each other).

Table 7.A.2. List of the TGTS attributes and their values

<table>
<tr><th>Attribute</th><th>Values (any value is possible if the list is not given)</th></tr>
<tr><td>trlemma</td><td>string</td></tr>
<tr><td>gender</td><td>ANIM|INAN|FEM|NEUT|NA|???</td></tr>
<tr><td>number</td><td>SG|PL|NA|???</td></tr>
<tr><td>degcmp</td><td>POS|COMP|SUP|NA|???</td></tr>
<tr><td>tense</td><td>SIM|ANT|POST|NA|???</td></tr>
<tr><td>aspect</td><td>PROC|CPL|RES|NA|???</td></tr>
<tr><td>iterativeness</td><td>IT1|IT0|NA|???</td></tr>
<tr><td>verbmod</td><td>IND|IMP|CDN|NA|???</td></tr>
<tr><td>deontmod</td><td>DECL|DEB|HRT|VOL|POSS|PERM
|FAC|NA|???</td></tr>
<tr><td>sentmod</td><td>ENUNC|EXCL|DESID|IMPER|INTER|NA|???</td></tr>
<tr><td>tfa</td><td>T|F|C|NA|???</td></tr>
<tr><td>func</td><td>|ACT|PAT|ADDR|EFF|ORIG|ACMP|ADVS|AIM|APP|APPS|ATT
|BEN|CAUS|CNCS|COND|CONJ|COMPL|CPR|CRIT|CSQ|CTERF
|DENOT|DES|DIFF|DIR1|DIR2|DIR3|DISJ|ETHD|EXT
|FRWH|GRAD|ID|INTF|INTT|HER|LOC|MANN|MAT|MEANS|MOD
|NORM|PAR|PREC|REAS|REG|RESL|RESTR|RHEM|RSTR|SUBS
|TFHL|THL|THO|TOWH|TPAR|TSIN|TTILL|TWHEN|VOC|VOCAT
|NA|SENT|???</td></tr>
<tr><td>gram</td><td>0|GNEG|DISTR|APPX|GPART|GMULT|VCT|PNREL|ON|BEF|AFT
|JAFT|INTV</td></tr>
<tr><td>reltype</td><td>CO|PA|NIL|???</td></tr>
<tr><td>fw</td><td>string</td></tr>
<tr><td>phraseme</td><td>string</td></tr>
<tr><td>del</td><td>ELID|ELEX|EXPN|NIL|???</td></tr>
<tr><td>quoted</td><td>QUOT|NIL|???</td></tr>
<tr><td>dsp</td><td>DSP|DSPP|NIL|???</td></tr>
<tr><td>coref</td><td>ID number (pointer)</td></tr>
<tr><td>cornum</td><td>ID number (pointer)</td></tr>
<tr><td>corstn</td><td>PREV|NIL|???</td></tr>
<tr><td>antec</td><td>all 'func' values</td></tr>
</table>

Chapter 8

AN HPSG-ANNOTATED TEST SUITE FOR POLISH

Małgorzata Marciniak, Agnieszka Mykowiecka, Adam Przepiórkowski, Anna Kupść

Institute of Computer Science, Polish Academy of Sciences

{mm, agn, adamp, aniak} @ipipan.waw.pl

Abstract The paper presents both conceptual and technical issues related to the construction of an HPSG test-suite for Polish. The test-suite consists of sentences of written Polish — both grammatical and ungrammatical. Each sentence is annotated with a list of linguistic phenomena it illustrates. Additionally, grammatical sentences are encoded in HPSG-style AVM structures. We describe also a technical organization of the database, as well as possible operations on it.

Keywords: Treebank, Test-suite, HPSG, Polish

1. AIMS AND DESIGN CONSTRAINTS

The aim of this paper is to describe **B**aza **R**ozbiorów **G**ramatycznych (BRG; Database of Grammatical Parses) — a test-suite of written Polish sentences, created as a part of the 3-year European Union CRIT-2 project, which ended in October 2000. The idea is based on the TSNLP project (Lehmann et al., 1996; Oepen et al., 1998), which resulted in the creation of test-suites for various European languages.

The test-suite contains utterances of written Polish. As a test-suite, BRG contains not only grammatical sentences but also ungrammatical utterances, violating various linguistic rules. They are hand-annotated with correctness markers, with names of linguistic phenomena and with HPSG-style Attribute-Value Matrices (AVMs) (see §4 below). Sentences included in BRG are elicited instead of, for example, being extracted from a text corpus. This allows us to represent in the test-suite also less common phenomena which rarely occur in real corpora and to reduce the number of lexical entries used in examples.

A. Abeillé (ed.), Treebanks: Building and Using Parsed Corpora, 129–146.

The immediate aim of the test-suite is to evaluate computational grammars of Polish. The empirical adequacy of parsers can be quantitatively evaluated by examining how they deal with respect to the data in the test-suite. Parsers can also be qualitatively evaluated by comparing the parses they produce to the exhaustive annotations contained in BRG.

In particular, the test-suite has been used so far for evaluation of the dependency grammar described in (Obrębski, 2002). Moreover, it will be used to evaluate and improve probably the largest existing computational grammar of Polish — the DCG-style grammar of (Świdziński, 1992) implemented in the AS parser, see (Bień et al., 2000).

We also intend to employ the test-suite to evaluate an HPSG (Head-driven Phrase Structure Grammar; (Pollard and Sag, 1994)) grammar of a fragment of Polish, which is currently being implemented. For the latter task, choosing an HPSG annotation scheme facilitates comparing parses with test-suite annotations, but there are also more general reasons for this decision. HPSG mechanisms, i.e., feature structures and a multiple inheritance type hierarchy, provide a uniform means for representing various types of linguistic information, including syntactic and morphosyntactic structures. HPSG is also one of the leading formalisms used in computational linguistics, so the annotation format should be readily understandable to computational linguists.

A longer-term application of this AVM-annotated test-suite concerns automatic grammar induction. Although induction of context-free grammars (CFG) on the basis of existing treebanks is a well-researched problem (e.g., Brill, 1993, Charniak, 1996), induction of attribute-value grammars, such as HPSG or Lexical-Functional Grammar (LFG) turns out to be a more difficult task. Recent years have, however, witnessed some progress in this respect; for example, (van Genabith et al., 1999, Frank et al, this volume) describe how to induce (the c-component of) LFG grammars on the basis of a treebank, (Osborne, 2000) describes methods of estimating a stochastic attribute-value grammar (with a CFG backbone) from a treebank, and (Johnson et al., 1999), (Johnson and Riezler, 2000), and (Riezler et al., 2000) describe various approaches to the induction of parameters in stochastic constraint-based grammars. A natural conclusion of these threads of work is the development of an algorithm for inducing attribute-value grammars, stochastic or otherwise, on the basis of AVM-banks like the one described in this paper. Once such an algorithm exists, it is possible that the present AVM-bank can be used for the automatic induction of an HPSG grammar of Polish.

2. CORRECTNESS AND COMPLEXITY MARKERS

Sentences contained in the database can be divided into several groups on the basis of their grammaticality and complexity (see also Bańko, 1990 for a discussion of test data selection). Each group is labeled with the name of a 'correctness marker'. These markers are defined and entered during the initialization of the database.

In this project we assume a two-step classification consisting of 6 markers. In the first step, sentences are divided into correct and incorrect. In the second step, the two groups of correct and incorrect sentences are partitioned into three subgroups each: basic constructions, complex constructions and very complex or peripheral constructions. The number of sentences labeled with each correctness and complexity marker is presented in Table 8.1.

During the evaluation of the formal grammar it is important to know how complicated the particular sentence is, as well as what kind of grammatical infelicity is represented in the analyzed sentence. For example, if a fundamental grammatical phenomenon is violated, e.g., the agreement between the verb and the nominative subject in *Chłopiec śpią* 'A boy sleep$_{pl}$', a sentence should be rejected by any parser of Polish. For this reason, it is important to mark a set of basic correct and incorrect sentences that any parser should get right. The following sentences illustrate our use of the complexity marker:

- correct–basic: *Jan widzi Marysię* 'John sees Mary.'
- correct–complex: *Po co i z kim chcesz tam jechać?* 'What for and with whom do you want to go there?'
- correct–peripheral: *Dzieci zjadły chleb i sera* 'The children ate bread$_{acc}$ and cheese$_{gen}$' (coordinated nouns are in different cases).
- incorrect–basic: *Jan czyta dobry książkę* 'John reads good$_{masc}$ book$_{fem}$.' (incorrect gender agreement)
- incorrect–complex: *Marysia jest najzwinniejsza jak kot* 'Mary is the most agile as a cat.' (incorrect use of comparison)
- incorrect–peripheral: *Matka*$_{fem}$ *i jej ukochane dziewczę*$_{neutr}$ *poszli*$_{masc-hum}$ *razem* 'Mother and her beloved girl went together.' (a very untypical agreement pattern between a coordinated nominative phrase and a verb; the correct sentence is the following: *Matka i jej ukochane dziewczę poszły*$_{non-masc-hum}$ *razem.*)

3. LINGUISTIC PHENOMENA

Each sentence in the test-suite is annotated with a list of linguistic phenomena (so-called indices) illustrated by this sentence. An incorrect sentence is labeled with phenomena which are violated (they are marked with (∗)), as well as with phenomena which can be observed in this sentence.

Table 8.1. Number of sentences

Marker	*Number*	*Marker*	*Number*
correct–basic	116	incorrect–basic	83
correct–complex	68	incorrect–complex	58
correct–peripheral	9	incorrect–peripheral	6
subtotal	193	*subtotal*	147

The classification of syntactic phenomena of Polish is constructed on the basis of similar classifications for German, English and French (Lehmann et al., 1996; Oepen et al., 1998), but it has been elaborated specifically for Polish (Marciniak et al., 2000). Although the database contains only a restricted number of clauses, they reflect a large number of syntactic phenomena characteristic for Polish, as well as their interactions. In the project, we distinguish the following nine main groups of phenomena:

- Types of utterances

  In this class we distinguish three types of core clauses: interrogative, imperative and declarative utterances.

  Interrogative sentences are divided into *yes/no* and *wh*-questions. *Yes/no* questions are further divided into those which are only marked with a question mark and those which begin with special question particles. *Wh*-questions are divided into regular and *in situ* questions, which in turn are subdivided into reprise and non-reprise questions.

  Imperative utterances are divided into those which contain imperative verb forms, those which begin with the special word *niech* 'let', and declarative sentences with the exclamation mark.

  Apart from core clauses, we describe also subordinate clauses, for which we indicate the way they are introduced. We distinguish, thus, indirect questions, relative clauses, and clauses introduced by complementizers (e.g., *że*, *żeby*).

- Verb types and forms

  This class of phenomena describes types of verbs (we distinguish proper verbs and quasi-verbs) and various phenomena related to verbal forms. This class includes also such properties of the verb as diathesis, aspect and tense.

The subclass Verb-Diathesis represents changes in the predicate-argument structure of the verb and includes passive, active and reflexive verb forms.

The Verb-Aspect subclass groups verbs according to their aspect, which, in Polish, is lexically (morphologically) encoded.

The Verb-Tense comprises phenomena related to tense forms. The formation of tenses differs if a perfective or imperfective verb form is used. Perfective verbs lack present tense forms and they can be used only in past and future tenses. Imperfective verbs have all tensed forms but the future tense form requires the auxiliary verb *być* 'to be'.

- Adjectives and Adverbs

  This small class comprises phenomena describing adjectival and adverbial forms according to degree and the way they are graded.

- Complementation

  This class reflects possible complementation frames of verbs, nouns, prepositions, adjectives, adverbs and numerals. We provide a classification of words' valences with respect to the number of arguments (from zero to four) and their type (nominal, prepositional, adverbial, numeral or verbal phrases). With respect to the subject requirement, we distinguish nominative, sentential and non-typical (dummy or non-nominative) subjects.

  For lexemes which have more than one requirement, each of them is represented by a separate phenomenon name.

- Modification

  In the first step, we classify modification types with respect to the type of the modified phrase. Thus, we distinguish: Modification-NP, Modification-VP, Modification-AdjP, Modification-AdvP and Modification-Num. These classes are then further divided with respect to the category of the modifier.

  Agreement principles (if any) which must hold between the modifier and the modified phrase are described in the Agreement class.

- Agreement

  We distinguish two basic types of agreement in Polish: agreement within NP and subject-predicate agreement. Agreement within NP is further divided according to the syntactic category of NP components, i.e., nouns, adjectives, pronouns, numerals, etc. Subject-predicate agreement depends on the form of the subject. If the subject is a coordinated phrase, usually two different verb forms are allowed.

A separate group of phenomena deals with agreement between elements of coordinated verbal, nominal, adjectival and numeral phrases.

- Coordination

  Within this group, we differentiate coordinated constructions according to the type of coordinated phrases (Coordination-NP, Coordination-VP, Coordination-AdjP, Coordination-Num, Coordination-AdvP, Coordination-Prep, Coordination-Pron-wh, Coordination-Clause) and then according to the type of the conjunction used. Conjunctions are divided into five classes: left-right, central, incorporational, serial disjunctive and serial conjunctive.

- Negation

  This class describes constituent (NP, Prep, Num, AdjP, AdvP) and sentential (C) negation.

  In sentential negation, we distinguish idiosyncratic negation of the existential copula *być* 'to be'. We represent also the so-called genitive of negation, i.e., the change to the genitive case of an accusative complement if the verb is negated. In Polish, the presence of an *n*-word, e.g., *nikt* 'nobody', *nigdzie* 'nowhere', usually triggers sentential negation. This phenomenon, known as negative concord, is also reflected in the classification.

- Word Order

  The linear order in Polish is relatively free but it is not unconstrained. The Word Order class captures several general facts of Polish linear order, e.g., relative clauses have to follow the noun phrases they modify, a conjunction has to occur in a place appropriate for its type. We deal also with the placement of the negative marker as well as verbal clitics.

Each of these phenomena groups is subdivided into more specific subgroups of various levels of specificity, thus forming a hierarchy of linguistic phenomena of Polish. The number of phenomena in each group is presented in Table 9.1.

Each of the most specific phenomena is illustrated with both grammatical and, if possible, ungrammatical Polish utterances (we assume that ungrammatical sentences have to be incorrect in all readings). Incorrect sentences can be related in BRG to their correct versions. The ungrammatical sentence *Jan iść* 'John go_{inf}' can be correlated with the correct sentence *Jan idzie* 'John goes', where the appropriate verb form is used or with the imperative sentence *Iść* 'Go', which cannot have a nominative subject. So the above incorrect sentence can be entered into BRG twice with different sets of indices.

Table 8.2. Number of linguistic phenomena

Phenomena group	*Number*
Types of utterances	43
Verb types and forms	34
Adjectives and Adverbs	10
Complementation	77
Modification	20
Agreement	24
Coordination	20
Negation	17
Word Order	19
Total	264

In order to illustrate the application of the hierarchy of phenomena, we present the list of phenomena for the sentence *Piotr daje piękne kwiaty Marysi* 'Peter gives beautiful flowers to Mary'. This sentence is annotated with the following indices:

C-Decl,
Compl-V-Valence-Two,
Compl-V-Comps-NP(acc),
Compl-V-Comps-NP(dat),
Compl-V-Subject-Nom-NP
Agreement-V-NPNom-reg,
Modification-NP-AdjP,
Adj-Cmp-degree-positive,
Agreement-NP-AdjP.

These annotations provide the following information: the sentence is declarative; it contains a verb with two complements which are nominal phrases: one in the accusative and the other in the dative case; the verb has a nominative subject, the finite verb and the subject follow the regular agreement rule; there is also an adjectival modifier in positive degree within a nominal phrase and the appropriate agreement rule between the noun and the adjective holds.

The incorrect sentence *Piotr daje piękny kwiaty Marysi* 'Peter gives beautiful$_{sing}$ flowers$_{pl}$ to Mary' is correlated in BRG with the correct sentence cited above. The incorrect sentence is labeled with the following indices:

$*$ C-Decl,
Compl-V-Valence-Two,

Compl-V-Comps-NP(acc),
Compl-V-Comps-NP(dat),
Compl-V-Subject-Nom-NP
Agreement-V-NPNom-reg,
Modification-NP-AdjP,
Adj-Cmp-degree-positive
∗ Agreement-NP-AdjP.

Two phenomena are violated: C-Decl (the whole sentence is incorrect) and Agreement-NP-AdjP (the agreement between *kwiaty piękny* does not hold).

The names of linguistic phenomena are organized into a hierarchy. The name of each phenomenon contains the name of its supertype, e.g. Agreement-NP subsumes the Agreement-NP-Adj class. Hence, it is possible to refer to an entire group of phenomena just by using a prefix included in all appropriate names.

4. ANNOTATION SCHEMA

Sentences (as well as wordforms, see §5 below) are annotated with AVMs, as used in HPSG.[1] In particular, each AVM is of a certain type, where possible types constitute a multiple inheritance type hierarchy. This type hierarchy specifies, for each type, its immediate subtypes and supertypes, as well as attributes appropriate for this type (and possible values of these attributes). A small part of the type hierarchy is given in Figure 8.1. It says that the type *sign* has two immediate subtypes, *word* and *phrase*, that there are two attributes appropriate for *sign* (and all its subtypes), i.e., PHON (with a value of type *string*) and SYNSEM (with a value of type *synsem*), and there are two additional attributes appropriate for *phrase*, i.e., *sign*-valued HEAD-DTR and *list-of-sign*-valued NON-HEAD-DTRS.

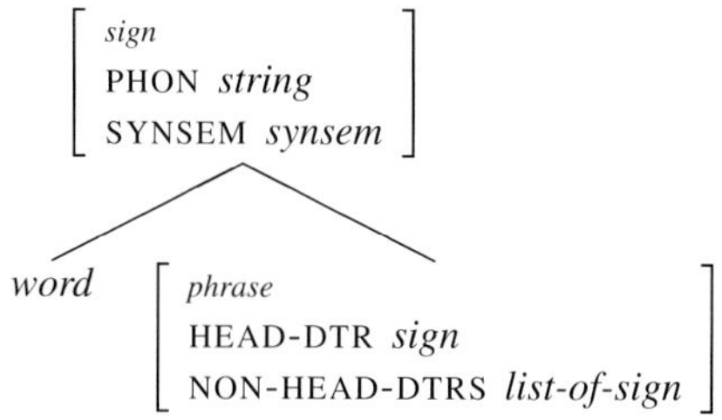

Figure 8.1. A part of the type hierarchy.

Each sentence is annotated with an AVM of type *phrase*, with the orthography of the sentence represented by the value of PHON,[2] the morphosyntactic, etc., information represented by SYNSEM and the constituency structure encoded (for headed phrases) via HEAD-DTR and NON-HEAD-DTRS. Deeper levels of AVM structures are consistent with current HPSG theory, e.g., SYNSEM objects contain LOCAL and NONLOCAL attributes; the objects which are values of the former have internal structure and contain CATEGORY, CONTENT and CONTEXT, etc.

Not all attributes assumed in current HPSG are represented in the current version of the test-suite. For example, pragmatic (CONTEXT) information is ignored, while semantic (CONTENT) information is represented only provisionally. Values of some attributes are adapted to Polish, e.g., the values of the morphosyntactic attribute GENDER (Czuba and Przepiórkowski, 1995) and the hierarchy of subtypes of the *substantive* type (Przepiórkowski, 1999).

Figure 8.2 contains an example of a (partial) annotation for the sentence *Janek widzi Marysię*. This sentence is assumed to have the phrase structure tree as in Figure 8.3.[3]

5. IMPLEMENTATION ISSUES

The HPSG test-suite for Polish is a database[4] of Polish sentences (the HPSG test-suite proper). Correct sentences are augmented with their (one or more) HPSG representations (AVM structures) constructed according to the HPSG signature. An additional, auxiliary, database contains Polish wordforms (a dictionary).

There are two text files restricting the content of the database and its interpretation. One of them contains an HPSG signature, i.e., the multiple inheritance hierarchy of types, and names of attributes appropriate for each type, as well as possible values of these attributes. The other file contains the hierarchy of linguistic phenomena of Polish covered by the test-suite.

The HPSG signature is converted into a database description. This signature should be created prior to the creation of the database but some modifications of it are also possible afterwards.

The dictionary is a separate part of the database. It consists of AVM structures of inflectional forms used in sentences contained in the test-suite. Each inflectional form is linked to the base form of the word. If the base form of some inflectional form is not present in the dictionary, the user is asked to enter it.

The most important groups of operations on the test-suite are entering, searching and viewing data. The main program window after opening a database is shown in Figure 8.4.

5.1 Entering data

Sentences with phenomena annotations can be added interactively and non-interactively from a text file. Figure 8.5 shows the window (*Nowe*

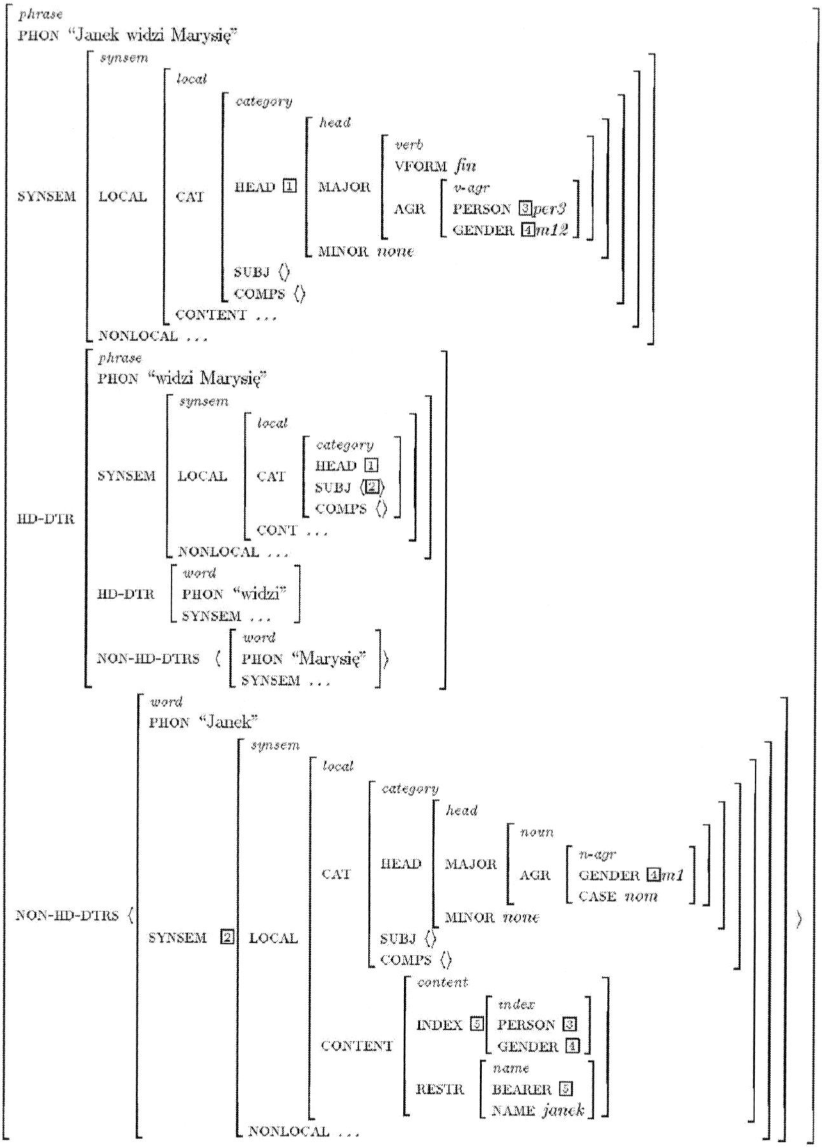

Figure 8.2. AVM structure of *Janek widzi Marysię*

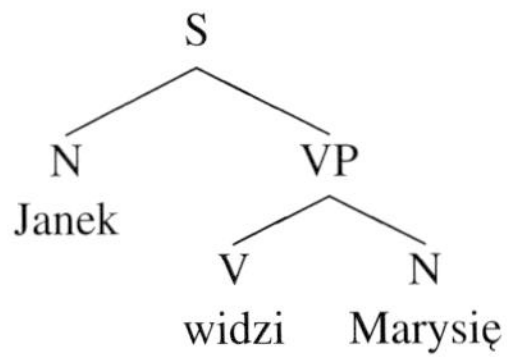

Figure 8.3. The phrase structure tree of *Janek widzi Marysię*

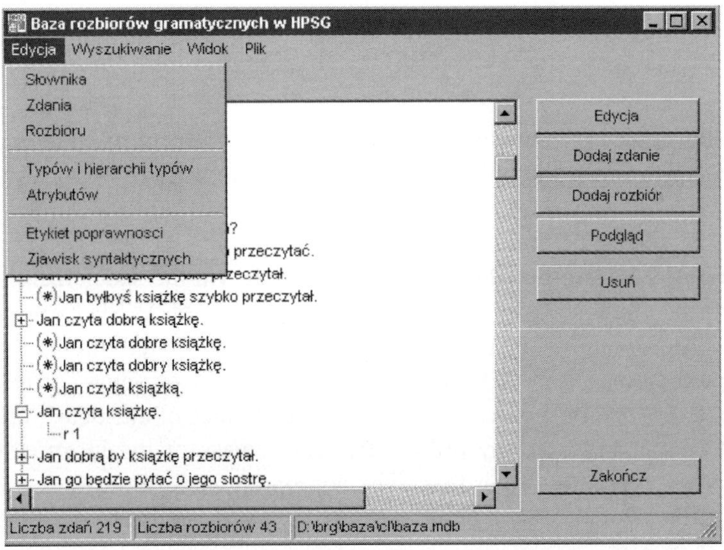

Figure 8.4. The main program window.

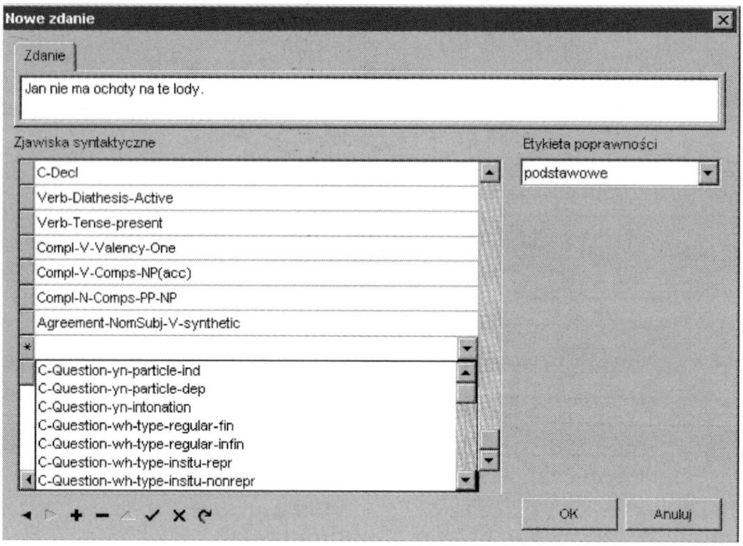

Figure 8.5. Sentence-entering window.

Zdanie) for entering a sentence (*Zdanie*) with the correctness marker (*Etykieta poprawności*) and the indices of linguistic phenomena (*Zjawiska syntaktyczne*). Correctness markers and names of linguistic phenomena can be entered manually or selected from the list.

Parses (AVMs) can be added only interactively via the specialized graphical interface. The interface facilitates the construction of AVMs by generating their parts semi-automatically. At every stage only a limited number of types is presented to the user. After choosing a type, a list of values of attributes appropriate for this type automatically pops up. Values of attributes must then be filled in manually, in any order. The correctness of the information entered this way is partially verified. The appropriateness of attribute values is automatically obtained. The consistent use of AVM labels (so-called tags) is checked.

To facilitate the input of complicated structures, it is possible to view the parse tree in another window during the edition process. Figure 8.6 presents a window in which an AVM representing the parse of the sentence *Jan czyta książkę* is being entered.

Each inflectional form not yet present in the dictionary must be entered into it before the parse is completed. Figure 8.7 presents a window containing the

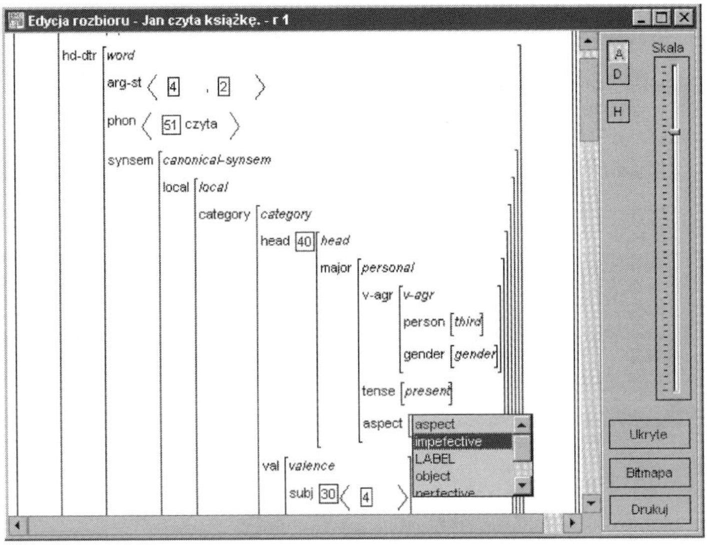

Figure 8.6. AVM entering window.

lexical entry of the word (*Słowo*) *Jana*, which is the genitive form of *Jan* and has only one description (*Opisy*) *jana1*.

5.2 Modifying data

The data in BRG can be modified by means of the same interface which is used for entering data. The following operations are possible:

- removing an index assigned to a sentence,
- adding a new index to a sentence,
- changing an attribute value in the parse of a sentence,
- adding a new parse to a sentence,
- removing a parse assigned to a sentence.

5.3 Search operations

There are several search operations which can be performed over the test-suite. In all cases, the search result is a list of sentences together with their

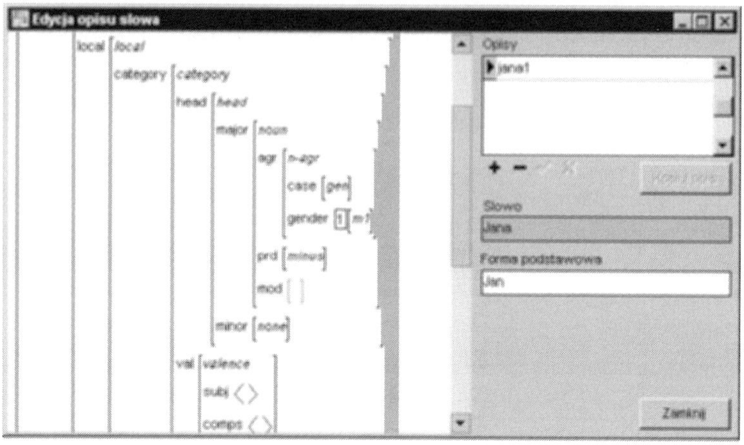

Figure 8.7. The lexicon window.

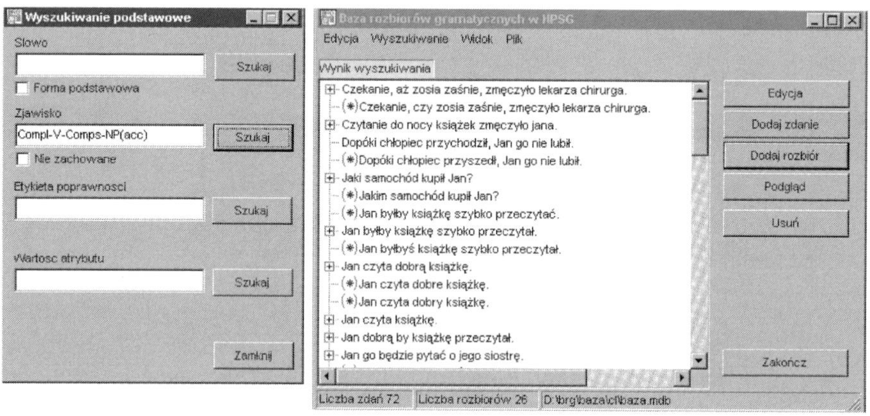

Figure 8.8. Simple query results.

parses. It is possible to output search results (sentences with indices) to a file as an ASCII text.

There are two ways of selecting data from a database. A simple query can consist of one word form, one base form of a word, one phenomenon name, one correctness marker or one name of an HPSG type. In Figure 8.8, we present an appropriate program window together with the main window containing the result of the search.

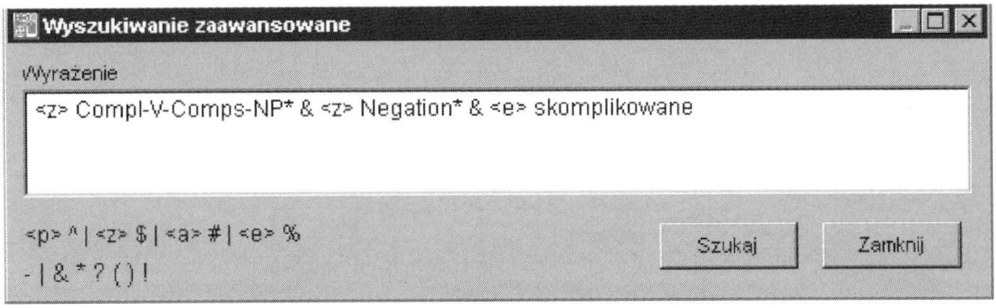

Figure 8.9. Advanced search window.

If this simple search mechanism is not sufficient, one can formulate a regular expression query being a combination of the equality and non-equality relations over word forms, phenomena names, type names and correctness markers. Figure 8.9 presents a sample query of this kind (<z> specifies a phenomenon name, <e> — a correctness marker). The result of this query is the set of sentences that contain verbs having noun phrases as their complements and any kind of negation-related phenomenon and are annotated with the correctness marker *skomplikowane* (i.e., correct-complex).

5.4 Viewing the test-suite

The parses of a sentence can be shown on the screen in two formats (in separate windows): as trees (see Figure 8.10) and as AVM structures (see Figure 8.2).

When viewing an AVM, it is possible to fold and unfold substructures, to hide selected attributes and to show the structure corresponding to a tag.

6. CONCLUSION

Our project is the first attempt at developing tools for evaluating the coverage of formal grammars of Polish. These tools are designed specifically for HPSG grammars, but the test-suite developed here can be equally useful for the evaluation of formal grammars developed within other frameworks, e.g., the DCG-style grammars of (Szpakowicz, 1986) and (Świdziński, 1992) or dependency grammars, see (Obrębski, 2002). Moreover, this project constitutes the first step towards creating a large-scale treebank for Polish, similar to that existing for Czech (Hajič, 1998; Hajič and Hajičová, 1997; http://ucnk.ff.cuni.cz/english/index.html).

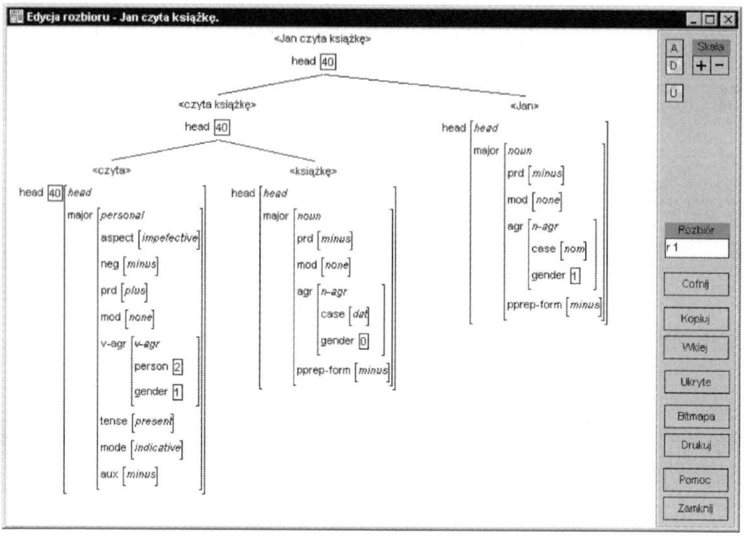

Figure 8.10. The tree structure.

Acknowledgments

Earlier versions of this this paper were presented at ATALA Workshop on Treebanks in Paris, June 1999, at the FDSL3 Conference held in Leipzig, 1999 and at the LREC2000 Conference in Athens. We would like to thank the audiences of these conferences, as well as Anne Abeillé and two anonymous reviewers for comments which led to many improvements in this paper.

Notes

1. The standard reference for AVMs, as used in HPSG, is Carpenter (1992).

2. The name of this attribute is a misnomer in the present context, but it was retained for consistency with standard HPSG (Pollard and Sag, 1994).

3. Such a tree representation is automatically generated from the AVM structure.

4. This database is implemented in Delphi (Borland) in the Microsoft Windows NT environment by Wiesław Bartkowski (Bartkowski, 2000).

References

Bańko, M. (1990). Niektóre problemy oceny adekwatności gramatyk (na przykładzie gramatyki Szpakowicza). *Studia Gramatyczne IX*, Prace Instytutu Języka Polskiego. Zakład narodowy im. Ossolińskich, Wroclaw.

Bartkowski, W. (2000). Komputerowa baza analiz gramatycznych w formalizmie HPSG. Master's thesis, Uniwersytet Warszawski, Wydział Matematyki, Informatyki i Mechaniki, Warszawa.

Bień, J. S., Szafran, K., Woliński, M. (2000). Experimental parsers of Polish. *Proceedings of FDSL 3*, Leipzig.

Brill, E. (1993). Automatic grammar induction and parsing free text: A transformation-based approach. *Proceedings of the 31st Annual Meeting of the Association for Computational Linguistics (ACL'93)*, Columbus, OH.

Charniak, E. (1996). Tree-bank grammars. In *AAAI-96 — Proceedings of the Thirteenth National Conference on Artificial Intelligence*, p. 1031–1036, Cambridge, MA. The MIT Press.

Czuba, K., Przepiórkowski, A. (1995). Agreement and case assignment in Polish: An attempt at a unified account. Technical Report 783, Institute of Computer Science, Polish Academy of Sciences.

Frank, A., Sadler, A., van Genabith, J., Way, A. (2003). From treebank resources to LFG F-Structures. This volume.

Hajič, J. (1998). Building a syntactically annotated corpus: The prague dependency treebank. In Hajičová, E. (ed), *Issues of Valency and Meaning. Studies in honour of Jarmila Panevowá*, p. 106–132. Karolinum, Prague.

Hajič, J. and Hajičová, E. (1997). Syntactic tagging in the Prague tree bank. *Proceedings of the Second European Seminar Language Applications for a Multilingual Europe*, Kaunas.

Johnson, M., Geman, S., Canon, S., Chi, Z., Riezler, S. (1999). Estimators for stochastic "unification-based" grammars. *Proceedings of the 37th Annual Meeting of the Association for Computational Linguistics (ACL'99)*, College Park, MD.

Johnson, M., Riezler, S. (2000). Exploiting auxiliary distributions in stochastic unification-based grammars. *Proceedings of the 1st Meeting of the North American Chapter of the Association for Computational Linguistics (ANLP-NAACL 2000)*, Seattle, WA.

Lehmann, S., Oepen, S., Regnier-Prost, S., Netter, K., Lux, V., Klein, J., Falkedal, K., Fouvry, F., Estival, D., Dauphin, E., Compagnon, H., Baur, J., Balkan, L., Arnold, D. (1996). TSNLP — test suites for natural language processing. *Proceedings of COLING 1996*, Kopenhagen.

Marciniak, M., Mykowiecka, A., Kupść, A., Węgiel, M. (2000). Klasyfikacja zjawisk syntaktycznych na potrzeby testowego zbioru wyrażeń języka polskiego. Technical Report 908, Institute of Computer Science, Polish Academy of Sciences.

Obrębski, T. (2002). *Automatyczna analiza składniowa języka polskiego z wykorzystaniem gramatyki zależnościowej*. PhD dissertation, Uniwersytet Adama Mickiewicza, Poznań.

Oepen, S., Netter, K., Klein, J. (1998). TSNLP — test suites for natural language processing. In Nerbonne, J. (ed), *Linguistic Databases*, CSLI Lecture Notes. CSLI Publications, Stanford.

Osborne, M. (2000). Estimation of stochastic attribute-value grammars using an informative sample. *Proceedings of COLING 2000*, Saarbrücken, Germany.

Pollard, C., Sag, I. A. (1994). *Head-driven Phrase Structure Grammar*. Chicago University Press, Chicago.

Przepiórkowski, A. (1999). *Case Assignment and the Complement-Adjunct Dichotomy: A Non-Configurational Constraint-Based Approach*. PhD thesis, Universität Tübingen, Germany.

Riezler, S., Prescher, D., Kuhn, J., Johnson, M. (2000). Lexicalized stochastic modeling of constraint-based grammars using log-linear measures and EM training. *Proceedings of the 38th Annual Meeting of the Association for Computational Linguistics*, Hong Kong.

Świdziński, M. (1992). *Gramatyka formalna języka polskiego*, volume 349 of *Rozprawy Uniwersytetu Warszawskiego*. Wydawnictwa Uniwersytetu Warszawskiego, Warszawa.

Szpakowicz, S. (1986). *Formalny opis składniowy zdań polskich*. Wydawnictwa Uniwersytetu Warszawskiego, Warszawa.

van Genabith, J., Way, A., Sadler, L. (1999). Semi-automatic generation of f-structures from treebanks. In Butt, M., Holloway King, T. (eds), *Proceedings of the LFG99 Conference*, Stanford, CA. CSLI Publications. http://www-csli.stanford.edu/publications/.

TREEBANKS FOR ROMANCE LANGUAGES

Chapter 9

DEVELOPING A SYNTACTIC ANNOTATION SCHEME AND TOOLS FOR A SPANISH TREEBANK

Antonio Moreno, Susana López, Fernando Sánchez
Universidad Autónoma de Madrid, Spain
{sandoval;susana;fernando}@maria.lllf.uam.es

Ralph Grishman
New York University, USA
grishman@cs.nyu.edu

Abstract This chapter will describe our experience developing specifications and tools for building a Syntactically Annotated Corpus (SAC) for Spanish newspaper texts. The initial corpus consists of 1,500 sentences extracted from *El País Digital* and *Compra Maestra*, with a total of 22,695 words. The paper will address several of the relevant topics for any SAC project, namely methodology, data selection, annotation scheme, tools, and experiments.

Keywords: Spanish, Annotation Scheme, Tools.

1. INTRODUCTION

We are developing the specifications and tools for building a Syntactically Annotated Corpus (SAC) of Spanish newspaper texts. The initial phase of the project started in December 1997 and currently the corpus consists of 1,500 syntactically annotated sentences extracted from newspapers. The team consists of two linguists (Moreno and López), who are responsible for the selection and annotation of the sentences, as well as for the decisions regarding the format and encoding strategies; and of two computational linguists (Sánchez and Grishman) who have developed the tools both for annotation and for validation. The starting point was a series of previous documents on syntactic annotation,

A. Abeillé (ed.), Treebanks: Building and Using Parsed Corpora, 149–163.

concretely (Marcus et al., 1993; Bies et al., 1995; EAGLES, 1996; Skut et al., 1997). First of all, we wanted to develop our own specifications incorporating the relevant features for Spanish into the general mainstream of corpus annotation. We treat this topic in section 3. Secondly, we wanted to base our specifications on the experience gained in annotating real text. The first 500 sentences were taken as a sample of the complexity and variety that we could find in newspaper texts. We took the sentences from two different sources (see next section) and we were seeking variety in the phenomena. We subsequently produced three different versions of the specifications, reflecting our experience with those sentences. The specifications are open to new additions and changes; we could even incorporate significant modifications to the current guidelines. Finally, in this preliminary stage of the corpus, we also wanted to explore and develop some tools for helping human annotators with the coding and debugging tasks. This experience will be explained in 4.

2. DATA SELECTION

The current corpus consists of 1,500 sentences taken from:

- **El País Digital**, the newspaper on-line edition. Sentences 1-50, 101-150 and 201-1500. Each one is an isolated sentence, without context.
- **Organización Consumidores y Usuarios (OCU)** magazines. Sentences 51-100 and 151-200. The sentences are integrated in a context of several paragraphs.

The fifty-fifty division of the first 200 sentences is intended for testing annotation within a pure syntactic environment and annotation with a discourse perspective. The average sentence length is 15.13 words/sentence. The sample has been taken selectively from the different sections of the sources, reflecting different styles. The variety and complexity is more evident in the first 500 sentences than in the last ones, since in the former case the goal was to test and refine the annotation scheme, while in the latter the objective was to enlarge the corpus. For this reason, the last 1,000 sentences tend to be less complex, that is, there is a smaller number of subordinate and embedded clauses, ambiguities, etc., and also those sentences usually are shorter. The selection has been made according to the linguists' criteria, seeking variety, but this decision may have caused the corpus to be biased to certain types of constructions. In order to solve this problem, in future phases the sentences will be chosen randomly[1]. The sources were chosen based on availability and legal permit. The main purpose of these 1,500 sentences was to develop the specifications and the tools; in subsequent phases of the treebank, new sources will be added. In the same fashion, future plans are to include other types of texts.

3. ANNOTATION SCHEME

This section will deal with three points: criteria for the identification of the linguistic units, the actual notation used in the treebank, and some strategies followed in the application of the scheme.

3.1 Identification of the linguistic units

We will discuss briefly some of the most relevant linguistic issues for any SAC in any language. Firstly, we will address how to handle complex constituents. Then, we will show how null elements are analyzed in our scheme.

Asymmetric constituents. Our scheme distinguishes the orthographic string from the lexical unit. Problems arise when the relation between them is asymmetric:

- **Multiwords**: many orthographic words to one lexeme.
- **Amalgams**: one orthographic word to many lexemes.

Multiterm constituents (i.e. several words forming a single unit) are problematic for a linear phrase structure representation. We have developed a specific treatment for the following phenomena in Spanish:

- *Verb periphrases*, which are a combination of TENSED VERB + PARTICLE [2] (a PREP or a C) + UNTENSED VERB (see Figure 9.1).
- *Lexicalization* (see example below for "hombres de paja", *men of straw*).

```
(N ''<hombres de paja>'' ''hombre_de_paja'' MASC PL))
```

- *Locutions* (the Spanish term for multiword) that can be adverbs (eg. "en efecto", *effectively*) prepositions (eg. "antes de", *before*) or conjunctions (eg. "tan pronto como", *as soon as*).
- *Time expressions*, *idioms*, and other typical constructions in newspaper texts (see 3.3).

In an amalgam more than one constituent is represented in a unique orthographic word. There are two typical cases in Spanish: the so-called *portmanteau* words ("del" = de + el, "al" = a + el), and the post-clitics ("dármelo" = dar + me + lo). In both cases, we want to express the fact that several units are involved and that on the surface they appear as one word.

```
(S
  (NP SUBJ MASC SG P3
    (N ''<Manuel>'' ''Manuel'' PROPER))
  (VP TENSED PRES MODAL SG P3
    (V ''<tiene que ir>'' ''ir'' TENSED PRES MODAL SG P3
      (AUX ''tener_que'' TENSED PRES SG P3)
      (V ''ir'' UNTENSED INFINITE))
    (PP A LOCATIVE
      (PREP ''<al>'' ''a'')
      (NP
        (ART ''el'' DEF MASC SG)
        (N ''<dentista>'' ''dentista'' MASC SG)))
    (NP TIME
      (ART ''<el>'' ''el'' DEF MASC SG)
      (N ''<viernes>'' ''viernes'' MASC SG))))
```

Figure 9.1. Periphrasis: "Manuel tiene que ir al dentista." *Manuel has to go to the dentist.*

In all these cases, our strategy is the same: to use an element of the feature description for the surface string, and another for the more abstract interpretation. This is the sample for a portmanteau word:

```
(PP
  (PREP ''<del>'' ''de'')
  (NP
    (ART ''el'' DEF MASC SG)
    (N ''<libro>'' ''libro'' MASC SG)))
```

where `''<del>''` represents the actual string, and `''de''` and `''el''` are the lexemes. Clitics in Spanish can appear before (preclitics) or after (postclitics) the verb. Preclitics are always separate words (*se lo dio*), and postclitics are always joined to the verb (*dárselo*). Annotating preclitics is not problematic, since they are pronouns, and therefore NPs. For postclitics we could split the input string into parts: "dar" "se" "lo". But we want to show that both, verb and clitic(s), constitute a compound. We mark this using the following format (some non-relevant features for the example have been ommited):

```
(VP UNTENSED INFINITE
  (V ''<drselo>'' ''dar''...  #CLITIC ID-1
    (NP
      (P ''se'' PERS P3 SG DISCONTINUOUS REF-1))
    (NP OBJ1
      (P ''lo'' PERS P3 SG DISCONTINUOUS REF-1))))
```

Null elements. We will follow basically the Penn Treebank scheme for empty elements, but we will only annotate **null subjects** (*) and **ellipsed material** (*?*) such as VP, PP, CL, etc. in coordinations, and also required objects. We do not mark traces (*T* in the Penn Treebank). Null subjects can be found in two different constructions:

- As a pro-drop language, Spanish usually omits implicit subjects, which are nevertheless recoverable from the verb agreement (see Figure 9.2).
- In the infinitive, participle and gerund clauses, which normally are referred to as *raising* and *control sentences*.

```
(S
  (NP * SUBJ PL P1)
  (VP TENSED PRES IND PL P1
    (V ''<Regresamos>'' ''regresar'' ...  PAST IND PL P1)
    (ADVP TIME
      (ADV ''<ayer>'' ''ayer''))))
```

Figure 9.2. "Regresamos ayer." *We came back yesterday*

In both cases we will use the same format:

```
(NP * FUNCTION FEATURE1 FEATURE2 ...)
```

For null subjects in sentences with a tensed main verb, the agreement features (i.e. number and person) are encoded. For null subjects in untensed sentences, we need to specify a **reference index (REF)** in the empty NP, and an identity index (ID) in the co-referenced NP (see Figure 9.3). The co-referenced index is not always easy to assign. In those cases where there is not a clear candidate for the ID feature, then it is not specified. We do not annotate NP movement in passives, as the Penn Treebank does, nor do we mark any trace (for motivation, see 3.3).

On the other hand, we use the Penn Treebank tag, ***?***, for marking any ellipsed element other than the empty subjects. However, we do not follow the Penn Treebank strategy of annotating ellipsis in comparatives, but only in coordinations. In addition, we include the REF feature in the null element, and the ID feature in the co-referenced one, as we do with null subjects in untensed sentences.

3.2 Notation

The Penn Treebank style has been chosen as a model for the format. The main reason was that that format can be easily handled by Treebank-trained parsers such as the Apple Pie Parser developed by the Proteus project at NYU[3]. The only significant innovation with respect to the Penn Treebank scheme is the addition of features. Thus, the annotation scheme is a combination of typical category (POS and phrase) tag with feature values that specify the syntactic information for each (terminal and non-terminal) element. We annotate different layers of information: syntactic categories (i.e., parts-of-speech such as NOUNS, ADJECTIVES, ...), syntactic functions (e.g. SUBJ, OBJ1 (direct object), OBJ2 (indirect object)...), morpho-syntactic features (i.e. number, gender, tense, etc.) and some semantic features (HUMAN, TIME, etc.). The actual

```
(S
  (NP SUBJ ID-1 SG P3
    (N ''<Juan>'' ''Juan'' PROPER SG P3))
  (VP TENSED PRES IND SG P3
    (V ''<quiere>'' ''querer'' TENSED PRES IND SG P3)
    (CL INFINITIVE OBJ1
      (NP * SUBJ REF-1)
      (VP UNTENSED INFINITE
        (V ''<leer>'' ''leer'' UNTENSED INFINITE)
        (NP OBJ1
          (ART ''<un>'' ''uno'' INDEF MASC SG)
          (N ''<libro>'' ''libro'' MASC SG)
          (PP DE
            (PREP ''<de>'' ''de'')
            (NP
              (N ''<Chejov>'' ''Chejov'' PROPER))))))))
```

Figure 9.3. "Juan quiere leer un libro de Chejov." *John wants to read a book by Chekhov.*

string is presented between `''<...>''`, and its lexeme is between `''...''`. All this information about each category is expressed in a unified format.[4] Lexical categories are represented as:

```
(CAT ''<string>'' ''lexeme'' FEATURE1 FEATURE2 ...  )
```

For the actual catalogue of allowed categories and features, we have developed an "Inventory of units", ordered by types. This typed inventory is described in (Moreno et al., 1999)[5]. In order to label non-terminal constituents, we follow a simple, vertical, indented format:

```
(CAT1 ...
  (CAT2 ...)
  (  ...   )
  (CATn ...))
```

3.3 Application strategies

In order to apply the annotation scheme, we have made some decisions:

- **Eliminate redundancy as much as possible**: To avoid duplication, the information is usually specified only once in the relevant layer. For instance, internal agreement features between a noun and its modifiers are not percolated up to the NP if they are not be used in further stages (for instance, the NP inside a PP). This strategy leads to **underspecification**, since not all syntactic details are included[6].

- **When there is an uncertainty about how to assign a given feature, prefer not to do it**. This attitude produces ambivalence, but we prefer that, better than making arbitrary decisions.

- **Reflect the surface syntax**: We are very cautious about empty categories, and how to annotate them. Only two kinds of null elements are labeled: null subjects and ellipsed material.

Some examples. An annotation scheme for a particular language must include some syntactic constructions that are unique for that language or for a cognate. However, those constructions are very frequent in corpora, as in the case of Spanish the so-called "se"-constructions. We will describe them here as an example of the annotation scheme coverage.

"Se"-constructions. One of the major problematic issues in Spanish is the one that involves the word "se". The actual categorial status of this word is rather problematic. Here we are going to treat it as a pronoun in the majority of cases, except when it functions as an intransitive marker or as an impersonal marker.

We have established five different annotations involving "se-constructions" depending on the kind of "se" that appears. These five annotations are the following ones:

- **"Se" that corresponds to "le"**: In this case, "se" is a pronoun that substitutes for "le" due to phonetic reasons. Example:"Se lo dio" (*He/she gave it to him/her*).

- **"Se" in a reflexive or reciprocal construction** This "se" is also treated as a pronoun, and as such it changes according to person and number ("me" SG P1, "te" SG P2, "se" SG P3, "nos" PL P1, "os" PL P2, "se" PL P3). When this pronoun appears, the subject and the patient of the action are the same. The difference between reflexive and reciprocal is a semantic one, so we are going to consider both equally. Example: "Yo me lavo" (*I wash myself*).

- **Pronominal or intrinsic "se"** This type of "se" appears in constructions where "se" is attached to the verb, that is, "se" is part of the verb; both appear together in the lexicon, for example "dormirse", "ponerse", etc. This type of "se" is going to be annotated as a compound word; it can precede or follow the verb, but we will treat it as a part of the verb either way. When the "se" precedes the verb, we will treat it as a pronoun with its own features plus the discontinuous and reference marks, to maintain its autonomy as a pronoun that forms part of the verb. If it follows the verb we will leave it that way, adding the feature #CLITIC.

```
(CL INFINITIVE
  (NP * SUBJ REF-1)
  (VP UNTENSED INFINITE
    (V ''<hacerse>'' ''hacerse'' UNTENSED #CLITIC)
    (PP CON OBL
      (PREP ''<con>'' ''con'')
      (NP
        (ART ''<el>'' ''el'' DEF MASC SG)
        (N ''<control>'' ''control'' MASC SG)))))
```

Figure 9.4. Pronominal "se": "... hacerse con el control..." *...to get control...*

```
(S
  (NP SUBJ MASC SG P3
    (ART ''<El>'' ''el'' DEF MASC SG)
    (N ''<libro>'' ''libro'' MASC SG))
  (VP TENSED PAST IND INTRANSITIVE SG P3
    (SE-MARK ''<se>'' ''se'' INTRANSITIVE)
    (V ''<rompi>'' ''romper'' TENSED PAST IND SG P3)))
```

Figure 9.5. Intransitive marker: "El libro se rompió"

```
(S IMPERSONAL
  (VP TENSED PRES IND SG P3
    (SE-MARK ''<se>'' ''se'' IMPERSONAL))
    (V ''<vende>'' ''vender'' TENSED PRES IND SG P3)
    (NP OBJ1
      (N ''<piso>'' ''piso'' MASC SG))))
```

Figure 9.6. Impersonal "se": "Se vende piso"

Example: "Tratan de hacerse con el control de la calle" (*They try to get control of the streets*). See Figure 9.4.

- **"Se" as an "intransitive-marker"** Here, what we have are three different constructions (that have been called "passive se", "inaccusative se" and "middle se") which have in common the loss of an argument. They are distinguishable by semantic means, but, as we are only concerned with syntactic criteria, they are to be annotated all the same. In this annotation, "se" is not treated as a pronoun but as a mark used to make intransitive constructions. Example: "El libro se rompió" (Figure 9.5).

- **Impersonal "se"** These constructions have the characteristic that there is no syntactic subject. "Se" is a pronoun that marks the impersonality. Example: "Se vende piso", *Apartment for sale*, literally "someone sells an apartment". (See Figure 9.6). As in the previous case, we use the category label SE-MARK, but with the feature IMPERSONAL instead of INTRANSITIVE.

Other relevant linguistic topics in corpora. Another frequent phenomena that usually appear in corpora of many languages are idiomatic expressions, dates and hours, math operators, scores and measures, foreign words, etc. In contrast with their apparent lack of interest for theoretical linguistics, they are important in corpus annotation. In general, all these structures are handled as multiwords (see 3.1) since they are considered to be a "block".

4. TOOLS

For the construction of the tree bank, we make use of a combination of tools and resources either developed by the group or obtained from the public domain. These tools and resources can be divided into:

1 Annotation tools:

- **A morphosyntactic annotation system**. This system uses MT-SEG, MULTEXT segmenter for texts[7]. This segmenter has been enhanced in a number of ways, including the addition of new resources, the identification of new text elements and better heuristics for sentence boundary identification. As a lexical resource, we use a 50,000 lemma lexicon accessed by a generating inflectional morphological component. Lexical analysis is reduced then to lexical look-up in the full form lexicon produced by the generator. This look-up strategy is complemented by a set of modules that handle complex phenomena (post-clitic pronouns, appreciative morphology, derivation...). Disambiguation is performed by means of a reductionist grammar. We are currently reusing the grammar developed within the *Constraint Grammar* formalism (Karlsson, 1995) as part of Ph.D. work described in (Fernando, 1997). This grammar (actually, the knowledge encoded in it) has been rewritten so as to be interpreted by a Perl program sequentially applying constraints found in the grammar. Constraints are distributed in five different grammars depending on reliability and complexity (locality v. long distance, mainly) of the rules. The approach to disambiguation favours recall rather than precision, so some disambiguation work is still left to the human posteditor, but the system rarely promotes an incorrect analysis.
- **A chunker** recognizing major phrases within the sentence. The grammar used by the chunker includes NPs, ADJPs, VPs, ADVPs, and PPs. These phrases can be recursively identified, so nesting of phrases is allowed up to a given maximum level. The chunker is applied after postediting the output from the annotation system.

Table 9.1. Error in feature assignment

	All categories	*ADJP*	*ADVP*	*NP*	*PP*	*VP*
Total number of cases	6364	592	262	2933	1503	1074
Total number of errors	672	51	70	457	35	59
Percentage of errors	10.5 %	8.6 %	26.7 %	15.6 %	2.3 %	5.4 %

Table 9.2. Types of errors

Types of errors	*All categories*	*ADJP*	*ADVP*	*NP*	*PP*	*VP*
Total	672	51	70	457	35	59
Missing features	422	22	29	333	25	13
Incorrect features	226	29	40	105	10	42
Unnecessary features	24	0	1	19	0	4

2 Debugging tools:

- **A graphical tree-drawer**. This tool, a public domain program called CLIG (Computational Linguistics Interactive Grapher[8]) allows the definition of clickable tree nodes which favors the drawing of nodes with just basic information so as to allow for rapid inspection of constituent structure, and then, by clicking on the relevant node(s) feature values can be checked. A program is used to automatically produce the forest of CLIG objects from treebank notation.
- **A feature checker** that controls the assignment of proper features for each category, described in the following section.
- **A phrase structure rule generator**, which is used to detect possible incorrect annotations. This is also described in the following section.

5. DEBUGGING AND ERROR STATISTICS

Using a small Perl program, we have managed to check and revise the features of the first 500 annotated sentences for an evaluation of the feature assignment. The data we have obtained are shown in Table 9.1[9]. We have also differentiated the types of errors made within each phrase (see Table 9.2). We can infer from this data that the most common errors are lack of features and replacement of features (that is, wrong features instead of correct features). This may be due to the various changes we have made during the elaboration of specifications for the project. What we learned from this is which phrases are the most prone to error with respect to our feature annotation scheme. Those are NPs and ADVPs, and the rest have low rates of error. Also, we have learned that there are some contradictory features such as PERFECT and IMPERFECT in the same verb head, which result from adding the features of an auxiliary verb and the features of the main verb, and percolating them up to the VP level. This evaluation allowed us to improve our performance in the next 500 sentences, since we concentrated on our previous errors. We have not conducted a proper evaluation for those new sentences yet, but our estimation is that the current percentage of error in assigning features is below 5%. This figure will be significantly reduced when we make use of a *feature checker*, based in the feature specifications. On the other hand, we use a phrase structure (PS) rule generator from the annotated sentences in order to detect "strange" combinations of constituents (for example, a clause made up of "ADVP V PP" instead of "C VP ADVP V PP"). This tool provides a different point of view to the coder, since it presents the results of the annotation. The PS rules generator has been useful for detecting some inconsistencies. Finally, we also use a graphical tree viewer called CLIG, which allows inspection of the annotated sentence. The tree viewer not only shows the branches and the categories, but also the features for each node. Like the rule generator, the tree viewer provides another way of approaching the corpus; both useful for the human annotator and the user.

We are currently involved in a complete evaluation of the 1,500 sentences. Some of the results suggest that changes in the guidelines will be needed (see next section).

6. CURRENT STATE AND FUTURE DEVELOPMENT

In this chapter, we have presented some of the basic problems that researchers encounter when developing an annotation scheme for a Spanish treebank. We have offered some possible solutions to these problems, but we have also detected some limitations in our approach. In particular, the scheme proposed is probably excessively fine-grained from a linguistic point of view. Producing a reasonable number of trees (over 10,000) will be an expensive task in terms of time and research staff. The advantages of our linguistically oriented approach (mainly the possibility of inferring a feature-based grammar and extracting syntactic structures by descriptive or theoretical linguistic principles) can only be envisaged as long-term goals. However, with the 1,500 annotated sentences we managed to run an experiment: to use the treebank to train a statistical parser, the Apple Pie Parser (Sekine, 1998). The experiment is reported in (Moreno et al., 2000). A stochastic context-free grammar was derived from 1,460 sentences, setting aside forty sentences for testing. The evaluation results obtained were 73.6% in recall, and 74.1% in precision. The most relevant conclusion we extracted was that restricting ourselves to a simple context-free skeleton instead of using the richer feature structures provided by the tree bank did not seem to be a major limitation on the performance of the trained parser. This fact, along with the difficulties mentioned above, suggests that it could be interesting to try a new approach. In particular, we are planning to develop two layers of annotation: one with only categorial and lexical information[10], and the other with the rich feature annotation. The idea is to test which type of information is more relevant for rule induction in Spanish. At the same time, concentrating on categorial/lexical information can speed up the process of tree annotation. In its current state, the treebank is not publicly available, although the annotation guidelines can be obtained from the project web page.

Recently López and Sánchez have left the project. Manuel Alcántara has conducted a complete revision of 1,500 sentences, and added a hundred sentences more to the treebank. Fernando Ares has translated the 1,600 parsed sentences into an XML format.

We are starting a new phase with new tools: for morphosyntactic annotation we are using GRAMPAL (Moreno and Goñi 1995) reimplemented in a Perl program by J.M. Guirao. Since the format has been moved to XML, the feature and POS validation is now performed by a XML parser. Moreno and Ares have defined a DTD for such a task, introducing some modifications in the annotation scheme.

Plans are to put the treebank in the public domain when the corpus reaches an acceptable size.

Acknowledgments

The research of Susana López has been supported by New York University. We want to thank El País Digital and Compra Maestra for letting us use their texts. We want to thank Lingsoft and especially Prof. Fred Karlsson for their permission to use the CG package during previous phases of this and other projects within Laboratorio de Lingüística Informática at UAM. Finally, we want to thank Karsten Konrad for putting his CLIG program in the public domain.

Notes

1. Another question related to this is whether 1,500 sentences are sufficient to consolidate an annotation scheme.
2. The particle does not occur in every case, like in *estar* + GERUND.

3. Future plans are to migrate to a standard like SGML/XML, as has been recently proposed for syntactically annotated corpora (Mengel et Lezius, 2000; Ide et al., 2000)

4. For free-order languages like Spanish, it could be appropiate to use two separate syntactic representations, one for the categorial and phrasal information, and the other for functional information. We have not chosen that representation because of simplicity and economy in the annotation process.

5. This is an 88-page report, for internal use. The specifications are available at the project WWW page: `http://www.lllf.uam.es/~sandoval/UAMTreebank.html`

6. However, after the experience with the 1,500 sentences, we are considering exploring the opposite approach: to promote redundancy, that is, to percolate features. The idea is to test which approach renders better results in training a parser.

7. This and other products from the MULTEXT project may be found in `http://www.lpl.univ-aix.fr/projects/multext/`.

8. CLIG is a grapher for visualizing linguistic data structures developed by Karsten Konrad in the Department of Computational Linguistics in Saarbrücken, Germany. CLIG is free for scientific purposes. The home page is `http://www.ags.uni-sb.de/~konrad/clig.html`.

9. The categories that have been considered are ADJPs, NPs, ADVPs, VPs, and, PPs. For this evaluation, we have not revised the head categories (e.g. N, Prep, V, etc.), nor major categories (e.g. S, CL).

10. Maybe incorporating a very selective feature information, such as agreement features

References

Bies, A., Ferguson, M., Katz, K., Macintyre, R. (1995). *Bracketing Guidelines for Treebank II Style Penn Treebank Project.*

Brants, T., Skut, S., Uszkoreit, H. (2003). "Syntactic annotation of a German newspaper corpus", in this volume.

EAGLES (1996): *Preliminary Recommendations for the Syntactic Annotation of Corpora.*

Ide, N., Bonhomme, P., Romary, L. (2000) "XCES: An XML-based Encoding Standard for Linguistic Corpora", *Proceedings of the Second International Conference on Language Resources and Evaluation (LREC)*, Athens, p. 831-835.

Karlsson, F. and Voutilainen, A. and Heikkilä, J. Anttila, A. (1995). *Constraint Grammar: a Language-Independent System for Parsing Unrestricted Text.* Berlin, Mouton de Gruyter.

Marcus, M, Santorini, B, Marcinkiewicz, M. A. (1993). Building a Large Annotated Corpus of English: The Penn Treebank, *Computational Linguistics*, 19, 2, p. 313-330.

Mengel, A., Lezius, W. (2000). "An XML-based representation format for syntactically annotated corpora", in *Proceedings of the Second International Conference on Language Resources and Evaluation (LREC)*, Athens, p. 121-126.

Moreno, A., López, S., Sánchez, F. (1999). *Spanish Tree Bank: Specifications. Version 4. 30 April 1999.* Internal document, Laboratorio de Lingüística Informática, UAM.

Moreno, A., Grishman, R., Lpez, S., Sánchez, F., Sekine, S. (2000). A Treebank of Spanish and its Application to Parsing, *Proceedings of the Second*

International Conference on Language Resources and Evaluation (LREC), Athens, p. 107-111.

Moreno, A. Goñi, J.M. (1995). GRAMPAL: A morphological model and processor for Spanish implements in Prolog, *Proceedings of the Joint Conference on Declarative Programming* (GULP-PRODE'95), Marina de Vietri, Italy.

Sánchez, F. (1997). *Análisis morfosintáctico y desambiguación en castellano*. Ph.D. Dissertation, Department of Linguistics, Universidad Autnoma de Madrid.

Sánchez, F. Ramírez, Declerck, Th. (1999). Integrated set of tools for robust text processing. *Proceedings of the VEXTAL Conference*, Venice.

Sekine, S. (1998). *Corpus-based Parsing and Sublanguage Studies*. Ph.D. Dissertation, Department of Computer Science, New York University.

Skut, W., Krenn, B., Brants, T., Uszkoreit, H. (1997). An Annotation Scheme for Free Word Order Languages, *Proceedings of the Fifth Conference on Applied Natural Language Processing (ANLP)*, Washington, D.C.

Appendix: Sample of trees

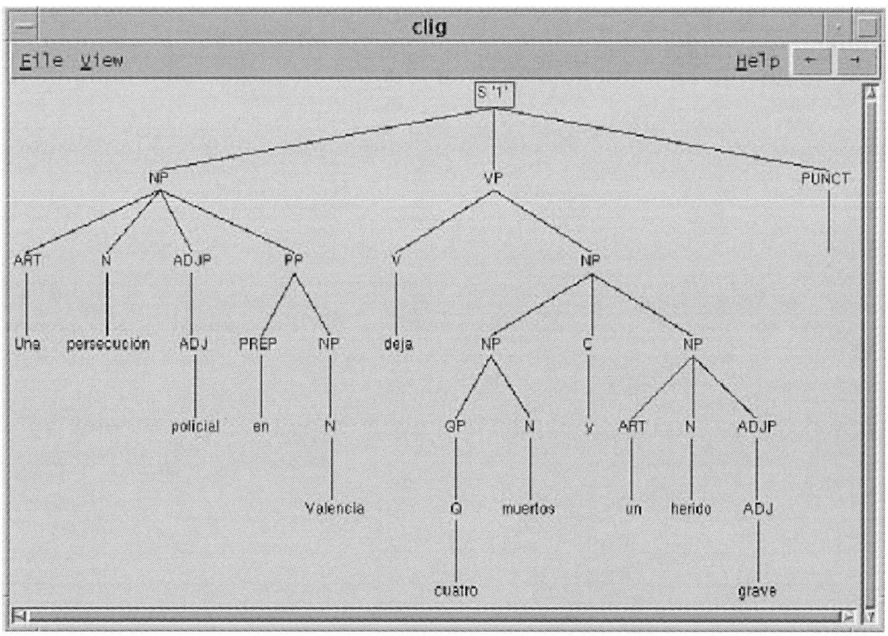

Chapter 10

BUILDING A TREEBANK FOR FRENCH

Anne Abeillé
UFRL, Université Paris VII, FRANCE
abeille@linguist.jussieu.fr

Lionel Clément
*Attol, Inria, Roquencourt, FRANCE**
lionel.clement@inria.fr

François Toussenel
UFRL, Université Paris VII, FRANCE
ftoussen@linguist.jussieu.fr

Abstract We present a treebank project for French. We have annotated a newspaper corpus of 1 Million words with part of speech, inflection, compounds, lemmas and constituency. We describe the tagging and parsing phases of the project, and for each, the automatic tools, the guidelines and the validation process. We then present some uses of the corpus as well as some directions for future work.

Keywords: Annotation Guidelines, Shallow Parser, French, Tagger, Tagset, Treebank

Introduction

Very few gold standard annotated corpora are currently available for French. We present a treebank project for French which started in 1997. We have annotated a newspaper corpus of 1 Million words (Abeillé & Clément 1999, Abeillé et al. 2000) with parts of speech, inflections, compounds, lemmas and constituency. We follow the EAGLES recommendations (von Rekowski 1996,

*Lionel Clément was at University Paris 7 while working on this project.

A. Abeillé (ed.), Treebanks: Building and Using Parsed Corpora, 165–187.

Ide & al. 1996, Sanfilippo & al. 1996, Kahrel & al. 1997) and develop specific annotation guidelines for French. Similarly to the Penn TreeBank (Marcus et al. 1993, Taylor et al. this volume), we distinguish a tagging and a parsing phase, and arrive at a process of automatic annotation followed by systematic manual validation and correction. Similarly to the Susanne Corpus (Sampson 1995, this volume) or the Prague treebank (Böhmova et al this volume), we rely on several types of morphosyntactic and syntactic annotations for which we define extensive guidelines. Our goal is to provide a theory neutral, surface oriented, error-free treebank for French. Due to the lack of robust reusable annotation tools at the beginning of the project, we chose to develop our own, which are also presented here.

1. THE TAGGING PHASE

As reported in (Abeillé & Clément 1999), we present the general methodology, the automatic tagging phase, the human validation phase and the final state of the tagged corpus.

1.1 Methodology

Choosing the corpus. The corpus consists of extracts from the daily newspaper *Le Monde*, ranging from 1989 to 1993, and covering a variety of authors and domains (economy, literature, politics, etc.), representative of contemporary written French. It comprises roughly 1 million tokens.

Choosing the tagset. We define a complete morphosyntactic tag as follows:

1 Part of Speech (POS), for example Determiner,

2 Subcategorization, for example possessive or cardinal,

3 Inflection, for example masculine singular,

4 Lemma (canonical form)

5 Parts (with similar morphosyntactic tags) for compounds

For parts of speech, we made traditional choices, except for weak pronouns that were given a POS of their own (Clitic) according to the generative tradition (Kayne 1975), and foreign words (in quotations) which receive a special POS (ET). Punctuations are divided between strong (clause markers) and weak (all the others). Most typographical signs (including %, numbers and abbreviations) are assigned a traditional POS (usually Common Noun).

We chose to annotate more than just parts of speech, for the following reasons. Some parts of speech are too inclusive (e.g. conjunctions or nouns) and further distinctions (called here "subcategories") are needed (e.g. proper and common for nouns, subordinating or coordinating for conjunctions), if one wants to use linguistically motivated distributional classes. Some words are unambiguous for parts of speech but ambiguous for such subcategories, for example *neuf* which can either be a numeral adjective (= nine) or a predicative adjective (= new), *lui* which can either be a strong personal pronoun (= him) or a weak clitic pronoun (= to him or to her), plus can either be a negative adverb (= not any more) or a simple adverb (= more).

Inflectional morphology also has to be annotated since morphological endings are important for grouping constituents (based on agreement marks) and also because many forms in French are ambiguous with respect to mood, person, number or gender. For example, the determiner ces (these) can be either masculine or feminine, the verb form *mange* (eat) can be either indicative or subjunctive, and either first or third person, or even 2nd person imperative.

We annotate lemmas because some ambiguities remain even after tagging: *suis* is an indicative verb form 1st person singular which can correspond to the lemma *être* (be) or to the lemma *suivre* (follow), and also because it is useful for corpus queries, as well as subsequent valence annotation or word sense disambiguation Compounds also have to be annotated since they may comprise words which do not exist otherwise (e.g. *insu* in the compound preposition *à l'insu de* = unbeknownst to) or exhibit sequences of tags otherwise non-grammatical (e.g. *à la va vite* = Prep + Det + finite verb + adverb, meaning ' in a hurry'), or sequences with different grammatical properties than expected from those of the parts: *peut-être* is a compound adverb made of two verb forms, a *peau rouge* (American Indian) can be masculine (although *peau* (skin) is feminine in French) and a *cordon bleu* (master chef) can be feminine (although *cordon* (ribbon) is masculine in French). Some sequences are ambiguous between compound and literal interpretations, although in corpora the compound interpretation often prevails:

(10.1) Paul veut bien que Marie vienne (Paul indeed wants Mary to come).

(10.2) Paul pleure bien que Marie vienne (Paul is crying although Marie is coming)

(10.3) Paul en fait a raison (Paul in fact is right)

(10.4) Paul en fait trop (Paul is acting too much)

In (10.1), there is no compound: *bien* is an adverb (well) and *que* a subordinating conjunction (that); whereas in (10.2) the same sequence *bien que* is a compound subordinating conjunction (although). In (10.3), the sequence *en fait* is a compound adverb (in fact), whereas in (10.4) the same sequence must be decomposed into *en* as a clitic and *fait* (does) as a finite verb.

Compounds are annotated with the same tagset as non-compounds, but tags are added for each of their parts. Since the borderline between compounds and free sequences is subject to much linguistic debate, we chose to also annotate the parts of the compounds. Tagging the parts as well is useful for specific studies on compounds, but also if a user wants to view our corpus ignoring some or all the compounds.

Our complete tagset comprises 218 tags, which are valid combinations of the labels presented in Table 10.1.

Table 10.1. Tagset of the tagged corpus

POS	Subcategory	Morphology	Description
A	cardinal, ordinal, poss, qualif., indef, inter	f,m + s,p + 1,2,3	Adjectives
Adv	-, inter, exclam, negative		Adverbs
CL	subj, refl, obj, -	f,m + s,p + 1,2,3	Clitic pronouns
C	subord, coord	-	Conjunctions
D	card, dem, def, indef, exclam, negative, poss, inter, partitive	f,m + s,p + 1,2,3	Determiners
ET	-	-	Foreign words
I	-		interjections
N	common, proper	f,m + s,p	Nouns
P	-	-	Prepositions
PRO	inter, pers, card, neg, poss, rel, indef	f,m + s,p + 1,2,3	Other Pronouns
PONCT	strong, weak	-	Punctuation
PREF	-	-	Prefixes
V	-	f,m + s,p + 1,2,3 + W, G, K, P, I, J, F, T, C, S, Y	Verbs

The tagging pipeline. The overall organization the tagging phase (cf. Figure 10.1) is more complex than just automatic tagging followed by human validation, because of the rich tagset we are using. For practical reasons, segmentation (for compounds) was done before tagging and lemmatization after tagging. For each phase, we try to minimize the number of tags involved, so in practice we define three different tagsets: a reduced one for the tagger (in order to minimize its errors), an enriched one for the annotators (so that all possible ambiguities are resolved but annotators don't have to make distinctions that are easy to perform automatically), and the full tagset for final formatting of the treebank. Mapping tools between these tagsets have thus been developed.

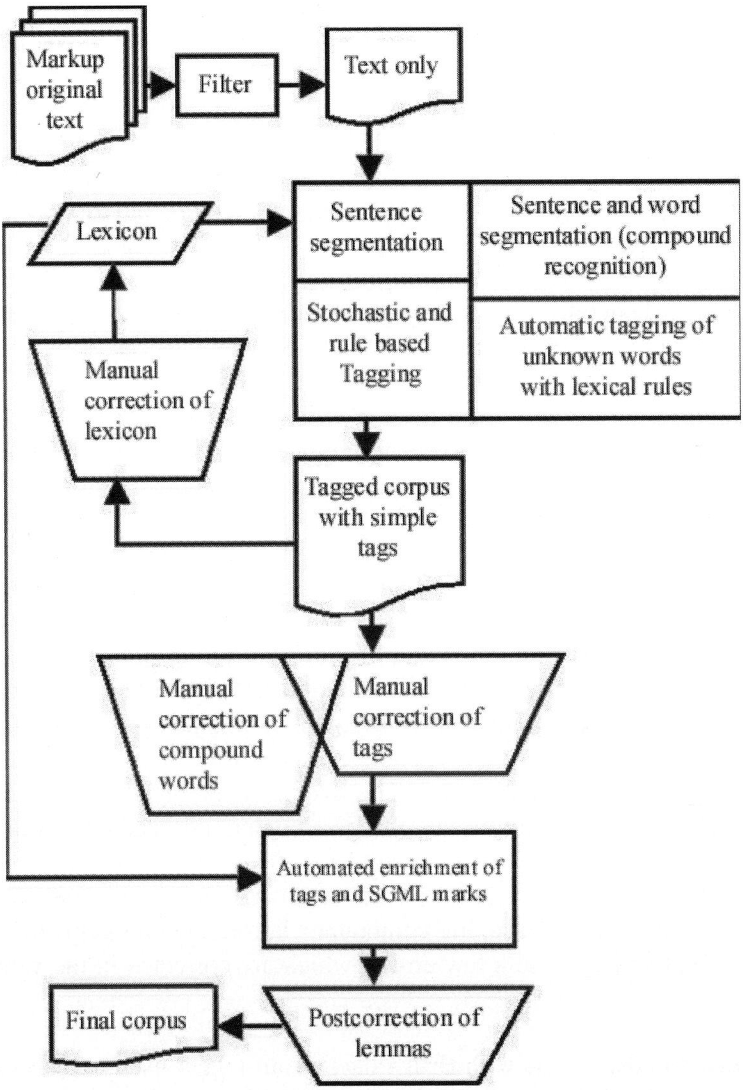

Figure 10.1. The tagging pipeline

1.2 Automatic tagging of the corpus

Given the lack of reusable annotation tools at the beginning of the project, we developed a morphosyntactic tagger for French (Reyes 1997, Clément 2001). Our tagger is based on Brill (1993) in that it has two phases (initial or dummy tagging, and context sensitive tag rewriting). The main difference with respect to a true Brill tagger is that we have added an external lexicon and rely mainly on manually written contextual rules. The tagger uses a reduced tagset for POS and morphology (103 tags), mainly derived from existing lexicons, with only a few simplifications for distinctions difficult to handle automatically (for example between interrogative and relative pronouns which are ambiguous forms in French).

The tagger's lexicon. The lexicon of the tagger comprises over 360,000 forms including 36,000 compounds. It comes from the lexicon we developed for our French Tree Adjoining grammar (FTAG, Candito 1999, Abeillé 2002), plus some extracts from the MULTEXT lexicon, from ABU lexicon (for proper names) and from INTEX for compounds (Silberztein 1993). It has been extended with most forms from the corpus (excluding numbers and specific proper names).

Segmentation. Our tagger comprises a sentence splitter and a tokenizer. The sentence splitter uses lexical data to properly distinguish between capital letters for proper names or beginning of sentence, between dots for acronyms or end of sentence, between hyphenation and linking dashes, etc. (cf. Silberztein 1993). As in English, word segmentation is always a problem since many compounds show up as separate words in French (*pomme de terre* = potato, *bien que* = although, etc.) The tokenizer thus reads the lexicon for compound recognition and groups the best compound candidates (choosing the longest one in case of several candidates; for example the compound adverb (or noun) *face à face* and not the compound preposition *face à* in the sequence *face à face*). Grouping compounds before tagging helps the tagger in most cases and leads to a few errors, which are corrected in the validation phase[1].

Unknown words. As with Brill's tagger, our tagger uses lexical rules for unknown words. We currently have 198 such rules corresponding to common suffixes for verbs, nouns, and adjectives. They are somewhat similar to a morphological analyzer. We also have regular expressions for numbers and proper nouns (acronyms). Since our lexicon has been extended as part of the project, most unknown words are foreign words and typographical errors.

Initial tagging. The initial (dummy) tagging is important since more than 40% of the words in our corpus receive more than one tag with the tagger's lexicon (and more than 20% more than two tags). In order to assign the best possible tag for each word, we rely on the trigram method using genotypes as data (cf. Tzoukerman 1995) and compute the probability of each tag for each word with a large unannotated corpus (of newspaper texts)[2].

Contextual retagging. The initial tag assigned to each word (by lexical lookup) can be changed depending on the context. The form *été* is assigned "Verb" (past participle) as its most probable tag, but must be retagged as Noun after a Determiner for example. Contrary to Brill's automatic rule induction approach (which gave poor results, cf. Reyes 1997, Abeillé & Clément 1999), we preferred to develop most of the contextual rules by hand, based on linguistic knowledge and corpus lookup. In order to accomodate the linguist's need for expressivity, we have added compositionality to the rule formalism, as well as three operators (for negation, for testing whether a tagset contains a specific tag, and to force a transformation even if a tag is not in the tagset of the word in the lexicon). We also added the possibility of having unifiable variables in the tag names (for morphological agreement). The tagger uses 322 contextual (retagging) rules[3].

The contextual rules cannot deal with compound/literal ambiguity (*carte bleue*: blue card or credit card) since they cannot modify the initial segmentation. The tagger does not handle lemmas, which are handled by a specific postprocessor. It processed our corpus with an error rate of about 8%.

1.3 Validating the tagged corpus

Word segmentation (compound recognition) had to be validated by systematic human scrutiny of the tagged corpus, as well as for each form (simple or compound) POS and inflection. Some subcategorization information, most lemmas and all parts of compounds depend only on lexical information (independently of the context) and were added automatically by lexical lookup (once compound segmentation, POS and morphology had been manually validated).

For the two main manual validation tasks (compound validation and tagging validation), very precise guidelines were written (Abeillé et al. 2000) and updated during the project. The reference tagged corpus was checked and corrected by two annotators (one after another) reading (some part of) the text in a longitudinal way, then some tools were applied to check the most difficult cases (for some frequent grammatical words such as *de* or *que*). Weekly meetings were also necessary to ensure consistency between annotators (more than fifteen persons were involved altogether). There were no remaining ambiguities at this level.

Validation of compounds. The automatic annotation for compounds was done by INTEX (Silberztein 1993) and by our tagger. We asked the annotators to validate the compound interpretation in context, to add compounds missing from our lexicons (especially for proper names) and to add discontinuous instances of compounds that could not be automatically found. We gave them guidelines about what to consider a compound based on linguistic tests (cf. Gross 1996), using morphological tests (parts not existing otherwise: *fi* in *faire fi de* (scorn)), syntactic tests (no internal modification or determination : *carte bleue* (credit card) / **carte très bleue* (very blue card) and semantic criteria such as opacity : en revanche (on the contrary; literally: in a revenge)). The well-known preference for compound interpretation was confirmed, except for function words, for which lots of candidate compounds turned out not to be compounds. For example *de plus* can be the compound adverb (all the more) but most of the time it was the preposition (*de*) followed by the adverb (*plus*). To our surprise, very few discontinuous compounds (*afin<justement>de* 'in order precisely to') were found in the corpus.

Annotating the parts of the compounds was done automatically with our compound lexicon.

Validation of tags. Our complete tagset comprises 218 tags (see Figure 10.1). Since most subcategories can be assigned unambiguously to a word (once its POS is known), we chose to simplify the tagset for the annotators. Possessive determiners, for example, can be ambiguous with other POS but not with other determiner subcategories, and the same for possessive pronouns; so the subcategory Possessive can be eliminated from the annotators' tagset. The tagset for the annotators was thus reduced to 122 tags, and they were presented with subcategories only in case of possible ambiguity (*neuf* as cardinal or qualifying adjective ('nine' or 'new'), *lequel* ('which') as interrogative or relative pronoun etc.). Annotators had to validate the output of the tagger and to add subcategories when needed. Most of the subcategories were added automatically afterwards with lexical lookup.

Difficult cases involved tagging numbers, tagging weak pronouns (clitics), choosing between adjective and past participle, between proper and common Noun (for unknown words), between Prep and (indefinite or partitive) Det (for *de*). For numbers, we depart from Multext guidelines in choosing the same tagset as for other words. The annotators thus had to choose between:

- determiner : *Deux hommes sont venus* (Two men came)
- pronoun : *Il en a accueilli deux* (He welcomed two of them)
- adjective : *Les deux hommes sont venus* (The two men came)
- noun : *Le joueur a misé sur le deux* (The player bet on the two)

For clitic pronouns, we simplified the usual case system and kept only nominative / objective / reflexive subcategories, since assigning the right case (or no case at all for uses as inherent clitics or mediopassive) is part of syntactic analysis and will be done (partly automatically) in the second phase of the project. Another difficulty is that most clitic forms in French are ambiguous with respect to gender (*je, leur, les...*) or number (*se*) or both (*y, en*). The annotator thus has to find their antecedent to properly annotate their morphosyntax.

Most of the difficult cases involved ambiguous grammatical words (such as *tous* 'all' or *que* 'that'), the tagging of which is a matter of debate among linguists since it depends on the syntactic analysis of notoriously complex constructions (cleft sentences, comparatives, etc.) In such cases, we made obviously debatable choices: our main goals were to be explicit (in the documentation), consistent (throughout the corpus) and theory neutral (so that our tagging is compatible with several syntactic analyses).

Validation of lemmas. The lemmas were not shown to the annotators. They were added automatically (using our lexicon) after the tag correction phase. At this stage, very few lemma ambiguities remained (*fils* NCmp from *fil* 'thread' or *fils* 'son' ...). They were resolved by hand. Some well known ambiguities such as *savons* (= *savon* 'soap' or *savoir* 'know'), *portes* (= *porte* 'door' or *porter* 'carry'), which are problematic for most lemmatizers, do not arise once the corpus has been tagged with parts of speech. The cost of validating 1 Million words was about 50 man-months (including tagger development). The average correction speed was 500 words per hour. This is much slower than that of the Penn Treebank (2000 words per hour) because of the compounds, and because of our richer tagset (the annotators were presented only 36 tags in the Penn Treebank).

2. THE PARSING PHASE

After the tagging phase was completed, we started the parsing phase of the project. We first present our annotation choices, then our tools for automatic syntactic annotation, and the validation phase. Human validation of constituency is now complete; current and future work includes functional annotation and XML formatting.

2.1 Syntactic annotation scheme

Contrary to tagging, precise language-specific guidelines are usually missing for syntactic annotation. In order to provide annotations that are reusable by researchers with various backgrounds, we chose to annotate both constituency and functional relations, starting with constituency.

Choosing the tagset. We chose surface and shallow annotations, compatible with various syntactic frameworks, and easily learnable for human annotators.

The following information will be contained in each syntactic tag :

1 Main category (e.g. S, PP, NP ...)

2 Possible subcategory (e.g. Rel for relative clauses)

3 Surface function (eg. Subj, Object for NPs)

4 Opening or closing boundaries (<>, </>)

5 Diathesis (e.g. passive) for verbal nuclei

For the moment we have only annotated phrasal names (category and subcategory) and phrasal (i.e. constituent) boundaries. The current syntactic tagset is shown in Table 10.2:

Table 10.2. Tagset of the parsed corpus

Phrasal category	Subcategorization	Description
<NP>, </NP>	-	Noun phrases
<VN>, </VN>	-	Verbal nucleus
<VP>, </VP>	-, inf, part	Infinitives and nonfinite clauses
<PP>, </PP>	-	Prepositional phrases
<AdP>, </AdP>	-	Adverbial phrases
<AP>, </AP>	-	Adjectival phrases
<SENT>, </SENT>	-	Sentences
<S>, </S>	-, int, sub, rel	Finite clauses
<COORD>, </COORD>	-	Coordinated phrases

We chose to only annotate major phrases, with little internal structure (we have determiners and modifying adjectives at the same level in the noun phrase for example). For the sake of simplicity, we make parsimonious use of unary phrases: we have unary NPs for proper names and pronouns, but not for bare common nouns, we have unary APs for predicative adjectives, but not for modifying ones, we have unary VNs for verbs but no unary AdP for Adverbs (see Abeillé et al. 2000). For rigid sequences of categories, such as dates or addresses, it is difficult to determine the head, and we have one global NP with no internal constituents.

We annotate certain phrases with a subcategory, which is important for functional annotation, for example relative or subordinate for embedded clauses.

We do not have discontinuous constituents. For discontinuous objects such as '*en ... trois*' in (10.5) or '*combien ... de pommes*' in (10.6), we will mark that they share the same Object function at the functional level, since a constituent made of a clitic (*en*) and a pronoun (*trois*) would not make sense from the syntactic point of view.

(10.5) `<NP> Paul:NP </NP> en:CL mange:V <NP> trois:PRO </NP>`

(Paul eats three of them)

(10.6) `Combien veux-tu <NP> de pommes </NP> ?`

(how many apples do you want ?)

In order to be as theory neutral as possible, we neither use empty categories, nor functional phrases (no DP or CP). We allow for headless phrases (elliptical NP lacking a head Noun as in (10.7) or sentential clauses lacking a verbal nucleus as in (10.8)).

(10.7) `Ce sont <NP> les:D meilleurs:A </NP>`

(they are the best)

(10.8) `plus vieille <Ssub> que:CS <NP> toi:PRO </NP> </Ssub>`

(older than you)

Unexpressed subjects (in infinitives or participials) will be marked at the functional level.

We made two specific choices, regarding verbal phrases, and regarding coordinated phrases, in accordance with some particularities of the French language.

For verbal phrases, we only annotate the minimal verbal nucleus (clitics, auxiliaries, negation and verb), because the traditional VP (with complements) is subject to much linguistic debate and is often discontinuous in French (like in Italian, cf Montemagni et al this volume):

(10.9) Les actions **qu'a mises** IBM **sur le marché** (the shares that IBM put on the market)

(10.10) Les actionnaires **décideront** certainement **une augmentation de capital** (the stock holders will certainly decide on an increase in capital)

In (10.9) the NP subject (IBM) is postverbal and precedes the locative complement (*sur le marché*). In (10.10), the adverb *certainement* is also postverbal and precedes the NP object (*une augmentation de capital*).

For coordination, we only mark a Coordinating phrase after a coordinating conjunction. We do not necessarily embed conjuncts inside a phrase since there are cases where there is none (10.11), and there are cases where the category of the phrase would be unspecified (10.12):

(10.11) `Paul va <NP>le lundi</NP> <PP>à <NP>la piscine</NP> </PP> <COORD> et <NP>le mardi</NP> <PP>au <NP>cinéma</NP></PP> </COORD>.`
(*Paul goes on Monday to the swimming pool and on Tuesday to the movies*)

(10.12) `Paul est <NP>médecin</NP> <COORD> et <AP>fier <VPinf>de l'être</VPinf></AP></COORD>`
(*Paul is a doctor and proud of it*)

We consider the first conjunct as the head and annotate each following conjunct with a specific category COORD[4].

The parsing pipeline. The following gives an overall view of the complete parsing phase[5]:

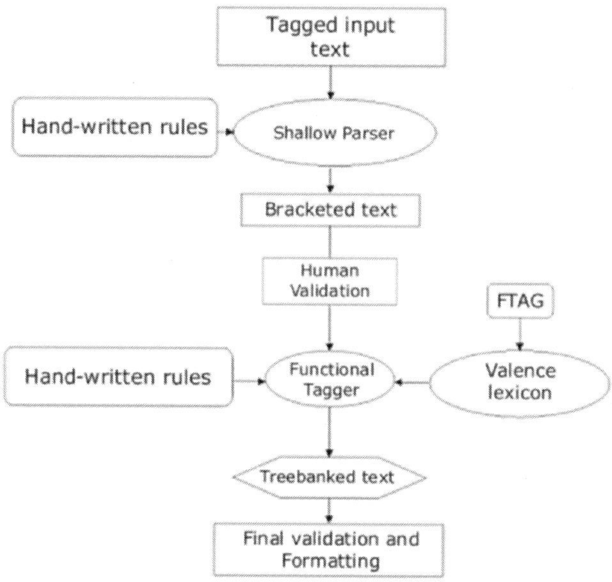

Figure 10.2. The parsing pipeline

2.2 Automatic parsing of the tagged corpus

We choose to use different tools for each task. We need a robust parser for marking major phrase boundaries and a functional tagger for marking syntactic functions (on major phrases) and valence (for each main verb).

For marking constituency, we do not use a classical parser, but have instead adapted specific tools more robust and more suited to our goal. We use a rule-based shallow parser (Kinyon 2001) which marks major phrase boundaries (NP, PP,), with limited embedding (and no recursion) (cf Abney 1991, Giguet 1998). It is designed to minimize errors, so it does not try to attach PPs or relative clauses. These attachments have to be added by the human annotators.

The shallow parser was first developed by Kinyon (2001) and adapted to the corpus by Toussenel (2001). We chose a rule-based parser which does not need a pre- existing treebank (contrary to probabilistic ones.

The shallow parser takes as input the tagged text, slightly simplified (discarding the lemma and the morphological information, but retaining some POS subcategories). It adds phrase boundaries in a left-to-right fashion. It was developed in Java for portability and currently comprises approximately 40 rules. Each rule has access to a limited context : the previous, current and next tag plus the label of the constituent(s) currently being processed. The main underlying idea is to rely on function words as triggers of constituent boundaries (e.g. when encountering a determiner, start a noun phrase (NP), or when encountering a clitic, start a Verbal nucleus)[6].

The shallow parser uses the same tagset as that in Table 10.2, except for Sint, which has to be added by the annotators, and INC (for unknown constituents), which is replaced in a postprocessing phase.

Following linguistic tradition, we consider as function words all words associated with a POS that labels a closed class : i.e., determiners, prepositions, clitics, pronouns (relative, demonstrative), conjunctions (subordination and coordination), auxiliaries, punctuation marks and adverbs that belong to a closed class (e.g. negation adverbs *"ne", "pas"*).

The general idea is that when one of these function words is encountered, an opening boundary for a new constituent is inserted in the text. Closing boundaries are added either naturally when a new constituent begins (e.g. NPs end when a new constituent starts), or triggered by a new function word (e.g. relatives and sentential complements end when a punctuation mark or a conjunction is encountered). Of course, some rules may refer to non function words (e.g. when encountering a proper noun, start an NP).

An example of a rule is the following:

```
When the current word is a preposition, look at the next word.
If this is a verb or a clitic or an adverb, then
     start <VPinf>.
Else start <PP>.
```

(First case) *le temps <**VPinf**> **de** <VN> parler </VN> soigneusement*
('the time for talking carefully')

(Second case) *<**PP**> **de** <NP> Moscou <NP> <PP>*
('from Moscow')

The shallow parser yields an output in linear time, since the input text is scanned just once, and constituent boundaries are added incrementally in a monotonic manner. Contrary to (Abney 1991), it does not establish a link between the constituent boundaries and the prosodic pattern in sentences. Contrary to (Ait- Mokhtar & Chanod 1997), it works in a strictly left-to-right fashion, and performs limited embedding (NPs embedded inside PPs , VN embedded inside a relative clause, itself embedded inside an NP) and limited attachment (e.g. coordination).

An evaluation has been done automatically by comparing the output of the parser with the corrected version of a set of 500 sentences (picked randomly from the corpus). For opening brackets, the recall is 92.9% and the precision is 96%, with 94% correct labels. For closing brackets, the recall is 58% and the precision is 60%, with 56.5% correct labels (cf. Toussenel 2001). Errors difficult to correct with access to a limited context involve mainly "missing" brackets (e.g. "*comptez-vous *ne pas le traiter*" appears as a single constituent, while there should be 2), while "spurious" brackets can often be eliminated by adding more rules (e.g. for multiple prepositions: "*de chez*"). For closing brackets, most of the errors are due to unattached constituents.

2.3 Validating the parsed corpus

For human validation, we defined precise guidelines, drawing on grammar books (cf. Grevisse & Goosse 1992) as well as numerous syntactic studies, especially in surface-based frameworks (cf Abeillé & Godard 2000). The annotators' task consists of the following steps:

1 checking (and enriching) the names of the syntactic tags,

2 checking (and possibly moving) the position of the syntactic tags.

The first check is usually done manually only on opening boundaries and the second check usually involves moving closing boundaries.

We are checking in a longitudinal way using an Emacs-based tool especially designed by Michel Simard and Lionel Clément called CAT. The tool presents the annotator with one phrase per line with automatic indentation according to the level of embedding. It enables the annotator to move opening or closing phrase boundaries, to view the sentences as a graphical tree, to change automatically opening and closing boundary names, and to view or hide full morphosyntactic tag of each word.

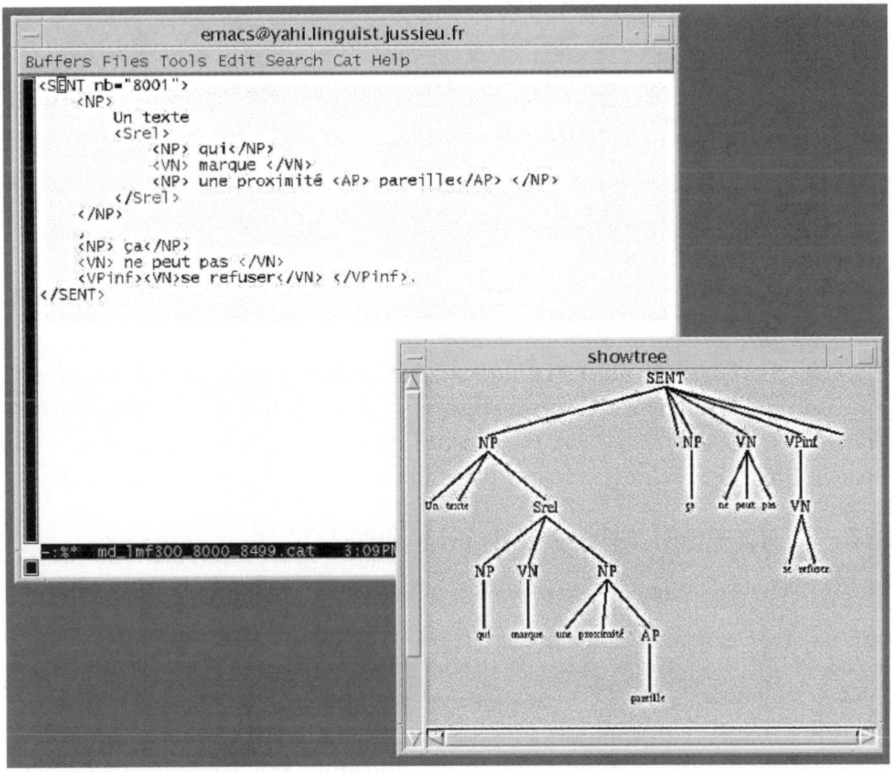

Figure 10.3. The CAT Validation tool for phrases

Most of the difficult cases involved PP attachment, Relative clause attachment or scope of coordination, for which a deep understanding of the sentences is necessary. We were agnostic about ambiguities remaining at the beginning of the project. But most of the ambiguities were resolved at the semantic level. The remaining ambiguities such as (10.13) are thus only spurious ones and we chose to get rid of them by the "attach high" heuristics (namely the second parse here).

(10.13) Paul écrit un livre sur les Indiens (Paul writes a book about Indians)

<NP>un livre <PP>sur <NP>les Indiens</NP></PP></NP>

or

<NP>un livre </NP> <PP>sur <NP>les Indiens</NP></PP>

Some mislabeled constituents were those introduced by other function words than those defined in the parser's rules, eg; NPs starting with quantificational adverbs or prepositions:

(10.14) <NP>environ:ADV trois cents:DET personnes :N</NP>
(approximately 300 people)

(10.15) Ils achetent <NP>jusqu'à:P 10 000:DET actions:N</NP>
(they buy up to 10,000 shares)

Some unexpected parsing errors came from remaining tagging errors that had escaped previous human validation. We checked using sample texts that different annotators were converging on the same parse, and usually one postchecking was sufficient for ensuring the quality of constituency annotation.

2.4 Syntactic formatting and search tools

The tagged corpus has been formatted in XML following the TEI and XCES guidelines (cf. Ide et al. 1996; see Appendix 2). The parsed corpus will be formatted in XML too (cf Ide and Romary this volume).

A search tool has been developed by L. Clément (Clément 2001) with a graphical interface, for linguists looking at specific words, expressions or constructions in French. This tool will be developed for syntactic annotation, too.

3. CURRENT STATE AND FUTURE WORK

3.1 Current state of the treebank

The automatically tokenized, tagged and parsed corpus has been manually validated and enriched (with longitudinal exhaustive checking by at least three different human annotators). The 1 Million tokens when annotated amount to 870,000 words, excluding punctuation signs, and clustering compounds into one word, for a total of 32,000 sentences with 37,000 different lemmas. The average number of words per sentence is 27 and the average number of internal constituents is 20. There are no remaining ambiguities, nor unknown words (the original typos have been corrected).

It is available in two versions :

- a light version with a reduced tagset in a compact format,
- a full version with a richer set of tags, lemmas, constituents, all in SGML

format (see appendix).

3.2 Using the treebank

The treebank is freely available for research purposes and is currently used by more than 10 licensees[7].

The tagged version has been used for evaluating a lemmatizer (Namer 2000), and for training stochastic taggers (cf. Langlais & Simart 2002). L. Clément used it to train a tagger based on Treetagger (Schmid 1994) as part of the RLT project. The parsed version has been used in collaboration with psycholinguistics at LPL (Aix) to check syntactic preferences (Abeillé et al 2001) and to train a connectionnist parser. Our guidelines have been reused for other projects (CLIF, Multitag) and will be used for the EASY project of parser evaluation for French (which is inspired by Carroll et al. this volume).

3.3 Future work

The treebank will be enriched with grammatical functions, associated with the major constituents. J. Steinlin has developed a rule-based functional tagger, which has to be fine-tuned to the corpus, and enriched with a valence lexicon, such as that developed within the FTAG project (cf. Barrier 1999). With such information, an automatic conversion of the constituent structures into dependency structures will also be possible.

4. CONCLUSION

We have presented a treebank project for French. We have developed a 1 M. word reference corpus for French (from newspaper texts) and annotated it with morphosyntax, lemmas, compounds and phrase boundaries. The automatic annotations have been validated by human annotators in several steps. The reference tagged corpus is a resource to be distributed in two versions: light (with a reduced tagset) or complete (with lemmas, constituent boundaries and full SGML markup). As part of the project, several resources have been developed:

- a tagger inspired by (Brill 1993) but with mostly hand-written rules, a sizeable external lexicon and a tokenizer (handling compounds),
- a shallow parser marking major phrase boundaries with limited embedding,

- guidelines for annotating constructions usually overlooked in grammar books (dates, measures, direct speech, unbalanced coordination)

The next step will be to annotate our corpus for functional relations, and to enrich our search tools. A longer term objective is the marking of some anaphoric relations (for pronouns) and of valence for verbs.

Acknowledgments

This project was mainly sponsored by the Institut Universitaire de France (IUF), but also by the CNRS (as part of the CLIF project), by LORIA (as part of the CALIN project) and by Aupelf-Uref (as part of the Francil Project). Many thanks are due to many people, including Claire Blanche-Benveniste, Nicolas Barrier, Martine Chéradame, Alexandra Kinyon, Patrick Paroubek, Rodrigo Reyes, Laurent Romary, Jacques Steinlin, Michel Simart, Jean Véronis, Eric Wehrli, and the annotators themselves.

Notes

1. We also did some lexicon tuning, taking out the compound adverb *sur ce* (colloquial 'then') for example since the corresponding sequence (Prep Det) was never a compound in the whole corpus.

2. The genotype of a word is the set of POS tags that can be assigned to it, i.e. [N:ms A:ms] is the genotype of the word /droit/ (right). [N:ms A:ms] and [A:ms N:ms] are the same genotype. Tzoukermann shows that words that share the same genotype also share (roughly) the same distribution.

3. INaLF's tagger, also based on Brill's tagger, uses about 335 rules, cf. (Lecomte & Paroubek 1996).

4. In final formatting, COORD can be replaced with the category of the first conjunct and Coord as a subcategory.

5. The last step with the functional tagger is currently being developed by J. Steinlin and N. Barrier.

6. In psycholinguistics, the role of function words in human sentence processing has been emphasized as early as (Kimball 1973), with the "new node principle" stating that "The construction of a new node is signaled by the occurrence of a grammatical function word".

7. We currently distribute one third (300,000 words= 10,000 sentences) of the corpus.

References

A. Abeillé (2002). *Une grammaire électronique du français*. CNRS Editions, Paris.

A. Abeillé, L. Clément (1999). A tagged reference corpus for French, *LINC'99 Proceedings*, EACL workshop, Bergen.

Abeillé A., D. Godard (2000). French word order and lexical weight, in R. Borsley (ed) *The Nature and Function of Syntactic Categories*, Syntax and Semantics, Academic Press, 325-358.

A. Abeillé., L. Clément, M. Chéradame, F. Toussenel (2000). Guides pour les Annotateurs - Mots simples - Mots composés - Constituants - Technical Reports, University Paris 7.

A. Abeillé, L. Clément, A. Kinyon, F Toussenel, (2001). The Paris 7 annotated corpus for French : some experimental results, in Wilson (ed) *Corpus Linguistics*, Lancaster.

A. Abeillé, J. Pynte, F. Toussenel, (2001). Constituent length and attachment preferences in French, *AMLAP*, Sarrebruck.

S. Abney (1991). Parsing by chunks. In Berwick et al (eds), *Principle-based Parsing*. Kluwer.

S. Aït-Mokhtar, J.P. Chanod (1997). Incremental Finite-State Parsing. *Proceedings of ANLP'97*, Washington, p. 72-79.

S. Barrier (1999). Repérage et classification de valences verbales, expériences avec FTAG, DEA thesis, University Paris 7.

A. Böhmova et al. (2003). The Prague Dependency treebank, this volume.

T. Brants, S. Skut, H. Uszkoreit (2003). Syntactic annotation of a German newspaper corpus, (this volume).

E. Brill (1993). A corpus-based approach to Language Learning, Ph.D. Dissertation, Department CIS, University of Pennsylvania.

J. Carroll, G. Minnen, T.Briscoe (2003). Parser evaluation using a grammatical relation annotation scheme (this volume)

M-H. Candito (1999). Représentation hiérarchique de grammaires lexicalisées: application au français et à l'italien, PhD Thesis, University Paris 7.

L. Clément (2001) Construction et exploitation d'un corpus syntaxiquement annoté pour le français, PhD Thesis, Paris 7.

S. Colonna (2001). Facteurs influençant la levée des ambigutés syntaxiques, PhD thesis, University of Provence.

E. Giguet 1998. Méthodes pour l'analyse automatique de structures formelles sur documents multilingues. PhD Thesis. Université de Caen.

M. Grévisse, A. Goosse (1992) *Le bon Usage*, Liège: Duculot.

G. Gross (1996). *Les expressions figées*, Ophrys, Gap.

N. Ide, J. Veronis, G. Priest-Dorman. (1996). Corpus Encoding Standard. EAGLES/MULTEXT.

N. Ide, L. Romary (2002) Encoding syntactic information, in this volume.

P. Kahrel, R. Barnett, G. Leech. (1997). Towards cross-linguistic standards or guidelines for the annotation of corpora. In *Corpus annotation*. Garside & al (eds). p. 231-243. Longman.

R. Kayne (1975). *French Syntax: the transformational cycle*. Current Studies in linguistics. MIT press.

J. Kimball (1973). Seven Principles of surface structure parsing in natural language. *Cognition* 2(1).

A. Kinyon (2001). A language independent shallow parser compiler. *Proceedings ACL-EACL Conference*, Toulouse.

P. Langlais, M. Simart (2002) Merging example-based and statistical machine translation: an experiment, *Proceedings of the 5th AMTA Conference*, Tiburon.

J. Lecomte, P. Paroubek (1996). Le catégoriseur d'E. Brill: mise en œuvre d'une version entraînée pour le français, Technical report, INaLF,Nancy.

M.Marcus, B. Santorini, M.-A. Marcinkiewicz (1993). Building a large annotated corpus of English : the Penn Treebank, *Computational Linguistics*, 19(2), 313-330.

F. Namer (2000). FLEMM : un analyseur flexionnel du français à base de règles, *TAL*, p. 41:2, p. 523-548.

U. von Rekowski (1996). ELM-FR : Specifications for French morphosyntax, lexicon specification and classification guidelines, EAGLES document.

R. Reyes (1997). Un Etiqueteur du français inspiré du taggeur de Brill, Rapport de stage, UFRL, Paris 7.

G. Sampson (1995). *English for the computer*. Oxford University Press.

G. Sampson (2003). Thoughts of two decades of drawing trees, in this volume.

A. Sanfilippo et al. 1996. EAGLES Subcategorization Standards. `http://www.icl.pi.cnr.it/EAGLES96/syntax/syntax.html`

H. Schmid (1994). Probabilistic part-of-speech tagging using decision treees, *Proceedings International Conference on new methods in Language processing*, Manchester.

M. Silberztein (1993). *Dictionnaires électroniques et analyse automatique de textes: le système INTEX*, Paris : Masson.

B. Srinivas, A. Joshi (1999). Supertagging: An approach to almost parsing, *Computational Linguistics*, 25-2: 237-266.

A. Taylor, M. Marcus, B. Santorini (2003). The Penn treebank: an overview, in this volume.

F. Toussenel (2001). Marquage de constituants sur un corpus français, résultats et exploitation linguistiques, DEA thesis, University Paris 7.

E. Tzoukermann, D. Radev, W. Gale (1995). Tagging French without lexical probabilities - combining linguistic knowledge and statistical learning, *Proceedings EACL SIGDAT Workshop*, Dublin.

Appendix

1. Sample extract

Sample text
Au cours de la conférence_de_presse qui a clos cette rencontre , le premier ministre est-allemand est revenu sur les incidents de lundi soir.
(During the press conference which ended this meeting, the East German Prime minister talked about Monday evening)

Tagged corpus (Light format: limited tagset, no lemmas) = Annotators' format

```
Au cours de             P+PNP
la                      Dfs
conférence_de_presse    NCfs+NPN
qui                     PROR3fs
a                       VP3s
clos                    VKms
cette                   Dfs
rencontre               NCfs
,
le                      Dms
premier_ministre        NCms+AN
est-allemand            Ams+XA
est                     VP3s
revenu                  VKms
sur                     P
les                     Dmp
incidents               NCmp
de                      P
lundi                   NCms
soir                    NCms
```

2. Tagged corpus (SGML final format, simplified for compounds)

cc: tags of parts for compounds

```
<w lemma=''au cours de'' cat=P cc=PCD >
     <w lemma=''à'' cat=''P''>Au</w>
     <w lemma=''le'' cat=''D''></w>
     <w lemma=''cours'' cat=''N''>cours</w>
     <w lemma=''de'' cat=''P''>de</w>
     </w>
<w lemma=''le'' cat=D subcat=def mph=fs >la</w>
<w lemma=''conference de presse'' cat=N subcat=comm mph=fs cc=NDN >
     <w lemma=''conférence'' cat=''N''>conférence</w>
     <w lemma=''de'' cat=''P''>de</w>
     <w lemma=''presse'' cat=''N''>presse</w>
```

```
     </w>
<w lemma=''qui'' cat=PRO subcat=R mph=fs >qui</w>
<w lemma=''avoir'' cat=V mph=P3s >a</w>
<w lemma=''clore'' cat=V mph=Kms >clos</w>
<w lemma=''ce'' cat=D subcat=dem mph=fs >cette</w>
<w lemma=''rencontre'' cat=N subcat=comm mph=fs >rencontre</w>
<w lemma='',,'' cat=PONCT >,</w>
<w lemma=''le'' cat=D subcat=def mph=ms >le</w>
<w lemma=''premier_ministre'' cat=N subcat=comm mph=ms cc=AN >
     <w lemma=''premier'' cat=''A''>premier</w>
     <w lemma=''ministre'' cat=''N''>ministre</w>
     </w>
<w lemma=''est-allemand'' cat=A mph=ms cc=XA >
     <w lemma=''est'' cat=''A''>est</w>
     <w lemma=''allemand'' cat=''A''>allemand</w>
</w>
<w lemma=''être'' cat=V mph=P3s >est</w>
<w lemma=''revenir'' cat=V mph=Kms > revenu</w>
<w lemma=''sur'' cat=P > sur</w>
<w lemma=''le'' cat=D subcat=def mph=mp > les</w>
<w lemma=''incident'' cat=N subcat=comm mph=mp> incidents</w>
<w lemma=''de'' cat=P > de</w>
<w lemma=''lundi'' cat=N subcat=comm mph=ms > lundi</w>
<w lemma=''soir'' cat=N subcat=comm mph=ms > soir</w>
```

3. Parsed corpus (simplified, without function annotation)

```
<SENT><PP>Au_cours_de:P
       <NP> la:Dfs conférence_de_presse:NC-fs
            <Srel> <NP>:SUJ qui:PROR-3fs </NP>
                        <VN> a:VP-3s clos:VK-ms </VN>
                        <NP> cette:D-fs rencontre:NC-fs </NP>
</Srel>
       </NP> </PP>  ,:PONCT
<NP>le:D-ms premier_ministre:NC-ms<AP>est-allemand:A-ms</AP></NP>
<VN>est:VP-3s revenu:VK-ms</VN>
<PP> sur:P <NP>les:D-mp incidents:NC-mp
        <PP> de:P <NP>lundi:NC-ms soir:NC-ms</NP></PP>
        </NP> </PP>
</SENT>
```

With graphical display :

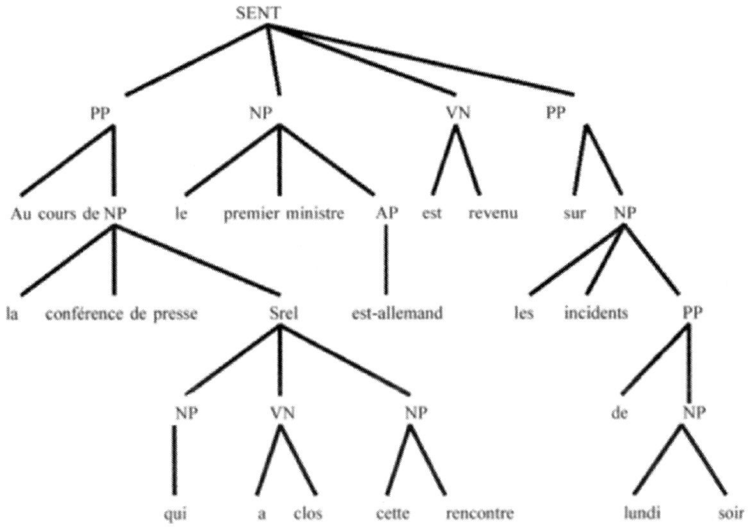

Chapter 11

BUILDING THE ITALIAN SYNTACTIC-SEMANTIC TREEBANK

Simonetta Montemagni, Francesco Barsotti, Marco Battista, Nicoletta Calzolari, Ornella Corazzari, Alessandro Lenci, Antonio Zampolli
ILC-CNR / CPR, Pisa (Italy)

Francesca Fanciulli, Maria Massetani, Remo Raffaelli
Synthema, Pisa (Italy)

Roberto Basili, Maria Teresa Pazienza, Dario Saracino, Fabio Zanzotto
"Tor Vergata" University / CERTIA, Rome (Italy)

Nadia Mana, Fabio Pianesi
ITC-IRST, Trento (Italy)

Rodolfo Delmonte
Venice University / CVR, Venice (Italy)

Abstract The paper reports on the design and construction of a multi-layered corpus of Italian, annotated at the syntactic and lexico-semantic levels, whose development is supported by dedicated software augmented with an intelligent interface. The issue of evaluating this type of resource is also addressed.

Keywords: Italian, Multi-layered Linguistic Annotation, Syntactic Annotation, Semantic Annotation, Annotation Software, Evaluation

A. Abeillé (ed.), Treebanks: Building and Using Parsed Corpora, 189–210.

1. INTRODUCTION

Linguistically annotated corpora nowadays have a crucial theoretical as well as applied role in Natural Language Processing (NLP). This paper describes a large scale effort to provide Italian with a multi-level annotated corpus, the Italian Syntactic-Semantic Treebank (henceforth referred to as ISST). ISST – which represents one of the main activities of an ongoing Italian national project, SI-TAL[1] – was developed by a consortium of companies and computational linguistics sites in Italy which represent a wide range of expertise in the computational linguistics field[2].

Expected uses for ISST range from NLP tasks (such as Information Retrieval, Word Sense Disambiguation, linguistic knowledge acquisition) to training (and/or tuning) of grammars and sense disambiguation systems, to the evaluation of language technology systems.

The final resource consists of a multi-layered corpus of Italian of 305,547 word tokens. A first evaluation of the resource was carried out in the framework of an automatic Italian-English machine translation system. Both annotation and evaluation activities were supported by software, including an intelligent interface, specifically developed for efficiently accessing and querying the large amount of textual data and related annotations.

2. ISST ARCHITECTURE

ISST has a four-level structure covering morpho-syntactic, syntactic and lexico-semantic levels of linguistic description. Syntactic annotation is distributed over two different levels: the constituent structure level and the functional relation level. The fourth level deals with lexico-semantic annotation, which is carried out in terms of sense tagging augmented with other types of semantic information.

Both syntactic and lexico-semantic annotations refer to the morpho-syntactically annotated text, which in turn is linked to the orthographic file with the text and mark-up of macrotextual organisation (e.g. titles, subtitles, summary, body of article, paragraphs).

The multi-level structure of ISST shows two main innovations with respect to other treebanks. While most treebanks are restricted to syntactic annotation only, ISST – together with e.g. the Sinica (Chen et al., this volume) and the Prague Dependency (Böhmová et al., this volume) treebanks – includes both syntactic and semantic annotation levels. However, whereas the Chinese and the Prague dependency treebanks conceive of semantic annotation as the marking of thematic-like structures, ISST presents a further innovation given the fact that semantic annotation is intended here as sense tagging of lexical heads. In this way, the prerequisites are set up for corpus-based investigations on the syntax-semantics interface: the linking of the syntactic and semantic annotation layers will permit, for instance, the identification of specific subcategorisation properties associated with a specific word sense, or of the semantic types associated with the functional positions of a given predicate.

The other innovative aspect of ISST concerns the distributed approach to syntactic annotation. In this respect, ISST differs from most treebanks, currently available or under construction for different languages, which adopt a unique syntactic representation layer, following either a constituency-based approach (see, among many others: Taylor et al., this volume; Marcus et al., 1993; Sampson, 1995, this volume; Greenbaum, 1996, Wallis, this volume; Moreno et al. 1999, this volume) or a dependency-based one (e.g. Karlsson et al., 1995), or a hybrid one combining features of both (e.g. Brants et al., this volume; Abeillé et al., this volume). ISST also differs from multi-level treebanks like the Prague Dependency Treebank (PTD). Whereas PTD annotation levels refer respectively to (a) the surface dependency relations and (b) the underlying sentence structure, ISST syntactic annotation levels are intended to provide orthogonal views of the same surface syntax.

3. ISST CORPUS

The ISST corpus consists of 305,547 word tokens reflecting contemporary language use. It includes two different sections:

1 a "balanced" corpus (215,606 tokens), exemplifying general language usage which consists of a selection of articles from newspapers (*La Repubblica* and *Il Corriere della Sera*) and periodicals, all selected to cover a high variety of topics (politics, economy, culture, science, health, sport, leisure, etc.);

2 a specialised corpus (89,941 tokens) from the financial domain, with articles taken from *Il Sole-24 Ore*.

All in all, they cover a 10 year time period (1985-1995).

4. ISST MORPHO-SYNTACTIC ANNOTATION

Morpho-syntactic annotation involves mark-up of morphological words with specification of part of speech, lemma, and morpho-syntactic features (such as number, person, gender, etc.). The adopted morpho-syntactic tagset conforms to the EAGLES international standard (Monachini and Calzolari, 1996) and includes 16 basic POS tags (see Appendix 1), which are further subdivided into 31 subtypes (to distinguish, for instance, between proper and common nouns, or demonstrative, possessive and clitic pronouns). The complete tagset, deriving from the combination of different POS subtypes with morpho-syntactic features, amounts to 236 different tags.

ISST morpho-syntactic annotation also includes treatment of (i) morphologically complex words such as cliticised verbs, e.g. *dammelo* lit. 'give+to_me+it', and (ii) basic multi-word expressions made up of contiguous sequences of words. The typology of multi-word expressions includes: expressions with words which do not occur separately, either foreign words (e.g. *prima_facie*) or Italian words which do not freely occur in texts (e.g. *chetichella* which only occurs in the adverbial locution *alla_chetichella* 'furtively'); expressions made up of sequences of tags not conforming to the general rules of grammar (e.g. *al_di_là* lit. 'at_of_there' meaning 'beyond' which is made up of two prepositions, the first of which also includes definiteness marking, followed by an adverb); expressions whose grammatical properties do not directly follow from their component words (e.g. multi-word prepositions such as *in_funzione_di* lit. 'in_function_of' meaning 'as'). Note, however, that in ISST other types of multi-word expressions are identified and marked at higher annotation levels (see section 6).

Morpho-syntactic annotation was previously carried out at ILC in the framework of the European projects PAROLE (Goggi et al., 1997) and ELSNET (Monachini and Corazzari, 1995). The text was automatically tagged by a stochastic tagger, the Pi-Tagger (Picchi, 1994); the output was then manually revised by a team of linguists.

5. ISST SYNTACTIC ANNOTATION

As already pointed out in section 2, ISST follows a distributed approach to syntactic annotation based on a monostratal view of syntax. ISST syntactic annotation levels are independent of each other: none of them presupposes the other, e.g. functional annotation is not built on top of constituent structure annotation. This makes it possible for the two annotation levels to be used (i.e. accessed and examined) independently. At the same time, they provide complementary information: in principle, combined views of the developed resource can be obtained, for example, by projecting functional information onto the constituent structure (see Montemagni et al., 2000).

The motivations for this "double track" approach to syntactic representation range from language-specific to more general.

This distributed approach to syntax is particularly suited to deal with some peculiarities of Italian syntax, namely:

- the syntactically free constituent order, which allows for considerable variation in the ordering of constituents at the sentence level;
- the pro-drop property: the subject of main verbs appears to be omitted in approximately 70% of the possible cases (Bates, 1976).

These two features together make a pure constituency-based representation of Italian unrestricted texts difficult: if on the one hand they can be handled in the annotation through the use of empty elements (either traces or pro-subjects), on the other hand their frequency of occurrence would make syntactic annotation less transparent and thus less intelligible. This is a well-known problem of syntactic annotation of free word order languages, see for instance (Brants et al., this volume).

ISST overcomes the problems of a pure constituency-based representation of Italian by decoupling functional information from the constituent structure. Hence, in ISST the treatment of word order variation does not interfere in any way with the representation of functional relations, i.e. the encoding of the latter becomes entirely separate from the order of constituents in the sentence. By the same token, subject omission is not accounted for at the level of constituent structure, but only at the functional level.

The distributed approach to syntactic annotation is also supported by the types of uses foreseen for ISST. In fact, ISST syntactic annotation levels are intended to be usable both in real applications and for research purposes, and to be compatible with different approaches to syntax, both dependency- and constituency-based, adopted in both theoretical and applied frameworks.

5.1 Constituency annotation

ISST constituency annotation departs from other constituency-based syntactic annotation schemes (e.g. the one adopted in the Penn Treebank) in a number of respects, mainly due to the distributed organisation of syntactic annotation.

Annotation at this level consists of the identification of phrase boundaries with labelling of constituent types. Given that functional relations are handled at a distinct level, ISST tree structures are shallow, as exemplified below for the sentence *lo scontro sulle cessioni legali è stato risolto per decreto* 'the clash on legal transfers has been resolved by decree':

```
(1) [F [SN lo scontro [SP sulle [SN cessioni [SA legali SA] SN] SP] SN]
    [IBAR e stato risolto IBAR] [COMPT [SP per [SN decreto SN] SP]
    COMPT] F]
```

In the constituent structure above, all the complements of the verb – the subject nominal constituent (SN), the verbal node (IBAR) and the complements node (COMPT) – are at the same level of embedding with respect to the sentence node (F). Similar observations hold for the internal structure of nominal constituents, where no hierarchical distinction is made among the head, the determiner and the complements and/or adjuncts (see the internal structure of the subject noun phrase in (1) above). Note also that, for verbal phrases, annotation is restricted to the minimal verbal nucleus (auxiliaries, negation, verb and clitics of inherently pronominal verbs), because the traditional notion of VP (which includes the verb complements) is not easily applicable to unrestricted Italian texts given the problem of discontinuity, which is so frequent that it becomes controversial whether the notion of VP is really useful for the purpose of corpus annotation.

Moreover, the fact that in ISST functional relations are dealt with at a distinct level instead of being defined in terms of constituent structures allows ISST to dispense with empty elements such as null subjects or traces, thus making constituent annotation more intelligible. In fact, the relevant information is recovered at the functional level, through a relation linking the displaced or omitted element to its governing head. Therefore, syntactic phenomena such as pro-drop and ellipsis, as well as cases of discontinuous or non canonical order of constituents (topicalisation, wh-questions, etc.) are not accounted for in terms of empty categories and coindexation as e.g. in the Penn Treebank but rather at the functional annotation level. Examples of constituency-based representations of these structures follow:

Ho cose più importanti di cui occuparmi '(I) have more important things to take care of'

```
(2) [F [IBAR Ho IBAR] [COMPC [SN cose [SA piu importanti SA] [F2 [SPD
    di cui [SV2 occuparmi SV2] SPD] F2] SN] COMPC] F]
```

Gli ordini di vendita stranieri hanno imboccato la strada che riporta al di là del confine 'the foreign selling orders took the way which goes back beyond the border'

```
(3) [F [SN Gli ordini [SPD di [SN vendita SN] [SA stranieri SA] SPD]
    SN] [IBAR hanno imboccato IBAR] [COMPT [SN la strada [F2 che [F
    [IBAR riporta IBAR] [COMPIN [SP al_di_la_del [SN confine SN] SP]
    COMPIN] F] F2] SN] COMPT] F]
```

Constituency annotation in ISST uses an inventory of 22 constituent types (see Appendix 2): specialised constituent names are used for a number of complements or adjuncts, in order to facilitate the mapping onto functional annotation.

Constituency annotation of ISST was performed in a semi-automatic way. First, the text was parsed by a Shallow Parser (Delmonte, 1999, 2000) whose task was that of building shallow syntactic structures for each safely recognisable constituent. In uncertain cases, no attachment was performed at this stage in order to avoid committing to structural decisions which might then reveal themselves to be wrong. The output of the shallow parser was then manually revised and corrected.

5.2 Functional annotation

Functional annotation in ISST is word-based, i.e. it is carried out independently of previous identification of phrasal constituents. The advantages of this choice include, on the theoretical front, the fact that ISST can be used as a reference resource for a wider variety of different annotation schemes, both constituency- and dependency-based ones (Lin, 1998). Moreover, word-based functional annotation is comparatively easy and "fair" for use in parsing evaluation since it overcomes some of the well-known shortcomings of constituency-based evaluation (see, among others: Carroll et al., 1998, this volume; Lin, 1998, this volume; Sampson, 2000).

We used FAME (Lenci et al., 1999, 2000) as the starting point for the development of the ISST functional annotation scheme[3]. FAME's main features are: (a) the hierarchical organisation of functional relations which makes provision for underspecified representations of highly ambiguous functional analyses, and (b) the modular coding architecture which is articulated over different information layers, each factoring out different but possibly interrelated linguistic facets of syntactic annotation. These features combined make FAME a meta-scheme, i.e. an annotation scheme which, beyond being a full-fledged annotation scheme, also acts as a sort of "metalanguage" for different annotation schemata.

The building blocks of FAME are functional relations which are expressed in terms of binary relations holding between two lexical heads. Note that FAME relations involve words belonging to major lexical classes only (i.e. non-auxiliary verbs, nouns, adjectives and adverbs); information about grammatical words (e.g. determiners, prepositions, auxiliaries) is encoded otherwise (see below).

Functional relations include dependency, i.e. head-dependent, relations such as subject and object, which – unlike constituency annotation – can also involve displaced elements, null subjects and elliptical material; the inventory of ISST dependency relations is given in Appendix 3. This dependency-based annotation scheme is augmented with other relation types dealing with constructions which cannot be interpreted in terms of head-dependent relationships, e.g. coordination phenomena, clause-internal co-reference etc. For the sake of paper length, only dependency relations are discussed below. A dependency relation is an asymmetric binary relation between two full words, a head and a dependent. Each dependency relation is modularly represented as follows:

```
(4) dep_type (head.<head_features>,
             dependent.<dep_features>)
```

where dep_type specifies the relationship linking the dependent to the head and features associated with the elements of the relation further specify relational information. Consider below the functional representation of the sentence *lo scontro sulle cessioni legali è stato risolto per decreto* 'the clash on legal transfers has been resolved by decree' (whose constituent structure representation is reported in (1) above):

```
(5)  sogg (risolvere.<diatesi=passiva>, scontro)
     mod (scontro, cessione.<intro=''su''>)
     mod (cessione, legale)
     mod (risolvere.<diatesi=passiva>, decreto.<intro=''per''>)
```

It can be observed that features convey, for instance, information about the preposition which introduces the dependent in a given relation (see the INTRO attribute), or about the diathesis of the verbal head. Other information types conveyed by features concern the open/closed predicative function of clausal dependents (in this way control information is also encoded), the semantic role of modifiers (e.g. temporal, locative), etc.

Unlike constituency annotation, at this level either the head or the dependent can correspond to elliptical material; this makes it possible to represent pro-drop phenomena:

Ho cose più importanti di cui occuparmi '(I) have more important things to take care of'

```
(6)  sogg (avere, .<pers=1, numb=sing>)
```

Note that this modular representation, distributed over relations and features, provides the prerequisites for ISST to be used as a reference annotation scheme which is compatible with a wide range of theories and thus mappable onto different syntactic representation formats (for more details on the intertranslatability of FAME into other syntactic representation formats see Lenci et al. 1999, 2000).

Annotation at the functional level was carried out manually.

6. ISST LEXICO-SEMANTIC ANNOTATION

The methodology for annotation at this level takes advantage of two previous experiments in semantic tagging carried out at ILC in the framework of the SENSEVAL initiative (Calzolari et al., 2000) and of the ELSNET resources task group activity (Corazzari et al., 2000).

The following inventory of annotation units is identified and distinguished in ISST:

- USS: sense units corresponding to single lexical items;
- USC: semantically complex units expressed in terms of multi-word expressions (e.g. compounds, support verb constructions, idioms);

- UST: title sense units corresponding to titles (of newspapers, books, shows, etc.).

Unlike USS and USC which are annotated at one level only, titles receive a two-level annotation: at the level of individual component words and as a single title unit. Note that in ISST lexico-semantic annotation is restricted to content words, in particular to nouns, verbs and adjectives and corresponding multi-word expressions.

Lexico-semantic annotation consists of the assignment of semantic tags, expressed in terms of attribute-value pairs. ISST semantic tags convey three different types of information:

1 sense of the target word(s) in the specific context: ItalWordNet (henceforth, IWN) is the reference lexical resource used for the sense tagging task (CPR et al., 2000). IWN, developed from the EuroWordNet lexicon (Alonge et al., 1998), includes a general part and a specialised one with financial and computational terminology;

2 other types of lexico-semantic information complementing IWN sense assignments, e.g. marking figurative usages, idiomatic expressions, evaluative suffixation, neologisms, proper nouns, etc.;

3 information about the tagging operation, mainly notes by the human annotator used to ease and speed up the annotation process and its revision. The human annotator can keep track of problematic cases (e.g. cases of indistinguishable IWN senses, of ambiguous corpus contexts, etc.). Input of this type may also be useful for discussion with the team of IWN lexicographers with a view to prospective revisions and updating of the lexical resource.

Note that through the taxonomical organisation of IWN word senses an implicit assignment is made to the semantic types of the IWN ontology. In this way, ISST sense tagging can also be seen as semantic tagging.

As for the annotation methodology for this level, in order to ensure the consistent tagging of polysemous words and USC, the annotation was manually performed 'per lemma' and not sequentially, that is, word by word following the text.

Annotation strategy. Each annotation unit is tagged with the relevant sense according to IWN sense distinctions. When more than one IWN sense applies to the context being tagged, arbitrary sense assignments are avoided by resorting to underspecified annotations (expressed, for instance, in terms of disjunction over different IWN senses).

Sense assignment is augmented through specification of lexico-semantic tags conveying information not explicitly included in the reference lexical resource or further specifying it. These additional semantic tags are used to mark:

- a US or USC used in a figurative sense (either metaphoric or methonymic): e.g. the metaphoric use of *fulmine* in *essere un fulmine* lit. 'to be a lightning bolt' meaning 'to be fast like a lightning bolt';
- a US semantically modified through evaluative suffixation (e.g. *porticciolo* 'small port', *borsone* 'a large bag');
- the semantic type (e.g. human entity, artifact, institution, location) of proper nouns, either US (e.g. *IBM* tagged as a 'group') or USC (e.g. *Nuova Zelanda* 'New Zealand' which can be assigned the type of 'place');
- the USC subtype, e.g. compound (e.g. *certificato di credito del tesoro* 'treasury certificate'), idiom (e.g. *essere la chiave di volta* 'to be the keystone'), support verb construction (e.g. *entrare in vigore* 'to come into effect');
- the UST subtype, e.g. title of an opera (e.g. *La Boheme*) or of a newspaper (e.g. *Il Corriere della Sera*).

Sense assignments combined together with additional lexico-semantic information make the ISST annotated corpus more than a mere list of instantiations of the senses attested in the reference lexical resource. This annotation strategy makes the annotated corpus a repository of interesting lexico-semantic information, especially concerning lexico-semantic facts which are excluded – either programmatically or just by chance – from the reference lexical resource.

Let us consider the case of non-lexicalised uses. Consider the following contexts, where the target word – marked in bold – is used metaphorically:

(7) *La nuova* ***arma*** *di vendetta è l'indifferenza*
'the new weapon of revenge is indifference'
(8) *Gli argentini ricominciano a mancare* ***appuntamenti*** *con la storia*
'Argentinians start to miss appointments with the history again'

The metaphoric use of target words is specified through a specific tag (FIGURATO=metaf). As to sense assignment, *arma* in (7) is assigned the appropriate figurative sense (IWN sense 2); by contrast, *appuntamenti* in (8), representing an instance of non-lexicalised metaphor, is linked to the literal sense. Through the interaction between sense and feature information lexicalised and non-lexicalised figurative uses can be singled out in ISST: namely, non-lexicalised metaphors are always linked to the literal sense. Similar observations hold in the case of semantic modification conveyed through evaluative suffixation: non-lexicalised cases are linked to the relevant sense of the stem word.

Feature assignment is also used to further specify sense distinctions which are left underspecified at the level of the reference lexical resource. Let us take the case of regular polysemies. Geographical proper nouns in the IWN lexicon are assigned a unique sense covering both the readings of 'group of people' and 'place'. Whenever possible, the annotator disambiguates between the two readings through the assignment of a specific feature as shown in the examples below:

(9) *La* ***Francia*** *si è sentita isolata*
'France felt isolated'
(10) *Perturbazione in arrivo dalla* ***Francia***
'Disturbance coming from France'

In both (9) and (10) *Francia* is assigned the underspecified IWN sense (sense 1); the two occurrences are then differentiated through the value assigned to the feature PROPER_NOUN which in (9) is assigned the 'group of people' value and in (10) the 'place' one.

It may also be the case that corpus annotation identifies multi-word expressions that are not recognised as such in the reference lexical resource, but behave as semantically complex units for the purposes of corpus annotation. This is the case of expressions such as *anni Sessanta* 'the sixties' which, being fully compositional and productive, do not appear as independent entries in the lexical resource. In this case, the annotator marks *anni Sessanta* as a USC with no specific sense assigned to it.

Corpus annotation can also shed light on the variability of multi-word expressions; in fact, multi-word expressions, going from compounds to support verb constructions and idiomatic expressions, when effectively used are prone to massive variation (Sinclair, 1996). To this end, semantically complex units, while being recorded in relation to a single lemma, are annotated as covering also modifiers which may optionally appear in the expression. Consider the example in (11) below where identified USC's correspond to the words marked in bold:

(11) ***tagliare le ali*** *a qn* 'to clip somebody's wings'
tagliare le ultime ali *a un paese* 'to clip the last wings of a country'

The grey areas spotted by these few examples in which corpus annotation either diverges from the lexical resource or further specifies it can be seen – in perspective – as the starting point for revisions and refinements of both the annotated corpus and the reference lexical resource. In this way, the annotated corpus proves to be a flexible resource, which is to some extent independent from the specific internal architecture of the lexicon selected as the reference resource. On the other hand, this type of corpus annotation can help to enrich or simply tune the reference lexical resource through the addition of missing entries (or simply variants) and senses.

7. THE MULTI-LEVEL LINGUISTIC ANNOTATION TOOL

The labour-intensive annotation task requires devoted tools to access efficiently the large amount of textual data and related annotations. From this perspective, both a data model and effective graphical representations are necessary. The annotation tool of ISST, GesTALt, features specific data models and graphical representations defined to comply with the different needs of the three levels of annotation. Building upon these data models, level-oriented subsystems are provided. The tool is also designed to ease the control of intra-level and inter-level coherence.

7.1 The linguistic data base

The ISST linguistic data model has been represented in the object-oriented formalism, which was selected for its flexibility. Defined data are directly used in the object-oriented database underlying GesTALt. For each level of annotation, a specific container was defined. The system (and its subsystems) manages a collection of documents, the corpus: this relation is represented in a class hierarchy. Moreover, the different level interpretations associated with sentences in the corpus are modelled respectively via the class of objects. To give the reader a flavor of the object modelling of linguistic structures, we present here the hierarchy describing constituency annotation (i.e. the class *synt_int*).

Constituency annotation is based on tree structures where both internal nodes and leaves are constituents (*const*). Leaves are called *basic constituents* (*b_const*), while internal nodes *complex constituents* (*c_const*). The resulting *synt_int sub-hierarchy* is depicted in Figure 11.1.

Complex constituents are collections of constituents, either basic or complex ones. A constituency-based syntactic interpretation is thus the complex constituent representing the interpretation of the whole sentence. This notion is modelled by the relation between the *c_const* class and the *synt_int* class in the hierarchy.

7.2 The visual representation of annotations

Managing the annotation of large sentences is cumbersome. Effective graphical representations are needed by both the annotator and the user to

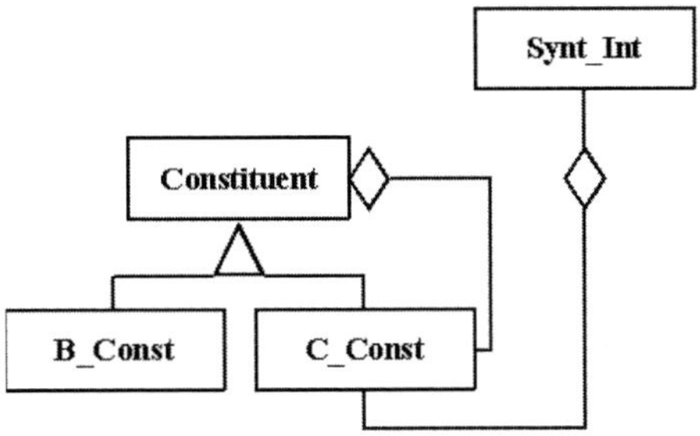

Figure 11.1. Syntactic interpretation

ease navigation in a complex information network. In what follows, the visual representation of syntactic and lexico-semantic annotations adopted within GesTALt is described.

Constituency-based Annotation. Constituency-based annotation is represented in terms of tree structures. A related manageable representation is thus needed within the annotation framework. Graphical tree representations can ease user interactions with the tree structures, i.e. retrieval and modification of encoded information.

Syntactic annotation of unrestricted texts involves long sentences (of 20 words or more). Sentence length (which determines the number of leaves) combined with the need for showing node tags may burden the tree diagram representation.

The visual representation defined for this annotation level is a *strip tree*, namely a tree described in strips (see Figure 11.2), which is similar to a bracketed representation but gives a hierarchical view of the structured information.

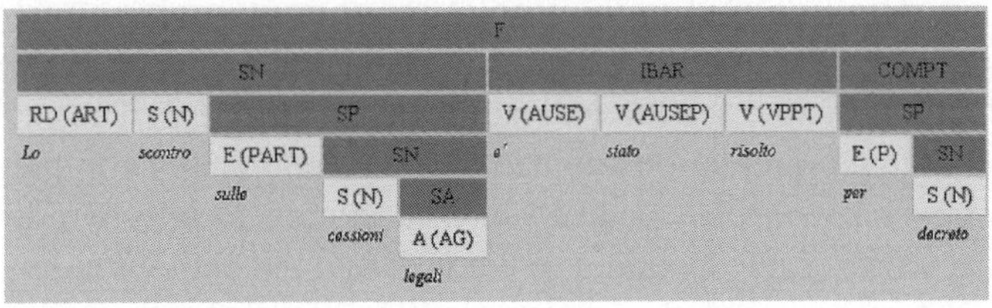

Figure 11.2. Strip tree

The annotation task at this level requires a convenient way of following the evolution of the tree structure. From this perspective, partial annotations have to be represented, and the transition from one partial annotation to another has to be supported.

Functional annotation. Dependency-based functional annotations are visualised in terms of graphs. Participants are represented as nodes and functional relations as arcs. Hence, the subsystem devoted to functional annotation has to manage mainly insertion/deletion of functional relations (i.e. arcs) connecting nodes. Given that ellipsis phenomena are accounted for at this annotation level (see section 5), another important functionality of this annotation module involves the insertion/deletion of nodes corresponding to elliptical material.

An example of functional annotation (sentence (2) above), as it appears in the graphical interface, is given in Figure 11.3:

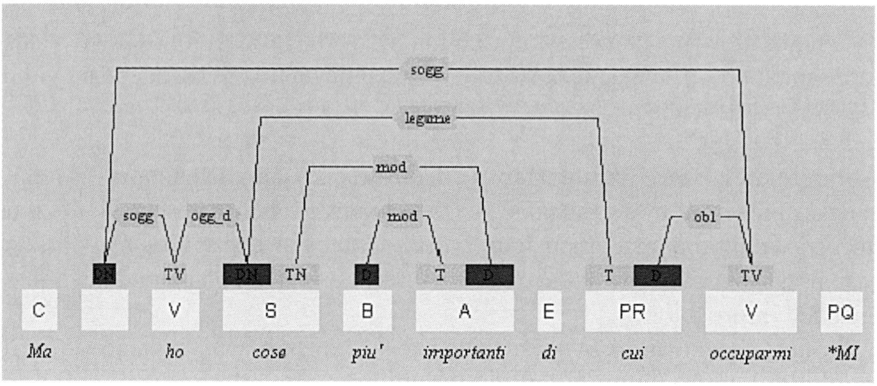

Figure 11.3. Planar graph

Functional relations are represented as directed labelled arcs linking words belonging to major lexical classes only; note that information about grammatical words is encoded in the feature structure describing each element of the relation. In the graphical interface, elliptical material is represented in terms of empty boxes: see the null subject in Figure 11.3. The example above also shows the representation adopted for morphologically complex forms: the word form *occuparmi* lit. 'occupy+me' is segmented into two different morphological words, corresponding to the verb and the clitic pronoun; annotation operates in fact on morphological words (see section 2).

Lexico-semantic annotation. The purpose of lexico-semantic annotation is to associate semantic tags to content words (namely, verbs, nouns and adjectives) and corresponding multi-word expressions. The graphical representation of lexico-semantic annotation is depicted in Figure 11.4.

Figure 11.4. The visual representation of lexico-semantic annotation

This figure shows a semantically tagged sentence where different types of semantic units can be seen. Boxes labelled as USS represent semantic units corresponding to individual words; the USC box marks the identified semantically complex unit, corresponding to the compound noun *cartone animato* 'cartoon', and the UST box identifies a semantic unit of type title. In the case of semantically complex units, annotation – which is performed at one level only – involves sequences of words which are not necessarily contiguous. As for title units, annotation is carried out both at the level of the component words and of the title unit. Note that, for each identified semantic unit, annotation is represented in terms of a feature structure specifying the types of information described in section 6 above.

7.3 GesTALt architecture

The GesTALt annotation workbench is the resulting system, made up of a pool of cooperating subsystems. The system manages the linguistic database sketched in section 7.1 and produces its output in standard XML.

The system is a suite consisting of specific applications: SinTAS for constituency annotation; FunTAS for functional annotation; SemTAS for lexico-semantic annotation; and ValTAS for evaluation and correction of inter- and intra-level annotations.

FunTAS, SinTAS, and SemTAS are stand-alone applications. The synthesis of the three subsystems is achieved in ValTAS, which needs the capabilities spread throughout the subsystems. The technology adopted for the development (object-oriented design), in conjunction with an *ad hoc* architectural design, allows easy reuse of the functionalities developed for the subsystems in the global (i.e. ValTAS) system.

The overall GesTALt architecture is shown in Figure 11.5, where the components are represented as boxes, and the interactions as arrows.

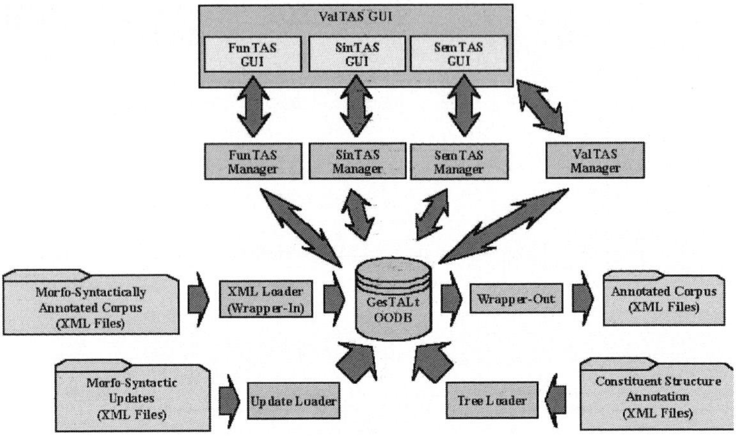

Figure 11.5. The visual representation of lexico-semantic annotation

The creating/translating flow of the object-oriented database (GestTALt-OODB) is shared by the subsystems. Information is downloaded from and uploaded to XML containers via specific wrappers (Wrapper-in and Wrapper-out). The GestTALt-OODB is the object-oriented database where the annotation of the different levels is stored respectively by FunTAS, SinTAS and SemTAS, together with the morphologically annotated corpus used as input by all annotation modules. Each subsystem, except for ValTAS which includes everything, is made up of specialised components. The graphical user interfaces based on the specific representations are depicted in the general architecture (FunTAS GUI, SinTAS GUI, SemTAS GUI and ValTAS GUI). Furthermore, the different ways of interacting with the database impose the design of special modules devoted to ad hoc navigation of the hierarchy (FunTAS Manager, SinTAS Manager, SemTAS Manager, and ValTAS Manager).

8. ISST EVALUATION

Information stored in ISST, particularly in the financial corpus, was used to improve an automatic Italian-English translation system, PeTra Word 2.0 ®, developed by Synthema and already on the market. The translation system is based on the Logical Grammars ("Slot Grammars") formalism (McCord 1980, 1989) and consists of three main components: the Italian language analyser (morphological analyser, monolingual dictionary and syntactic parser), the transfer component (bilingual dictionary and structural transfer rules) and the English generator. Improvements were mainly concerned with mono- and bi-lingual dictionaries, the Italian grammar and the transfer rules.

Dictionaries were revised on the basis of corpus evidence. In particular, dictionary coverage was enlarged by adding missing specialised entries and by improving already existing ones; associated translations were also added to the bilingual dictionary. A crucial aspect of this enrichment was concerned with multi-word expressions: multi-word expressions annotated in ISST at the different levels were evaluated and eventually added to PeTra's dictionaries according to the system constraints, in terms of either individual entries or particular constructions associated with component words. This addition was essential for the analysis of multi-word adverbs or prepositions which could not be parsed otherwise (such as *al di là di*) and for the recognition of compound words which cannot be literally translated (such as *codice fiscale* 'taxpayer's code number'). ISST lexico-semantic annotation was also used to revise and improve the structure of the hierarchical semantic dictionary used e.g. for lexical transfer disambiguation.

Let us turn now to improvements at the level of analysis and transfer rules. Before the tuning of the system with ISST, the grammar already had a good coverage (i.e. 88% on unrestricted texts). In spite of this fact, there were syntactic constructions attested in the ISST corpus which were analysed incompletely or incorrectly: this also follows from the fact that the subcorpus selected for evaluation is a specialised one, containing syntactic structures not currently used in standard Italian. ISST was first examined to check grammar coverage: accessing ISST on the basis of functional relations which correspond to the slots, it was possible to study the features associated with them and their constituency-based representation. In this way, the main features of an uncovered syntactic structure were identified and included both in the grammar rules and at the level of syntactic transfer.

The adopted evaluation methodology can be summarised as follows: identification of a thematically homogeneous subcorpus; translation of the subcorpus before and after tuning; classification of translated sentences into correct translation, inaccurate translation (requiring minor revisions), wrong translation, sentence which could not be translated; analysis and comparison of the results obtained before and after the system tuning. It came out that correctness of results increased by 17%. By comparing the classification results in the two translation runs (before and after tuning) it was observed that the number of correctly translated sentences increased by 45%, and the number of inaccurate translations by 40%. As a consequence, the number of wrong translations decreased by 38%, and of untranslated sentences by 79%. This overall improvement of translation results led to a significant reduction (about 18%) of the time required for the manual revision of the translations.

9. CONCLUSION

The final tested version of ISST is now available together with the annotation and browsing software specifically developed within the project. ISST consists of 89,941 word tokens annotated at the constituency structure level, 305,547 at the functional level and 81,236 content words at the lexico-semantic level (corresponding to 69,972 identified semantic units). For about one third of the ISST corpus (namely the financial part) there are four annotation layers available simultaneously. The annotated corpus is also available in XML format. An overall description of achieved results can be found in (Montemagni and Pazienza, 2001).

Completion of course refers to the goals set up within the SI-TAL project, since resources like ISST require continuous refinement and extension. In fact, treebanks and NLP resources by their very nature should be regarded as open-ended enterprises. Two possible extensions might be envisaged, both along the horizontal dimension and along the vertical one. As for the former, ISST coverage can obviously be extended by adding new annotated texts, as well as spoken data and domain-specific corpora. On the other hand, vertical extensions might involve the enrichment of information encoded for existing annotation levels or – most importantly – the addition of new annotation layers (e.g. annotation of anaphoric relations or of discourse structure).

Notes

1. SI-TAL was a joint enterprise working towards an integrated suite of tools and resources for Italian Natural Language Processing, funded by the Italian Ministry of Science and Research (MURST) and coordinated by the Consorzio Pisa Ricerche (CPR).

2. Different partners were in charge of different aspects of the project: ILC-CNR/CPR, Venice University/CVR and ITC-IRST were in charge of the annotation, "Tor Vergata" University/CERTIA of the design and construction of the annotation software and Synthema of the evaluation of the developed resource.

3. FAME originated as a revision of a de facto standard, i.e. the functional annotation scheme developed in the framework of the LE-2111 SPARKLE project (Carroll et al., 1996), a revision first carried out to comply better with the basic requirements of parsing evaluation (in the framework of the LE4-8340 ELSE project), and then to make the scheme suitable for annotation of unrestricted Italian texts.

References

Abeillé A., Clément L., Toussenel F., (2003). Building a treebank for French. This volume.

Alonge A., Calzolari N., Vossen P., Bloksma L., Castellon I., Martì T., Peters W., (1998). The Linguistic Design of the EuroWordNet Database. *Computers and the Humanities* 32, 2-3, p. 91-115.

Bates E., (1976). *Language and Context: Studies in the Acquisition of Pragmatics*, New York, Academic Press.

Brants T., Skut W., Uszkoreit H., (2003). Syntactic annotation of a German newspaper corpus. This volume.

Böhmová A., Hajic J., Hladká B., Panenová J., (2003). The Prague Dependency Treebank: a three-level annotation scenario. This volume.

Calzolari N., Corazzari O., (2000). Senseval/Romanseval: the framework for Italian. *Computers and the Humanities*, vol. 34, n. 1-2, p. 61-78.

Carroll J., Briscoe T., Calzolari N., Federici S., Montemagni S., Pirrelli V., Grefenstette G., Sanfilippo A., Carroll G., Rooth M., (1996). *Specification of Phrasal Parsing*, SPARKLE Deliverable 1.1.

Carroll J., Briscoe E., Sanfilippo A., (1998). Parser Evaluation: a Survey and a New Proposal. *Proceedings of LREC*, Granada, p. 447-454.

Caroll J., Minnen G., Briscoe T., (2003). Parser evaluation using a grammatical relation annotation scheme. This volume.

Chen K., Luo C., Gao Z., Chang M., Chen F., Chen C., (2003). Sinica Treebank. This volume.

Corazzari O., Calzolari N., Zampolli A., (2000). An Experiment of Lexical-Semantic Tagging of an Italian Corpus. *LREC-2000 Proceedings*, Athens.

Corazzari O., Monachini M., (1995). *ELSNET: Italian Corpus Sample*, ILC, Pisa.

CPR, ITC-IRST, Quinary, (2000). *ItalWordNet: Rete semantico-lessicale per l'italiano*. SI-TAL, Specifiche Tecniche di SI-TAL, Manuale Operativo, Capitolo 2.

Delmonte R., (1999). From Shallow Parsing to Functional Structure. *Atti del Workshop AI*IA* "Elaborazione del Linguaggio e Riconoscimento del Parlato", IRST Trento, p. 8-19.

Delmonte R., (2000). Shallow Parsing and Functional Structure in Italian Corpora. *LREC-2000 Proceedings*, Athens.

Goggi S., Biagini L., Picchi E., Bindi R., Rossi S., Marinelli R., (1997). *Italian Corpus Documentation*, LE-PAROLE WP2.11, ILC, Pisa.

Greenbaum S. (ed.), (1996). *English Worldwide: The International Corpus of English*, Oxford, Clarendon Press.

Karlsson F., Voutilainen A., Heikkila J., Anttila A. (eds.), (1995). *Constraint Grammar, a language-independent system for parsing unconstrained text*. Berlin and New York, Mouton de Gruyter.

Lenci A., Montemagni S., Pirrelli V., Soria C., (1999). FAME: a Functional Annotation Meta-scheme for Multimodal and Multi-lingual Parsing Evaluation. *Proceeding of the ACL99 Workshop on Computer-Mediated Language Assessment and Evaluation in NLP*, University of Maryland.

Lenci A., Montemagni S., Pirrelli V., Soria C., (2000). Where opposites meet. A Syntactic Meta-scheme for Corpus Annotation and Parsing Evaluation. *LREC-2000 Proceedings*, Athens.

Lin D., (1998). A dependency-based method for evaluating broad-coverage parsers. *Natural Language Engineering*, 4(2), p. 97-114.

Lin D., (2003). Dependency-based evaluation of MINIPAR. This volume.

Marcus M., Marcinkiewicz M.A., Santorini B., (1993). Building a Large Annotated Corpus of English: The Penn Treebank. *Computational Linguistics*, 19(2), p. 313-330.

McCord M.C., (1980). Slot Grammars. *Computational Linguistics*, vol. 6, p. 31-43.

McCord M.C., (1989). Design of LMT: A Prolog-based Machine Translation System. *Computational Linguistics*, vol 15, p. 33-52.

Monachini M., Calzolari N., (1996). *Synopsis and Comparison of Morphosyntactic Phenomena Encoded in Lexicons and Corpora. A Common Proposal and Application to European Languages*. EAGLES Recommendations. Pisa, ILC.

Montemagni S., Barsotti F., Battista M., Calzolari N., Corazzari O., Zampolli A., Fanciulli F., Massetani M., Raffaelli R., Basili R., Pazienza M.T., Saracino D., Zanzotto F., Mana N., Pianesi F., Delmonte R., (2000). The Italian Syntactic- Semantic Treebank: Architecture, Annotation, Tools and Evaluation. *Proceedings of the COLING Workshop on "Linguistically Interpreted Corpora (LINC-2000)*", Luxembourg, 6 August 2000, p. 18-27.

Montemagni S., and Pazienza M.T. (eds), (2001) *Atti del Workshop su "La Treebank sintattico-semantica dell'italiano in SI-TAL"*. 7° Congresso della Associazione Italiana per l'Intelligenza Artificiale (AI*IA 2001), Bari, 26 settembre 2001.

Moreno A., López A., Sánchez F., (1999). *Spanish Tree Bank: Specifications*, Version 4, Manuscript.

Moreno A., López A., Sánchez F., Grishman R., (2003). Developing a syntactically annotation scheme and tools for a Spanish treebank. This volume.

Picchi E., (1994). Pi-Tagger: A tagger and lemmatizer for Italian. *EURALEX-94 Proceedings*, Amsterdam.

Sampson G., (1995). *English for the Computer*, Oxford, Clarendon Press.

Sampson G., (2000). A proposal for improving the measurement of parse accuracy. *International Journal of Corpus Linguistics*, vol. 5, n. 1, p. 53-68.

Sampson G., (2003). Thoughts on two decades of drawing trees. This volume.

Sinclair J., (1996). The Empty Lexicon. *International Journal of Corpus Linguistics*, 1, p. 99-119.

SI-TAL, (2000). Specifiche Tecniche di SI-TAL. Manuale Operativo. ILC, Pisa.

Taylor A., et al. (2003). The Penn Treebank: an overview. This volume.

Wallis S., (2003). Completing parsed corpora from correction to evolution. This volume.

Appendix

1. Morpho-syntactic tagset

Tag	Description
S	Nouns
V	Verbs
A	Adjectives
P	Pronouns
T	Predeterminers
D	Determiners
R	Articles
B	Adverbs
E	Prepositions
C	Conjunctions
N	Numerals
I	Interjections
@@	Punctuation
SA	Abbreviations
X	Residuals

2. Syntactic constituents tagset

Constituent type	Description
F	Sentence
SN	noun phrase, including its complements and/or adjuncts
SA	adjectival phrase, including its complements and/or adjuncts
SP	prepositional phrase
SPD	prepositional phrase *di* 'of'
SPDA	prepositional phrase *da* 'by, from'
SAVV	adverbial phrase, including its complements and/or adjuncts
IBAR	verbal nucleus with finite tense and all adjoined elements like clitics, adverbs and negation
SV2	infinitival clause
SV3	participial clause
SV5	gerundive clause
FAC	sentential complement
FC	coordinate sentence (also ellipsed and gapped)
FS	subordinate sentence
FINT	+wh interrogative sentence
FP	punctuation marked, parenthetical or appositional sentence
F2	relative clause

Constituent type	Description
CP	dislocated or fronted sentential adjuncts
COORD	coordination with coordinating conjunction as head
COMPT	transitive/passive/ergative/reflexive complement
COMPIN	intransitive/unaccusative complement
COMPC	copulative/predicative complement

3. Hierarchy of dependency relations

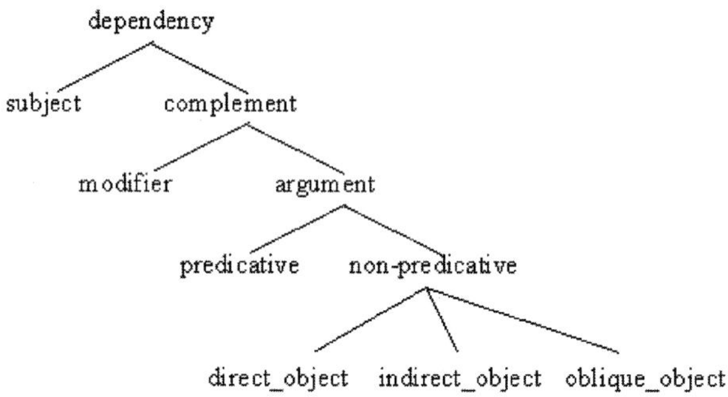

Chapter 12

AUTOMATED CREATION OF A MEDIEVAL PORTUGUESE PARTIAL TREEBANK

Vitor Rocio, Mário Amado Alves, J. Gabriel Lopes
CENTRIA, Departamento de Informática, Faculdade de Ciências e Tecnologia
Universidade Nova de Lisboa, Portugal

Maria Francisca Xavier, Graça Vicente
Faculdade de Ciências Sociais e Humanas
Universidade Nova de Lisboa, Portugal

Abstract The growing trend towards corpus-based linguistics has led researchers to manually annotate large quantities of text. The human effort involved in this task is often enormous, and requires highly specialised linguistically trained manpower. According to our point of view, another approach should be followed, using this highly trained manpower in other activities, more rewarding and creative, in a constructive dialogue among the various kinds of expertise needed for overcoming our ignorance about languages. As an experiment, we used tools and linguistic resources previously built for Contemporary Portuguese for partially automating the process of partial annotation of a Medieval Portuguese corpus. In this paper, we describe the tools used (POS tagger, lexical analyser and partial parser) and demonstrate that the similarities between a language at two different time periods is sufficient for bootstrapping and acquiring lexical knowledge from the partially parsed, automatically annotated corpus.

Keywords: Automatic Corpus Annotation, Tool Reuse, Lexical Analysis, Partial Parsing, Lexicon Extraction

1. INTRODUCTION

Syntactic annotation of electronically available corpora has been, in recent years, a major task in the linguistics and computational linguistics communities. For linguists, treebanks, along with appropriate search tools, are useful for studying various language phenomena. Computational linguists use tree-

A. Abeillé (ed.), Treebanks: Building and Using Parsed Corpora, 211–227.

banks for automatically learning lexicons and grammars and training statistically based tools.

The manual creation of treebanks is a labour-intensive task, even with the help of computational tools. In this paper, we adopt another approach: using robust tools and resources developed for a similar language for partially annotating the corpus.

In our particular case, we were interested in the syntactic annotation of 12th and 13th century Medieval Portuguese (MP) texts. There was, however, a great deficit of language-specific computational resources available for the task. Namely, no computational grammar existed, and only a very small lexicon with words belonging to closed syntactic categories had been prepared. So we took the innovative stance of applying to MP existing resources and tools built for Contemporary Portuguese (CP), namely a wide- coverage grammar, a (language independent) POS tagger generator, a lexical analyser and a partial parser.

MP and CP differ mainly in their lexicons, especially in word spelling: MP takes more liberties in spelling, with many words having two, three or more different spellings. MP also uses outdated grammatical constructions such as subject-object-verb word order (in CP the canonical order is subject- verb-object).

This cross-language reuse strategy was possible thanks to our tools' robustness (Rocio and Lopes, 1999a; Rocio and Lopes, 1999b; Rocio et al., 2000). In fact, when first analysing CP, we were faced with lexicon incompleteness, spelling errors, wrong POS-tagging and other problems that prevented us from obtaining full parses for the corpus sentences. Nevertheless, a lot of useful information about the causes of full parsing failure was automatically gathered from the partial parses obtained. Our goal is to integrate a set of fault finders in a multi-agent architecture to automatically detect and correct faults leading to partial parsing (Balsa 1998; Balsa and Lopes, 2000).

Whereas other authors (Marcus et al., 1993; Hobbs et al., 1997) use resources that are language-specific and even domain-specific (law, technical, news, etc.), our approach is domain independent and resistant to language variations (temporal and spatial). The system adapts itself to accommodate specific language features.

While other authors have re-used existing parsers for other languages (Moreno et. al., this volume; Böhmová et al., this volume), none has gone, as far as we know, to the extent of using the same grammar.

2. THE PARSED CORPUS OF MEDIEVAL PORTUGUESE TEXTS

The Partial Parsed Corpus of Medieval Portuguese is a fraction of the Computerised Corpus of Medieval Portuguese the CIPM , which has about three million words. The CIPM includes Late Latin texts from the 9th to the 12th century and Portuguese texts from the 12th to the 16th century[1].

The electronic partial syntactic analysis described here was done on a POS tagged corpus of Old Portuguese non-literary texts amounting to 78,037 words. The corpus used in this experiment includes the following texts: *Notícia d'Auer*, one text from the 12th century, and several texts from the 13th century: *Notícia de Torto*; *Testamento de D. Afonso II*; *Chancelaria de D. Afonso III*; *Tempos dos Preitos*; several 13th century texts published in *História do Galego-Português* and in the Appendix of *Clíticos na História do Português.*

This corpus corresponds to a group of the oldest Portuguese texts in prose known so far. They are technical documents, namely wills, donations and laws, considered to be of a particular interest for studies in historical linguistics, history and culture.

The first task consisting of POS tagging these texts was not a simple one. Medieval Portuguese texts are not orthographically normalised. They have many editorial annotations and their capital letters and punctuation, when present, do not always correspond to the contemporary system, which makes them confusing for the purposes of the current research.

As far as the graphic variants are concerned, a word may have several spellings in just one text. For instance, in the small sample transcribed and translated below, the noun "convent" and the preposition "to" have two forms each: "conuẽto/conuento" and "a/ad".

Nevertheless, the necessary preparation of the Medieval corpora did not involve any kind of graphic normalisation before being tagged and parsed. However, some conversions were carried out on medieval corpora with textual annotations by an automatic system in order to obtain a text format compatible with the tagger and the parser (which runs on tagged corpora). The details on the (semi-automatic) preparation of the corpus are given in section 3.

For the sake of illustration, the first paragraph of one text in the corpus is transcribed together with its literal translation:

<E HGP1; D 1262; GCorunha; T Nendos1>

Inno nome de D(eu)s, am(en). Conoszuda cousa segia a tod(os) aq(ue)lles

(In the name of God, Amen. Known thing be to all those)

q(ue) este scripto uirẽ y oyrẽ commo eu Aras Diaz, filo de Diago Láá,

(who this writing see and hear as I Aras Diaz, son of Diago Láá,)

por mĩ & por miña uoz & eu Marina Rod(r)iguit, fila de Ma(ri)na Diaz

(by me and by my voice and I Marina Rod(r)iguit, daugther of Ma(ri)na Diaz)

q(ue) foy da Regueyra, por nos & por nossas uozes, a uos, ffrey Pááyo,

(who was from Regueyra, by us and by our voices, to you, Friar Pááyo,)

vestiaro de Subrado ĩ uoz & ĩ nome de Don Johan Perez, abbade de

(responsible for the wardrobe of Subrado, in voice and in name of Don Johan Perez, abbot of)

```
Subrado, & du conuẽto desse meesmo lugar, damos & offeremos au dito
```
(Subrado, & of the convent of that same place, (we) give and donate to the mentioned)
```
abbade & conuento & a Deus & ad Santa Maria i& ad suas uirtudes & áás
```
(abbot & convent & to God & to Saint Mary & to her virtues & to the)
```
outras que sam dus outros santos & santas eno subredito moesteyro quanta
```
(other ones that belong to the other male and female saints in the mentioned monastery all the)
```
herdade & uoz & iuyr & possissom & sinurio nos auemos & á áuer
```
(heritage & voice and rights & possession & ownership we have and receive)
```
devemos ena igrigia de Santa Maria de Chãtada & som duas septimas de
```
(must in the church of Santa Maria de Chãtada & (they) are two seventh of)
```
huna noa.
```
(one nineth.)

The analysis of this very long and complex sentence shows, crucially, four situations of non-basic word order:

1 The sentence "commo [...] huna noa" is the subject of the matrix clause. It is an extraposed constituent with 119 words, which is basically generated as the subject of the small clause selected by the copular verb "segia" (be).

2 The predicate phrase – "Conoszuda cousa" (Known thing) – is on the left of the copular verb, instead of being on its right, as it would be the case in CP. The MP word order should be associated with the complement-verb order, which is also characteristic of MP and is non-existent in CP.

3 In the predicate expression, there is also a modification of the basic word order: the copular verb – "segia" – occurs between the two complements of the predicate head "conoszuda": "Conoszuda cousa segia a todos" (Known thing be to all).

4 In the relative clause "que este scripto uire y oyre " (who this writing see and hear), the direct object "este scripto" is on the left of the verbal sequence, instantiating the order subject-object-verb, which does not exist in CP.

The basic word order of the above complex sentence (the order in which the constituents – or empty categories forming chains with them – are semantically interpreted) would then be the following: "[ ] segia [ ] conoszuda cousa a todos aquelles (...) commo (...)". This is, obviously, a very difficult sentence to be analysed by an electronic tool.

The main goal of the project for the creation of a Parsed Corpus of Medieval Portuguese is in fact twofold. One important issue is to build a Treebank of Medieval Portuguese. This will enable linguists to access syntactically annotated

Portuguese historic data, in a more efficient and accurate manner. It will also facilitate the comparison of data from other Treebanks, which will contribute to obtaining a deeper knowledge of variation and change cross-linguistically. The other also important issue is, naturally, the advancement of research in computational linguistics concerning the development of the electronic tools described in the remaining sections of this text.

3. TOOLS AND COMPUTATIONAL RESOURCES

The method used to analyse the MP corpus is basically the same one used to analyse the CP corpus, with the difference that we took into account the lack of lexicon information for MP. So, we rely on the use of a lexical analyser that overcomes many of the lexicon limitations. We describe in detail the lexical analyser in subsection 3.2 and the partial parser in subsection 3.3. Part-of-speech tagging, described in subsection 3.1, is applied before lexical and syntactic analysis.

3.1 Tokenisation and POS tagging

Manually tagged samples of a minimum of 10,000 words for each text had to be prepared for training a neural-network based part-of-speech tagger and for the automatic extraction of the first dictionaries (Marques and Lopes, 1996; Marques, 2000). The tagger then attributed a set of 24 part of speech tags to the words of the whole corpus (plus 4 tags for punctuation) – see Table 12.1 –, enlarging the dictionary automatically. Mistagged words resulting from the automatic classification of the corpus were manually corrected and inserted in the dictionary. Unknown words could also be inserted in the dictionary. Contractions were also manually analysed - for instance, [[Inno]] and [[da]] - were expanded as, respectively, em_P = o_AD and de_P = a_AD[2].

A small excerpt (not a full sentence) of the POS tagged corpus can be seen below:

Conuzuda_VPP cousa_NC seya_V a_P todos_PI como_QU eu_PES Pedro _NP Paez_NP d*_P Arregeyro_NP por_P m$\tilde{j}$_PES &_C por_P todos_PI meus_POS fillos_NC &_C por_P toda_PI mina_POS uoz_N de_P bõ_A corazũ_NC &_C de_P boa_A uóóntade_NC dou_V &_C firmemẽte_ADV outorgo_V por_P min*_POS alma_NC ...

*(Known thing be to all as I Pedro Paez d*Arregeyro by me and by all my children and by my voice of good heart and of good will (I) give and firmly grant by my soul...)*

The tasks of POS tagging the training corpora followed by the manual correction of the tagged corpus required people well prepared to do linguistic

Table 12.1. Part-of-speech tags

Tag	Meaning
A	adjective
AD	definite article
ADV	adverb
AI	indefinite article
C	conjunction
CARD	cardinal number
CARDR	roman cardinal number
I	interjection
N	noun
NC	common noun
NP	proper name
ORD	ordinal number
P	preposition
PCL	clitic personal pronoun
PD	demonstrative pronoun
PES	personal pronoun
PI	indefinite pronoun
POS	possessive pronoun
PR	relative pronoun
V	verb
VINF	infinitive verb
VN	gerundive verb
VPP	past participle verb
QU	qu-word (corresponding to wh-word in English
PTO	period
VIRG	comma
DPTO	colon
SS	no meaning (used for irrelevant punctuation)

analysis and with a reasonable knowledge of Old Portuguese. In fact, the texts of the 13th century of CIPM present many difficulties: ambiguities, discontinuities, multi-word units, extremely long sentences with multiple embeddings, successive coordinations and appositions, as well as sentences generated by a grammatical system which handles null subjects and objects, moved constituents, clitics (proclitics, enclitics and mesoclitics), different constituent orders, namely SVO and SOV, finiteV+non-finiteV and non-finiteV+finiteV, long distance clitic climbing and interpolations between the clitic and the verb of all sorts of constituents (Fiéis, 2000).

3.2 Lexical analysis

The bootstrapping of lexical knowledge was provided by a small morphocentric lexical knowledge-base (LKB) containing the classes of grammatical word forms (GWF), inflexional affixes and inflexion rules described in Table 12.2.

Table 12.2. Classes in the LKB

class		extension (number of entries)	
1. articles		31	GWFs
2. pronouns		153	GWFs
3. irregular verb forms		47	GWFs
4. verb inflexion suffixes		597	suffixes
5. general noun inflexion rule		4	suffixes
	total:	832	forms

Classes 1-4 were acquired, using standard tools, and set in tables and lists in a printing-oriented proprietary format (Microsoft Word), but with HTML-exportation capability. The printed form helped humans perform direct verification of the data. Figure 12.1 shows an excerpt of one of the source tables for verb inflexion. In the data cells, an hyphen (-) indicates a suffix, and a hash sign (#) denotes the backward deletion of one character (the other non- letter characters have no special meaning). Of course the lexical analyser implements this semantics.

The exported HTML form of these source tables and lists was used to transfer them into the database module of the lexical analyser. Some normalisation also took place in this phase, e.g. field Pax with values (Figure 12.1) was mapped onto normalised Person and Number values (Table 12.3).

Class 5 of the LKB represents the two alternations -o/a, -0/s (for masculine/feminine, singular/plural respectively), well known for Contemporary Portuguese, and also seemingly pervasive in Medieval Portuguese. This class of the LKB was directly encoded in the program module of the lexical analyser

Indicative	Pax	1st Conjugation (*verbs in –ar*)	2nd Conjugation (*verbs in –er*)	3rd Conjugation (*verbs in –ir*)
Present	1	-##o -##o´ -##u -##/o/	-##o -##o´	-##o
	2	-#s	-#s	-##es
	3	-#	-#	-##e
	4	-#mos -#m(os) -#moss -#m(us) -#/mos/ -#mus	-#m(os) -#mos -#mus -#m(us)	-#mos -#m(os)
	5	-#des	-#des -#dess -#ejs	-#des
	6	-#~ -#m -#n -#(m)	-#m -#~ -#n -#[n]	-##en -##e~ -##em

Figure 12.1. Source table excerpt: verb inflexion suffixes

(in a stunning example of hacking taking its rightful place in language engineering).

Table 12.3 describes the complete set of features of lexical analysis utilised, after normalisation. The microstructure, or schema, of each class in the LKB is essentially a proper subset of this set of features, or fields.

To simplify formalisation, implementation, integration and explanation of the lexical analyser, each lexical knowledge item (LKI) is viewed as a tuple of all the features in Table 12.3, with the domain of every feature extended with special values for not applicable and no value. In the interest of clarity, in this paper we use a blank space for these special values.

The lexical analyser applies the knowledge contained in the LKB to each input condition, to produce a set of solutions, as exemplified in Figure 12.2 (Tem values PRI and PPI represent *Present Indicative* and *Past Participle Indicative* respectively).

The input to the lexical analyser is the output from the POS-tagger, namely the set of information {Ort, Tag} associated with each token in the corpus. This LKI carries the only POS disambiguation information in the system, so it is ranked high in the set of solutions. If it is compatible with the knowledge in

Table 12.3. Features of lexical analysis

Symbol	Name	Description
Ort	(Ortho)graphic form	character string in ISO Latin-1 alphabet
Cat	Part-Of-Speech	see table 1
Tem	Tense	PRI=present indicative, PPI=past participle indicative,...
Pes	Person	1,2,3=1st,2nd,3rd person
Num	Number	s=singular, p=plural
Gen	Gender	m=masculine, f=feminine
Gra	Degree	inflexional degree of adjectives and adverbs[3]
Can	Canonical form	infinitive for verbs, singular masculine for others
Tag	Tag	POS-tag passed from the POS-tagger; same domain as Cat
Cnd	Condition	+/- = tuple (is / is not) the input condition
Lex	Lexical	+/- = tuple (is / is not) a lexical entry in the LKB
Reg	Regular	+/- = tuple (is / is not) from a rule in the LKB
Val	Value	ranking value in a group of solutions; an integer value

	Ort	Cat	Tem	Pes	Num	Gen	Gra	Can	Ptc	Sub	Tag	Cnd	Lex	Reg	Val
input	Ego										PES				
output	Ego	PES		1	s				eu		PES		+		110
	Ego	PES									PES	+			100
	Ego	V	PRI	1	s			Eger			PES			+	1
	Ego	V	PRI	1	s			Egir			PES			+	1
	Ego	V	PPI	3	s	m		Egar			PES			+	1

Figure 12.2. Example lexical analysis

the LKB, it is enriched with that knowledge; otherwise, alternate solutions are produced.

The output from the lexical analyser is the input to the syntactic analyser. Because the latter is a logic program, a set of solutions as input suits it well: the solutions are sequenced by descending order of Val, and we leave backtracking to do its job.

The relative ranking of the solutions is a delicate issue. After some thought and experimentation we arrived at the ranking criteria in Table 12.4, which could probably still be improved. The values are added together to yield the rank (Val) of each solution, so the absolute numbers are not important: it only matters that they relate to each other by some order of magnitude.

Table 12.4. Ranking criteria for solutions of lexical analysis

condition	**value**
+Cnd and intractable Tag (i.e. Tag not a Cat in the LKB)	1000
Cat=Tag, i.e. the solution respects the POS-tagger choice	100
+Lex	10
-Lex but +Reg, i.e. Ort is derivable by a rule in the LKB	1

From a more abstract point of view, the LKB defines a space of LKIs. This definition is done intensionally for the most part, because the main knowledge consists of suffixes and rules. It is the job of the lexical analyser to search this space for the LKIs that unify with the input condition. And that it does efficiently and elegantly. For example, the analyser handles the out of vocabulary (OOV) problem by applying affixation rules or, failing that, resorting to the POS-tagger information.

3.3 Syntactic analysis

A cascaded partial parser (Rocio & Lopes, 1999; Rocio et al., 2000) was used to partially annotate the MP corpus. The same parser had been used for CP, plus a lexicon with circa 1,000,000 entries and a DCG grammar with 250 compactly written rules. This system is robust enough to resist errors in the input text, wrong or missing lexical information and wrong or missing POS tagging.

For our first experiment with MP, we simply replaced the CP lexicon with the lexical analyser described in the previous section. The system worked normally, producing partial parses for the input text, even if they were more partial than for CP. In section 3, we will characterise the output of the parser, and point out its strengths and weaknesses.

Despite only having 250 rules, the grammar used has a large coverage due to its high degree of factorisation. For instance, to cope with the large variety of subcategorisation frames, we built a specific language that is used to describe the argument syntax of a particular word (noun, verb or adjective). Pointers to these descriptions are stored in the lexicon and the parser interprets them to determine which constituents are the word's arguments. Table 12.5 shows some of these descriptions, for intransitive verbs (0), verbs with only one nominal complement (1), verbs with both nominal complement and one prepositional complement (2), and verbs with either a noun phrase or a subordinate clause as complement (3).

Table 12.5. Subcategorization class descriptions

Identifier	**Description**
0	[]
1	or ([np])
2	and ([np, pp])
3	or ([np, sub_c])

The parser itself is a cascade with 3 levels, the first being a finite state transducer that identifies very specific structures: proper names, dates and compound prepositions and adverbials. The application of this transducer to the example tagged text shown in the previous section produces an NP (proper name) tag for the sequence (*Pedro Paez d* Arregeyro*).

The second parsing level uses the DCG grammar mentioned above. This level identifies main constituents: noun phrases, verb phrases, prepositional phrases, adjective phrases and adverbial phrases, in the usual CP word order. Finally, the third level identifies constituents involving constituent movement: relative clauses, interrogative clauses, verb nuclei with clitic pronouns, and topicalised verbs and prepositional phrases. Both the second and the third levels build a full sentence analysis where possible.

The set of possible syntactic tags (Table 12.6) is small since we encode most of the information in the arguments of first-order logic terms, following the factorisation philosophy used in the grammar. The tags shown in table 4 are the term functors. For a sample of the information encoded in the arguments see the output text in the next section.

Partial parsing is achieved by storing partial results in a table or chart while parsing. Our level 2 and 3 parsers were implemented using the DyALog logic program compiler (de la Clergerie et Lang, 1994; Pardo et al. 1999), which incorporates a very efficient tabulation method. The parser's speed is, on average, 250 words per second. This means that we can partially parse one million words in slightly more than one hour.

Another important feature of the parsing machinery is the way it views parsing as a deduction task (cf. Shieber et al., 1995; Rocio and Lopes, 1998). This allows us to use it as an abduction/diagnosis mechanism in order to extract in-

Table 12.6. Syntactic categories

Category	Meaning
s	complete sentence
pp	prepositional phrase
np	noun phrase
rel_np	relative noun phrase
number	number
verb	verb phrase nucleus
vp	verb phrase
adj_p	adjective phrase
adv_p	adverbial phrase
conj	conjunction

formation from partial parses given hypothetical initial premises. For instance, we can introduce alternative hypotheses for verb subcategorisation and, after the parsing has finished, pick the one that leads to the best solution (a full or less partial parse, in this case).

This is an extremely useful technique that has been applied to CP in order to extract subcategorisation frames for verbs and nouns, to correct wrong POS tagging and to identify multi-word units. In MP, it was used to extract gender and number information for nouns and adjectives, as reported in the following section.

4. EVALUATION

The combination of both methods described in the previous section was applied to a subset of the MP corpus with 15,716 words.

An example of the partial parsed output for the tagged input sample shown in section 3.1 can be seen below:

```
<Conuzuda cousa>
np(3+sin+fem,np(nucleus(det([]),adj_p([verb(past+part,'Conuzer')]),cousa),n_args([]))).
<seya>
vp(v(seyar,active,pres+_,indic,_,pos),[],v_args([arg(dir,[])]))
<a todos>
pp(a,np(_+plu+masc,[todos],[]))
<como>
conj(como,como,_,sub+_,_)
<eu>
np(1+sin+_,[eu],[])
```

```
<Pedro Paez d* Arregeyro>
np(3+sin+masc,np(name(det([]),['Pedro','Paez','d*','Arregeyro']),n_args([])))
<por mj̃>
pp(por,np(1+sin+_,['mj̃'],[]))
<&>
conj(&,&,_,coord+_,_)
<por todos meus fillos>
pp(por,np(3+plu+masc,np(nucleus(det([todos,meus]),[],fillos,[]),n_args([]))))
<&>
conj(&,&,_,coord+_,_)
<por toda mina uoz>
pp(por,np(3+sin+fem,np(nucleus(det([toda,mina]),[],uoz,[]),n_args([]))))
<de bõ corazũ>
pp(de,np(3+sin+masc,np(nucleus(det([]),adj_p('bõ'),'corazũ',[]),n_args([]))))
<&>
conj(&,&,_,coord+_,_)
<de boa uóóntade>
pp(de,np(3+sin+fem,np(nucleus(det([]),adj_p(boa),'uóóntade',[]),n_args([]))))
<dou>
vp(v(doar,active,pres+_,indic,_,pos),[],v_args([arg(dir,[])]))
<&>
conj(&,&,_,coord+_,_)
<firmemente outorgo>
vp(v(outorgar,active,pres+_,indic,_,pos),['firmemẽte'],v_args([arg(dir,[])]))
<por min* alma>
pp(por,np(3+sin+fem,np(nucleus(det(['min*']),[],alma,[]),n_args([]))))
```

The output is a sequence of "chunks" together with their respective syntactic tags, in the form of a logic term. Besides the syntactic category (which is the functor of the term), the tags encode also agreement information and the syntactic tree of the chunk.

The partial parsing solutions obtained were inspected in order to check for their correctness. The problems identified reveal attachment problems not decidable at the syntactic level, incompleteness of the lexicon and incorrect or insufficient POS tagging.

We tackled lexicon incompleteness by using the lexical analyser described in the previous section on tagged text. However, morphology alone is often not enough to define features such as noun/adjective gender and number or verb tense. For instance, nouns *uoz, corazũ* and *uóóntade* (in the example) are exceptions to the rule that states that masculine nouns end in o and feminine nouns end in –a.

By using the information in partial parses, we were able to extract gender and number information for 42% of the noun occurrences in the test corpus. As can be seen from the example output, gender and number information is easily obtained for *uoz, corazũ* and *uóóntade* from the agreement features of the phrases they occur in.

One of the problematic features of the corpus text is the ambiguity between apposition and coordination, which must be often decided at a super-syntactic level. Linked to this problem is the orthographic variety and ambiguity of the lexical items. To illustrate, an apposed noun phrase is separated from its main NP by a comma, or just a blank (e.g. *eu Pedro Paez d* Arregeyro*), while coordinated NPs are separated by a comma, an ampersand (&) or by a coordinative conjunction, which may have different orthographies (*e, y, i, j*). To add to the confusion, both appositions and coordinations may involve a sequence of several NPs, attached to each other in non-trivial ways.

Another problem is the large variety of word orders in MP: much more frequently than in CP, word orders such as subject-object-verb (derived from Latin) occur rather than the canonical order, subject-verb-object.

POS tagging errors also influence the output of the parser. For instance, mistagging the preposition “a” as the article “a” (feminine singular) will lead to an incorrect parse. The ambiguity of punctuation does not allow the parser to discriminate among its possible syntactic roles when using the same tag for the same punctuation symbol. Commas, for instance, as mentioned above, may indicate either a coordinated conjunction or an apposed NP.

Other attachment problems, such as PP-attachment or argument attachment that are subject to semantic/pragmatic or subcategorisation information also lead to partial parses, as can be seen in the example. These problems will be solved with the diagnosis system (Lopes et al. 1999) mentioned in the previous section. We are now starting to tackle these problems, but the very fact that we became aware of them justifies the work involved.

5. CONCLUSION

With the completion of the work reported in this paper, our computational knowledge of MP, notably its lexicon, has attained a high level. With the continued processing of the annotated corpus we expect that knowledge to advance further. Namely, the application of techniques for revising the grammar is now possible.

Other automatic language treatment tools are being developed that will increase our methods' accuracy and performance, besides giving rise to other kinds of annotations: a multi-word unit identifier (Ferreira da Silva et al., 1999) and a system that learns verb subcategorisation from POS tagged corpora (Marques et al., 1998; Marques, 2000).

The continued development of a multi-agent diagnosis architecture (Balsa, 1998; Balsa & Lopes, 2000; Rocio & Lopes, 1999a; Lopes et al., 1999) is allowing us to extract and cross-validate several kinds of information, such as subcategorisation frames (not only for verbs), POS tagging errors and multi-word units.

Future work will also include the evaluation of our hypothesis (cross- language resource reusability) by applying the system to other languages similar to Portuguese, obvious candidates being those of the Romance family.

Notes

1. The building up of CIPM started in 1993. Anthony Kroch and Anne Taylor were then starting to build the Penn Treebank for Middle English with texts from the Helsinki Corpus. The CIPM has been developed with the coordination of M.F. Xavier of Centro de Linguística da Universidade Nova de Lisboa (CLUNL) and has been financially supported by FCT-MCT. The CIPM will be available online by the end of the year 2000.

2. The POS tagged corpus is also useful for the project of the Dictionary of Medieval Portuguese, whose first publication Dicionário de Verbos Portugueses do Século 13 was organised and edited by M.F. Xavier, G. Vicente and M.L. Crispim (Xavier et al., 1999b). This dictionary has also been funded by FCT-MCT and will also be available online soon.

3. Not used in any of the bootstrapping classes; but included here only for completion of the inflexional morphology features subset {Tem,Pes,Num,Gen,Gra}

References of texts in CPIM parsed corpus

NT – *Notícia de Torto* (ca. 1214) from CINTRA, L. F. Lindley (1990). *Boletim de Filologia*, vol. XXXI, pp. 37-41 (texto cr-tico).

TL, TT – *Testamento de D. Afonso II* (1214) from CASTRO, Ivo (1991). *Curso de História da L-ngua Portuguesa*, Lisboa, Universidade Aberta, pp. 197-202.

CA – *Chancelaria de D. Afonso III* (1255) from DUARTE, Luiz F.: (1986) *Os Documentos em Português da Chancelaria de D. Afonso III (Edição)*, Dissertação de Mestrado, F.L.U.L. pp.68-295.

TP – *Tempos dos Preitos* from FERREIRA, J. Azevedo (ed.) (1986). *Tempos dos Preitos. Edição e estudo linguístico dos "Tempos dos Preitos"* in Roudil, Jean *Summa de los Neuve Tiempos de los pleitos. Édition et étude d'une variation sur un thème*, Paris, Klincksieck, pp. 151-169.

HGP – 13th century texts (1262-1300) from MAIA, Clarinda de Azevedo (1986). *História do Galego-Português*, Coimbra, INIC. pp.19-295.

CHP – 12th and 13th century texts (nd, 1243-1300) from MARTINS, Ana Maria (1994). Clíticos na História do Português. Apêndice Documental. PhD thesis, Universidade de Lisboa.

References

Balsa, J. (1998). A hierarchical Multi-agent system for Natural Language Diagnosis. *Proceedings of the 13th European Conference on Artificial Intelligence*. Henri Prade, ed.. John Willey & Sons, 1998.

Balsa, J.; Lopes, J. G. (2000). A Distributed Approach for a robust and evolving NLP system. *Proceedings of the NLP 2000 Conference*, Patras, Greece, D. N Christodoulakis, ed.

Böhmová, Alena et al. (2003). The Prague Dependency Treebank: a three-level annotation scenario. *This volume*.

de la Clergerie, Eric; Lang, Bernard (1994). LPDA: Another Look at tabulation in logic programming. *Proceedings of the International Conference on Logic Programming*, Prague.

Ferreira da Silva, Joaquim; Lopes, J. Gabriel; Xavier, M.Francisca; Vicente, Graça (1999). Relevant Expressions in Language Corpora. *Actes de l'atelier* "Corpus et Traitement Automatique des Langues: Pour une réflexion méthodologique" (TALN'99), Cargèse, Corse (France). Anne Condamines, Cécile Fabre and Marie-Paule Péry-Woodley, eds. p. 86–94.

Fiéis, M. Alexandra (2000). Interpolation in Medieval Portuguese. *Proceedings of Lexicon & Grammar* International Congress of Linguistics, Lugo.

Hobbs, Jerry R. et al. (1997). FASTUS: A cascaded finite-state transducer for extracting information from natural-language text. In *Finite-State Language Processing*, E. Roche and Y. Schabes, ed., MIT Press, pp. 383-406.

Lopes, J. Gabriel; Rocio, Vitor; Balsa, Joco (1999). Overcoming lexical information incompleteness, *Proceedings of the First Portuguese Workshop* on Computational Linguistics, Maria Antónia Mota, ed., Associação Portuguesa de Linguística.

Marcus, Mitchell P.; Santorini, Beatrice; Marcinkiewicz, Mary Ann (1993). Building a large annotated corpus of English: The Penn Treebank, *Proceedings of the 31st Annual Meeting of the Association of Computational Linguistics* (ACL'93).

Marques, Nuno; Lopes, J. Gabriel (1996). Using Neural Nets for Portuguese Part-of-Speech Tagging. *Proceedings of the 5th International Conference on the Cognitive Science of Natural Language Processing*. Dublin City University.

Marques, Nuno; Lopes J. Gabriel; Coelho, Carlos A. (1998). Learning Verbal Transitivity using LogLinear Models, *Proceedings of the Tenth European Conference on Machine Learning* (ECML-98), Lecture Notes in Artificial Intelligence, Springer Verlag.

Marques, Nuno (2000). Uma metodologia para a modelação estatística da subcategorização verbal. PhD thesis. Faculdade de Ciências e Tecnologia, Universidade Nova de Lisboa, 2000.

Moreno, A., López, S., et Sánchez F., (2003). Developing a syntactic annotation scheme and tools for a Spanish treebank. This volume.

Pardo, M. A.; Souto; D.C.; Vilares, M.; de la Clergerie; E. (1999). Tabular Algorithms for TAG Parsing. *Proceedings of EACL'99.*

Rocio, Vitor; Lopes, J. Gabriel (1998). Partial parsing, deduction and tabling, Actes des premières Journées sur la Tabulation en Analyse Syntaxique et Déduction (*Proceedings of the Workshop on Tabulation in Parsing and Deduction*), Bernard Lang, ed., INRIA, Rocquencourt.

Rocio, Vitor; Lopes, J. Gabriel (1999a). An infra-structure for diagnosing causes for partially parsed natural language input, *Proceedings of the 6th International Symposium on Social Communication*, Santiago de Cuba, pp. 550-554, Editorial Oriente.

Rocio, Vitor; Lopes, J. Gabriel (1999b). Cascaded Syntactic Partial Analysis. *Proceedings of the First Portuguese Workshop on Computational Linguistics*, Maria Antónia Mota, ed. Associação Portuguesa de Linguística.

Rocio, Vitor; de la Clergerie, Eric; Lopes, J. Gabriel (2000). Tabulation for multi-purpose partial parsing. *Journal Grammars. To appear.*

Shieber, S.M.; Schabes, Y.; Pereira, F. (1995). Principles and Implementation of Deductive Parsing. *Journal of Logic Programming.*

Xavier, M.Francisca; Vicente, Graça; Crispim, M. de Lourdes. (1999). Dicionário de Verbos do Século 13, Lisboa, Centro de Linguística da Universidade Nova de Lisboa.

Treebanks for other languages

Chapter 13

SINICA TREEBANK

Design criteria, representational issues and implementation

Keh-Jiann Chen, Chi-Ching Luo, Ming-Chung Chang, Feng-Yi Chen, Chao-Jan Chen, Chu-Ren Huang

Academia Sinica, Taiwan

{kchen,airport,mjchung,apple,richard}@iis.sinica.edu.tw

hschuren@ccvax.sinica.edu.tw

Zhao-Ming Gao

National Taiwan University

zmgao@ncnu.edu.tw

Abstract This paper describes the design criteria and annotation guidelines of the Sinica Treebank. The three design criteria are: Maximal Resource Sharing, Minimal Structural Complexity, and Optimal Semantic Information. One of the important design decisions guided by these criteria is the encoding of thematic role information. We discuss the representational and methodological issues based on our design criteria.

Keywords: Annotation Guidelines, Chinese, Treebank, Thematic Roles.

1. INTRODUCTION

The Penn Treebank (Marcus et al. 1993) initiated a new paradigm in corpus-based research. It has enabled and motivated corpus and computational linguistic research based on information extractable from structurally annotated corpora. Recently, research has focused on the following two issues: first, when and how can a structurally annotated corpus of language X be built? Second, what information should or can be annotated? A good sample of issues in these two directions can be found in this volume.

A. Abeillé (ed.), Treebanks: Building and Using Parsed Corpora, 231–248.

The construction of the Sinica Treebank deals with both issues. First, it is one of the first structurally annotated corpora of Mandarin Chinese. In fact, the Sinica Treebank was simultaneously released with the Penn Chinese Treebank (Xia et al., 2000). Second, the Sinica Treebank annotation includes thematic role information in addition to syntactic categories. In this paper, we will discuss the design criteria and annotation guidelines of the Sinica Treebank. We will also discuss how some notoriously difficult structures can be dealt with based on these design criteria and annotation guidelines.

2. DESIGN CRITERIA

There are three important design criteria for the Sinica Treebank: Maximal Resource Sharing, Minimal Structural Complexity, and Optimal Semantic Information.

First, to achieve maximal resource sharing, the construction of the Sinica Treebank is bootstrapped from existing Chinese computational linguistic resources. The textual material is extracted from the tagged Sinica Corpus[1] (Chen et al. 1996). Thus, the tasks and issues involving tokenization/word segmentation and category assignment have been previously resolved. Moreover, the segmentation and tagging of the Sinica Corpus have undergone vigorous post-editing. Hence the precision of category-assignment is much higher than with automatically tagged corpora. In addition, since the same research team has been carrying out the tagging of the Sinica Corpus and the annotation of the Sinica Treebank, consistency of the interpretation of texts and tags is ensured. For structure-assignment, an automatic parser (Chen 1996) was applied before human post-editing.

Second, the criterion of Minimal Structural Complexity is proposed to ensure that the assigned structural information can be shared regardless of a user's theoretical presupposition. It is observed that theory-internal motivations often require abstract intermediate phrasal levels (such as in various versions of the X-bar theory). Other theories may also call for an abstract covert phrasal category (such as INFL in the GB theory for Chinese). In either case, although the phrasal categories are well-motivated within the theory, their significance cannot be maintained in the context of other theoretical frameworks. Since a primary goal of annotated corpora is to serve as the empirical base for linguistic investigations, it is desirable to annotate structural divisions that are the most commonly shared among theories. We concluded that the minimal basic level structures are the ones that are shared by all theories. Thus our annotation is designed to achieve the least amount of structural complexity. All abstract phrasal levels are eliminated and only canonical phrasal categories are marked.

Third, a critical issue involving the Treebank construction as well as theories of NLP is how much semantic information, if any, should be incorporated.

The original Penn Treebank took a fairly straightforward syntactic approach. A purely semantic approach, though tempting in terms of theoretical and practical considerations, has not been attempted yet. A third approach is to annotate partial semantic information, especially pertaining to argument relations. This is an approach shared by us and the Prague Dependency Treebank (e.g. Böhmová and Hajičova, this volume). In this approach, the thematic relation between a predicate and an argument is marked in addition to grammatical category. Note that the predicate-argument relation is usually grammatically instantiated and generally considered to be the semantic relation that interacts most closely with syntactic behavior. This allows optimal semantic information to be encoded without going far beyond the partially automatic process of argument identification.

3. REPRESENTATION OF LEXICO-GRAMMATICAL INFORMATION: ICG

The first crucial decision towards the actual implementation of the Treebank construction was the choice of a representational model. Based on our own design criteria, we were looking for a framework that would allow us to share maximal resources, annotate minimal levels without losing information, and provide optimal semantic information. In terms of formalisms, these criteria clearly recommend a lexicon-driven and information-based theory, such as HPSG (Pollard and Sag, 1994). A lexicon-driven grammar allows lexically encoded information to be directly merged with the structural representation. Hence it allows maximal resource-sharing between lexical and structural databases. It also allows lexical semantic information (if annotated) to be attached to the trees. Although not a theoretical necessity, lexicon-driven grammars also tend to have a flatter structure which ensures a more direct mapping of lexical information. On the other hand, an information-based theory is designed to facilitate maximal information sharing and reduce structural complexity. Such theories also usually allow semantic and syntactic descriptions to be manipulated uniformly (as information). Given the choices among the many lexicon-driven and information-based formalisms, the Sinica Treebank chose to adopt Information-based Case Grammar (ICG, Chen & Huang 1994, 1996, Chen 1996) because there exists a fully ICG-annotated lexicon with rich syntactic and semantic information for Mandarin Chinese. This was completed by the Chinese Knowledge Processing (CKIP) group over a period of 5 years (CKIP 1993 /1997, Chen and Huang 1996). By adopting ICG, we were able to access its rich lexical database when assigning tree structures and thematic information. Although a theoretically more commonly accepted framework, such as HPSG, is not adopted, we believe that the annotated information can be easily transferred and comparative studies will be possible.

ICG was developed to represent the complex constraint relations between words in Chinese. In addition to retaining immediate dominancy, linear precedence, and the feature-based representation of GPSG (Gazdar et al., 1985), the head-driven principle of HPSG (Pollard 1994), and the lexicalist approach of CUG (Uszkoreit 1987), ICG stipulates that each lexical entry contains both semantic and syntactic features, and also how these features may be used (Chen 1996). Thus, the ambiguities of syntactic structures can be resolved by semantic preference checking. For each phrasal head, the syntactic and semantic constraints of the phrase are expressed by formation rules and linear ordering rules for thematic roles, which are illustrated in example (1). The grammatical information is simplified for easy illustration.

(1) *jiao* "ask"

- Semantic:
  - meaning : "ask"
  - features:
  - arguments:
    - AGENT: feature:+HUMAN
    - GOAL(1): feature:+HUMAN
    - THEME:
      - feature:+EVENT
      - argument:AGENT(1)
  - adjuncts: time, location, manner
- Syntactic
  - class: $V_{NP,VP}$
  - constraints:
    - form:
      - time[{NP,DM,PP,ADV}, +time]
      - location[{PP,ADV}, +location]
      - manner [ADV,+manner]
    - BP: AGENT[NP] < * < GOAL[NP] < THEME[VP]
    - AP:
      - 1. {time, location} < *
      - 2. AGENT < manner < *

The above grammatical representation matches sentences such as (2a) by taking *jiao* 'ask' as the head verb. The matched tree structure is given as in (2b).

(2a) *Ta jiao Li-si jian qiu*
He ask Lisi pick ball.
"He asked Lisi to pick up the ball."

(2b) S(agent:NP(Head:Nhaa:*Ta* 'He') | Head:$V_{NP,VP}$:*jiao* 'ask' | goal:NP(Head:Nba: *Li-si*) | theme:VP(Head:VC2: *jian* 'pick' | goal:NP(Head:Nab:*qiu* 'ball')))

The representation of the tree structure in (2b) has the advantages of maintaining phrase structure rules and the syntactic and semantic dependency relations. Under the framework of ICG, the matching processes will be achieved by a head-driven parser. The parser begins with the identification of the potential phrasal heads of input, which is guided by phrasal patterns registered in the heads. Once the heads are located, the syntactic and semantic restrictions between words are also identified (Chen 1996).

4. ANNOTATION GUIDELINE

Annotation guidelines were drafted based on the ICG representation to fulfill the design criteria. The basic structure of a tree in a treebank is a hierarchy of nodes with categorical denotation. As in any standard phrase structure grammar, the lexical (i.e. terminal) symbols are defined by the lexicon (CKIP 1993). Following the recent lexicon-driven and information-based trends in linguistic theory, linguistic information will be projected from encoded lexical information. Please refer to CKIP (1993) for the definition of lexical categories that we followed. We give below the inventory of the restricted set of phrasal categories used and their interpretations. This set defines the domain of expressed syntactic information (instead of projected or inherited information). A complete list of tags is given in the Appendix.

4.1 Defining phrasal categories

There are 6 non-terminal phrasal categories annotated in the Sinica Treebank.

(3) Phrasal Categories

1 An *S* is a complete tree headed by a predicate (i.e. S is the start symbol).

2 A *VP* is a phrase headed by a predicate. However, it lacks a Subject and cannot function alone.

3 An *NP* is headed by an N

4 A *GP* is a phrase headed by locational noun or locational adjunct. Since the thematic role is often determined by the governing predicate and not encoded locally, nominal phrases are given a tentative role of DUMMY so that it can inherit the correct role from the main predicate.

5 A *PP* is headed by a preposition. The thematic role of its argument is inherited from the mother; hence its argument is marked with DUMMY.

6 An *XP* is a conjunctive phrase that is headed by a conjunction. Its syntactic head is the conjunction. However, since the actual category depends on the interactive inheritance from possibly non-identical conjoined elements, X in XP stands for an under specified category.

4.2 Defining inheritance relations

Following unification-based grammatical theories, categorical assignments in the Sinica Treebank is both lexicon-driven and head-driven. In principle, all grammatical information is lexically encoded, while structurally heads indicate the direction of information inheritance, as well as defining possible predicate-argument relations. However, since the notion 'head' can have several different linguistic definitions, we attempt to allow at least the discrepancy between syntactic and semantic heads. In the Sinica Treebank, three different kinds of grammatical heads are annotated.

(4) Heads

1. Head: indicates a grammatical head in an endocentric phrasal category. Unless a different semantic head is explicitly marked, Head marks a category that serves simultaneously as both the syntactic and semantic head of the construction.
2. head: indicates a semantic head, which does not simultaneously function as a syntactic head. For instance, in constructions involving grammaticalized 'particles,' such as in the 'VP-de' construction, the grammatical head ('de' in this case) does not carry any semantic information. In these cases, head marks the semantic head ('VP' in this case) to indicate the flow of content information.
3. DUMMY: indicates the semantic head(s) whose categorical or thematic identity cannot be locally determined. The two most likely scenarios involving DUMMY are 1) in a coordination construction, where the head category depends on the sum of all conjuncts, and 2) in a non-NP argument phrase, such as PP, where the semantic head carries a thematic role assigned not by the immediate governing syntactic head ('P' in this case), but by a higher predicate. In these cases, DUMMY allows a parser to determine the correct categorical/thematic relation later, while maintaining the same local structure.

4.3 Beyond simple inheritance

When simple inheritance fails, the following principles derived from our design criteria serve to predict the structural assignments of a phrasal category: Default Inheritance, Sisters Only, and Left First.

Default inheritance. This principle deals primarily and most effectively with coordinations and conjunctions. The theoretical motivation of this account follows Sag et al.'s (1985) proposal. In essence, the category of a conjunctive construction must be inherited from its semantic heads. However, since conjunctions are not restricted to the same categories, languages must have principled ways to determine the categorical identity when different semantic heads carry different information.

First, in the trivial case when all head daughters are of the same category, the mother will inherit that category. Second, when the different head daughters are actually elaborations of the same basic category (e.g. both Nd and Ne are elaborations of N), then the basic category is the default inheritance category for the mother. This can be illustrated by (5).

(5) [[[*da4*]VH13 [*er2*]Caa [*yuan2*]VH11]V]VP

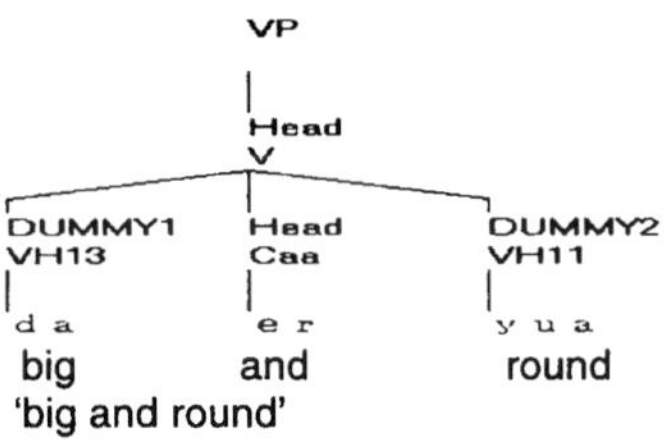

Third, when other inheritance mechanisms fail to provide a clear categorical choice, default inheritance is activated. There are two default hierarchies to deal with when the head daughters are all lexical categories (6a), and when they are all phrasal categories (6b). If there is a disparity between the lexical and phrasal categories, then a lexical category will be expanded to a phrasal category first.

(6) Default Inheritance Hierarchy for Categories

> **(a)** Lexical Categories: V > N > P > Ng
>
> **(b)** Phrasal Categories: S > VP> NP> PP> GP

When phrasal conjuncts are involved, S is the privileged category since it is the start symbol of the grammar. VP comes next since its structural composition is identical to that of S. If the structure involved is not a predicate (i.e. head of a sentence), then it must be a role. For argument roles, NP's are more privileged than PP's, and PP's are more privileged than GP's. (7) is an instance of the application of this default hierarchy.

(7) [[[*da4liang4*]Neqa [*er2*]Caa [*feng1sheng4*]VH11]V]VP
big-quantity and bountiful
"bountiful and of big quantity"

When lexical conjuncts are involved, the same principle is used. The priority is given to the predicate head of the sentence. When possible argument roles differ, a nominal category is the default. An illustrative example can be found in (8).

(8) [[*wei4lan2 de tian1kong1*]NP [yu3]Caa [*zhu1qun2 biao1han4*]S]S
aqua-blue DE sky and people ferocious
"That the sky being aqua blue and that the people being ferocious..."

Sisters only. Following most current linguistic theories, argument roles and adjunct complements must be sisters of a lexical head. However, driven by our design criteria of minimal structural complexity, no same level iteration is allowed. Thus these arguments and adjuncts can be located by the straightforward definition of sisterhood: that they share the same mother-daughter relation with the head. The result is a flat structure.

Left First. This principle is designed to account for more than two sisters without having to add hierarchical complexity. Hence, the default interpretation of the internal structure of multiple sisters is that the internal association goes from left to right.

4.4 Structural annotation of thematic information

A thematic relation contains a compact bundle of syntactic and semantic information. Although thematic relations are lexically encoded on a predicate, they can only be instantiated when that information is projected to phrasal arguments. In other words, the only empirical evidence for the existence of a thematic relation is a realized argument. However, a realized argument cannot by itself determine the thematic relation. The exact nature of the relation must be determined based on the lexical information from the predicate as well as by checking of the compatibility of that realized argument. Since structural information alone cannot determine thematic relations, prototypical structural annotation, such as in the original Penn Treebank, does not include thematic roles since they contain non-structural information. On the other hand, in theories where lexical heads drive the structural derivation/construction (e.g. ICG, HPSG, and LFG), thematic relations are critical. Hence, we encode realized thematic relations on each phrasal argument. The list of thematic relations lexically-encoded on the head predicate is consulted whenever a phrasal argument is constructed, and a contextually appropriate relation sanctioned by the lexical information is created. It is worth noting that in our account, we not only mark the thematic relations of a verbal predicate, but we also mark the thematic relations governed by a deverbal noun, among others. Also note that the argument of a preposition is marked with the placeholder DUMMY. This is because a preposition only governs an argument syntactically, while its thematic relation is determined by a higher verb.

(9) Thematic Roles: Classification and Inventory

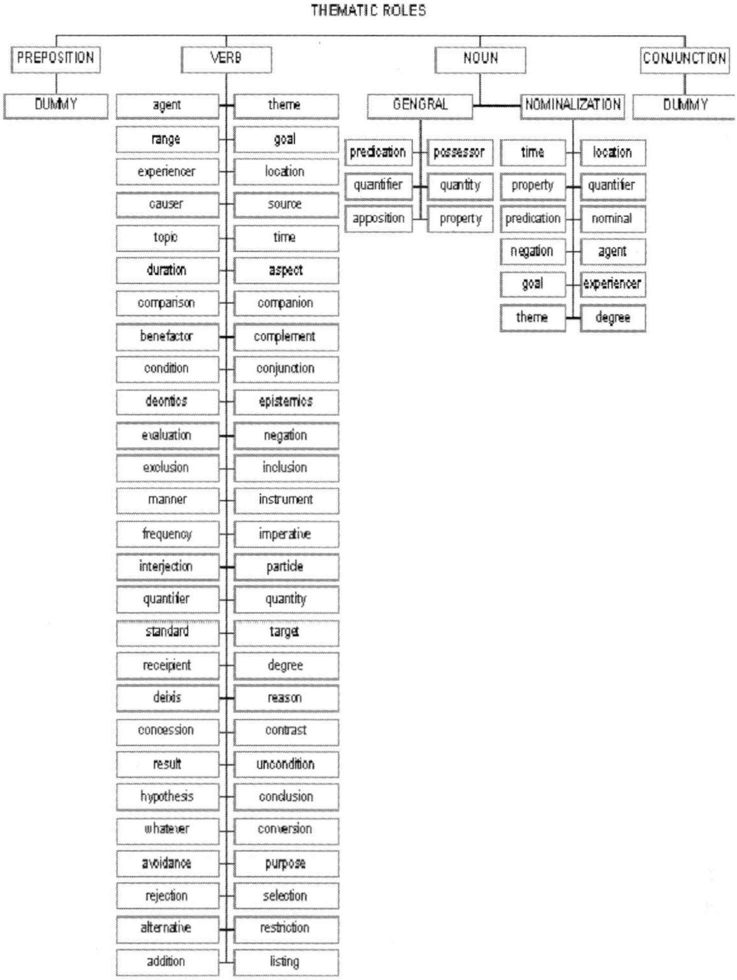

5. IMPLEMENTATION

In order to achieve efficient and consistent sentential structure annotations, the strategy of automatic parsing followed by manual post-editing is adopted. Under the framework of ICG, the lexical entries contain the linguistic information in accordance with the criterion of Minimal Syntactic Complexity and Optimal Semantic Information. The parsing process begins with the word identification, and the initialization of lexical information from an ICG-based lexicon (CKIP 1993). The head-driven chart parser begins with identification of the potential phrasal heads of the input and then constructs candidates of phrasal structures according to the encoded grammatical information of each head word (Chen 1996). The ambiguities of syntactic structures can be resolved by semantic preference checking. Therefore, in addition to the bracketing, not only syntactic categories but also thematic roles are annotated. For instance, the sentence in example (10a) has many verbs which are potentially the matrix verb, but the parser generates only one parsed tree (10b).

(10a) *tamen da che dao Wu Lai kao rou*
they take vehicle to Wu Lai roast meat
"They go to Wu Lai by bus to have a barbeque."

(10b) S(agent: NP(Head: Naeb: *tamen* 'they') | Head:VC2: *da* 'take' | goal:NP(Head: Nab: *che* 'vehicle') | complement:VP(Head:VC1: *dao* 'to' | goal: NP(Head: Nca: *Wulai* 'Wulai') | complement: VP(Head: VC2: *kao* 'roast' | goal: NP(Head: Naa: *rou* 'meat'))))

5.1 Automatic parsing and manual post-editing

After automatic bracketing and annotating of input, many ambiguous and partially correct parsed sentences are generated, so manual post-editing is required to modify them and to pick the correct structures[1]. From 1997 to 2000, 6 annotators who majored in linguistics or Chinese were responsible for this labor-intensive editing. To be consistent in manual editing, we created an editing tool and set up principles to be followed for special constructions. Annotators were encouraged to present and solve problems case by case in their regular weekly meetings. In addition, they had to check and cross-check all structural sentences to ensure inter-annotator consistency and adherence to the annotation guidelines and principles.

5.2 On-line post-editing tools

We created an on-line tool to edit automatic parsed sentences. Three main functions are included in this editing tool.

(a) Conversion:

To avoid making mistakes and to work more efficiently in editing, the

[1]For computer parsing results of the 5-million-word Sinica Corpus with a total of 477,891 sentences, the distribution of well-formed and ill-formed constructions is listed as follows:

Total	Well-Formed	Ill-Formed	Yield Rate
477,891	325,276	152,615	68%

Of 325,276 well-formed sentences recognized by the computer parsing process, the number of sentences without ambiguity is 244,078 and that of sentences with ambiguity is 81,198. Among the sentences with ambiguous results, the distributions are:

Total	1 result	2 results	3 results	more than 3 results
325,276	204,078	79,491	28,076	13,631

first function of this tool is to change the liner form of parsed sentences into graphic tree structures. The linear form of example (10b) is converted into the tree structure as in example (11).

(11) Tree structure of example (10b)

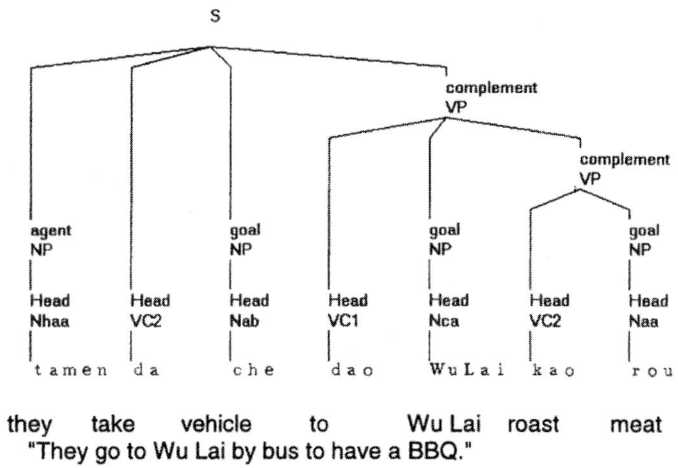

(b) Modification:

This tool provides users with a more convenient way to modify the structure. They can move, delete, modify, or add the whole sub-trees directly, if needed. In addition, this tool allows annotators to create new structural trees without any automatic parsing.

(c) Error correction:

The final function, which is under construction, is error correction. The function will perform grammar and format checking as well as search and find sentences that are similarly misparsed and then automatically correct them.

6. REPRESENTATIONAL ISSUES: PROBLEMATIC CASES AND HOW THEY ARE SOLVED

Some constructions in Mandarin Chinese involve notorious representational issues. For example, there are multiple thematic roles to express different semantic relations simultaneously in topicalized constructions. In addition, constructions with nominal predicates that are ill-formed syntactically but well-formed semantically will fail in the automatic matching process. For more consistent annotation, we set up guidelines for the constructions that pose problems in our representational model case by case. The treatments of topicalization and constructions with nominal heads are presented in the following two subsections.

6.1 Topicalization

A topic may or may not be subcategorized, so it is not easy to give a definite role name to those with multiple roles. Therefore, two different labels are coded according to the following conditions.

1 When the topic of one sentence is not the subcategorized argument, it is just coded as a topic. An example is given in (12)

2 When one subcategorized argument of the head is topicalized, it is annotated as a topic with an additional feature, namely topic [+thematic role]. The example is given in (13).

(12a) *zhe yi zhong shi wo de jingyan zui fengfu*
this one kind thing I DE experience most abundant
"I am highly experienced for this kind of thing."

(12b) this one kind thing I DE experience most abundant "I am highly experienced for this kind of thing."

In the sentence, *zhe yi zhong shi* 'this kind of thing' is not the subcategorized argument of the verb *fenfu* 'abundant', so it is annotated as a *topic*.

(13a) *zhe yi zhong yu wo zui xihuan chi*
this one kind fish I most like eat
"I like to eat this kind of fish most."

(13b) this one kind fish I most like eat
"I like to eat this kind of fish most."

In this sentence, the object of the verb *chi* 'eat' *zhe yi zhong yu* 'this kind of fish', is fronted and topicalized, so it is annotated as *topic [+theme]*.

6.2 Construction with nominal predicate

Chinese sentences do not necessarily contain a verbal head. In addition to being the head of an NP, nominal constructions may function as predicates of sentences. Like well-formed sentences, the constructions with nominal heads should be annotated as S and not as NP. However, these constructions with nominal predicates are regarded as ill formed in automatic parsing. Thus, we encode nominal constructions as S when one of the following conditions is met.

1 The concept or meaning of the construction with a nominal head is time.

2 The construction with a nominal head takes an adverbial modifier, which is event related.

Compare example (14) with (15). The head of (14) is '28 years old', which has to do with the concept of time. In addition, it takes a time adjunct, *yi* 'already'. On the contrary, (15) is coded as an NP because it does not take any time related modifier with the construction.

(14)

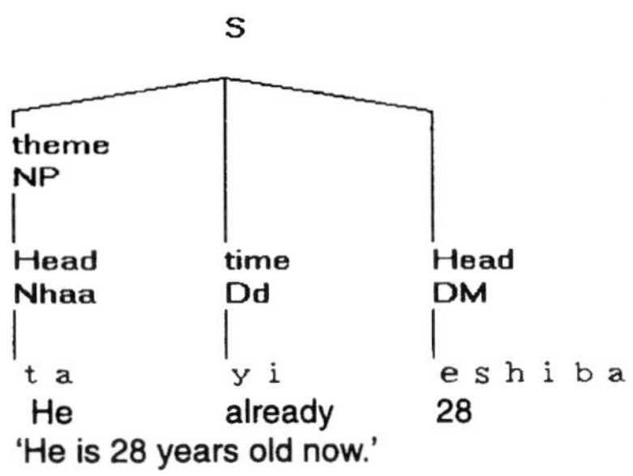

(15)

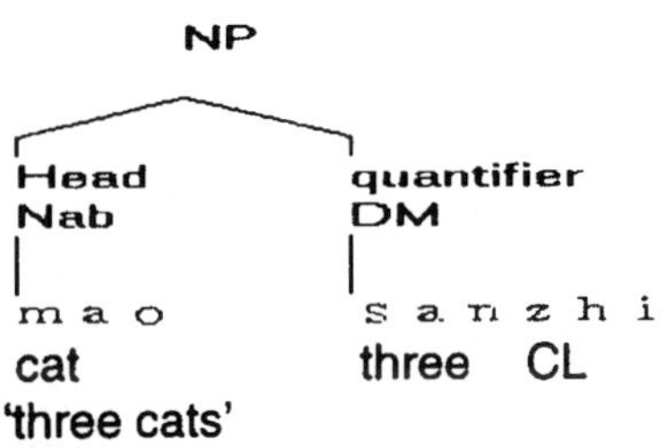

7. CURRENT STATUS OF THE SINICA TREEBANK AND FUTURE WORK

Following the given criteria and principles, we have already finished annotating 38,725 Chinese structural trees containing 239,532 words, and covering subject areas that include politics, traveling, sports, finance, and society, etc. This version of the Sinica Treebank (1.0) was released in November, 2000. A small subset of it (1,000 sentences) is available for researchers to download from the website `http://godel.iis.sinica.edu.tw/CKIP/trees1000.htm`. The complete Sinica Treebank is not downloadable but can be licensed. The license information is available from `http://rocling.iis.sinica.edu.tw/ROCLING/Treebank/Treebank_cf.htm`.
A searchable interface is also being developed and tested for researchers to directly access the complete treebank information.

As an annotated corpus, one of the most important roles that a treebank can play is to serve as a shared source of data for linguistic, and especially syntactic studies. Following the example of the successful Sinica Corpus, we are developing an on-line interface for extraction of grammatical information from the Sinica Treebank. Although the users that we have in mind are (theoretical) linguists with little computational background, we hope that non-linguists can also benefit from the ready availability of such grammatical information. And of course, computational linguists should also be able to use this interface for quick reference before a more in-depth study of an annotated corpus.

In addition to the expansion work performed locally, we are also exploring the possibility of combining resources in the Penn Chinese Treebank and the Sinica Treebank. The two Chinese treebanks each have several desirable characteristics. The Penn Chinese Treebank largely follows the Penn Treebank annotation convention (Xia 2000), therefore allows direct contrastive studies with several other treebanks following the same tradition. It also means that several established treebank tools can be applied to it. The Penn Chinese Treebank data is taken from People's Daily. Thus it has more uniformity and can serve as a good source of a language model for standard formal language use in the PRC (People Republic of China). The Sinica Treebank, on the other hand, is slightly bigger and offers the additional thematic information. It is also extracted from a balanced corpus largely based on Taiwan sources, and the data contains more stylistic and genre variations. Taking into account the labor-intensive nature of treebank building, as well as the clearly desirable goal of combining the advantages from both treebanks, we are collaborating with the University of Pennsylvania team to try to convert annotated data from one format to another. The idea is to automatically convert shared annotation content, to be followed by manual correction and/or addition for full annotation in either format. Preliminary work, done by Xia Fei at the University of Pennsylvania, has promising results. We hope that this research will not only be a first step toward resource sharing, but will also be a groundbreaking theoretical study in treebank conversion.

The construction of the Sinica Treebank is only a first step towards application of structurally annotated corpora. Continuing expansion and correction will make this database an invaluable resource for linguistic and computational studies of Chinese.

Acknowledgments

We would like to thank Kathleen Ahrens, as always, for her comments and editing of this paper. We would also like to thank participants at the 1999 ATALA Treebank Conference, especially Anne Abeillé and Annie Zaenen, for their comments. In addition, we would like to thank the participants of the

2000 2nd International Workshop on Chinese Language Processing, as well as the 2000 Research on Computational Linguistics (ROCLING) Conference, especially Martha Palmer, for their input and suggestions. Various parts of this paper were presented at the mentioned three conferences above as well as at CKIP seminars. Any remaining errors are, of course, our own responsibility.

Notes

1. http://www.sinica.edu.tw/kiwi.sh

References

Böhmová, Alena, Eva Hajičová, et al. (2003). *The Prague Dependency Treebank: a three-level annotation scenario*. This Volume.

Brants, Thorsten, Wojciech Skut, Hans Uszkoreit. (2003). "Syntactic Annotations of a German Newspaper Corpus." In Abeillé (Ed). This volume.

Chen, Feng-Yi, Pi-Fang Tsai, Keh-Jiann Chen, Chu-Ren Huang. (2000). Sinica Treebank. [in Chinese] *Computational Linguistics and Chinese Language Processing*. 4.2, p. 87–103.

Chen, Keh-Jiann. (1996) A Model for Robust Chinese Parser. *Computational Linguistics and Chinese Language Processing*. 1.1, p. 183–204.

Chen, Keh-Jiann. (1992). Design Concepts for Chinese Parsers. *3rd International Conference on Chinese Information Processing*. p. 1–22.

Chen, Keh-Jiann, Shing-Huan Liu, Li-Ping Chang, Yeh-Hao Chin. (1994). A Practical Tagger for Chinese Corpora. *Proceedings of ROCLING VII*. p. 111–126.

Chen, Keh-Jiann, Shing-Huan Liu. (1992). Word Identification for Mandarin Chinese Sentences. *Proceedings of COLING-92*, p. 101–105.

Chen, Keh-Jiann, Chi-Ching Luo, Zhao-Ming Gao, Ming-Chung Chang, Feng-Yi Chen, Chao-Ran Chen. (1999). The CKIP Chinese Treebank: Guidelines for Annotation. In Abeillé (Ed). p. 85–96.

Chen, Keh-Jiann, Chu-Ren Huang, Li-Ping Chang, Hui-Li Hsu. (1996). Sinica Corpus: Design Methodology for Balanced Corpora. *Proceedings of the 11th Pacific Asia Conference on Language, Information, and Computation (PACLIC II)*, Seoul Korea. p. 167–176.

Chen, Keh-Jiann, Chu-Ren Huang. (1996). Information-based Case Grammar: A Unification-based Formalism for Parsing Chinese. *Journal of Chinese Linguistics Monograph Series* No. 9. Chu-Ren Huang, Keh-Jiann Chen, Benjamin K. T'sou Eds. *Readings in Chinese Natural Language Processing*. p. 23–45. Berkeley: JCL.

Chen, Keh-Jiann, Chu-Ren Huang. (1994). Features Constraints in Chinese Language Parsing. *Proceedings of ICCPOL '94*. p. 223–228

CKIP (Chinese Knowledge Information Processing). (1993). *The Categorical Analysis of Chinese*. [in Chinese] CKIP Technical Report 93-05. Nankang: Academia Sinica.

Gazdar, G, E. Klein, G.K. Pullum, I. A. Sag. (1985). *Generalized Phrase Structure Grammar*. Cambridge: Blackwell, and Cambridge, Mass: Harvard University Press.

Huang, Chu-Ren, Keh-Jiann Chen, Feng-Yi Chen, Keh-Jiann Chen, Zhao-Ming Gao, Kuang-Yu Chen. (2000). Sinica Treebank: Design Criteria, Annotation Guidelines, and On-line Interface. *Proceedings of 2nd Chinese Language Processing Workshop(Held in conjunction with the 38th Annual Meeting of the Association for Computational Linguistics, ACL-2000)*. Hong Kong. p. 29–37.

Huang, Chu-Ren, Keh-Jiann Chen, Feng-Yi Chen, Li-Li Chang. (1997). Segmentation Standard for Chinese Natural Language Processing. *Computational Linguistics and Chinese Language Processing*. 2.2. p. 47–62

Lin, Fu-Wen. (1992). *Some Reflections on the Thematic System of Information-based Case Grammar (ICG)*. [In Chinese.] CKIP Technical Report No. 92-01. Nankang: Academia Sinica.

Marcus, Mitchell P., Beatrice Santorini, Mary Ann Marcinkiewicz. (1993). Building a large annotated corpus of English: The PENN Treebank. *Computational Linguistics*, 19.2. p. 313–330.

Piollard, C. , I. A. Sag. (1994). *Head-Driven Phrase Structure Grammar*. Stanford: Center for the Study of Language and Information, Chicago Press.

Pustejovsky, J. (1985). *The Generative Lexicon*. MIT Press.

Sag, Ivan, Gerald Gazdar, Thomas Wasow, and Steven Weisler. 1985. Coordination and How to Distinguish Categories. *Natural Language and Linguistic Theory*. 3. p. 117–171.

Tseng, Shin-Shyeng, Meng-Yuan Chang, Chin-Chun Hsieh, Keh-Jiann Chen. (1988). Approaches on An Experimental Chinese Electronic Dictionary. *Proceedings of 1988 International Conference on Computer Processing of Chinese and Oriental Languages*, p. 371–74.

Uszkoreit, Hans (1986). Categorial Unification Grammars. *Proceedings of COLING'86*. Bonn: University of Bonn. Also appeared as Report No. CSLI-86-66. Stanford: Center for the Study of Language and Information.

Xia, Fei. (2000a). *The Segmentation Guidelines for the Penn Chinese Treebank (3.0)*. IRCS Report 00-06. Philadelphia, PA: University of Pennsylvania.

Xia, Fei. (2000b). *The Part-of-Speech Tagging Guidelines for the Penn Chinese Treebank (3.0)*. IRCS Report 00-07. Philadelphia, PA: University of Pennsylvania.

Xia, Fei, Martha Palmer, Nianwen Xue, Mary Ellen Okurowski, John Kovarik, Fu-Dong Chiou, Shizhe Huang, Tony Kroch, Mitch Marcus. (2000). Developing Guidelines and Ensuring Consistency for Chinese Text Annotation. *Proceedings of the Second International Conference on Language Resources and Evaluation (LREC-2000)*, Athens, Greece.

Xia, Fei, Chunghye Han, Martha Palmer, Aravind Joshi. (2000). Comparing Lexicalized Treebank Grammars Extracted from Chinese, Korean, and English. *Proceedings of 2nd Chinese Language Processing Workshop (Held in conjunction with the 38th Annual Meeting of the Association for Computational Linguistics, ACL-2000)*. p. 52–59. Hong Kong.

Xue, Nianwen, Fei Xia. (2000). *The Bracketing Guidelines for the Penn Chinese Treebank (3.0)*. IRCS Report 00-07. Philadelphia, PA: University of Pennsylvania.

Appendix: Syntactic Categories

*A :**NON-PREDICATIVE ADJVECTIVE**
*Caa , Cab, Cba, Cbaa, Cbab, Cbb, Cbba, Cbbb, Cbc, Cbca, Cbcb :**CONJUNCTION**
*Daa, Dab (quantity), Dbaa, Dbab, Dbb, Dbc (modal), Dc (negation), Dd (time), Dfa, Dfb (degree), Dg (locative), Dh (manner), Di (aspect), Dj (interrogative), Dk (sentential adverb) :**ADVERB**
*I :**INTERJECTION**
Naa (Mass Noun), Nab (Common Noun), Nac(Abstract Noun, Countable), Nad (Abstract Noun), Naea, Naeb(Group Noun), Nba, Nbc(Proper Noun), Nca, Ncb, Ncc, Ncda, Ncdb(Location Noun), Nd(Time Noun) :**NOUN**
*Neu, Nes, Nep, Neqa, Neqb :**DETERMINATIVE**
*Nfa, Nfb, Nfc, Nfd, Nfe, Nff, Nfg, Nfh, Nfi :**MEASURE WORD / CLASSIFIER**
*Ng :**POSTPOSITION WORD**
*Nhaa, Nhab, Nhac, Nhb, Nhc :**PRONOUN**
*P01 ~ P65 :**PREPOSITION**
*Ta, Tb, Tc, Td :**PARTICLE [VERB]**
*VA11, VA12, VA13, VA2, VA3, VA4 :**ACTIVE INTRANSITIVE VERB**
*VB11, VB12, VB2 :**PSEUDO ACTIVE TRANSITIVE VERB**
*VC1, VC2, VC31, VC32, VC33 :**ACTIVE TRANSITIVE VERB**
*VD1, VD2 :**DITRANSITIVE VERB**
*VE11, VE12, VE2 :**ACTIVE VERB WITH SENTENTIAL OBJECT**
*VF1, VF2 :**ACTIVE VERB WITH VP OBJECT**
*VG1, VG2 :**CLASSIFICATORY VERB**
*VH11, VH12, VH13, VH14, VH15, VH16, VH17, VH21, VH22 :**STATIVE INTRANSITIVE VERB**
*VI1, VI2, VI3 :**PSEUDO STATIVE TRANSITIVE VERB**
*VJ1, VJ2, VJ3 :**STATIVE TRANSITIVE VERB**
*VK1, VK2 :**STATIVE VERB WITH SENTENTIAL OBJECT**
*VL1, VL2, VL3, VL4 :**STATIVE VERB WITH VP OBJECT**

Chapter 14

BUILDING A JAPANESE PARSED CORPUS*

While Improving the Parsing System

Sadao Kurohashi
Graduate School of Information Science and Technology
University of Tokyo
kuro@kc.t.u-tokyo.ac.jp

Makoto Nagao
Kyoto University
nagao@kuee.kyoto-u.ac.jp

Abstract In January 1996, we started a project to construct a Japanese parsed corpus and to simultaneously improve a morphological analyzer and a dependency structure analyzer. In this project, human annotators not only correct the erroneous analyses produced by the parsing system, but also improve the parsing system/grammar: finding problematic fixed expressions, picking out phrases which have exceptional functions, classifying unseen types of clauses, and so on. The project ended in July 2000 with the release of an enhanced version of the Japanese parsing system and 40,000 sentences of parsed corpus.

Keywords: Corpus Annotation, Japanese Parser, Japanese Newspaper Corpus

1. INTRODUCTION

Corpus-based methods have become a central paradigm in present-day NLP. Corpus-based NLP usually takes the following steps:

*This paper is an extended version of a paper with the same title paper that appeared in the proceedings of First International Conference on Language Resources & Evaluation (LREC '98).

A. Abeillé (ed.), Treebanks: Building and Using Parsed Corpora, 249–260.

1 plain corpora are first assigned tags automatically (this paper limits the scope to part-of-speech tags and syntactic tags),

2 those tags are corrected by human annotators, making correctly tagged corpora,

3 tagged corpora are used to construct or improve an NLP system/grammar[2].

Corpus construction projects so far have not fully exploited the automatic parser. In the case of Penn Treebank Project (Marcus et al., 1993), the employed parser, Fidditch (Hindle, 1989), was only expected to chunk the input into a string of trees, not to make a whole syntactic tree for the input. The annotators' task was then to glue together the syntactic chunks produced by the parser. In the case of ATR/Lancaster Treebank Project (Black et al., 1996), the parser employed produced the 'parse forest' for the input, and it was left to the annotators to choose the proper parse within the forest.

However, if a parser is available which can make a unique parse for the input accurately, the situation changes. One advantage in using such a powerful parser is the reduction of the annotators' labor. Furthermore, there is another important advantage in using a powerful parser. If annotators correct the unique parses of the inputs, the process is almost equivalent to the detailed investigation of the performance of the parser. Accordingly, deficiencies of the system and/or grammar can be found simultaneously with the corpus construction process. That is, steps 2 and 3 above can be to some extent merged.

Apparently, the accuracy of the original parser is very important. If the parser produces erroneous analyses often, it is hard to locate the essential problem of the parser, and also the manual correction process becomes much more troublesome. In the case of Japanese language processing, we have developed a morphological analyzer, JUMAN, and a dependency structure analyzer, KNP (Kurohashi and Nagao, 1994), and have been improving them continuously. Consequently, their performance in producing unique parses for real world texts has been very close to the satisfactory level. In January 1996 we started a project of constructing a Japanese parsed corpus and improving the morphological analyzer and the dependency analyzer simultaneously. This paper describes the several achievements of the project, which successfully ended in July 2000.

2. OVERVIEW OF THE PROJECT

2.1 Information assigned to the Corpus

The syntactic information in the corpus is based on dependency relations defined on *bunsetsu* units, according to the parser employed, KNP. *Bunsetsu* is a commonly used linguistic unit in Japanese traditional grammar, consisting

* 0 1D					
沸点 ふってん 沸点	名詞	普通名詞	*	*
(*hutten* 'the boiling point'	Noun	Common Noun)		
が が が	助詞	格助詞	*	*
(*ga*	Postposition	Case Marker)		
* 1 4P				
高い たかい 高い	形容詞	*	イ形容詞アウオ段	基本形
(*takai* 'high'	Adjective		I-adjective-type	Basic form)
、 、 、	特殊	読点	*	*
((comma)	Special Symbol	Comma)		
* 2 3D				
多く おおく 多く	副詞	*	*	*
(*ooku* 'many'	Adverb)			
の の の	助詞	名詞接続助詞	*	*
(*no*	Postposition	Nominal-connector)		
* 3 4D				
物質 ぶっしつ 物質	名詞	普通名詞	*	*
(*busshitsu* 'substance'	Noun	Common Noun)		
を を を	助詞	格助詞	*	*
(*wo*	Postposition	Case Marker)		
⋮ ⋮ ⋮				

Figure 14.1. An example sentence with the morphological and syntactic information.

of one or more adjoining content words and zero or more following functional words. The English equivalents for bunsetsu would be a small noun phrase, a prepositional phrase, a verb phrase consisting of auxiliary verbs and a main verb, and so on. The dependency grammar formalism has been used in KNP because of its suitability to Japanese language in the parsing process. Furthermore, it has an important advantage in corpus construction; lack of internal, artificial nodes, like NP, VP, makes the annotators' task much easier.[3] The information assigned in the parsed corpus is as follows:

Morphological Information:

- boundaries between words,
- pronunciation, basic form, POS, conjugation type, conjugation form of each word.[4]

Syntactic Information:

- boundaries between bunsetsus,
- governor bunsetsu of each bunsetsu, and one of the following three relations between the bunsetsu and the governor bunsetsu:

D: predicate-argument/adjunct relation or head-modifier relation,

P: coordination relation,

A: appositive relation.

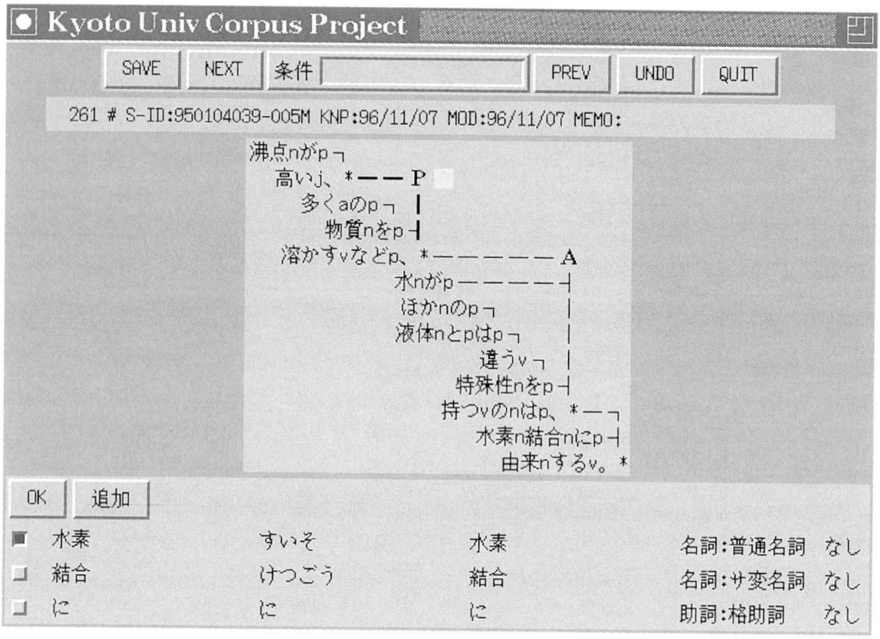

Figure 14.2. User interface for manual correction.

Figure 14.1 shows an example sentence with full information in the corpus (this is the format for distribution; parenthesized lines are inserted for the gloss, not included in the corpus). The original sentence is composed of words in the first column. Each line starting with a word shows its morphological information; each item in a line shows a word occurring in the original sentence, pronunciation, basic form, upper level POS, lower level POS, conjugation type, and conjugation form, respectively. A line starting with '*' shows a bunsetsu-boundary. The number next to '*' shows the ID of a bunsetsu consisting of the words between the line and the next '*' line; the next number and the character shows the ID of its governor bunsetsu and their type of relation.

For example, the 0th bunsetsu, "(*hutten* 'the boiling point') (*ga* 'case marker')", depends on the 1st bunsetsu, " (*takai* 'high')", with the D relation (predicate-argument/adjunct relation).

This information is first assigned by JUMAN and KNP automatically, and then corrected by annotators using a mouse-based interface (Figure 14.2). The upper part of the interface window is for the dependency analysis correction;

the lower part of the interface window is for the correction of the morphological analyses and the bunsetsu segmentation. The upper part of Figure 14.2 shows the dependency structure of the example sentence in Figure 14.1.

2.2 Achievements of the Project

The project started in January 1996 and successfully finished in July 2000. In the first six months, we intensively modified the morphological analyzer JUMAN (see Section 3). Then, in the next six months, we modified the Japanese dependency structure analyzer KNP (see Section 4). In this period, we also made a mouse-based interface for manual correction, and did some trials of manual correction. Then, we actually started the manual correction process in January 1997.

As the original text of the corpus, we have been using the Mainichi Newspaper, which is a general, daily, paper edition newspaper and can be regarded as an example of standard contemporary written Japanese.

One annotator participated in the project for the first 15 months, then another annotator for the remaining 40 months. Both of them received their master's degree in Japanese linguistics. The average speed of their correction (morphological and syntactic information together) was approximately 40 sentences ($\simeq$ 1,000 tokens) per hour.

During three and half years of the manual correction process, in the beginning we had a weekly meeting to discuss the problems of the system/grammar and modified them periodically. After that, both JUMAN and KNP became rather accurate and stable, and in the second half of the project we just did small modification to them.

In September 1997, we released the first version of the corpus consisting of about 10,000 sentences. In June 1998, the second version of about 20,000 sentences and in July 2000, the final version of about 40,000 sentences (950,000 tokens) were released. The first half of the final version (about 20,000 sentences) is a collection of all articles from January 1st to 17th in 1995; the other half is the editorials of the whole year 1995. We also released enhanced versions of JUMAN and KNP whenever significant modifications were made.

3. MORPHOLOGICAL ANALYZER JUMAN

A robust morphological analysis is needed for the Japanese language since Japanese sentences have no explicit separators between words and the words such as verbs and adjectives have complex conjugation. The Japanese morphological analyzer JUMAN was first developed in 1992 based on the Japanese grammar book (Masuoka and Takubo, 1989). At the first stage of the project, we intensively modified JUMAN, making it accurate enough as a basic tool for corpus construction.

3.1 Basic Algorithm of JUMAN

Japanese morphological analysis is usually done using bigram information, which is often referred to as connectivity of pairs of words. JUMAN first recognizes all the possible character combinations which constitute a word in the given input by consulting the word dictionary. The size of the word dictionary is about 200,000. The dictionary derives from the EDR Japanese Word Dictionary (Japan Electronic Dictionary Research Institute Ltd., 1993) and our in-house modifications. Then, JUMAN finds possible connections between adjacent words by checking the connectivity dictionary.

In many cases, however, there are many possible word segmentation patterns for the input which meet the connectivity constraints. To handle this problem, costs are assigned to each word (or class of words) and each connectivity between words in JUMAN. The higher the cost, the lower the word frequency, or the frequency of the two words in an adjacent position. By summing up those costs, JUMAN determines the most plausible answer (the most plausible word string) for the input.

3.2 Handling of Fixed Expressions

The erroneous analyses of the above algorithm are mainly due to the cost calculation, that is, when the correct answer is not assigned the minimal cost. In the conventional version of JUMAN, the only way of resolving such erroneous analyses was to adjust the costs of some specific words and/or connectivities. However, such a fine adjustment often causes side effects; a cost adjustment for an erroneous analysis might cause other erroneous analyses to other inputs. For this reason, the total performance of the conventional version of JUMAN could not be improved further using such cost adjustments.

The erroneous analyses by cost calculation often occur for a long string of *kana* characters (Japanese alphabet). This is because a small set of *kana* characters are used much more frequently than *kanji* characters (Chinese characters) in Japanese lexicon. However, strings of *kana* characters usually correspond to some fixed expressions consisting of two or more words, and in most cases their segmentations are not ambiguous when they are seen as a whole. Accordingly, if the system can handle a word string as a whole, defining its total cost and its connectivity, most of the erroneous analyses by cost calculation can be resolved without side effects.

The main modification we made to JUMAN in the project was the enhancement of the system to handle a word string as a whole, and to find and enter problematic fixed expressions which were analyzed incorrectly by the normal cost calculation. Some examples are as follows:

- *tameshi* ‘instance’ *ga* ‘case marker’ *nai* ‘there is no’

- *ka* 'if' *dou* 'how' *ka* 'if'
- *ni* 'case marker' *mo* 'also' *sukoshi* 'some'

For example, if the word string "*tameshi ga nai*" has not been registered in the dictionary, "*tameshiganai*" is incorrectly segmented into "*tame* 'for' *shiganai* 'poor' " by the normal cost calculation.

The registration of such problematic expressions has been continued in the corpus construction process, and the current dictionary in JUMAN contains about 200 fixed expressions.

3.3 Accuracy of JUMAN

To evaluate the current accuracy of JUMAN, the automatic analyses by JUMAN and the manually corrected corpus of about 40,000 sentences were compared. The counting is based on the words in the manually corrected analyses, and only the upper level of POS classifications are compared. By these criteria, the current accuracy of JUMAN is 99.0%.

We have to say this is a closed test, since JUMAN was modified by looking at the corpus. However, as mentioned in the preceding section, JUMAN was rather stable and only small changes were made during the second half period of the corpus tagging, and the accuracy of JUMAN is almost the same for the first half and the second half of the corpus. In this sense, the above score can be seen as a kind of open-test score for newspaper domain texts. (We would like to make the same claim for the KNP accuracy reported in the next section.)

4. DEPENDENCY STRUCTURE ANALYZER KNP

Simultaneously with the construction of a Japanese parsed corpus, another goal of the project is to make the Japanese dependency analyzer KNP more accurate. In the following, several aspects of KNP are discussed, including recent improvements.

4.1 Basic Grammar Formalism of KNP

KNP is based on a dependency grammar defined on the bunsetsu unit. The advantage of this strategy is as follows:

- The bunsetsu is a proper linguistic unit of a grammar for the following reasons:
  - The syntactic behavior of bunsetsus is much clearer (more specified) than that of words so that a grammar construction based on the bunsetsu is easier than one based on the word unit.
  - The behavior of some bunsetsus cannot be explained compositionally from its components (words). For example, "*kaku* 'write'

mono 'thing' *no* 'of' " means 'through writing'. In such cases, it is natural to assign a syntactic function to a bunsetsu, not to a word.

- Japanese nominal arguments have complex properties: order flexibility and omissibility. The dependency grammar formalism can cope with these properties. This is because the dependency relation between a predicate and an argument remains as it is, even if arguments are scrambled or some of them are omitted.[5]

The procedure of KNP consists of the following steps:

1. KNP first converts a word string segmented by JUMAN into a bunsetsu string. This process can be done by checking the POS of words without ambiguity in most cases.

2. The regular-expression pattern rules described in the next section are applied to bunsetsus to give features which specify their syntactic behavior. KNP contains about 600 rules currently.

3. KNP identifies the head of each bunsetsu by referring to their features. The Japanese language is head-final, that is, a bunsetsu depends on another bunsetsu to its right (not necessarily the adjacent bunsetsu). Accordingly, syntactic ambiguity in the dependency grammar formalism arises when a bunsetsu can depend on two or more bunsetsus which follow in a sentence. KNP resolves such ambiguity by using several heuristic rules described in the following sections.[6]

4.2 Treatment of Exceptional Bunsetsus

In some contexts, certain bunsetsus do not behave as defined by pure syntax. For example ([$\cdots$] establishes a context):

- *dekiru* 'can do' *dake* 'only' [*shizukani* 'quietly']
  — works as an adverb like 'as $\cdots$ as possible'.
- *utsukushiku* 'beautiful' [*saku* 'bloom']
  — works as an adverb like 'beautifully'.
- [$\cdots$ *wo* 'case marker'] *henkan* 'transformation' ,
  — works as a verb like 'transform'.
- [$\cdots$ *wo* 'case marker'] *megutte* 'tour'
  — works as a postposition like 'as to'.

When a bunsetsu behaves exceptionally like in the above examples, it can usually be recognized by checking the surrounding bunsetsus. Therefore, we added a regular-expression pattern matching facility to KNP so that several features marking exceptionality can be given to a bunsetsu according to its local context.[7] A regular-expression pattern consists of:

- a pattern for the bunsetsu to which some feature is given (a pattern for a bunsetsu specifies the word sequence in the bunsetsu),
- patterns for the preceding bunsetsu sequence,
- patterns for the following bunsetsu sequence.

For example, if a bunsetsu consists of two words, *dekiru* 'can do' and *dake* 'only', and the next adjacent bunsetsu consists of a verb or an adjective, the bunsetsu is given a *non-predicate feature*. A bunsetsu with this feature is not treated as a predicate though the POS of its content word is verb, so that it does not govern nominal arguments.

There must be many other expression like the above examples, and it is important in the step-by-step improvement of the parser to find such expressions and treat them appropriately in the grammar. This can be done along with the manual correction of syntactic analyses during corpus construction.

4.3 Treatment of Coordinate Structures

Coordinate structures (CSs) pose a serious problem for syntactic analysis. This is because not only do CSs themselves have complex scope ambiguity, but also sentences with CSs tend to be long and the combination of scope ambiguities and the intrinsic syntactic ambiguities in long sentences can easily cause combinatorial explosion.

To solve this problem, we have developed a unique, efficient method of resolving CS scope ambiguities (Kurohashi and Nagao, 1994). The underlying assumption of this method is that conjoined phrases/clauses/sentences exhibit parallelism, that is, we have a certain similarity in the sequence of words and their grammatical structures as a whole. Based on this assumption, we devised a dynamic programming algorithm which identifies conjuncts by finding the two most similar word sequences on the left and the right of a conjunction.

This method can determine CS scope accurately, which leads to a substantial reduction of the syntactic ambiguity in a sentence. Therefore, KNP analyzes CSs in the input first by using this method, and then it determines the dependency structure of the input keeping the identified CS's scope.

4.4 Treatment of Subordinate Clauses

Another serious problem in parsing sentences is the treatment of subordinate clauses. When there are three or more clauses in a sentence, we have to determine their scope. In the dependency grammar formalism, the scope of clauses can be expressed by dependency relations among the predicates of the clauses as follows (note that a predicate is final in a clause):

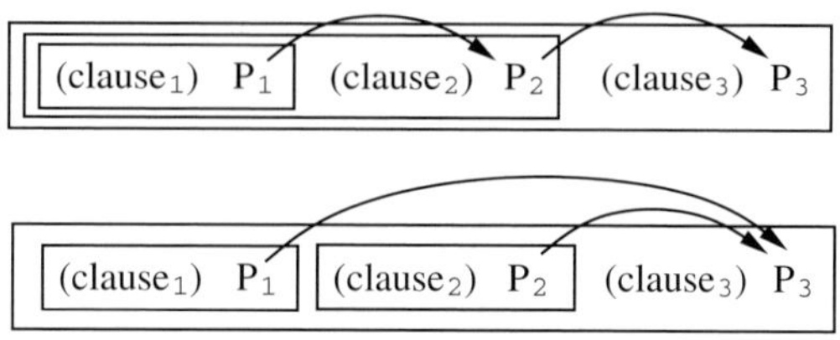

For this problem, Minami proposed a very effective preference rule (Minami, 1993). He classified several types of clauses into three classes depending on their strength, e.g., *-keredo* 'although ⋯' is classified into the strongest class, *-tsutsu* 'while ⋯' is classified into the weakest class. Based on his clause classification, he claimed that a weaker clause cannot contain a stronger clause in its scope, that is, the predicate in a stronger clause does not depend on the predicate in a weaker clause.

This claim fits the behavior of Japanese clauses very well, i.e., it works almost as a constraint. The problem with adopting Minami's study to the real parsing is that he just listed representative types of clauses for each class. In the project, therefore, we extended Minami's clause classification to provide good coverage of real world texts, and incorporated the preference rule based on the clause classification into KNP.

4.5 The Remaining Problem

KNP can resolve ambiguities in coordinate structures and subordinate clauses as described in the preceding sections. Now, the major remaining ambiguity is the predicate-argument relation in embedded sentences. This ambiguity occurs, for example, when the input is "N_1 V_1 N_2 V_2", and N_1 can depend either on V_1 or V_2, satisfying the dependency constraint.

This type of ambiguity can be resolved by using case-frame information, which specifies what types of nouns can fill each case slot of a predicate. However, there is no Japanese case-frame dictionary of wide coverage so far. Accordingly, KNP currently uses the naive preference rule which treats a bunsetsu that can depend on two or more bunsetsus as if it depended on the nearest one only. This rule is almost the same as the *right association* principle in parsing English sentences.

One of our on-going projects is to automatically construct a case-frame dictionary from raw corpora by using JUMAN and KNP, and to incorporate the dictionary into KNP (Kawahara and Kurohashi, 2000).

4.6 Accuracy of KNP

To evaluate the current accuracy of KNP, the automatic analyses by KNP and the manually corrected corpus of about 40,000 sentences were compared. The counting was based on pairs of bunsetsus which have a dependency relation in the manually corrected analyses. To evaluate the native performance of KNP, if the morphological analysis of both or either bunsetsu in a pair is incorrect, the pair is removed from the counting. Furthermore, we removed the pair of the last bunsetsu and the second to last bunsetsu in each sentence, since this pair is always analyzed correctly based on the head-final feature. As for the remaining pairs of bunsetsus in the manually corrected analyses, if the same dependency relation exists in the automatically analyzed corpora, it is counted as a correct analysis; if not, it is counted as an incorrect analysis. By these criteria, the current accuracy of KNP is 91.1%.

5. CONCLUSION

This paper has described the corpus project at Kyoto University, i.e., the construction of a Japanese parsed corpus and simultaneous improvement of the morphological analyzer JUMAN and the dependency analyzer KNP.

In our project, annotators not only correct the erroneous analyses produced by the parsing system, but also improve the parsing system/grammar: finding problematic fixed expressions for the morphological analysis, picking out bunsetsus which have exceptional functions, classifying unseen types of clauses, and so on.

The results of our project, namely JUMAN, KNP and the parsed corpus, have already been used by several researchers and groups internationally. The latest versions of them are available from `http://www-nagao.kuee.kyoto-u.ac.jp/`.

Notes

1. This paper is an extended version of a paper with the same title paper that appeared in the proceedings of First International Conference on Language Resources & Evaluation (LREC '98).

2. Although unsupervised learning using plain corpora is promising, supervised learning using tagged corpora is much more effective and reliable (Pereira and Schabes, 1992).

3. The NEGRA project of constructing a German treebank is similar to our approach, in the sense that dependency links between minimal phrases (in our case, bunsetsu) are annotated (Brants et al., this volume).

4. The Japanese morphological grammar in JUMAN has 43 POS-tags, 33 conjugation types, and about 15 conjugation forms for each conjugation type. For the POS tagset, a two level classification is used. For example, "Noun" defined as the upper level class is classified into "Common Noun", "Proper Noun", "Adverbial Noun", and so on.

5. An HPSG variant with the enhanced treatment of SUBCAT feature can also handle these characteristics (Mitsuishi et al., 1998). However, so far we do not think that a costly unification calculation and a rigid formalism are suitable or necessary for parsing real world texts.

6. KNP assumes projectivity (no crossing dependency links), which actually holds in most Japanese sentences. However, when human annotators correct the automatic analyses, they are allowed to assign crossing links.

7. This matching facility is also used to assign general features to bunsetsus, such as nominal, verbal, indicator of a coordination, types of clauses, and so on.

References

Black, E., Eubank, S., Kashioka, H., Magerman, D., Garside, R., Leech, G. (1996). Beyond skeleton parsing: producing a comprehensive large-scale general-English treebank with full grammatical analysis. *Proceedings of the 16th COLING*, p. 107–112.

Brants, T., Skut, W., Uszkoreit, H. (2003). Syntactic annotation of a German newspaper corpus. In *This volume*.

Hindle, D. (1989). Acquiring disambiguation rules from text. *Proceedings of the 27th Annual Meeting of ACL*, p. 118–125.

Japan Electronic Dictionary Research Institute Ltd. (1993). *EDR Electronic Dictionary Specifications Guide*.

Kawahara, D., Kurohashi, S. (2000). Japanese case structure analysis by unsupervised construction of a case frame dictionary. *Proceedings of the 18th COLING*, p. 432–438.

Kurohashi, S., Nagao, M. (1994). A syntactic analysis method of long Japanese sentences based on the detection of conjunctive structures. *Computational Linguistics*, 20(4).

Marcus, M. P., Santorini, B., Marcinkiewicz, M. A. (1993). Building a large annotated corpus of English: the Penn Treebank. *Computational Linguistics*, 19(2), p. 313–330.

Masuoka, T., Takubo, Y. (1989). *Basic Japanese grammar*. Kuroshio Publishing, Tokyo.

Minami, F. (1993). *A grammar of contemporary Japanese*. Taishukan Publishing, Tokyo.

Mitsuishi, Y., Torisawa, K., Tsujii, J. (1998). HPSG-style underspecified Japanese grammar with wide coverage. *Proceedings of the 17th COLING and the 36th Annual Meeting of ACL*, p. 876–880.

Pereira, F., Schabes, Y. (1992). Inside-outside re-estimation from partially bracketed corpora. *Proceedings of the 30th Annual Meeting of ACL*, p. 128–135.

Chapter 15

BUILDING A TURKISH TREEBANK

Kemal Oflazer
Faculty of Engineering and Natural Sciences
Sabancı University
Istanbul, Turkey
oflazer@sabanciuniv.edu

Bilge Say
Informatics Institute
Middle East Technical University
Ankara, Turkey
bsay@ii.metu.edu.tr

Dilek Zeynep Hakkani-Tür, Gökhan Tür
AT&T Labs-Research,
180 Park Avenue,
Florham Park, NJ, 07928, USA
{hakkani,tur}@research.att.com

Abstract We present the issues that we have encountered in designing a treebank architecture for Turkish along with rationale for the choices we have made for various representation schemes. In the resulting representation, the information encoded in the complex agglutinative word structures are represented as a sequence of inflectional groups separated by derivational boundaries. The syntactic relations are encoded as labeled dependency relations among segments of lexical items marked by derivation boundaries. Our current work involves refining a set of treebank annotation guidelines and developing a sophisticated annotation tool with an extendable plug-in architecture for morphological analysis, morphological disambiguation and syntactic annotation disambiguation.

Keywords: Treebanks, Dependency Syntax, Turkish, Agglutinative Languages

A. Abeillé (ed.), Treebanks: Building and Using Parsed Corpora, 261–277.

INTRODUCTION

In the last few years, treebank corpora such as the Penn Treebank (Marcus et al., 1993; Taylor et al., this volume) or the Prague Dependency Treebank (Böhmová et al., this volume) have become a crucial resource for building and evaluating natural language processing tools and applications. Although the compilation of such structurally annotated corpora is time-consuming and expensive, the eventual benefits outweigh this initial cost. With a set of future applications in mind, we have undertaken the design of a treebank corpus architecture for Turkish, which we believe encodes the lexical and structural information relevant to Turkish. In this chapter we present the issues that we have encountered in designing a treebank for Turkish along with rationale for the representational choices we have made. In the resulting representation, the information encoded in complex agglutinative word structures is represented as a sequence of inflectional groups separated by derivational boundaries. A tagset reduction is not attempted as any such reduction leads to the removal of potentially useful syntactic markers, especially in the encoding of derived forms. At the syntactic level, we have opted to just represent relationships between lexical items (or rather, inflectional groups) as dependency relations. The representation is extendable so that relations between lexical items can be further refined by augmenting syntactic relations using finer distinctions which are more semantic in nature.

1. TURKISH: MORPHOLOGY AND SYNTAX

Turkish is a Ural-Altaic language, having agglutinative word structures with productive inflectional and derivational processes. Derivational phenomena have rarely been addressed in designing tagsets, and in the context of Turkish, this may pose challenging issues, as the number of forms one can derive from a root form may be in the millions (Hankamer, 1989).

Turkish word forms consist of morphemes concatenated to a root morpheme or to other morphemes, much like beads on a string. Except for a very few exceptional cases, the surface realizations of the morphemes are conditioned by various morphophonemic processes such as vowel harmony, vowel and consonant elisions. The morphotactics of word forms can be quite complex when multiple derivations are involved. For instance, the derived modifier `sağlamlaştırdığımızdaki`[1] would be represented as[2]:

```
sağlam+Adj^DB
      +Verb+Become^DB
      +Verb+Caus+Pos^DB
      +Noun+PastPart+A3sg+Pnon+Loc^DB
      +Adj
```

Marking such a word as an adjective and ignoring anything that comes before the last part of speech would ignore the fact that the stem is also an adjective which may have syntactic relations with preceding words such as an adverbial modifier, or that there is an intermediate causative (hence transitive) verb which may have an object NP or a subject NP to its left.

A recent experiment that we conducted on about 250,000 Turkish words in news text revealed that there were over 6,000 distinct morphological feature combinations when root morphemes were ignored. Although this is less than the much larger numbers quoted by Hankamer who considered the generative capacity of the derivations, it is nevertheless much larger than the distinctions encoded by the tagsets of languages like English or French. What is important is not the size of the potential tagset, but rather

- the fact that there is no a priori limit on it as the next set of million words that one looks at may contain another 6,000 distinct feature combinations, and
- the nature of the derivational information.

On the syntactic side, although Turkish has unmarked SOV constituent order, it is considered a free-constituent order language as all constituents including the verb, can move freely as demanded by the discourse context with very few syntactic constraints (Erguvanlı, 1979). Case marking on nominal constituents usually indicates their syntactic role. Constituent order in embedded clauses is substantially more constrained but deviations from the default order, however infrequent, can still be found. Turkish is also a pro-drop language, as the subject, if necessary, can be elided and recovered from the agreement markers on the verb. Within noun phrases, there is a loose order with specifiers preceding modifiers, but within each group, order (e.g., between cardinal and attributive modifiers) is mainly determined by which aspect is to be emphasized. For instance the Turkish equivalents of *two young men* and *young two men* are both possible: the former being the neutral case or the case where youth is emphasized, while the latter is the case where the cardinality is emphasized. A further but relatively minor complication is that various verbal adjuncts may intervene in well-defined positions within NPs causing discontinuous constituents.

2. WHAT INFORMATION NEEDS TO BE REPRESENTED?

We expect this treebank to be used by a wide variety of "consumers", ranging from linguists investigating morphological structure and distributions, syntactic structure, and constituent order variation, to computational linguists extracting language models or evaluating parsers, etc. We would therefore employ an extensible multi-tier representation, so that any future extensions can be easily incorporated if necessary. Similar concerns have also been addressed in the French Treebank (Abeillé et al., this volume).

2.1 Representing Morphological Information

At the lowest level we would like to represent three main aspects of a lexical item:

- The word itself, e.g., `evimdekiler`, (those in my house).
- The lexical structure, as a sequence of free and bound morphemes (including any morphophonological material elided on the surface, and meta symbols for relevant phonological categories), e.g.,

  `ev+Hm+DA+ki+lAr`

  (where for instance `D` represents a set of dental consonants, `H` a set of high-vowels and `A` represents the set of non-round front vowels, which are resolved to their surface realizations when the phonological context is taken into account.)
- The morphological features encoded by the word as a sequence of morphological and POS feature values all of which except the root are symbolic, e.g.,

  `ev+Noun+A3sg+P1sg+Loc^DB+Adj^DB+Noun+Zero+A3pl+Pnon+Nom`

  A point to note about this representation is that, information that is conveyed covertly by zero-morphemes that is not explicit in the lexical representation, is represented here. (e.g., if a plural marker is not present then the noun is singular hence `+A3sg` is the feature supplied even though there is no overt morpheme.) A comprehensive list of morphological feature symbols is given in Appendix.

The first two components of the morphological information do not require any more details for the purposes of this presentation. The third component with its relation to lexical tag information needs to be discussed further.

The prevalence of productive derivational word forms is a challenge if we want to represent such information using a finite (and possibly reduced) tagset. The usual approaches to tagset design typically assume that the morphological information associated with a word form can be encoded using a finite number of cryptically coded symbols from some set whose size ranges from few tens (e.g., the Penn Treebank tagset (Marcus et al., 1993)) to hundreds or even thousands (e.g., the Prague Treebank tagset, (Hajič, 1998; Böhmová et al., this volume)). But, such a finite tagset approach for languages like Turkish inevitably leads to loss of information. The reason for this is that the morphological features of intermediate derivations can contain markers for syntactic relationships. Leaving out this information within a fixed-tagset scheme may prevent crucial syntactic information from being represented.

For these reasons we have decided not to compress in any way the morphological information associated with a Turkish word and represent such words as a sequence of *inflectional groups* (IGs hereafter), separated by `^DB`s denoting derivation boundaries. Thus a word would be represented in the following general form:

$\texttt{root+Infl}_1\texttt{\^{}DB+Infl}_2\texttt{\^{}DB+}\cdots\texttt{\^{}DB+Infl}_n$

where the $\texttt{Infl}_i$ denote relevant inflectional features including the part-of-speech for the root or any of the subsequent derived forms, if any. For instance, the derived modifier `sağlamlaştırdığımızdaki` (with the parse given earlier) would be represented by the 6 IGs:

1. `sağlam+Adj`
2. `+Verb+Become`
3. `+Verb+Caus+Pos`
4. `+Adj+PastPart+P1sg`
5. `+Noun+Zero+A3sg+Pnon+Loc`
6. `+Adj`

Note that the set of possible IGs is finite and these can be compactly coded into (cryptic) symbols, but we feel that apart from saving storage, such an encoding serves no real purpose while the resulting opaqueness prevents facilitated access to component features.

Although we have presented a novel way of looking at the lexical structure, the reader may have received the impression that words in Turkish have overly complicated structures with many IGs per word. Various statistics actually indicate that this is really not the case. For instance the statistics presented in Table 15.1, compiled from an approximately 850,000 word corpus of Turkish news text, indicate that on average the number of IGs per word is less than 2. Thus, for instance modeling each word uniformly with 2 IGs may be a very good approximation for statistical modeling (Hakkani-Tür, 2000).

Table 15.1. Parse and IG Statistics from a Turkish Corpus

	All tokens	**All but high frequency function words and and punctuation**
Morph. Parses per Token	1.76	1.93
IGs per Parse	1.38	1.48
% Tokens with single parse	55	45
% Parses with 1 IG	72	65
% Parses with 2 IGs	18	23
% Parses with 3 IGs	7	9
% Parses with > 3 IGs	3	3
Max Number of IGs in a parse	7	7
Distinct IGs ignoring roots	2448	

Turkish is also very rich in lexicalized and non-lexicalized collocations (Oflazer and Kuruöz, 1994; Oflazer and Tür, 1996). The lexicalized collocations are much like what one would find in other languages. On the other hand, non-lexicalized collocations can be divided into two groups:

1 In the first group, we have compound and support verb formations where there are two or more lexical items the last of which is a verb. Even though the other components can themselves be inflected, they can be assumed to be fixed for the purposes of the collocation and the collocation assumes its inflectional features from the inflectional features of the last verb which itself may undergo any morphological derivation or inflection process. For instance, the idiomatic verb *kafa çek-* (`kafa+Noun+A3sg+Pnon+Nom çek+Verb+...`) (literally, to pull head) means *to get drunk*, and these two tokens essentially behave together as far as syntax goes.[3]

2 The second group of non-lexicalized collocations involve full or partial duplication of verb, adjective or noun forms. For instance, the aorist marked verb sequence

gelir gelmez (`gel+Verb+Pos+Aor+A3sg gel+Verb+Neg+Aor+A3sg`)

actually functions as a temporal adverbial meaning *as soon as ... comes*. Note that these formations (usually involving full or partial reduplications of strings of the sort $\omega\ \omega$, $\omega\ x\ \omega$ or $\omega x\ \omega z$) are beyond the formal power of finite state mechanisms, hence are not dealt within the finite state morphological analyzer. (See Oflazer and Kuruöz, 1994 or Oflazer and Tür, 1996, for a list of such non-lexicalized collocations.)

2.2 Representing Syntactic Relations

We would like to represent syntactic relations between lexical items (actually between inflectional groups as we will see in a moment) using a simple dependency framework. Our arguments for this choice essentially parallel those of recent studies on this topic (Hajič, 1998; Böhmová et al., this volume; Skut et al., 1997; Brants et al., this volume; Lepage et al., 1998). Free constituent ordering and discontinuous phrases make the use of constituent-based representations rather difficult and unnatural. It is however possible to use constituency where it makes sense and bracket sequences of tokens to mark segments in the texts whose internal dependency structure would be of little interest. For instance, collocations, time–date expressions or multiword proper names (which incidentally do not follow Turkish noun phrase rules so have to be treated specially anyway) are examples whose internal structure is of little syntactic concern, and can be bracketed a priori as chunks and then related to other constituents. Such features have also been proposed for the French Treebank (Abeillé et al., this volume). If necessary, any further constituent-based representation can be extracted from the dependency representation (Lin, 1995).

An interesting observation that we can make about Turkish is that, when a word is considered as a sequence of IGs, syntactic relation links only emanate from the last IG of a (dependent) word, and land on one of the IGs of the (head) word to the right (with minor exceptions), as exemplified in Figure 15.1. A second observation is that, (again with minor exceptions), the dependency links between the IGs, when drawn above the IG sequence, do not cross (although this is not a concern here).[4] Figure 15.3 shows a dependency tree for the following sentence in Figure 15.2, laid on top of the words segmented along IG boundaries. Note for instance that, for the word *büyümesi* the previous two words link to its first (verbal) IG, while its 2nd IG (infinitive nominal) links to the final verb as subject.

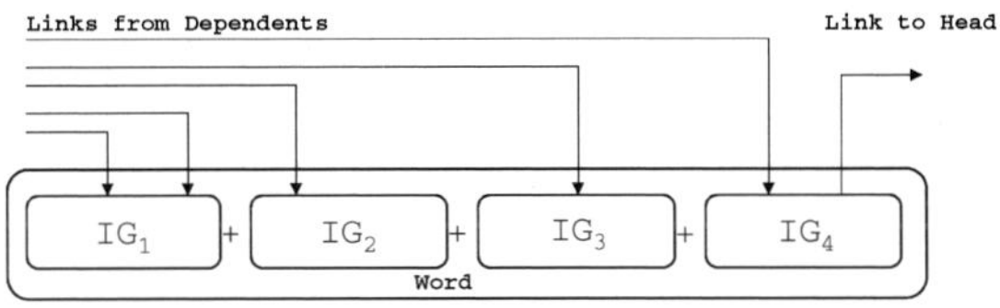

Figure 15.1. Links and Inflectional Groups

(1) Bu eski bahçe-de+ki
`bu(this)+Det eski(old)+Adj bahçe(garden)+A3sg+Pnon+Loc^DB+Adj`
The growth of the rose

gül-ün böyle
`gül(rose)+Noun+A3sg+Pnon+Gen böyle(like-this)+Adv`
like this in this old garden impressed everybody very much.

büyü+me-si
`büyü(grow)+Verb+Pos^DB+Noun+Inf+A3sg+P3sg+Nom`

herkes-i çok
`herkes(everybody)+Pron+A3sg+Pnon+Acc çok(very)+Adv`

etkile-di.
`etkile(impress)+Verb+Pos+Past+A3sg`

Figure 15.2. Example Turkish Sentence

The syntactic relations that we have currently opted to encode in our syntactic representation are the following:

1. Subject	2. Object
3. Modifier (adv./adj.)	4. Possessor
5. Classifier	6. Determiner
7. Dative Adjunct	8. Locative Adjunct
9. Ablative Adjunct	10. Instrumental Adjunct

Some of the relations above perhaps require some more clarification. *Object* is used to mark objects of verbs and the nominal complements of postpositions. A *classifier* is a nominal modifier in nominative case (as in *book cover*) while a *possessor* is a genitive case-marked nominal modifier. For verbal adjuncts, we indicate the syntactic relation with a marker paralleling the case marking though the semantic relation they encode is not only determined by the case marking but also the lexical semantics of the head noun and the verb they are attached to. For instance a dative adjunct can be a *goal*, a *destination*, a *beneficiary* or a *value carrier* in a transaction, or a *theme*, while an ablative adjunct may be a *reason*, a *source* or a *theme*. Although we do not envision the use of such detailed relation labels at the outset, such distinctions can certainly be useful in training case-frame based transfer modules in machine translation systems to select the appropriate prepositions in English for instance.

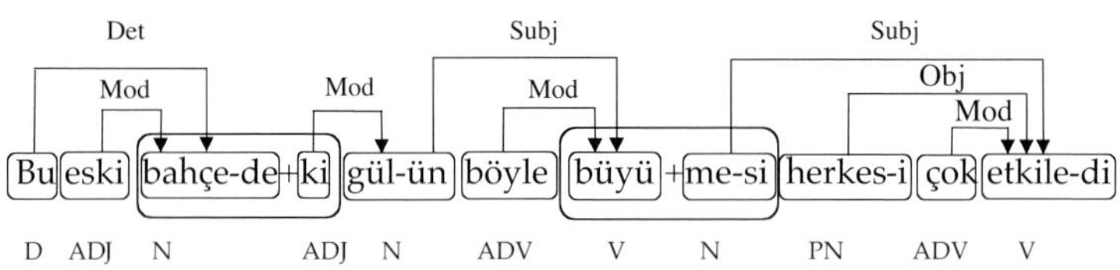

Last line shows the final POS for each word.

Figure 15.3. Dependency structure for a sample Turkish Sentence

2.3 Example of a Treebank Sentence

In this section we present the detailed representation of a Turkish sentence in the treebank. Each sentence is represented by a sequence of the attribute lists of the words involved, bracketed with tags `<S>` and `</S>`.[5] Figure 15.4 shows the treebank encoding for the sentence given earlier. Each word is bracketed by `<W>` and `</W>` tags. The `IX` denotes the number or index of the word. `LEM` denotes the lemma of the word, as one would find in a dictionary. For verbs, this is typically an infinitive form, while for other word classes it is usually the root word itself. `MORPH` indicates the morphological structure of the word as a sequence of morphemes, essentially corresponding to the lexical form.

```
<S>
<W IX=1 LEM=''bu'' MORPH=''bu'' IG=[(1, ''bu+Det'')]
REL=[(3,1,(DETERMINER)]> Bu </W>

<W IX=2 LEM=''eski'' MORPH=''eski'' IG=[(1, ''eski+Adj'')]
REL=[3,1,(MODIFIER)]> eski> </W>

<W IX=3 LEM=''bahçe'' MORPH=''bahçe+DA+ki'' IG=[(1,
''bahçe+A3sg+Pnon+Loc'') (2, ''+Det'')] REL=[4,1,(MODIFIER)]> bahçedeki
</W>

<W IX=4 LEM=''gül'' MORPH=''gül+nHn'' IG=[(1,''gül+Noun+A3sg+Pnon+Gen'')]
REL=[6,1,(SUBJECT)]> gülün </W>

<W IX=5 LEM=''böyle'' MORPH=''böyle'' IG=[(1,''böyle+Adv'')]
REL=[6,1,(MODIFIER)]> böyle </W>

<W IX=6 LEM=''büyümek'' MORPH=''büyü+mA+sH'' IG=[(1,''büyü+Verb+Pos'') (2,
''+Noun+Inf+A3sg+P3sg+Nom'')] REL=[9,1,(SUBJECT)]> büyümesi </W>

<W IX=7 LEM=''herkes'' MORPH=''herkes+yH'' IG=[(1,''herkes+Pron+A3sg+Pnon+Acc'')]
REL=[9,1,(OBJECT)]> herkesi </W>

<W IX=8 LEM=''çok'' MORPH=''çok'' IG=[(1,''çok+Adv'')]
REL=[9,1,(MODIFIER)]> çok </W>

<W IX=9 LEM=''etkilemek'' MORPH=''etkile+DH'' IG=[(1,
''etkile+Verb+Pos+Past+A3sg'')] REL=[]> etkiledi </W>

</S>
```

Figure 15.4. Sample treebank encoding a Turkish sentence

The morphemes may involve meta-symbols (mentioned earlier) for indicating any phonological classes of symbols. IG is a list of pairs of an integer and an inflectional group. REL encodes the relationship of this word, as indicated by its last inflection group, to an inflectional group of some other word. The first component of REL is the index of a word, the second component is the number of the inflection group in that word that the current word's last IG is linked to, and the third component is a list of relation labels for any possible syntactic (e.g., dative adjunct) and semantic (e.g., destination) relationships between the IGs involved. For example, the 4th and 5th words in the sentence are the subject and adverbial modifier, respectively, of the verb in the first IG of the 6th word, while the 2nd IG of the same word (6) is the subject of the main verb of word 9. We have only used simple syntactic relation names in the example but more certainly can be added. For instance adjectival modifiers can be further classified into attributive, cardinal, etc., while an object may further be marked as theme or patient, as discussed earlier.

A collocation would be represented by coalescing the information of individual components. For instance, the non-lexicalized collocation *gelir gelmez* and its adjunct

(2)

ev+e	gel+ir	gel+me+z
`ev+Noun+A3sg+Pnon+Dat`	`gel+Verb+Pos+Aor+A3sg`	
	`gel+Verb+Neg+Aor+A3sg`	

...as soon as ...comes to the house ...

would be represented as

```
   ...
<W IX=5 LEM=''ev'' MORPH=''ev+yA'' IG=[(1,''ev+A3sg+Pnon+Dat'')]],
   REL=[6,1,(DATIVE-ADJ,DEST)]> eve </W>

<W IX=6 LEM=''gelmek'' MORPH=''gel+Hr gel+mA+z''
   IG=[(1, ''gel+Verb+Pos'')(2, ''+Adv+AsSoonAs'')],
   REL=[...]> gelir gelmez  </W>
   ...
```

where it should be noted that the non-lexicalized collocation has been treated as a derivational process and an adverbial IG `+Adv+AsSoonAs` has been created.

3. THE ANNOTATION TOOL

We have implemented a first version of treebank annotation tool that lets an annotator semi-automatically annotate a Turkish text. A snapshot of the user interface of this tool is given in Figure 3.

At the top, the annotator sees the sentence as text along with the previous and the next sentences, if any. The main window below contains the morphological analyses of the tokens with ambiguous analyses being listed vertically below the token. The annotator then performs a manual morphological disambiguation by selecting the appropriate analysis by ticking its box.[6]. The IGs of the selected analysis are then listed side by side, in the middle of the lower window, with the morphological features in an IG being listed vertically (see the entries above the rightmost word bracketed with ==). The annotator then proceeds with a drag and drop interaction, clicking on a source IG, starting a link and then dropping the end of the link on the target IG. At this point a pop-up menu forces the annotator to select a link type as shown in Figure 15.5. In a future version, this linking will be done in a more intelligent fashion with the destination IG and the contents of the label pop-up menu being determined by the source IG.

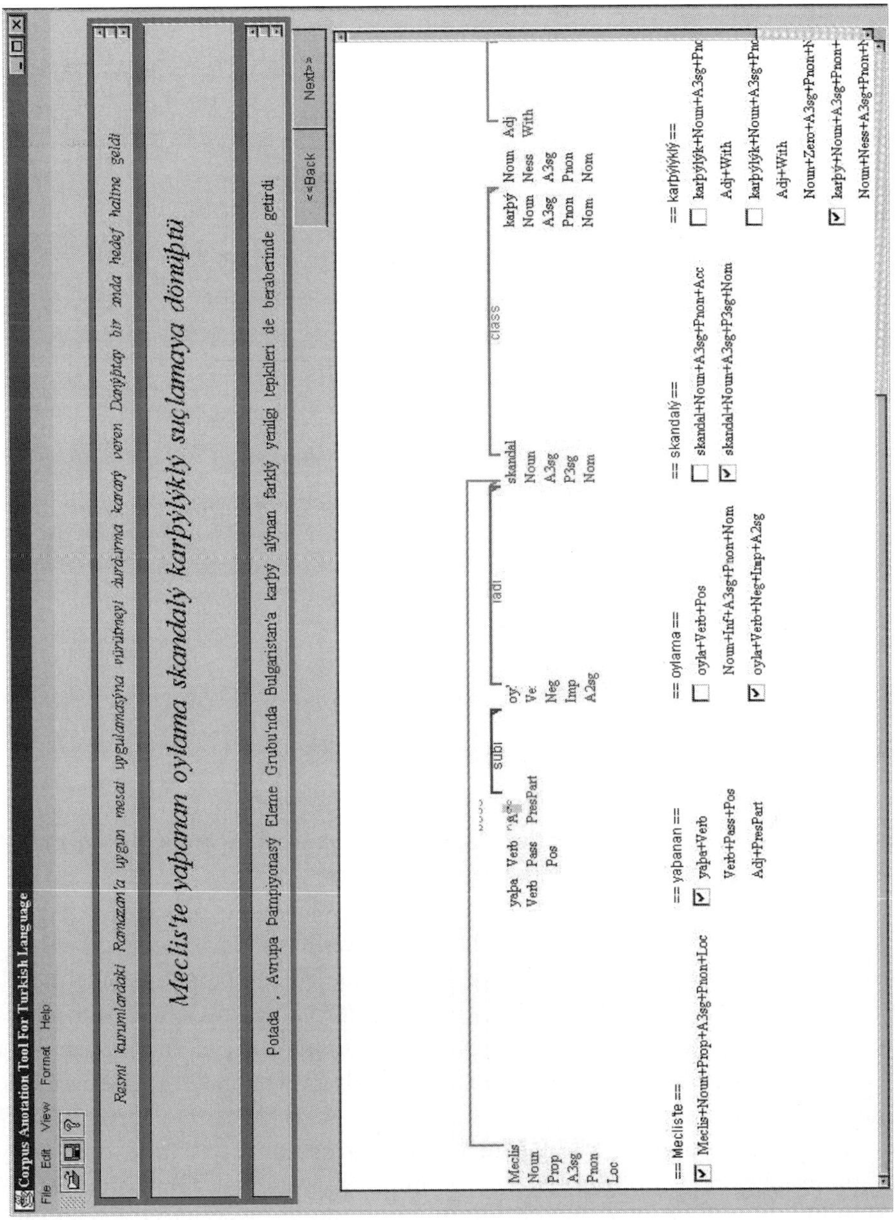

Figure 15.5. The user interface of the treebank annotation tool

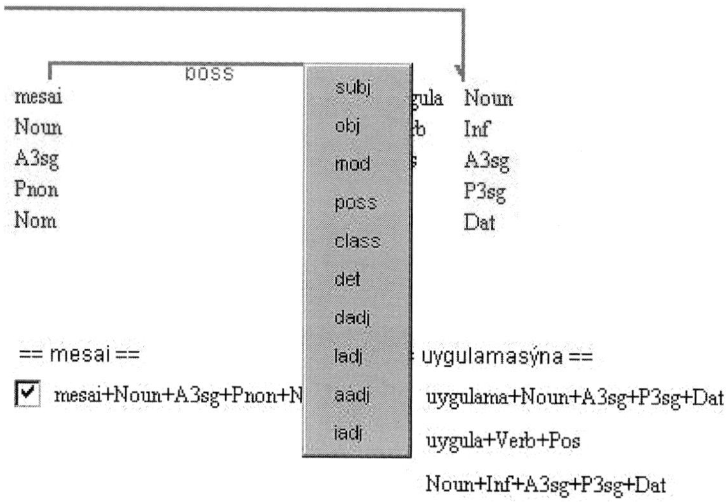

Figure 15.6. Selecting the link type

4. SOME DIFFICULT ISSUES

Turkish is a pro-drop language, and the subject (and usually various other constituents) may be elided on the surface. In the case of subjects, the information is recoverable from the agreement marker on the verbs. Since we aim to capture just the surface relations, such covert cases are not marked. The case of verb ellipsis is a bit more tricky. In these cases we have constituents which do not have a surface governor. We have for the time being opted to handle these cases by explicitly entering a dummy constituent (with a null surface form but nevertheless a token) linked with a special link to the parallel verb, indicating its elided status. Then the constituents of the elided verb can be attached to this dummy constituent.

Headless constructions such as coordinating conjunctions have been one of the weaker points of dependency grammar approaches. Our solution for describing coordinate conjunction constructs essentially follows (Järvinen and Tapanainen, 1998). For a sequence of IGs like

$$D_1 \ldots C \ldots D_2 \ldots C \ldots\ldots D_k \ldots H$$

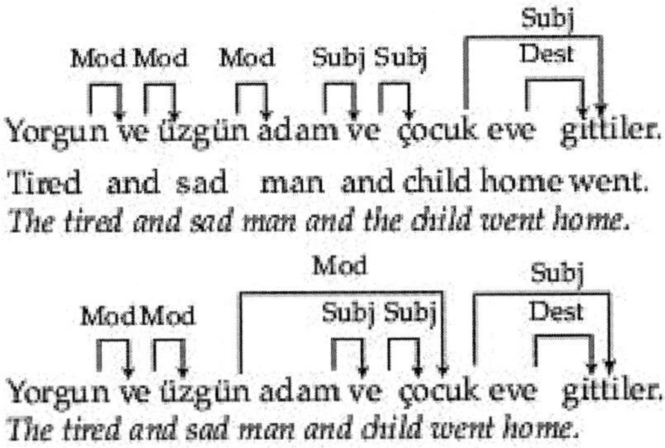

Figure 15.7. Linking conjoined constituents

where the D_i are the dependent IGs that are coordinated and the Cs are the conjunction IGs (for , (comma), *and* and *or*), and H is the head IG, we effectively thread a "long link" from D_1 to H. If the link between D_k and H is labeled with l, then dependent D_i links to the following C with link l, and this C links to D_{i+1} with l. One feature of Turkish simplifies this threading a bit: the left conjunct IG has to immediately precede the conjunction IG (except for the very unlikely case of verbal coordination in inverted constituent orders). Figure 4 shows the links for encoding two possible interpretations of conjunction scope for a simple Turkish sentence.

5. CONCLUSIONS AND FUTURE WORK

Our work to date has concentrated on resolving the issues in encoding Turkish treebanks, developing annotation guidelines and tools for semi-automatic annotation. There are certainly other theoretical issues especially in the dependency representations of various problematic constructs. As of summer of 2002, the annotation process has itself produced a preliminary treebank with only about 1500 sentences annotated using the annotation tools we have developed.

The annotation tool provides for full morphological analysis but for limited conservative morphological disambiguation (Oflazer, 1994; Oflazer and Tür, 1997). It will allow the annotator to modify the selection if an error has been in the automatic annotation process. It will also suggest possible dependency links by eliminating the impossible dependency links than can not occur between two words with given morphological analyses (suggested by our work on dependency parsing of Turkish (Oflazer, 1999). If the annotator does agree with the automatically selected links, then nothing else needs to be done. Otherwise the annotator has the option to correct and manually add the correct links. Using this tool, we expect to complete about 20,000 in the next 18 months with multiple annotators working in parallel.

Acknowledgments

This work is supported by a grant from TÜBİTAK, the Turkish Scientific and Technical Research Council (Grant No: EEEAG-199E026).

Notes

1. Literally, "(the thing existing) at the time we caused (something) to become strong". Obviously this is not a word that one would use everyday. Turkish words (excluding noninflecting frequent words such as conjunctions, clitics etc) found in typical text average about 10 letters in length.

2. Please refer to the comprehensive list of morphological features given in Appendix for the semantics of some of the non-obvious symbols used here.

3. Though they may be separated by various clitics, in which case the collocation cannot be recognized by simple local means.

4. This however does not mean that there no non-projective constructs in Turkish. There are a number of constructs, such as an adverbial modifying a verb, cutting in between a modifier and the head noun making up the subject NP. These, however, are very rare. Our representation does not have any restriction regarding projectivity and lets us represent the crossing links in such cases.

5. Words in this context may also be lexicalized or non-lexicalized collocations.

6. The input to the annotator is actually morphologically preprocessed with each token already having been analyzed in all its ambiguity. This same file could also be run through a morphological disambiguator module (Hakkani-Tür et al., 2000). If this disambiguator makes any mistakes (and it does), our current tool does not let us correct an incorrectly disambiguated morphological analyses yet, so we have opted not to disambiguate for the time being.

References

Abeillé, A., Clément, L., Toussenel, F. (2003). Building a treebank for french. This volume.

Böhmová, A., Hajič, J., Panenová, B. H. J., Böhmova, A., Hajicova, E. (2003). The Prague Dependency Treebank. This volume.

Brants, T., Skut, W., Uszkoreit, H. (2003). Syntactic annotation of a German newspaper corpus. This volume.

Erguvanlı, E. (1979). *The Function of Word order in Turkish*. PhD thesis, University of California, Los Angeles.

Hajič, J. (1998). Building a syntactically annotated corpus: The Prague Dependency Treebank. In Hajicova, E., (ed), *Issues in Valency and Meaning: Studies in Honour of Jarmila Panenova*. Karolinum – Charles University Press, Prague.

Hakkani-Tür, D. Z. (2000). *Statistical Language Modeling for Turkish*. PhD thesis, Bilkent University, Department of Computer Science, Ankara, Turkey.

Hakkani-Tür, D. Z., Oflazer, K., Tür, G. (2000). Statistical morphological disambiguation for agglutinative languages. In *Proceedings of COLING*. ICCL.

Hankamer, J. (1989). Morphological parsing and the lexicon. In Marslen-Wilson, W., (ed), *Lexical Representation and Process*. MIT Press.

Järvinen, T., Tapanainen, P. (1998). Towards an implementable dependency grammar. *Proceedings of COLING/ACL'98 Workshop on Processing Dependency-based Grammars*, p. 1–10.

Lepage, Y., Shin-Ichi, A., Susumu, A., Hitoshi, I. (1998). An annotated corpus in Japanese using Tesnière's structural syntax. *Proceedings of COLING-ACL'98 Workshop on the Processing of Dependency-based Grammars*.

Lin, D. (1995). A dependency-based method for evaluation broad-coverage parsers. *Proceedings of IJCAI'95*.

Marcus, M., Santorini, B., Marcinkiewitz, M. A. (1993). Building a large annotated corpus of English: The Penn Treebank. *Computational Linguistics*, 19, p. 313–330.

Oflazer, K. (1994). Two-level description of Turkish morphology. *Literary and Linguistic Computing*, 9(2).

Oflazer, K. (1999). Dependency parsing with an extended finite state approach. *Proceedings of ACL'99, the 37th Annual Meeting of the Association for Computational Linguistics*.

Oflazer, K., Kuruöz, İ. (1994). Tagging and morphological disambiguation of Turkish text. *Proceedings of the* 4th *Applied Natural Language Processing Conference*, p. 144–149. ACL.

Oflazer, K., Tür, G. (1996). Combining hand-crafted rules and unsupervised learning in constraint-based morphological disambiguation. In Brill, E. and Church, K., (eds), *Proceedings of the ACL-SIGDAT Conference on Empirical Methods in Natural Language Processing*.

Oflazer, K., Tür, G. (1997). Morphological disambiguation by voting constraints. *Proceedings of ACL'97/EACL'97, The 35th Annual Meeting of the Association for Computational Linguistics*.

Skut, W., Krenn, B., Brants, T., Uszkoreit, H. (1997). An annotation scheme for free word order languages. *Proceedings of Fifth Conference on Applied Natural Language Processing*.

Taylor, A., Marcus, M., Santorini, B. (2003). The Penn Treebank: an overview. This volume.

Appendix: Turkish Morphological Features

In this section we provide a list of morphological features used in the encoding of about 9,000 possible IGs that can be produced by our morphological analysis. Although not all of these have been used in examples used in this chapter, we feel it is useful for conveying to the reader the wealth of the information Turkish lexical forms encode.

- **Major Parts of Speech**: `+Noun, +Adj, +Adv, +Conj, +Det, +Dup, +Interj, +Ques, +Verb, +Postp, +Num, +Pron, +Punc.` (the category `+Dup` contains onomatopoeic words which only appear as duplications in a sentence.)
- **Minor Parts of Speech**: These typically follow a major POS to further subdivide that class, or to indicate the kind of derivation involved.
  - After `+Num`: `+Card, +Ord, +Percent, +Range, +Real, +Ratio, +Distrib, +Time.`
  - After `+Noun`: `+Inf, +PastPart, +FutPart, +Prop, +Zero.`
  - After `+Adj`: `+PastPart, +FutPart, +PresPart.`
  - After `+Pron`: `+DemonsP, +QuesP, +ReflexP, +PersP, +QuantP.`
- The following (mostly semantic) markers are used after derivations to indicate the kind of derivation involved:
  - After `+Adv` derived from verbs: `+AfterDoingSo, +SinceDoingSo, +As (he does it), +When, +ByDoingSo, +While, +AsIf, +WithoutHavingDoneSo.`
  - After `+Adv` derived from Adjectives: `+Ly` (equivalent to the English *+ly* derivation.)
  - After `+Adv` derived from temporal nouns: `+Since`
  - After `+Adj` derived from nouns: `+With, +Without, +SuitableFor, +InBetween, +Rel.`
  - After `+Noun` derived from adjectives: `+Ness` (as in red vs. redness)
  - After `+Noun` derived from nouns: `+Agt` (someone involved in some way with the stem noun), `+Dim` (Diminutive),
  - After `+Verb` derived from nouns or adjectives: `+Become` (to become like the noun or adjective in the stem) `+Acquire` (to acquire the noun in the stem)
  - A `+Zero` appears after a zero morpheme derivation.
- Nominal forms (Nouns, Derived Nouns, Pronouns, Participles and Infinitives) get the following additional inflectional markers:
  1 **Number/Person Agreement**: `+A1sg, +A2sg, +A3sg, +A1pl, +A2pl, +A3pl.`
  2 **Possessive Agreement**: `+P1sg, +P2sg, +P3sg, +P1pl, +P2pl, +P3pl, +Pnon` (no overt agreement).
  3 **Case**:`+Nom, +Acc, +Dat, +Abl, +Loc, +Gen, +Ins.`
- Adjectives (lexical or derived) do not take any inflection, except `+Adj+PastPart` and `+Adj+FutPart` will have a `+Pxxx` (possessive agreement as above) to mark verbal agreement. Any other inflection to adjectives implies type-raising to nouns and the inflection goes onto the noun after a zero-morpheme derivation.

- Verbs have two sets of markers which are treated as derivations:

  1 **Voice**: `+Pass, +Caus, +Reflex, +Recip`, (A verb form may have multiple causative markers).

  2 **Compounding/Modality**: `+Able` (able to verb), `+Repeat` (verb repeatedly), `+Hastily` (verb hastily), `+EverSince` (have been verb-ing ever since), `+Almost` (almost verb-ed but did not), `+Stay` (stayed frozen while verb-ing), `+Start` (start verb-ing immediately)

- Verbs also get the following inflectional markers:

  1 **Polarity**: `+Pos, +Neg`

  2 **Tense-Aspect-Mood**: A finite verb may have 1 or 2 of `+Past` (past tense), `+Narr` (narrative past tense), `+Fut` (future tense), `+Aor` (Aorist, may indicate habitual, present, future, you name it), `+Pres` (present tense, for predicative nominals or adjectives), `+Desr` (desire/wish), `+Cond` (conditional), `+Neces` (Necessitative, must), `+Opt` (optative, let me/him/her verb), `+Imp` (imperative), `+Prog1` (Present continuous, process), `+Prog2` (Present continuous, state).

  3 Verbs also have person and number agreement markers (see nominal forms earlier) and an optional copula marker.

II

USING TREEBANKS

Chapter 16

ENCODING SYNTACTIC ANNOTATION

Nancy Ide
Department of Computer Science, Vassar College, Poughkeepsie, New York 12604-0520, USA
ide@cs.vassar.edu

Laurent Romary
LORIA/CNRS, Campus Scientifique, B.P. 239, 54506 Vandoeuvre-les-Nancy, FRANCE
romary@loria.fr

Abstract There is a widely recognized need for a general framework for linguistic annotation that is flexible and extensible enough to accommodate different annotation types and different theoretical and practical approaches, while at the same time enabling their representation in a "pivot" format that can serve as the basis for comparative evaluation, merging, and the development of reusable editing and processing tools. To address this need, we have developed a framework composed of an abstract model for a variety of different annotation types (e.g., morpho-syntactic tagging, syntactic annotation, coreference annotation, etc.), which can be instantiated in different ways depending on the annotator's approach and goals. The results have been incorporated into XCES (Ide et al., 2000), the XML instantiation of the Corpus Encoding Standard (Ide 1998a,b), which provides a ready-made, standard encoding format together with a data architecture designed specifically for linguistically annotated corpora.

Keywords: Corpus Annotation Standards, Extended Markup Language, Resource Description Framework

1. INTRODUCTION

Building a treebank requires several choices concerning annotation format. First, the annotator(s) must determine the *annotation scheme*, consisting of morpho-syntactic labels and syntactic constituent types together with general structural principles for the annotation, as dictated by the theory or model that informs the annotation. Second, the annotator must decide on an *encoding*

A. Abeillé (ed.), Treebanks: Building and Using Parsed Corpora, 281–296.

scheme, that is, the physical representation of the annotation information in a physical document with tags, attributes, etc., as well as representation of both immediate and long-distance dependencies among constituents. Finally, the annotator must choose a data architecture for the primary text and its annotations, which dictates whether annotations are interspersed throughout the document containing the primary text or stored in one or more additional documents linked to the primary text. As the chapters in the previous section of this book demonstrate, these choices can differ considerably from project to project, even for the same language (see for example, Taylor et al., this volume; Wallis, this volume).

It is widely recognized that the proliferation of annotation schemes runs counter to the need to re-use language resources, and that standards for linguistic annotation are becoming increasingly mandatory. In particular, there is a need for a general framework for linguistic annotation that is flexible and extensible enough to accommodate different annotation types and different theoretical and practical approaches, while at the same time enabling their representation in a "pivot" format that can serve as the basis for comparative evaluation of parser output, such as PARSEVAL (Harrison, et al., 1991), as well as the development of reusable editing and processing tools.

To address this need, we have developed such a framework consisting of an abstract model for a variety of different annotation types (e.g., morpho-syntactic tagging, syntactic annotation, co-reference annotation, etc.), which can be instantiated in different ways depending on the annotator's approach and goals. We have implemented both the abstract model and various instantiations using XML schemas (Thompson, et al., 2000), and the Resource Definition Framework (RDF) (Lassila and Swick, 2000) and RDF schemas (Brickley and Guha, 2000), which enable description and definition of abstract data models together with means to interpret, via the model, information encoded according to different conventions. The results have been incorporated into XCES (Ide, et al., 2000a), the XML instantiation of the Corpus Encoding Standard (Ide, 1998a,b). XCES provides a ready-made, standard encoding format together with a data architecture designed specifically for linguistically annotated corpora.

By exploiting the power of XML and RDF to implement an abstract model for instantiations of specific annotation schemes, XCES provides a flexible and extensible mechanism for encoding a wide variety of linguistic annotations that is based on emerging standards for data representation and interchange. As such, it has a broader scope and applicability than existing annotation frameworks such as ATLAS (Bird, et al, 2000), which define specific XML formats for encoding annotations and rely on internally-developed mechanisms for associating semantics with annotation categories. The XCES framework, on the other hand, takes data abstraction a step farther than existing frameworks by assuming that project-specific formats (including, for example, the ATLAS format) will be translated into the generic XML representation for the purposes of interchange, merging and comparison, and manipulation via generic tools. Furthermore, XCES relies on RDF to define annotation semantics, thus ensuring built-in support via web-based tools. It is also closely related to on-going work within the International Standards Organization (ISO) on the development of representation frameworks for terminology (Terminological Markup Framework[1], ISO project no. 16642) and language resources (TC37SC4). Thus XCES provides a framework that is developing in step with international standards and guarantees reusability without limiting the annotator's choice of representation.

2. XCES

The eXtensible Markup Language (XML) is the emerging standard for data representation and exchange on the World Wide Web (Bray, Paoli, & Sperberg-McQueen, 1998). Although at its most basic level XML is a document markup language directly derived from SGML (i.e., allowing tagged text (elements), element nesting, and element references), various features and extensions of XML make it a far more powerful tool for data representation and access. For example, the eXtensible Style Language (XSL) provides a powerful transformation language (XSLT) (Clark, 1999) that can be used to convert any XML document into another document (either another XML document or a document marked-up with HTML, etc.) by selecting, rearranging, and adding information to it, in order to serve any application that relies on part or all of its contents. Also, XML's provision for accessing part or all of multiple DTDs in a single document provides an elegant means to represent and manipulate multiple documents representing a text and its annotations.

XCES[2], the XML instantiation of the Corpus Encoding Standard (Ide, 1998a, b), is part of the EAGLES Guidelines developed by the Expert Advisory Group on Language Engineering Standards (EAGLES)[3]. XCES is designed to be optimally suited for use in language engineering research and applications, and to serve as a widely accepted set of encoding standards for corpus-based work in natural language processing applications. The standard specifies a minimal encoding level that corpora must achieve to be considered standardized in terms of descriptive representation (marking of structural and typographic information), provides a suite of DTDs and XML schemas for encoding basic document structure and linguistic annotation, and specifies a corresponding data architecture for linguistically annotated corpora.

We are currently developing a comprehensive framework for linguistic annotation within the XCES which exploits the capabilities of the XML environment, with the ultimate goal of providing a fully-specified web-based format that enables maximal inter-operability among not only annotations of the same phenomena, but across annotation types. We aim to provide an environment in which annotations can be easily defined (and validated), rather than to dictate the use of specific annotation values, elements, etc. To this end, we are developing the following:

- a repository of existing annotation formats for a variety of linguistic features and, where necessary, XML schemas to instantiate them together with XSLT scripts to transduce between different formats.
- XML schemas to instantiate a hierarchically specified structural model for annotations, beginning at the most abstract level and then defining derived types for general classes of annotation (e.g., speech, discourse, morpho-syntax, etc.). Precise annotation values will be specified in schemas at the lowest level of the hierarchy that can be used "off the shelf" by corpus annotators or modified to suit specific needs. Because types and sub- types are specified in an increasingly precise hierarchy, it is relatively trivial to back up one or more levels of abstraction and define new sub-types, and variant types can be easily created from existing ones by defining new derived or extended types.
- Because XML-encoded annotated corpora are increasingly used for interchange between individual processing and analytic tools, for commonly used tools we are developing XSLT scripts for mapping, and extraction of annotated data, import/export of (partially) annotated material, and integration of results of external tools into existing annotated data in XML.

3. SYNTACTIC ANNOTATION: CURRENT PRACTICE

At the highest level of abstraction, syntactic annotation schemes must represent the following kinds of information:

1 *Category information*: labeling of components based on syntactic category (e.g., noun phrase, prepositional phrase), syntactic role (subject, object), etc.;

2 *Dependency information*: relations among components, including constituency relations, grammatical role relations, etc.

For example, the annotation in Figure 16.1, drawn from the Penn Treebank II (Taylor, et al., this volume; Marcus et al., 1993) (hereafter, PTB), uses LISP-like list structures to specify constituency relations and provide syntactic category labels for constituents. Some grammatical roles (subject, object, etc.) are implicit in the structure of the encoding: for instance, the nesting of the

NP "the front room" implies that the NP is the object of the first prepositional phrase, whereas the position of the NP "him" following and at the same level as the VP node implies that this NP is the grammatical object. Additional processing (or human intervention) is required to render these relations explicit. Note that the PTB encoding provides some explicit information about grammatical role, in that "subject" is explicitly labeled (although its relation to the verb remains implicit in the structure), but most relations (e.g., "object") are left implicit. Relations among non-contiguous elements demand a special numbering mechanism to enable cross-reference, as in the specification of the NP-SBJ of the embedded sentence by reference to the earlier NP-SBJ-1 node in the PTB example.

```
((S        (NP-SBJ-1 Jones)
           (VP followed)
           (NP him)
           (PP-DIR        into
                  (NP the front room))
           ,
           (S-ADV (NP-SBJ *-1)
                  (VP     closing
                          (NP the door)
                          (PP     behind
                                  (NP him)))))
.))
```

Figure 16.1. Penn Treebank in-line annotation for the sentence "Jones followed him into the front room, closing the door behind him."

Although they differ in the labels and in some cases the function of various nodes in the tree, many of the annotation schemes described in this volume provide a similar constituency-based representation of relations among syntactic components. In contrast, pure dependency schemes (e.g., Sleator and Temperley, 1993; Tapanainen and Jarvinen, 1997; Jarvinen, this volume; Böhmova et al., this volume; Carroll, et al., this volume) do not provide a constituency analysis but rather specify grammatical relations among elements explicitly; for example, the sentence "Paul intends to leave IBM" could be represented as shown in Figure 16.2, where the predicate is the relation type, the first argument is the head, the second the dependent, and additional arguments may provide category-specific information (e.g., introducer for prepositional phrases, etc.). Although dependency schemes do not rely on hierarchical nesting etc. to indicate relations, a projective dependency structure can be mapped into a hierarchical tree structure, which enables construction of a syntax tree. So-called "hybrid systems" (e.g., Basili, et al., 1999; Grefenstette, 1999; Brants et al., this volume) combine constituency analysis and functional dependencies, usually producing a shallow constituent parse that brackets major phrase types and identifies the dependencies between heads of constituents. Such systems (e.g. the NEGRA Corpus, Brants, et al., this volume) allow for crossing branches in their representations; these can be easily converted to well-formed tree structures with traces.

```
subj(intend, Paul, _)
xcomp(intend, leave, to)
subj(leave, Paul)
dobj(leave, IBM _)
```

Figure 16.2. Dependency annotation as used by Carroll, Minnen, and Briscoe

4. A MODEL FOR SYNTACTIC ANNOTATION

The goal in the XCES is to provide a framework for annotation that is theory and tagset independent. We accomplish this by treating the description of any specific syntactic annotation scheme as a process involving several knowledge sources that interact at various levels. The process allows one to specify, on the one hand, the informational properties of the scheme (i.e., its capacity to represent a given piece of information), and, on the other, the way the scheme can be instantiated (e.g., as an XML document). FIG 16.3 shows the overall architecture of the XCES framework for syntactic annotation.
Two knowledge sources are used to define the abstract model:

Data Category Registry (DCR): Within the framework of the XCES we are establishing an inventory of data categories for syntactic annotation, initially based on the EAGLES Recommendations for Syntactic Annotation of Corpora (Leech et al., 1996). Data categories are defined using RDF descriptions that formalize the properties associated with each. The categories are organized in a hierarchy, from general to specific. For example, a general *dependent* relation may be defined, which may be refined as a more precise value such as *argument* or *modifier*; *argument* in turn may have the possible values *subject*, *object*, or *complement*; etc[4]. Note that RDF descriptions function much like class definitions in an object-oriented programming language: they provide, effectively, templates that describe how objects may be instantiated, but do not constitute the objects themselves. Thus, in a document containing an actual annotation, several objects with the type *argument* may be instantiated, each with a different value. The RDF schema ensures that each instantiation of argument is recognized as a sub-class of *dependent* and inherits the appropriate properties.

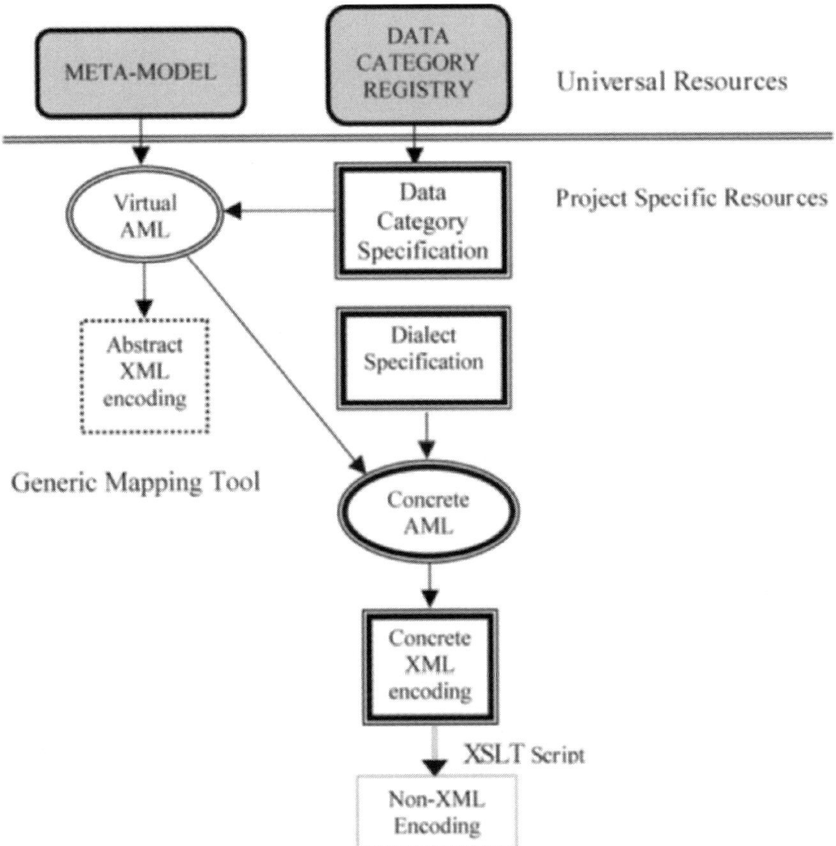

Figure 16.3. Overall architecture of the XCES annotation framework

Meta-model: a domain-dependent abstract structural framework for syntactic annotations, capable of fully capturing all the information in a specific annotation scheme. The meta- model for syntactic annotations is described below in section 4.1.

Two other knowledge sources are used to define a project-specific format for the annotation scheme, in terms of its expressive power and its instantiation in XML:

Data Category Specification (DCS): describes the set of data categories that can be used within a given annotation scheme, again using RDF syntax. The

DCS defines constraints on each category, including restrictions on the values they can take (e.g., "text with markup"; a "picklist" for grammatical gender, or any of the data types defined for XML (see Thompson, et al., 2000), restrictions on where a particular data category can appear (level in the structural hierarchy – see section 4.1). The DCS may include a subset of categories from the DCR together with application-specific categories additionally defined in the DCS. The DCS also indicates a level of granularity based on the DCR hierarchy.

Dialect specification: defines, using XML schemas, the project-specific XML format for syntactic annotations. The specifications may include

- *Data category instantiation styles*: Data categories may be realized in a project-specific scheme in any of a variety of formats. For example, if there exists a data category NounPhrase, this may be realized as a <NounPhrase> element (possibly containing additional elements), a typed element (e.g. <cat type="NounPhrase">), tag content (e.g., <cat>NounPhrase</cat>), etc.

- *Data category vocabulary*: Project-specific formats can utilize, for a given style, names different from those in the Data Category Registry; for instance, a DCR specification for NounPhrase can be expressed as "NP" or "SN" ("syntagme nominal", in French) in the project-specific format, if desired.

- *Expansion structures*: A project-specific format may alter the structure of the annotation as expressed using the meta-model. For example, it may be desirable for processing or other reasons to create two sub-nodes under a given <struct> node, one to group features and one to group relations (see section 4.1).

The combination of the meta-model and the DCS defines a **virtual annotation markup language (AML)**. Any information structure that corresponds to a virtual AML has a canonical expression as an XML document; therefore, the inter-operability of different AMLs is dependent only on their compatibility at the virtual level. As such, virtual AML is the hub of the annotation framework: it defines a *lingua franca* for syntactic annotations that can be used to compare and merge annotations, as well as enable design of generic tools for visualization, editing, extraction, etc.

The combination of a virtual AML with the Dialect Specification provides the information necessary to automatically generate a **concrete AML** representation of the annotation scheme, which conforms to the project-specific format provided in the Dialect specification. XSLT filters translate between the representations of the annotation in concrete and virtual AML, as well as between non-XML formats (such as the LISP-like PTB notation) and concrete AML[5].

4.1 The Meta-Model

For syntactic annotation, we can identify a general, underlying model that informs current practice: specification of constituency relations (with some set of application-specific names and properties) among syntactic or grammatical components (also with a set of application-specific names and properties), whether this is modeled with a tree structure or the relations are given explicitly.

Because of the common practice for syntactic annotation utilizing trees, together with the natural tree-structure of markup in XML documents, we provide a meta-model for syntactic markup that follows this approach. The model is instantiated using the following tags:

- *<struct>* represents a node (level) in the tree. <struct> elements may be recursively nested at any level to reflect the structure of the corresponding syntax tree. In the virtual AML, <struct> elements are not typed (i.e., associated via attributes with specific data categories such as *Sentence, NounPhrase*, etc.), although a project-specific XML schema can provide this information. Attributes include
  - *type* : annotation type (e.g., "syntax"), where necessary[6]
  - *ID*: unique identifier for the node
  - *ref* : node this <struct> node represents (for implicit structures)
- *<feat>* (feature) is used to provide information attached to the node in the tree represented by the enclosing <struct> element. A type attribute on the <feat> element identifies the data category of the feature. The tag may contain a string that provides an appropriate value for the data category (e.g., for type=CAT the value might be "NP") or <feat> can be recursively refined to describe complex structures. Alternatively, it may point via a target attribute to an object in another document that provides the value. Note that this allows the possibility for generating a single instantiation of an annotation value in a separate document that can be referenced as needed within the annotation document.
- *<alt>* is used to provide one or more alternative annotations, where necessary.
- *<rel>* is used to point to a non-contiguous related element, e.g., to identify dependencies explicitly by pointing to the related <struct> node.

The <rel> element has the following attributes, which correspond to the dependency scheme proposed in Carroll, Minnen, and Briscoe (this volume):

- *type* : gives the type of relation (e.g., "subj")
- *head* : specifies the node corresponding to the head of the relation
- *dependent* : specifies the node corresponding to the dependent of the relation
- *introducer* : specifies the node corresponding to an introducing word or phrase
- *initial* : gives a thematic or semantic role of a component, e.g., "subj" for the object of a by-phrase in a passive sentence.
- *target* : pointer to node(s) corresponding to related objects, for non-oriented relations (e.g., ellipses, verb-less sentences, conjunction). Note that this attribute can be used to handle crossing branches, as in trees in the NEGRA Corpus (Brants, et al., this volume), by linking the associated nodes.

■ <*seg*> points to the data to which the annotation applies. In the XCES, we recommend the use of *stand-off annotation* – i.e., annotation that is maintained in a document separate from the primary (annotated) data. A *target* attribute on the <seg> element uses XML Pointers (Xpointer) (Daniel, et al., 2001) to specify the location of the relevant data.

The hierarchy of <struct> elements corresponds to the nodes in a phrase-structure analysis. The grammar underlying the annotation therefore specifies constraints on embedding that can be instantiated with XML schema, which can then be used to prevent or detect tree structures that do not conform to the grammar. Conversely, grammar rules implicit in annotated treebanks, which are typically not annotated according to a formal grammar, can be extracted using tools for automatic DTD generation. Although the context-free rules defined in the derived XML DTD would in most cases fail to represent all of the constraints on alternative right-hand sides, the rules in the DTD nonetheless provide a starting point for determining the grammar underlying the treebank annotations.

Figure 16.4 shows the annotation from the PTB (Figure 16.1) rendered in the abstract XML format. The words in the original sentence are given on the right in italics for reference. Note that in this example, relations are encoded only when they appear explicitly in the original annotation. Heads of these relations, which are implicit in the original, are encoded explicitly here (marked in boldface in Figure 16.1). Note also that the <feat> element associated with the implicit subject of the embedded sentence ([Jones]), also given in boldface, is included here to reflect the contents of the original PTB encoding, although the information is redundant since it appears within the <struct> node to which the reference applies.

A strict dependency annotation encoded in the abstract format uses a "flat" hierarchy and specifies all relations explicitly with the rel attribute, as shown in Figure 16.5[7].

5. USING THE XCES SCHEME

Despite its apparent complexity, the framework outlined in the previous section is intended to reduce overhead for annotators and users. Part of the work of the XCES is to provide XML support (e.g., development of XSLT scripts, XML schemas, etc.) for use by the research community, thus eliminating the need for XML expertise at each development site. Also, with XML at its core, the XCES framework builds on emerging standards for data interchange for which there is widespread support; common scripts and tools can be developed, reducing the "reinventing of the wheel" that is commonplace in the area of corpus annotation at present. Because XML-encoded annotated corpora are increasingly used for interchange between individual processing and analytic tools, for commonly used tools we are developing XSLT scripts for mapping, and extraction of annotated data, import/export of (partially) annotated material, and integration of the results of external tools into existing annotated data in XML. Tools for editing annotations in the abstract format, which automatically generate virtual AML from Data Category and Dialect Specifications, are already under development in the context of work on the Terminological Markup Language, and a tool for automatically generating RDF specifications for user-specified data categories has already been developed in the SALT project[8]. Several freely distributed interpreters for XSLT have also been developed (e.g., XT[9] , Xalan[10]). As XML use becomes more widespread, more and more reusable tools and resources (including web-based applications) are becoming available. In practice, then, annotators and users of annotated corpora will rarely see XML and RDF instantiations of annotated data; rather, they will access the data via interfaces that automatically generate, interpret, and display the data in easy-to-read formats.

The abstract model that captures the fundamental properties of syntactic annotation schemes provides a conceptual tool for assessing the coherence and consistency of existing schemes and those being developed. The abstract model enforces clear distinctions between implicit and explicit information (e.g., functional relations implied by structural relations in constituent analyses), and phrasal and functional relations. It is alarmingly common for annotation schemes to represent these different kinds of information in the same way, rendering their distinction computationally intractable (even if they are per-

```
<struct id="s0">
    <feat type="Cat">S</feat>
    <struct id="s1">
        <rel type="SBJ" head="s2"/>
      <feat type="Cat">NP</feat>
        <seg target="xptr(substring(/p/s[1]/text(),1,5))"/>                  Jones
    </struct>
    <struct id="s2">
        <feat type="Cat">VP</feat>
        <seg target="xptr(substring(/p/s[1]/text(),7,8))"/>                 followed
    </struct>
    <struct id="s3">
        <feat type="Cat">NP</feat>
        <seg target="xptr(substring(/p/s[1]/text(),16,3))"/>                   him
    </struct>
    <struct id="s4">
        <rel type="DIR" head="s2"/>
        <feat type="Cat">PP</feat>
        <seg target="xptr(substring(/p/s[1]/text(),20,4))"/>                  into
        <struct id="s5">
                <feat type="Cat">NP</feat>
                <seg target="xptr(substring(/p/s[1]/text(),25,14))"/> the room
        </struct>
    </struct>
    <struct id="s6">
        <rel type="ADV" head="s2"/>
        <feat type="Cat">S</feat>
        <struct id="s7" ref="s1">
            <rel type="SBJ" head="s8"/>                                   [Jones]
            <feat type="Cat">NP</feat>
        </struct>
        <struct id="s8">
            <feat type="Cat">VP</feat>
            <seg target="xptr(substring(/p/s[1]/text(),41,7))"/>        closing
         <struct id="s9">
            <feat type="Cat">NP</feat>
            <seg target="xptr(substring(/p/s[1]/text(),49,8))"/>        the door
            <struct id="s10">
                <rel type="DIR" head="s8"/>
                <feat type="Cat">PP</feat>
                <seg target="xptr(substring(/p/s[1]/text(),57,6))"/>  behind
                <struct id="s11">
                    <feat type="Cat">NP</feat>
                    <seg target="xptr(substring(/p/s[1]/text(),64,3))"/>him
                </struct>
            </struct>
        </struct>
    </struct>
</struct>
```

Figure 16.4. Abstract XML encoding for the PTB example in Figure 16.1.

```
<struct>
  <rel type="subj"  head="mySentence.xml#w2" dependent="mySentence.xml#w1"/>
  <rel type="xcomp" head="mySentence.xml#w2" dependent="mySentence.xml#w4"
                    introducer="mySentence.xml#w3"/>
  <rel type="subj"  head="mySentence.xml#w4" dependent="mySentence.xml#w1"/>
  <rel type="dobj"  head="mySentence.xml#w4" dependent="mySentence.xml#w5"/>
</struct>
```

Figure 16.5. Abstract XML encoding for the dependency annotation in Figure 16.2.

fectly understandable to the informed human reader). Hand-developed annotation schemes used in treebanks are often described informally in guidebooks for annotators, leaving considerable room for variation; for example, Charniak (1996) notes that the PTB implicitly contains more than 10,000 context-free rules, most of which are used only once. Comparison and transduction of schemes becomes virtually impossible under such circumstances. While requiring that annotators make relations explicit and consider the mapping to the XCES abstract format increases overhead, we feel that the exercise will help avoid such problems and can only lead to greater coherence, consistency, and inter-operability among annotation schemes.

The most important contribution to inter-operability of annotation schemes is the Data Category Registry. By mapping site-specific categories onto definitions in the Registry, equivalences (and non-equivalences) are made explicit. Again, the provision of a "standard" set of categories, together with the requirement that scheme-specific categories are mapped to them where possible, will contribute to greater consistency and commonality among annotation schemes.

6. CONCLUSION

The framework presented here for syntactic annotation is intended to allow for variation in annotation schemes while at the same time enabling comparison and evaluation, merging of different annotations, and development of common tools for creating and using annotated data. We have developed an abstract model for annotations that is capable of representing the necessary information while providing a common encoding format that can be used as a pivot for combining and comparing annotations, as well as an underlying format that can be manipulated and accessed with common tools. The details presented here provide a look "under the hood" in order to show the flexibility and representational power of the abstract scheme; however, the intention is that annotators and users of syntactic annotation schemes can continue to use their own or other formats with which they are comfortable, and translation into and out of the abstract format will be automatic.

The XCES framework for linguistic annotation is built around some relatively straightforward ideas: separation of information conveyed by means of structure and information conveyed directly by specification of content categories; development of an abstract format that puts a layer of abstraction between site-specific annotation schemes and standard specifications; and creation of a Data Category Registry to provide a reference set of annotation categories. The emergence of XML and related standards, together with RDF, provides the enabling technology. We are, therefore, at a point where the creation and use of annotated data and concerns about the way it is represented can be treated separately – that is, researchers can focus on the question of *what* to encode, independent of the question of *how* to encode it. The end result should be greater coherence, consistency, and ease of use and access for linguistic annotated data.

Notes

1. http://www.loria.fr/projets/TMF
2. http://www.xml-ces.org
3. http://www.ilc.pi.cnr.it/EAGLES/home.html
4. Cf. the hierarchy in Figure 17.1 (Carroll, Minnen, and Briscoe, this volume).
5. Strictly speaking, an application-specific format could be translated directly into the virtual AML, eliminating the need for the intermediary concrete AML format. However, especially for existing formats, it is typically more straightforward to perform the two-step process.
6. For some annotation types, <struct> elements are typed; see, for example, the Terminological Markup Framework (http://www.loria.fr/projects/TMF).
7. For the sake of readability, this encoding assumes that the sentence "Paul intends to leave IBM" exists in a separate document named mySentence.xml and is marked up as <s1><w1>Paul</w1><w2>intends</w2><w3>to</w3><w4>leave</w4><w5>IBM</w5></s1>.
8. http://www.loria.fr/projets/SALT
9. (Clark, J., 1999). XT Version 1991105. http://www.jclark.com/xml/xt.html
10. http://www.apache.org

References

Basili, R., Pazienza, M. T., Zanzotto, F.M. (1999). Lexicalizing a Shallow Parser. *Proceedings TALN'99*, Cargèse, Corsica, p. 25-34.

Bird, S., Day, D., Garafolo, J., Henderson, J., Laprun, C., Liberman, M. (2000). ATLAS: A Flexible and Extensible Architecture for Linguistic Annotation. *Proceedings of the Second Language Resources and Evaluation Conference (LREC)*, Athens, Greece, p. 1699-1706

Böhmová , A., Hajič, J., Hajicová, E., Hladká , B. (2003). The Prague Dependency Treebank: a three-level annotation scenario. This volume.

Biron, P., Malhotra, A. (2000). XML Schema Part 2: Datatypes. W3C Candidate Recommendation. `http://www.w3.org/TR/xmlschema-2/`.

Brants, T., Skut, W., Uszkoreit, H. (2003). Syntactic Annotation of a German Newspaper Corpus. This volume.

Bray, T., Paoli, J., Sperberg-McQueen, C.M. (eds.) (1998). Extensible Markup Language (XML) Version 1.0. W3C Recommendation. `http://www.w3.org:TR/1998/REC-xml-19980210`.

Brickley, D. Guha, R.V. (2000). Resource Description Framework (RDF) Schema Specification 1.0. W3C Candidate Recommendation, 27 March 2000. `http://www.w3.org/TR/rdf-schema/`.

Carroll, J., Minnen, G., Briscoe, T. (2003). Parser Evaluation Using a Grammatical Relation Annotation Scheme. This volume.

Clark, J. (ed.) (1999). XSL Transformations (XSLT). Version 1.0. W3C Recommendation. `http://www.w3.org/TR/xslt`.

Daniel, R., DeRose, S., Maler, E. (2001). XML Pointer Language (XPointer) Version 1.0. W3C Recommendation. `http://www.w3.org/TR/xptr`.

Grefenstette, G. (1999). Shallow Parsing Techniques Applied to Medical Terminology Discovery and Normalization. *Proceedings of IMIA WG6, Triennial Conference on Natural Language and Medical Concept Representation.* Phoenix, AZ.

Harrison, P., Abney, S., Black, E., Flickinger, D., Gdaniec, C., Grishman, R., Hindle, D., Ingria, B., Marcus, M., Santorini, B., Strzalkowski, T. (1991). Evaluating syntax performance of parser/grammars of English. *Proceedings of the Workshop on Evaluating Natural Language Processing Systems*. 29th Meeting of the Association for Computational Linguistics, Berkeley, CA, p. 71-77.

Ide, N. (1998a). Encoding Linguistic Corpora. *Proceedings of the Sixth Workshop on Very Large Corpora*, 9-17.

Ide, N. (1998b). Corpus Encoding Standard: SGML Guidelines for Encoding Linguistic Corpora. *Proceedings of the First International Language Resources and Evaluation Conference*, p. 463-70.

Ide, N., Bonhomme, P., Romary, L. (2000). XCES: An XML-based Standard for Linguistic Corpora. *Proceedings of the Second Language Resources and Evaluation Conference (LREC)*, Athens, Greece, p. 825-30.

Järvinen, T. (2003). Bank of English and Beyond: Hand-crafted Parsers for Functional Annotation. This volume.

Lassila, O. Swick, R. (1999) Resource Description framework (RDF) Model and Syntax Specification. W3C Recommendation. `http://www.w3.org/TR/REC-rdf-syntax`.

Leech, G, Barnett, R., Kahrel, P. (1996). EAGLES Recommendations for the Syntactic Annotation of Corpora. EAG-TCWG-SASG/1.8. `http://www.ilc.pi.cnr.it/EAGLES/segsasg1/segsasg1.html`.

Marcus, M., Santorini, B., Marcinkiewicz, M.A. (1993). Building a Large Annotated Corpus of English: The Penn Treebank. *Computational Linguistics*, 19, 2, p. 313-30.

Sleator, D., Temperley, D., (1993). Parsing English with a Link Grammar. *Proceedings of the 3rd International Confernece on Parsing Technologies*, IWPT'93.

Tapanainen, P., Jarvinen, T. (1997). A Non-projective Dependency Parser. *Proceedings of ANLP'97*, Washington D,C., p. 64-71.

Taylor, A., Marcus, M., Santorini, B. (2003). The Penn Treebank: An Overview. This volume.

Thompson, H., Beech, D., Maloney, M. Mendelsohn, N. (eds.) (2000). XML Schema Part 1: Structures. W3C Candidate Recommendation, 24 October 2000. `http://www.w3.org/TR/xmlschema-1/`.

Wallis, S. (2003). Completing Parsed Corpora: From Correction to Evolution. This volume.

Evaluation with treebanks

Chapter 17

PARSER EVALUATION

Using a Grammatical Relation Annotation Scheme

John Carroll
Cognitive and Computing Sciences, University of Sussex, Brighton BN1 9QH, UK
johnca@cogs.susx.ac.uk

Guido Minnen*
Motorola Human Interface Laboratory, Schaumburg, IL 60196, USA
Guido.Minnen@motorola.com

Ted Briscoe
Computer Laboratory, University of Cambridge, Pembroke Street, Cambridge CB2 3QG, UK
ejb@cl.cam.ac.uk

Abstract We describe a recently developed corpus annotation scheme for evaluating parsers that avoids some of the shortcomings of current methods. The scheme encodes grammatical relations between heads and dependents, and has been used to mark up a new public-domain corpus of naturally occurring English text. We show how the corpus can be used to evaluate the accuracy of a robust parser, and relate the corpus to extant resources.

Keywords: Corpus Annotation Standards, Evaluation of NLP Tools, Parser Evaluation

1. INTRODUCTION

The evaluation of individual language-processing components forming part of larger-scale natural language processing (NLP) application systems has recently emerged as an important area of research (see e.g. Rubio, 1998; Gaiz-

*This work was carried out while the second author was at the University of Sussex.

A. Abeillé (ed.), Treebanks: Building and Using Parsed Corpora, 299–316.

auskas, 1998). A syntactic parser is often a component of an NLP system; a reliable technique for comparing and assessing the relative strengths and weaknesses of different parsers (or indeed of different versions of the same parser during development) is therefore a necessity.

Current methods for evaluating the accuracy of syntactic parsers are based on measuring the degree to which parser output replicates the analyses assigned to sentences in a manually annotated test corpus. Exact match between the parser output and the corpus is typically not required in order to allow different parsers utilising different grammatical frameworks to be compared. These methods are fully *objective* since the standards to be met and criteria for testing whether they have been met are set in advance.

The evaluation technique that is currently the most widely-used was proposed by the Grammar Evaluation Interest Group (Harrison *et al.*, 1991; see also Grishman, Macleod and Sterling, 1992), and is often known as 'PARSEVAL'. The method compares phrase-structure bracketings produced by the parser with bracketings in the annotated corpus, or 'treebank'[1] and computes the number of bracketing matches M with respect to the number of bracketings P returned by the parser (expressed as precision M/P) and with respect to the number C in the corpus (expressed as recall M/C), and the mean number of 'crossing' brackets per sentence where a bracketed sequence from the parser overlaps with one from the treebank (i.e. neither is properly contained in the other).

Advantages of PARSEVAL are that a relatively undetailed (only bracketed), treebank annotation is required, some level of cross framework/system comparison is achieved, and the measure is moderately fine-grained and robust to annotation errors. However, a number of disadvantages of PARSEVAL have been documented recently. In particular, Carpenter and Manning (1997) observe that sentences in the Penn Treebank (PTB; Marcus, Santorini and Marcinkiewicz, 1993) contain relatively few brackets, so analyses are quite 'flat'. The same goes for the other treebank of English in general use, SUSANNE (Sampson, 1995), a 138K word treebanked and balanced subset of the Brown corpus. Thus crossing bracket scores are likely to be small, however good or bad the parser is. Carpenter and Manning also point out that with the adjunction structure the PTB gives to post noun-head modifiers *(NP (NP the man) (PP with (NP a telescope)))*, there are zero crossings in cases where the VP attachment is incorrectly returned, and *vice-versa*. Conversely, Lin (1998) demonstrates that the crossing brackets measure can in some cases penalise mis-attachments more than once, and also argues that a high score for phrase boundary correctness does not guarantee that a reasonable semantic reading can be produced. Indeed, many phrase boundary disagreements stem from systematic differences between parsers/grammars and corpus annotation schemes that are well-justified within the context of their own theories. PARSEVAL does attempt to circumvent this problem by the removal from consideration of bracketing information in constructions for which agreement between analysis schemes in practice is low: i.e. negation, auxiliaries, punctuation, traces, and the use of unary branching structures.

However, in general there are still major problems with compatibility between the annotations in treebanks and analyses returned by parsing systems using manually-developed generative grammars (as opposed to grammars acquired directly from the treebanks themselves). The treebanks have been constructed with reference to sets of informal guidelines indicating the type of structures to be assigned. In the absence of a formal grammar controlling or verifying the manual annotations, the number of different structural configurations tends to grow without check. For example, the PTB implicitly contains more than 10000 distinct context-free productions, the majority occurring only once (Charniak, 1996). This makes it very difficult to accurately map the structures assigned by an independently-developed grammar/parser onto the structures that appear (or should appear) in the treebank. A further problem is that the PARSEVAL bracket precision measure penalises parsers that return more structure than the treebank annotation, even if it is correct (Srinivas, Doran and Kulick, 1995). To be able to use the treebank and report meaningful PARSEVAL precision scores such parsers must necessarily 'dumb down' their output and attempt to map it onto (exactly) the distinctions made in the treebank[2]. This mapping is also very difficult to specify accurately. PARSEVAL evaluation is thus *objective*, but the results are not *reliable*.

In addition, since PARSEVAL is based on measuring similarity between phrase-structure trees, it cannot be applied to grammars which produce dependency-style analyses, or to 'lexical' parsing frameworks such as finite-state constraint parsers which assign syntactic functional labels to words rather than producing hierarchical structure.

To overcome the PARSEVAL grammar/treebank mismatch problems outlined above, Lin (1998) proposes evaluation based on dependency structure, in which phrase structure analyses from parser and treebank are both automatically converted into sets of dependency relationships. Each such relationship consists of a modifier, a modifiee, and optionally a label which gives the type of the relationship. Atwell (1996), though, points out that transforming standard constituency-based analyses into a dependency-based representation would lose certain kinds of grammatical information that might be important for subsequent processing, such as 'logical' information (e.g. location of traces, or moved constituents). Srinivas, Doran, Hockey and Joshi (1996) describe a related technique which could also be applied to partial (incomplete) parses, in which hierarchical phrasal constituents are flattened into chunks and the relationships between them are indicated by dependency links. Recall and precision are defined over dependency links. Sampson (2000) argues for an approach to evaluation that measures the extent to which lexical items are fitted correctly into a parse tree, comparing sequences of node labels in paths up to the root of the tree to the corresponding sequences in the treebank analyses.

The TSNLP (Lehmann *et al.*, 1996) project test suites (in English, French and German) contain dependency-based annotations for some sentences; this allows for "generalizations over potentially controversial phrase structure configurations" and also mapping onto a specific constituent structure. No specific annotation standards or evaluation measures are proposed, though.

2. GRAMMATICAL RELATION ANNOTATION

In the previous section we argued that the currently-dominant constituency-based paradigm for parser evaluation has serious shortcomings[3]. In this section we outline a recently-proposed annotation scheme based on a dependency-style analysis, and compare it to other related schemes. In the next section we describe a 10,000-word test corpus that uses this scheme, and we then go on to show how it may be used to evaluate a robust parser.

Carroll, Briscoe and Sanfilippo (1998) propose an annotation scheme in which each sentence in the corpus is marked up with a set of grammatical relations (GRs), specifying the syntactic dependency which holds between each head and its dependent(s). In the event of morphosyntactic processes modifying head-dependent links (e.g. passive, dative shift), two kinds of GRs can be expressed: (1) the initial GR, i.e. before the GR-changing process occurs; and (2) the final GR, i.e. after the GR-changing process occurs. For example, *Paul* in *Paul was employed by Microsoft* is both the initial object and the final subject of *employ*.

In relying on the identification of grammatical relations between headed constituents, we of course presuppose a parser/grammar that is able to identify heads. In theory this may exclude certain parsers from using this scheme, although we are not aware of any contemporary computational parsing work which eschews the notion of head and moreover is unable to recover them. Thus, in computationally-amenable theories of language, such as HPSG (Pollard and Sag, 1994) and LFG (Kaplan and Bresnan, 1982), and indeed in any grammar based on some version of X-bar theory (Jackendoff, 1977), the head plays a key role. Likewise, in recent work on statistical treebank parsing, Magerman (1995) and Collins (1996) propagate information on each constituent's head up the parse tree in order to be able to capture lexical dependencies. A similar approach would also be applicable to the Data Oriented Parsing framework (Bod, 1999).

The relations are organised hierarchically: see Figure 17.1. Each relation in the scheme is described individually below.

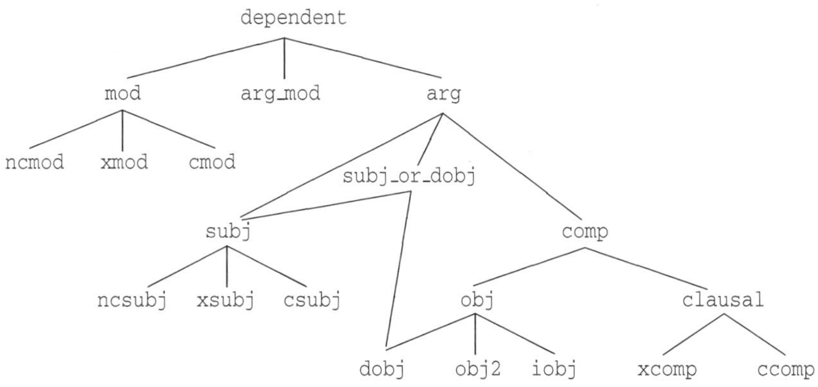

Figure 17.1. The grammatical relation hierarchy.

dependent(introducer, head, dependent). This is the most generic relation between a head and a dependent (i.e. it does not specify whether the dependent is an argument or a modifier). E.g.

dependent(in, live, Rome)	Marisa lives in Rome
dependent(that, say, leave)	I said that he left

mod(type, head, dependent). The relation between a head and its modifier; where appropriate, **type** indicates the word introducing the dependent; e.g.

mod(_, flag, red)	a red flag
mod(_, walk, slowly)	walk slowly
mod(with, walk, John)	walk with John
mod(while, walk, talk)	walk while talking
mod(_, Picasso, painter)	Picasso the painter

The **mod** GR is also used to encode the relationship between an event noun (including deverbal nouns) and its participants; e.g.

mod(of, gift, book)	the gift of a book
mod(by, gift, Peter)	the gift ... by Peter
mod(of, examination, patient)	the examination of the patient
mod(poss, doctor, examination)	the doctor's examination

cmod, xmod, ncmod. Clausal and non-clausal modifiers may (optionally) be distinguished by the use of the GRs **cmod/xmod**, and **ncmod** respectively, each with slots the same as **mod**. The GR **ncmod** is for non clausal modifiers; **cmod** is for adjuncts controlled from within, and **xmod** for adjuncts controlled from without, e.g.

xmod(without, eat, ask)	he ate the cake without asking
cmod(because, eat, be)	he ate the cake because he was hungry
ncmod(_, flag, red)	a red flag

arg_mod(type, head, dependent, initial_gr). The relation between a head and a semantic argument which is syntactically realised as a modifier; thus in English a 'by-phrase' in a passive construction can be analysed as a 'thematically bound adjunct'. The **type** slot indicates the word introducing the dependent: e.g.

arg_mod(by, kill, Brutus, subj)	killed by Brutus

arg(head, dependent). The most generic relation between a head and an argument.

subj_or_dobj(head, dependent). A specialisation of the relation **arg** which can instantiate either subjects or direct objects. It is useful for those cases where no reliable bias is available for disambiguation. For example, both *Gianni* and *Mario* can be subject or object in the Italian sentence

Mario, non l'ha ancora visto, Gianni
'Mario has not seen Gianni yet'/'Gianni has not seen Mario yet'

In this case, a parser could avoid trying to resolve the ambiguity by using **subj_or_dobj**, e.g.

subj_or_dobj(vedere, Mario)
subj_or_dobj(vedere, Gianni)

An alternative approach to this problem would have been to allow disjunctions of relations. We did not pursue this since the number of cases where this might be appropriate appears to be very limited.

subj(head, dependent, initial_gr). The relation between a predicate and its subject; where appropriate, the **initial_gr** indicates the syntactic link between the predicate and subject before any GR-changing process:

subj(arrive, John, _)	John arrived in Paris
subj(employ, Microsoft, _)	Microsoft employed 10 C programmers
subj(employ, Paul, obj)	Paul was employed by IBM

With pro-drop languages such as Italian, when the subject is not overtly realised the annotation is, for example, as follows:

subj(arrivare, Pro, _)	arrivai in ritardo '(I) arrived late'

in which the dependent is specified by the abstract filler **Pro**, indicating that person and number of the subject can be recovered from the inflection of the head verb form.

csubj, xsubj, ncsubj. The GRs **csubj** and **xsubj** indicate clausal subjects, controlled from within, or without, respectively. **ncsubj** is a non-clausal subject. E.g.

csubj(leave, mean, _)	that Nellie left without saying good-bye meant she was angry
xsubj(win, require, _)	to win the America's Cup requires heaps of cash

comp(head, dependent). The most generic relation between a head and complement.

obj(head, dependent). The most generic relation between a head and object.

dobj(head, dependent, initial_gr). The relation between a predicate and its direct object—the first non-clausal complement following the predicate which is not introduced by a preposition (for English and German); **initial_gr** is **iobj** after dative shift; e.g.

dobj(read, book, _)	read books
dobj(mail, Mary, iobj)	mail Mary the contract

iobj(type, head, dependent). The relation between a predicate and a non-clausal complement introduced by a preposition; **type** indicates the preposition introducing the dependent; e.g.

iobj(in, arrive, Spain)	arrive in Spain
iobj(into, put, box)	put the tools into the box
iobj(to, give, poor)	give to the poor

obj2(head, dependent). The relation between a predicate and the second non-clausal complement in ditransitive constructions; e.g.

obj2(give, present)	give Mary a present
obj2(mail, contract)	mail Paul the contract

clausal(head, dependent). The most generic relation between a head and a clausal complement.

xcomp(type, head, dependent). The relation between a predicate and a clausal complement which has no overt subject (for example a VP or predicative XP). The **type** slot indicates the complementiser/preposition, if any, introducing the XP. E.g.

xcomp(to, intend, leave)	Paul intends to leave IBM
xcomp(_, be, easy)	Swimming is easy
xcomp(in, be, Paris)	Mary is in Paris
xcomp(_, be, manager)	Paul is the manager

Control of VPs and predicative XPs is expressed in terms of GRs. For example, the unexpressed subject of the clausal complement of a subject-control predicate is specified by saying that the subject of the main and subordinate verbs is the same:

subj(intend, Paul, _) xcomp(to, intend, leave) *subj(leave, Paul, _)* dobj(leave, IBM, _)	Paul intends to leave IBM

When the proprietor dies, the establishment should become a corporation until it is either acquired by another proprietor or the government decides to drop it.

cmod(when, become, die)
ncsubj(die, proprietor, _)
ncsubj(become, establishment, _)
xcomp(become, corporation, _)
mod(until, become, acquire)
ncsubj(acquire, it, obj)
arg_mod(by, acquire, proprietor, subj)
cmod(until, become, decide)
ncsubj(decide, government, _)
xcomp(to, decide, drop)
ncsubj(drop, government, _)
dobj(drop, it, _)

Figure 17.2. Example sentence and GRs (SUSANNE rel3, lines G22:1460k–G22:1480m).

ccomp(type, head, dependent). The relation between a predicate and a clausal complement which does have an overt subject; **type** is the same as for **xcomp** above. E.g.

ccomp(that, say, accept)	Paul said that he will accept Microsoft's offer
ccomp(that, say, leave)	I said that he left

Figure 17.2 gives a more extended example of the use of the GR scheme.

The scheme is application-independent, and is based on EAGLES lexicon/syntax standards (Barnett *et al.*, 1996), as outlined by Carroll, Briscoe and Sanfilippo (1998). It takes into account language phenomena in English, Italian, French and German, and was used in the multilingual EU-funded SPARKLE project[4]. We believe it is broadly applicable to Indo-European languages; we have not investigated its suitability for other language classes.

The scheme is superficially similar to a syntactic dependency analysis in the style of Lin (1998, this volume). However, the scheme contains a specific, defined inventory of relations. Other significant differences are:

- the GR analysis of control relations could not be expressed as a strict dependency tree since a single nominal head would be a dependent of two (or more) verbal heads (as with *ncsubj(decide, government, _) ncsubj(drop, government, _)* in the Figure 17.2 example *...the government decides to drop it*);
- any complementiser or preposition linking a head with a clausal or PP dependent is an integral part of the GR (the **type** slot);

- the underlying grammatical relation is specified for arguments "displaced" from their canonical positions by movement phenomena (e.g. the **initial_gr** slot of *ncsubj* and *arg_mod* in the passive *...it is either acquired by another proprietor...*);

- semantic arguments syntactically realised as modifiers (e.g. the passive by-phrase) are indicated as such—using *arg_mod*;

- conjuncts in a co-ordination structure are distributed over the higher-level relation (e.g. in *...become ... until ... either acquired ... or ... decides...* there are two verbal dependents of *become*, *acquire* and *decide*, each in a separate *mod* GR;

- arguments which are not lexically realised can be expressed (e.g. when there is pro-drop the dependent in a *subj* GR would be specified as **Pro**);

- GRs are organised into a hierarchy so that they can be left underspecified by a shallow parser which has incomplete knowledge of syntax.

Both the PTB and SUSANNE contain functional, or predicate-argument annotation in addition to constituent structure, the former particularly employing a rich set of distinctions, often with complex grammatical and contextual conditions on when one function tag should be applied in preference to another. For example, the tag TPC ("topicalized")

> "— marks elements that appear before the subject in a declarative sentence, but in two cases only: (i) if the fronted element is associated with a *T* in the position of the gap. (ii) if the fronted element is left-dislocated [...]"

(Bies *et al.*, 1995: 40). Conditions of this type would be very difficult to encode in an actual parser, so attempting to evaluate on them would be uninformative. Much of the problem is that treebanks of this type have to specify the behaviour of many interacting factors, such as how syntactic constituents should be segmented, labelled and structured hierarchically, how displaced elements should be co-indexed, and so on. Within such a framework the further specification of how functional tags should be attached to constituents is necessarily highly complex. Moreover, functional information is in some cases left implicit[5], presenting further problems for precise evaluation. Given the above caveats, Table 17.2 compares the types of information in the GR scheme and in the PTB and SUSANNE. It might be possible partially or semi-automatically to map a treebank predicate-argument encoding to the GR scheme (taking advantage of the large amount of work that has gone into the treebanks), but we have not investigated this to date.

Table 17.1. Correspondence between the GR scheme and the functional annotation in the Penn Treebank (PTB) and in SUSANNE.

Relation	PTB	SUSANNE
dependent	–	–
mod	TPC/ADV etc.	p etc.
ncmod	CLR/VOC/ADV etc.	n/p etc.
xmod		
cmod		
arg_mod	LGS	a
arg	–	–
subj	–	–
ncsubj	SBJ	s
xsubj		
csubj		
subj_or_dobj	–	–
comp	–	–
obj	–	–
dobj	(NP following V)	o
obj2	(2nd NP following V)	
iobj	CLR/DTV	i
clausal	PRD	–
xcomp		e
ccomp		j

3. CORPUS ANNOTATION

We have constructed a small English corpus for parser evaluation consisting of 500 sentences (10,000 words) covering a number of written genres. The sentences were taken from the SUSANNE corpus, and each was marked up manually by two annotators. Initial markup was performed by the first author and was checked and extended by the third author. Inter-annotator agreement was around 95% which is somewhat better than previously reported figures for syntactic markup (e.g. Leech and Garside, 1991). Marking up was done semi-automatically by first generating the set of relations predicted by the evaluation software from the closest system analysis to the treebank annotation and then manually correcting and extending these. Although this corpus is without doubt too small to train a statistical parser on or for use in quantitative linguistics, it appears to be large enough for parser evaluation (next section). We may enlarge it in future, though, if we encounter a need to establish statistically significant differences between parsers performing at a similar level of accuracy.

The mean number of GRs per corpus sentence is 9.72. Table 17.2 quantifies the distribution of relations occurring in the corpus. The split between modifiers and arguments is roughly 60/40, with approximately equal numbers of subjects and complements. Of the latter, 40% are clausal; clausal modifiers are almost as prevalent. In strong contrast, clausal subjects are highly infrequent (accounting for only 0.2% of the total). Direct objects are 2.75 times more frequent than indirect objects, which are themselves 7.5 times more prevalent than second objects.

Table 17.2. Frequency of each type of GR (inclusive of subsumed relations) in the 10,000-word corpus.

Relation	*# occurrences*	*% occurrences*
dependent	4690	100.0
mod	2710	57.8
ncmod	2377	50.7
xmod	170	3.6
cmod	163	3.5
arg_mod	39	0.8
arg	1941	41.4
subj	993	21.2
ncsubj	984	21.0
xsubj	5	0.1
csubj	4	0.1
subj_or_dobj	1339	28.6
comp	948	20.2
obj	559	11.9
dobj	396	8.4
obj2	19	0.4
iobj	144	3.1
clausal	389	8.3
xcomp	323	6.9
ccomp	66	1.4

The corpus contains sentences belonging to three distinct genres. These are classified in the original Brown corpus as: *A*, press reportage; *G*, belles lettres; and *J*, learned writing. Genre has been found to affect the distribution of surface-level syntactic configurations (Sekine, 1997) and also complement types for individual predicates (Roland and Jurafsky, 1998). However, we observe no statistically significant difference in the *total* numbers of the various grammatical relations across the three genres in the test corpus.

4. PARSER EVALUATION

To investigate how the corpus can be used to evaluate the accuracy of a robust parser we replicated an experiment previously reported by Carroll, Minnen and Briscoe (1998), using a statistical lexicalised shallow parsing system. The system comprises:

- an HMM part-of-speech (PoS) tagger (Elworthy, 1994), which produces either the single highest-ranked tag for each word, or multiple tags with associated forward-backward probabilities (which are used with a threshold to prune lexical ambiguity);
- a robust, finite-state, inflectional morphological analyser for English (Minnen, Carroll and Pearce, 2000);
- a wide-coverage unification-based 'phrasal' grammar of English PoS tags and punctuation (Briscoe and Carroll, 1995);
- a fast unification parser using this grammar, taking the results of the tagger as input, and performing probabilistic disambiguation (Briscoe and Carroll, 1993) based on structural configurations in a treebank (of 4600 sentences) derived semi-automatically from SUSANNE; and
- a set of lexical entries for verbs, acquired automatically from a 10 million word sample of the British National Corpus, each entry containing subcategorisation frame information and an associated probability (for details see Carroll, Minnen and Briscoe, 1998).

The grammar consists of 455 phrase structure rules, in a formalism which is a syntactic variant of a Definite Clause Grammar with iterative (Kleene) operators. The grammar is 'shallow' in that:

- it has no *a priori* knowledge about the argument structure (subcategorisation properties etc.) of individual words, so for typical sentences it licenses many 'spurious' analyses (which are disambiguated by the probabilistic component); and
- it makes no attempt to fully analyse unbounded dependencies.

However, the grammar does express the distinction between arguments and adjuncts, following X-bar theory (e.g. Jackendoff, 1977), by Chomsky-adjunction to maximal projections of adjuncts ($XP \rightarrow XP\ Adjunct$) as opposed to 'government' of arguments ($X1 \rightarrow X0\ Arg_1 \ldots Arg_n$).

The grammar is 'robust' to phenomena occurring in real-world text. For example, it contains an extensive and systematic treatment of punctuation incorporating the text-sentential constraints described by Nunberg (1990), many of which (ultimately) restrict syntactic and semantic interpretation (Briscoe and Carroll, 1995). The grammar also incorporates rules specifically designed to overcome limitations or idiosyncrasies of the PoS tagging process. For example, past participles functioning adjectivally are frequently tagged as past participles, so the grammar incorporates a rule which analyses past participles as adjectival premodifiers in this context. Similar idiosyncratic rules are included for dealing with gerunds, adjective-noun conversions, idiom sequences, and so forth.

The coverage of the grammar—the proportion of sentences for which at least one analysis is found—is around 80% when applied to the SUSANNE corpus. Many of the parse 'failures' are due the parser enforcing a root *S*(entence) requirement in the presence of elliptical noun or prepositional phrases in dialogue. We have not relaxed this requirement since it increases ambiguity, our primary interest at this point being the extraction of lexical (subcategorisation, selectional preference, and collocation) information from full clauses in corpus data. Other systematic failures are a consequence of differing levels of shallowness across the grammar, such as the incorporation of complementation constraints for auxiliary verbs but the lack of any treatment of unbounded dependencies.

The parsing system reads off GRs from the constituent structure tree that is returned from the disambiguation phase. Information is used about which grammar rules introduce subjects, complements, and modifiers, and which daughter(s) is/are the head(s), and which the dependents. This information is easy to specify since the grammar contains an explicit, determinate rule-set. Extracting GRs from constituent structure would be much harder to do correctly and consistently in the case of grammars induced automatically from treebanks (e.g. Magerman, 1995; Collins, 1996).

In the evaluation we compute three measures for each type of relation against the 10,000-word test corpus (Table 17.3). The evaluation measures are precision, recall and F-score of parser GRs against the test corpus annotation. (The F-score is a measure combining precision and recall into a single figure; we use the version in which they are weighted equally, defined as $(2 \times precision \times recall)/(precision + recall)$.) GRs are in general compared using an equality test, except that we allow the parser to return *mod*, *subj* and *clausal* relations rather than the more specific ones they subsume, and to leave unspecified the filler for the **type** slot in the *mod*, *iobj* and *clausal* relations[6]. The **head** and **dependent** slot fillers are in all cases the base forms of single head words, so for example, 'multi-component' heads such as names are reduced to a single word; thus the slot filler corresponding to *Bill Clinton* would be *Clinton*. For real-world applications this might not be the desired behaviour—one might instead want the token *Bill_Clinton*—but the analysis system could easily be modified to do this since parse trees contain the requisite information.

Table 17.3. GR accuracy of parsing system, by relation.

Relation	*Precision (%)*	*Recall (%)*	*F-score*
dependent	75.1	75.2	75.1
mod	73.7	69.7	71.7
ncmod	78.1	73.1	75.6
xmod	70.0	51.9	59.6
cmod	67.4	48.1	56.1
arg_mod	84.2	41.0	55.2
arg	76.6	83.5	79.9
subj	83.6	87.9	85.7
ncsubj	84.8	88.3	86.5
xsubj	100.0	40.0	57.1
csubj	14.3	100.0	25.0
subj_or_dobj	84.4	86.9	85.6
comp	69.8	78.9	74.1
obj	67.7	79.3	73.0
dobj	86.3	84.3	85.3
obj2	39.0	84.2	53.3
iobj	41.7	64.6	50.7
clausal	73.0	78.4	75.6
xcomp	84.4	78.9	81.5
ccomp	72.3	74.6	73.4

5. DISCUSSION

The evaluation results can be used to give a single figure for parser accuracy: the F-score of the *dependent* relation (75.1 for our system). However, in contrast to the three PARSEVAL measures (bracket precision, recall and crossings), the GR evaluation results also give fine-grained information about levels of precision and recall for groups of, and single relations. The latter are particularly useful during parser/grammar development and refinement to indicate the areas in which effort should be concentrated. Lin (this volume), in a similar type of dependency-driven evaluation, also makes an argument that dependency errors can help to pinpoint parser problems relating to specific closed-class lexical items.

In our evaluation, Table 17.3 shows that the relations that are extracted most accurately are (non-clausal) subject and direct object, with F-scores of 86.5 and 85.3 respectively. This might be expected, since the probabilistic model contains information about whether they are subcategorised for, and they are the closest arguments to the head predicate. Second and indirect objects score much lower (53.3 and 50.7), with clausal complements in the upper area between the two extremes. We therefore need to look at how we could improve the quality of subcategorisation data for more oblique arguments.

Modifier relations have an overall F-score of 71.7, three points lower than the combined score for complements, again with non-clausal relations higher than clausal. Many non-clausal modifier GRs in the test corpus are adjacent adjective-noun combinations which are relatively easy for the parser to identify correctly. In contrast, some clausal modifiers span a large segment of the sentence (for example the GR *cmod(until, become, decide)* in Figure 17.2 spans 15 words); despite this, clausal modifier precision is still 67–70%, though recall is lower. Precision of *arg_mod* (representing the displaced subject of passive) is high (84%), but recall is low (only 41%). The problem shown up here is that many occurrences are incorrectly parsed as prepositional *by*-phrase indirect objects.

6. SUMMARY

We have outlined and justified a language-and application-independent corpus annotation scheme for evaluating syntactic parsers, based on grammatical relations between heads and dependents. We have described a 10,000-word corpus of English marked up to this standard, and shown how it can be used to evaluate a robust parsing system and also highlight its strengths and weaknesses. The corpus and evaluation software that can be used with it are publicly available online at `http://www.cogs.susx.ac.uk/lab/nlp/carroll/greval.html`.

Acknowledgments

This work was funded by UK EPSRC project GR/L53175 'PSET: Practical Simplification of English Text', and by an EPSRC Advanced Fellowship to the first author. We would like to thank Antonio Sanfilippo for his substantial input to the design of the annotation scheme.

Notes

1. Subsequent evaluations using PARSEVAL (e.g. Collins, 1996) have adapted it to incorporate constituent labelling information as well as just bracketing.

2. Gaizauskas, Hepple and Huyck (1998) propose an alternative to the PARSEVAL precision measure to address this specific shortcoming.

3. Note that the issue we are concerned with here is parser *evaluation*, and we are not making any more general claims about the utility of constituency-based treebanks for other important tasks they are used for, such as statistical parser training or in quantitative linguistics.

4. Information on the SPARKLE project is at `http://www.ilc.pi.cnr.it/sparkle.html`.

5. "The predicate is the lowest (right-most branching) VP or (after copula verbs and in 'small clauses') a constituent tagged PRD" (Bies *et al.*, 1995: 11).

6. The implementation of the extraction of GRs from parse trees is currently being refined, so these minor relaxations will be removed soon.

References

Atwell, E. (1996). Comparative evaluation of grammatical annotation models. In R. Sutcliffe, H. Koch, A. McElligott (Eds.), *Industrial Parsing of Software Manuals*, p. 25–46. Amsterdam, Rodopi.

Barnett, R., Calzolari, N., Flores, S., Hellwig, P., Kahrel, P., Leech, G., Melera, M., Montemagni, S., Odijk, J., Pirrelli, V., Sanfilippo, A., Teufel, S., Villegas, M., Zaysser, L. (1996). *EAGLES Recommendations on Subcategorisation.* Report of the EAGLES Working Group on Computational Lexicons. Available at `ftp://ftp.ilc.pi.cnr.it/pub/eagles/lexicons/synlex.ps.gz`.

Bies, A., Ferguson, M., Katz, K., MacIntyre, R., Tredinnick, V., Kim, G., Marcinkiewicz, M., Schasberger, B. (1995). *Bracketing Guidelines for Treebank II Style Penn Treebank Project.* Technical Report, CIS, University of Pennsylvania, Philadelphia, PA.

Bod, R. (1999). *Beyond Grammar.* Stanford, CA: CSLI Press.

Briscoe, E. and Carroll, J. (1993). Generalised probabilistic LR parsing for unification-based grammars. *Computational Linguistics*, 19(1), p. 25–60.

Briscoe, E., Carroll, J. (1995). Developing and evaluating a probabilistic LR parser of part-of-speech and punctuation labels. *Proceedings of the 4th ACL/SIGPARSE International Workshop on Parsing Technologies*, p. 48–58. Prague, Czech Republic.

Carpenter, B. and Manning, C. (1997). Probabilistic parsing using left corner language models. *Proceedings of the 5th ACL/SIGPARSE International Workshop on Parsing Technologies*, p. 147–158. MIT, Cambridge, MA.

Carroll, J., Briscoe E. and Sanfilippo, A. (1998). Parser evaluation: a survey and a new proposal. *Proceedings of the International Conference on Language Resources and Evaluation*, p. 447–454. Granada, Spain.

Carroll, J., Minnen, G. and Briscoe, E. (1998). Can subcategorisation probabilities help a statistical parser?. *Proceedings of the 6th ACL/SIGDAT Workshop on Very Large Corpora*, p. 118–126. Montreal, Canada.

Charniak, E. (1996). Tree-bank grammars. *Proceedings of the 13th National Conference on Artificial Intelligence, AAAI'96*, p. 1031–1036. Portland, OR.

Collins, M. (1996). A new statistical parser based on bigram lexical dependencies. *Proceedings of the 34th Meeting of the Association for Computational Linguistics*, p. 184–191. Santa Cruz, CA.

Elworthy, D. (1994). Does Baum-Welch re-estimation help taggers?. *Proceedings of the 4th ACL Conference on Applied Natural Language Processing*, p. 53–58. Stuttgart, Germany.

Gaizauskas, R. (1998). Evaluation in language and speech technology. *Computer Speech and Language*, 12(3), p. 249–262.

Gaizauskas, R., Hepple M., Huyck, C. (1998). Modifying existing annotated corpora for general comparative evaluation of parsing. *Proceedings of the LRE Workshop on Evaluation of Parsing Systems*. Granada, Spain.

Grishman, R., Macleod, C., Sterling, J. (1992). Evaluating parsing strategies using standardized parse files. *Proceedings of the 3rd ACL Conference on Applied Natural Language Processing*, p. 156–161. Trento, Italy.

Harrison, P., Abney, S., Black, E., Flickinger, D., Gdaniec, C., Grishman, R., Hindle, D., Ingria, B., Marcus, M., Santorini, B., Strzalkowski, T. (1991). Evaluating syntax performance of parser/grammars of English. *Proceedings of the Workshop on Evaluating Natural Language Processing Systems*, p. 71–77. 29th Annual Meeting of the Association for Computational Linguistics, Berkeley, CA.

Jackendoff, R. (1977). *X-bar Syntax*. Cambridge, MA: MIT Press.

Kaplan, R., Bresnan, J. (1982). Lexical-Functional Grammar: a formal system for grammatical representation. In J. Bresnan (Eds.), *The Mental Representation of Grammatical Relations*, p. 173–281. Cambridge MA: MIT Press.

Leech, G. (1991). Running a grammar factory: the production of syntactically analysed corpora or "treebanks", in Johansson et al (eds) English computer corpora, Berlin, Mouton de Gruyter, p. 15-32.

Lehmann, S., Oepen, S., Regnier-Prost, S., Netter, K., Lux, V., Klein, J., Falkedal, K., Fouvry, F., Estival, D., Dauphin, E., Compagnion, H., Baur, J., Balkan, L., Arnold, D. (1996). TSNLP — test suites for natural language processing. *Proceedings of the 16th International Conference on Computational Linguistics, COLING'96*, p. 711–716. Copenhagen, Denmark.

Lin, D. (1998). A dependency-based method for evaluating broad-coverage parsers. *Natural Language Engineering*, 4(2), p. 97–114.

Lin, D. (2002) Dependency-based evaluation of MINIPAR, This volume.

Magerman, D. (1995). Statistical decision-tree models for parsing. *Proceedings of the 33rd Annual Meeting of the Association for Computational Linguistics*, p. 276–283. Boston, MA.

Marcus, M., Santorini, B., Marcinkiewicz, M. (1993). Building a large annotated corpus of English: The Penn Treebank. *Computational Linguistics*, 19(2), p. 313–330.

Minnen, G., Carroll, J., Pearce, D. (2000). Robust, applied morphological generation. *Proceedings of the 1st ACL/SIGGEN International Conference on Natural Language Generation*, p. 201–208. Mitzpe Ramon, Israel.

Nunberg, G. (1990). *The Linguistics of Punctuation*. CSLI Lecture Notes 18, Stanford, CA.

Roland, D., Jurafsky, D. (1998). How verb subcategorization frequencies are affected by corpus choice. *Proceedings of the 17th International Conference on Computational Linguistics, COLING-ACL'98*, p. 1122–1128. Montreal, Canada.

Pollard, C., Sag, I. (1994). *Head-driven Phrase Structure Grammar*. Chicago, IL: University of Chicago Press.

Rubio, A. (Ed.) (1998). *International Conference on Language Resources and Evaluation*. Granada, Spain.

Sampson, G. (1995). *English for the Computer*. Oxford, UK: Oxford University Press.

Sampson, G. (2000). A proposal for improving the measurement of parse accuracy. *International Journal of Corpus Linguistics*, 5(1), p. 53–68.

Sekine, S. (1997). The domain dependence of parsing. *Proceedings of the 5th ACL Conference on Applied Natural Language Processing*, p. 96–102. Washington, DC.

Srinivas, B., Doran, C., Hockey B., Joshi A. (1996). An approach to robust partial parsing and evaluation metrics. *Proceedings of the ESSLLI'96 Workshop on Robust Parsing*, p. 70–82. Prague, Czech Republic.

Srinivas, B., Doran, C., Kulick, S. (1995). Heuristics and parse ranking. *Proceedings of the 4th ACL/SIGPARSE International Workshop on Parsing Technologies*, p. 224–233. Prague, Czech Republic.

Chapter 18

DEPENDENCY-BASED EVALUATION OF MINIPAR

Dekang Lin
Department of Computing Science
University of Alberta
Edmonton, Alberta, Canada T6G 2H1
lindek@cs.ualberta.ca

Abstract In this paper, we first present a dependency-based method for parser evaluation. We then use the method to evaluate a broad-coverage parser, called MINIPAR, with the SUSANNE corpus. The method allows us to evaluate not only the overall performance of the parser, but also its performance with respect to different grammatical relationships and phenomena. The evaluation results show that MINIPAR is able to cover about 79% of the dependency relationships in the SUSANNE corpus with about 89% precision.

Keywords: English, Parser Evaluation, Dependency, Susanne Corpus

1. INTRODUCTION

With the emergence of broad-coverage parsers, quantitative evaluation of parsers becomes increasingly important. It is generally accepted that quantitative parser evaluation should be conducted by comparing the parser-generated parse trees (we call them **answers**) with manually constructed parse trees (we call them **keys**). A commonly used method (Black et al., 1991) is to compare the phrase boundaries between answers and keys. (Lin, 1995; Lin, 1998) argued that there are many problems with this approach. For example, a single attachment error may lead to multiple incorrect phrase boundaries. More seriously, nonsensical parses may get rather high phrase-boundary scores. We proposed a dependency-based evaluation scheme in which both the answers and keys were converted into dependency trees and the evaluation scores were computed according to the set of dependency relationships in the answers and the keys.

A. Abeillé (ed.), Treebanks: Building and Using Parsed Corpora, 317–329.

In this paper, we present the results of using such a scheme to evaluate MINIPAR, which is a descendent of PRINCIPAR (Lin, 1993; Lin, 1994). MINIPAR adopted some of the ideas in the Minimalist Program (Chomsky, 1995), such as bare phrase structure and economy principles.

2. DEPENDENCY-BASED PARSER EVALUATION

A dependency relationship (Hays, 1964; Hudson, 1984; Mel'čuk, 1987; Bömová et al., this volume) is an asymmetric binary relationship between a word called **head** (or governor, parent), and another word called **modifier** (or dependent, daughter). Dependency grammars represent sentence structures as a set of dependency relationships. Normally the dependency relationships form a tree that connects all the words in a sentence. A word in the sentence may have several modifiers, but each word may modify at most one word. The root of the dependency tree does not modify any word. It is also called the head of the sentence.

For example, (18.1) is a dependency structure of a sentence. The head of the sentence is "have". There are four pairs of dependency relationships, depicted by four arcs from heads to modifiers.

(18.1)

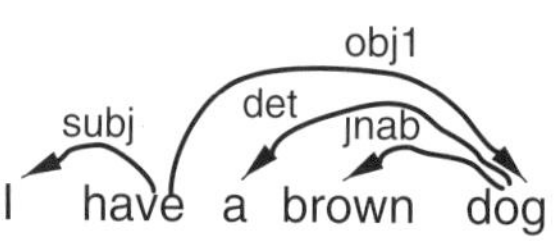

We use a list of tuples to represent a dependency tree. Each tuple represents a node in the dependency tree and has the following format
`(word category [head] [relationship])`
where:

- `word` is the word represented by the node,
- `category` is the lexical category of `word`,
- `head` specifies which word is modified by `word`, and
- `relationship` is a label assigned to the dependency relationship, for example, `subj` (subject), `adjn` (adjunct), `cmpl` (complement), `spec` (specifier), *etc.*

The fields `head` and `relationship` are optional. The `head`-field consists of a position indicator followed by a word. The position indicator takes one of the following values: {`<`, `>`, `<<`, `>>`, `<<<`, ...}. If the `head`-field is "$\underbrace{<\ldots<}_{n}$ w", the head of `word` is the *n*th occurrence of `w` to the right of the modifier. The meaning of "$\underbrace{>\ldots>}_{n}$ w" is similarly defined in the opposite direction.

For example, in the following sentence:

(18.2) The book Alex is reading is the same as the one I am reading

the word "book" modifies the second "is" to its right. Its `head`-field in the dependency tree should be: "`<< is`".

The dependency tree in (18.1) is represented by the following tuples:

(18.3)

Modifier	Category	Head	Type
I	N	< have	subj
have	V		
a	Det	< dog	spec
brown	Adj	< dog	adjn
dog	N	> have	comp

2.1 Evaluation Measures and Procedure

Once the answer and the key are both represented as dependency trees, we can compare them on a word-by-word basis and calculate two scores:

recall: the percentage of dependency relationships in the key that are also found in the answer.

precision: the percentage of dependency relationships in the answer that are also found in the key.

Table 18.1 shows the dependency-based evaluation result for the key-answer pair in (18.4). Except for the word "Alex", all the other words are assigned the same head in the answer as in the key. Therefore, both the precision and recall of the answer are 5/6.

Table 18.1. Dependency-based evaluation of the structures in (18.4)

Key				Answer				correct
word	cate	head	rel	word	cate	head	rel	
Kim	N	< promised	subj	Kim	N	< promised	subj	yes
promised	V			promised	V			
Alex	N	> promised	obj1	Alex	N	< bring	subj	no
to	Aux	< bring	aux	to	Aux	< bring	aux	yes
bring	V	> promised	obj2	bring	V	> promised	obj1	yes
some	Det	< wine	spec	some	Det	< wine	spec	yes
wine	N	> bring	obj1	wine	N	> bring	obj1	yes

(18.4)

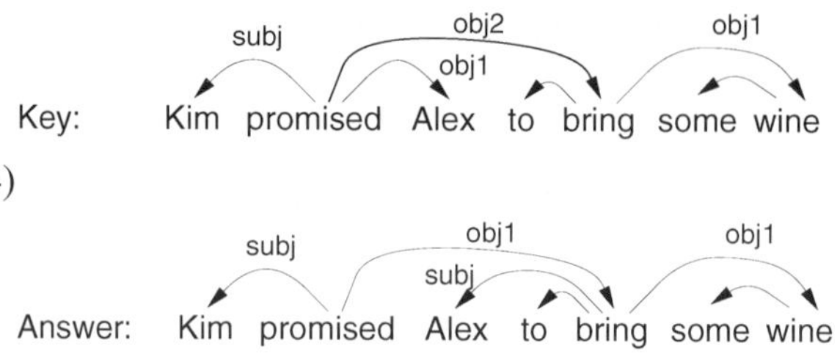

The above evaluation ignores the labels assigned to the dependency relationships. This is analogous to ignoring constituency labels in phrase boundary based evaluations (Black et al., 1991). If both the answer and the key use the same set of dependency labels or a mapping between equivalent labels can be established, labels can be incorporated into the evaluation algorithm by requiring not only that a word modify the same word in the answer as in the key, but also that the dependency relationships have the same or equivalent labels. For example, if the labels were taken into account in Table 18.1, the precision and recall of the answer would be 4/6.

When both the answer and the key are full parses, each of them have $N - 1$ dependencies, where N is the number of words in the sentence. That means that the precision and recall value will be the same. Therefore, in our earlier proposal (Lin, 1995), the ratio between the number of correct dependencies and the number of words was adopted as the evaluation metric. However, a number of situations exist in which the number of dependency relationships in the answer may not be the same as in the key:

- Due to differences in tokenization, the answer and key may be segmented into different numbers of words. For example, under one scheme, a hyphenated word is treated as a single token. In another, the hyphens and the word they separate are regarded as individual tokens.
- When we selectively evaluate different aspects of a parser, only a subset of the dependencies participates in the evaluation.
- Although it is safe to assume that the key is always a fully connected dependency tree, the answer may consist of several fragments of dependency trees.

The precision and recall measures are more flexible under these circumstances.

3. EVALUATION OF MINIPAR WITH SUSANNE CORPUS

3.1 MINIPAR

MINIPAR is a principle-based English parser (Berwick et al., 1991). Like PRINCIPAR (Lin, 1993), MINIPAR represents the grammar as a network.

where the nodes represent grammatical categories and the links represent types of syntactic (dependency) relationships. The grammar network consists of 35 nodes and 59 links. Additional nodes and links are created dynamically to represent subcategories of verbs. MINIPAR employs a message passing algorithm that essentially implements distributed chart parsing. Instead of maintaining a single chart, each node in the grammar network maintains a chart containing partially built structures belonging to the grammatical category represented by the node. The grammatical principles are implemented as constraints associated with the nodes and links.

The lexicon in MINIPAR is derived from WordNet (Miller et al., 1990). With additional proper names, the lexicon contains about 130K entries (in base forms). The lexical entry of a word lists all possible parts of speech of the word and its subcategorization frames (if any). The lexical ambiguities are handled by the parser instead of a tagger. Like chart parsers, MINIPAR constructs all possible parses of an input sentence. However, it outputs a single parse tree with the highest ranking. Although the grammar is manually constructed, the selection of the best parse tree is guided be the statistical information obtained by parsing a 1GB corpus with MINIPAR.

3.2 SUSANNE

The SUSANNE corpus (Sampson, 1995; Sampson, this volume) is a subset of the Brown Corpus of American English. It contains parse trees of 64 of the 500 texts in the Brown Corpus of American English. The texts are evenly distributed over the following four Brown genre categories:

A	press reportage;
G	belles lettres, biography, memoirs, etc.;
J	"learned" (technical and scholarly prose);
N	adventure and Western fiction.

While the SUSANNE corpus is not large enough for the purpose of statistical training, it is much larger and much more diverse than the testing corpora used in previous evaluation of broad coverage parsers (e.g., Magerman, 1995; Collins, 1996; Collins, 1997). Compared with other possible alternatives such as the PennTreebank (Marcus et al., 1993), the SUSANNE corpus offers several advantages:

- The PennTreebank is made up solely of Wall Street Journal sentences. The SUSANNE corpus contains a wide variety of texts, including news articles, letters and biographies, scientific and technical writing, and fiction.
- The SUSANNE corpus puts more emphasis on precision and consistency, which are more important properties than quantity for parser evaluation purposes.

SUSANNE corpus, as well as the Penn TreeBank II, not only labels the categories of phrases, but also the functional roles, such as subjects, direct/indirect objects, and temporal adjuncts. For example, if a phrase is labeled `Ns:s`, it means that the phrase belongs to the category `Ns` and its role is the logical subject. This information can be used to determine how well a parser recognizes predicate-argument relationships, or how good it is at prepositional phrase attachment.

3.3 Evaluation Results

Table 18.2 summarizes the results of evaluating MINIPAR with the SUSANNE corpus. The second and the third column in Table 18.2 are the number of sentences in each category and their average lengths. Since each category contains roughly the same number of words, there are fewer sentences in categories with longer sentences. The precision, recall and the error rate are calculated by summing up the total number of errors and the total number of dependency relationships in the corpus or a subcorpus, rather than by averaging the measures for individual sentences.

Table 18.2. Results of evaluating MINIPAR

Category	no. of sentences	avg. length	precision	recall	avg. words per second*
A	1614	22.12	88.60	81.81	292
G	1525	23.74	88.76	77.15	335
J	1398	25.27	88.28	79.95	339
N	2566	13.92	88.54	75.29	319
All categories	7103	20.15	88.54	78.58	320

*on a Pentium II 300 with 128 MB memory.

In the development of MINIPAR, as well as PRINCIPAR, we only used news articles and example sentences from linguistics textbooks to test and debug the parser and the grammar. It is not surprising that MINIPAR performed visibly better on category A than on the others. It is also worth noting that the greatest differences in performance were in recall, while the precision remains almost constant across different categories. One possible explanation for this is that the lower recall values of categories G, J and N (compared with Category A) are due to less complete coverage of linguistic phenomena in those categories. However, when the structure of a sentence is indeed covered by the parser, the parser has similar likelihood of generating correct dependency relationships as in category A.

Another interesting observation is that even though the sentences in category N (fiction) are much shorter than the sentences in other categories, MINIPAR's recall in this category is lower than in other categories. This seems to contradict the intuition that shorter sentences are easier to parse.

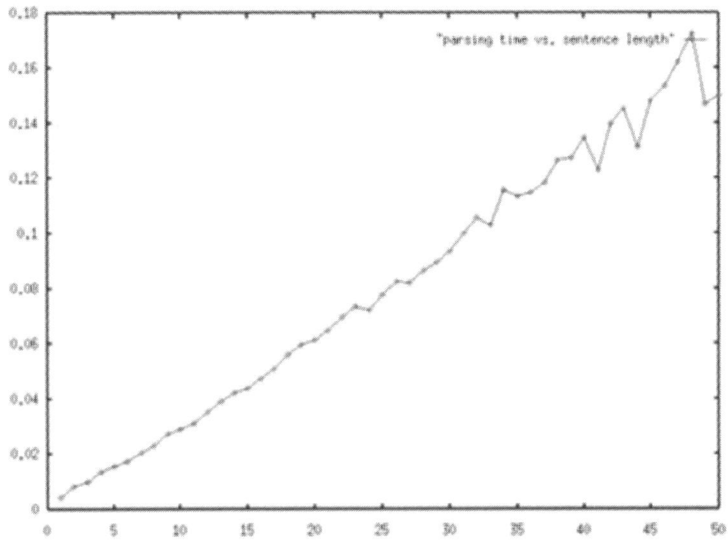

Figure 18.1. Sentence length vs. parsing time (in seconds)

The timing results in Table 18.2 shows that MINIPAR is very efficient. It is able to parse about 300 words per second on a Pentium II 300 with 128M memory. In contrast, Magerman's statistical parser (Magerman, 1995) processes about 1.86 words per second on a SGI R4400 with 160M memory. His result is obtained by limiting sentence length to 40 words, whereas we parsed all the sentences in the SUSANNE corpus, in which the longest sentence contains 215 words.

Figure 18.1 plots the average parsing time for sentences with a given length (from 1 to 50). Surprisingly, the parsing time looks linear to the number of words in the sentence. The linear parsing time can also be observed in Table 18.2.

4. SELECTIVE EVALUATION

An advantage of the dependency-based evaluation method is that it allows us to evaluate the parser performance with respect to specific types of dependency relationships, such as predicate-argument, or prepositional attachment. This can be achieved by comparing a subset of the words in the answer and the key, instead of all the words.

Assuming that the dependency relationships are labeled, we can use the labels to select a subset of the dependency relationships. Consider the example in Table 18.1. The labels "obj1" and "obj2" are assigned to the dependency relationships between verbs and their first and second objects. If we only include a word in the evaluation if the dependency between the word and its parent is labeled "obj1" or "obj2", the precision and recall values will tell us how the parser performed on verb-object relationships.

(18.5)

Key			Answer		
head	modifier	label	head	modifier	label
promised	Alex	obj1			
promised	bring	obj2	promised	bring	obj1
bring	wine	obj1	bring	wine	obj1

For example, by restricting the dependency relationships to those with "obj1" or "obj2" label, only the dependency relationships in (18.5) are selected from the dependency relationships in Table 18.1. Therefore, the recall and precision of the verb-object dependency in Table 18.1 are 66.7% and 100% respectively. If a dependency in the answer is only considered to be correct if it has the same label as the head, the recall will be 33.3% and the precision will be 50%. Similarly, if we score the subject relationships in Table 18.1, the recall is 100%, but the precision is 50%.

Table 18.3 summarizes the evaluation results of different types of dependency relationships. The second and third column in Table 18.3 contain the total numbers of dependency relationships belonging to the given type in the MINIPAR outputs and in the SUSANNE corpus respectively.

Table 18.3. Evaluation of different types of dependency relations

Dependency Type	Total in Answer	Total in Key	Precision	Recall
Subject	10328	11917	88.7%	78.4%
Complement	8557	7031	87.9%	71.8%
PP attachment	15629	16344	77.9%	72.2%
Relative Clause	1588	1135	51.8%	55.8%
Conjunction	3404	4810	67.1%	49.6%

Table 18.3 shows that the dependency relationships that involve systematic attachment ambiguities, such as PP attachments, relative clauses and conjunctions have much lower precision and recall than predicate-argument relationships. This is because MINIPAR resolves attachment ambiguities by "Minimal Attachment" and "Right Association." However, many of the ambiguities can only be resolved on semantic grounds.

The selective evaluation can be carried out further by considering a parser's performance with respect to a word. For example, Table 18.4 shows evaluation scores for the ten most frequent prepositions.

Table 18.4. Prepositional attachments

Prep	Total in Answer	Total in Key	Precision	Recall
of	4227	4636	95.2%	91.8%
in	2533	2684	70.5%	60.7%
to	1025	1353	73.0%	69.3%
for	930	1059	68.7%	64.4%
with	892	824	74.6%	66.7%
on	745	662	68.1%	60.1%
by	746	697	80.3%	71.8%
at	610	561	67.0%	58.7%
from	597	532	77.8%	69.5%
as	332	362	53.9%	58.1%

While most of the prepositions have similar precision and recall, the score for "of" is much better than others and the score for "as" is significantly lower than others. The errors involving "of" can be classified into the following categories:

- Extraposition: MINIPAR does not handle extraposition of prepositional phrases. For example, the head of "of" in (18.6) is "murder" in SUSANNE, but is "1935" in MINIPAR output.

  (18.6) the murder in 1935 of her son-in-law

- Quotation marks: MINIPAR fails to parse a sentence when there is a quotation mark after a preposition. For example,

  (18.7) In the area of "community health services" ...

- Clausal complement: MINIPAR also fails when the complement of a preposition is a wh-clause. For example,

  (18.8) a body of legal principle which by and large was made up of what Western nations could do in the world arena

- Conjunction: MINIPAR generates a different tree than the dependency tree derived from SUSANNE analysis when a conjunction is modified by a prepositional phrase. An example is shown in Figure 18.2. Such differences are due to a difference in representation rather than genuine parser errors. We did not deliberately transform the SUSANNE analysis of [NP and NP of NP] into a different dependency structure than MINIPAR outputs. It is simply a result of our translation rules that deals with conjunctions and prepositional phrase attachments. While it is not hard to modify the translation rules to reconcile such a difference, the large number of such differences makes it hard to fix all of them.

a. dependency analysis derived from SUSANNE   b. MINIPAR output

Figure 18.2. Different analysis of conjunctions in SUSANNE and MINIPAR.

Selective evaluation may also be carried out if the nodes in constituency trees are also labeled with grammatical roles. However, it may still be necessary to identify the head node in a constituent, so that a constituent in parser outputs may be considered to match a constituent in the key even if they have different spans. For example, the verb-object relation in

(18.9)

Ans: $[_{\text{S}}$ $[_{\text{NP-SUBJ}}$ I] $[_{\text{VP}}$ saw $[_{\text{NP-OBJ}}$ a man] with a telescope]]

Key: $[_{\text{S}}$ $[_{\text{NP-SUBJ}}$ I] $[_{\text{VP}}$ saw $[_{\text{NP-OBJ}}$ a man with a telescope]]]

should be considered to be correct even though the object NPs in the answer and key have different spans. By identifying the head in every constituent, we implicitly transform the constituency trees into dependency trees.

5. RELATED WORK

The main obstacle in parser evaluation is that different grammatical theories and different parsers may have different notions of what constitutes a correct parse. The best one can do is to compare a common factor, i.e., information that is encoded in all types of parse trees. In our approach, the common factor is the set of dependency relationships in the answer and the key. In the phrase boundary based evaluation methods the common factor is the set of phrase boundaries identified by parse trees.

The phrase boundaries in the answer and the key are treated as two sets (A and K respectively). The phrase boundary based evaluation computes the following measures:

Recall: The percentage of phrase boundaries in the key that are also found in the answer ($\frac{|A \cap K|}{|K|}$).

Precision: The percentage of phrase boundaries in the answer that are also found in the key ($\frac{|A \cap K|}{|A|}$).

Suppose (18.10a) is the key and (18.10b) is the answer. They each contain six phrases. Five of the phrases in the key are also found in the answer and five of the phrases in the answer are also found in the key. Therefore, the precision and recall are both 5/6.

(18.10)

a. [Kim [promised [Alex] [to bring [some wine]]]]

b. [Kim [promised [Alex [to bring [some wine]]]]]

Table 18.5. Dependency-based evaluation of structures in Figure 18.3

Key				Answer				correct
word	cate	head	rel	word	cate	head	rel	
a	Det	< screen	det	a	Det	< bib	det	no
bib	N	< summary	nn	bib	N	< appeared	subj	no
summary	N	< screen	nn	summary	N	< screen	subj	yes*
screen	N	< appeared	subj	screen	V	> summary	rel	no
appeared	V			appeared	V			

*assuming labels are ignored

Compared with the recall/precision of phrase boundaries, the recall/precision measures of dependency relationships are intuitively more meaningful. The phrase boundaries themselves are not used directly in semantic interpretation. Getting the phrase boundaries right is not even a necessary condition for semantic interpretation. Consequently, it is hard to predict how missing or spurious phrase boundaries affect semantic interpretation. On the other hand, since semantic dependencies are embedded in syntactic dependencies, the semantic interpretation process should be more sensitive to the percentage of correct syntactic dependencies than the percentage of correct phrase boundaries.

Consider the two parse trees "Answer" and "Key" in Figure 18.3. The answer treats the word "screen" as a verb and "summary screen" as a relative clause modifying the noun "BIB." The answer is obviously a very poor parse of the sentence. It is unlikely that the sentence can be interpreted correctly on the basis of this analysis. However, according to the phrase-boundary scores proposed in (Black et al., 1991), the answer has 100% recall and 75% precision. In contrast, Table 18.5 shows the dependency-based evaluation of the two parses in Figure 18.3. Both the recall and precision of the answer are 25%, which are appropriate for a very bad parse.

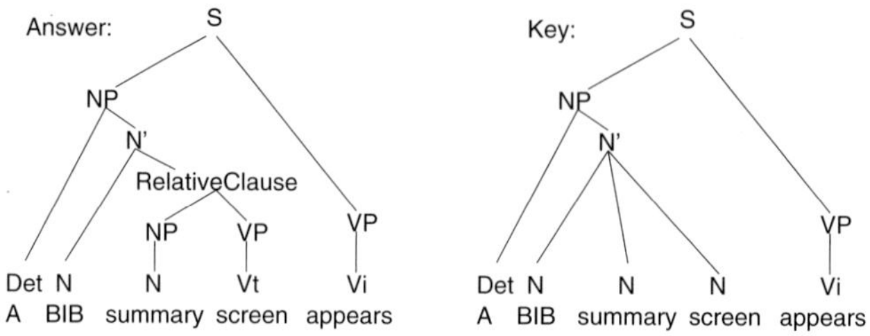

Figure 18.3. Two parse trees of "A BIB summary screen appears"

More recently, (Carroll et al., 1999) proposed a parser evaluation scheme similar to (Lin, 1995). Instead of comparing unlabeled dependency trees, Carroll *et al.* extracted relational tuples that represent a set of labeled dependency relationships between content words. One advantage of their scheme is the possibility of evaluating the deep-level grammatical relationships in structures involving 'moved' elements, such as passive and relative clauses.

6. CONCLUSIONS

We presented a dependency-based evaluation of a principle-based broad-coverage parser, called MINIPAR. The dependency-based method offers several advantages over previous methods that rely on the comparison of phrase boundaries. By evaluating a selected subset of dependencies, we can measure parser performance with respect to different types of grammatical relationships, or different types of lexical properties. Our evaluation shows that MINIPAR is able to achieve about 89% precision and 79% recall.

References

Bömová , A., Hajič, J., Hajicová, E., Hladká , B. (2003). The Prague Dependency Treebank: A Three level Annotation Scenario. In Abeillé, Anne (ed.) *Treebanks: Building and Using Syntactically Annotated Corpora*, Kluwer Academic Publishers, this volume.

Berwick, R. C., S. P. Abney, C. Tenny (eds.) (1991). *Principle-Based Parsing: Computation and Psycholinguistics*. Kluwer Academic Publishers.

Black, E., S. Abney, D. Flickenger, C. Gdaniec, R. Grishman, P. Harrison, D. Hindle, R. Ingria, F. Jelinek, J. Klavans, M. Liberman, M. Marcus, S. Roukos, B. Santorini, T. Strzalkowski (1991). A Procedure for Quantitatively Comparing the Syntactic Coverage of English Grammars. *Proceedings of Speech and Natural Language Workshop*. p. 306–311.

Carroll, J., G. Minnen, T. Briscoe (1999). Corpus Annotation for Parser Evaluation. *Proceedings of the EACL Workshop on Linguistically Interpreted Corpora*. Bergen, Norway.

Chomsky, N. (1995). *The Minimalist Program*. MIT Press.

Collins, M. J. (1996). 'A New Statistical Parser Based on Bigram Lexical Dependencies'. *Proceedings of the 34th Annual Meeting of the Association for Computational Linguistics*. Santa Cruz, CA, p. 184–191.

Collins, M. J. (1997). Three Generative, Lexicalized Models for Statistical Parsing. *Proceedings of the 35th Annual Meeting of the Association for Computational Linguistics*. Madrid, Spain, p. 16–23.

Hays, D. (1964). Dependency theory: a formalism and some observations. *Language* **40**, p. 511–525.

Hudson, R. (1984). *Word Grammar*. Oxford, England: Basil Blackwell Publishers Limited.

Lin, D. (1993). Principle-based Parsing without Overgeneration. *Proceedings of ACL–93*. Columbus, Ohio, pp. 112–120.

Lin, D. (1994) PRINCIPAR—An Efficient, Broad-coverage, Principle-based Parser. *Proceedings of COLING–94*. Kyoto, Japan: p. 482–488.

Lin, D. (1995) A Dependency-based Method for Evaluating Broad-coverage Parsers. *Proceedings of IJCAI-95*. Montreal, Canada, p. 1420–1425.

Lin, D. (1998). A Dependency-based Method for Evaluating Broad-Coverage Parsers. *Journal of Natural Language Engineering*, p. 97–114.

Magerman, D. (1995). Statistical Decision-Tree Model for Parsing. *Proceedings of ACL-96*. Cambridge, MA, p. 276–283.

Marcus, M. P., B. Santorini, M. A. Marcinkiewicz (1993). Building a large annotated corpus of English: the Penn Treebank. *Computational Linguistics* **19**(2), p. 313–330.

Mel'čuk, I. A. (1987). *Dependency syntax: theory and practice*. Albany: State University of New York Press.

Miller, G. A., R. Beckwith, C. Fellbaum, D. Gross, K. J. Miller (1990). 'Introduction to WordNet: An on-line lexical database'. *International Journal of Lexicography* **3**(4), p. 235–244.

Sampson, G. (2003). Thoughts on two decades of drawing trees. This volume.

Sampson, G. R. (1995). *English for the Computer*. Oxford University Press.

Grammar induction with treebanks

Chapter 19

EXTRACTING STOCHASTIC GRAMMARS FROM TREEBANKS

Rens Bod
School of Computing, University of Leeds
Leeds LS2 9JT
UK
and Institute for Logic, Language and Computation
University of Amsterdam
rens@science.uva.nl

Abstract The Data-Oriented Parsing (DOP) model employs an annotated corpus or treebank directly as a stochastic grammar. New input is parsed by combining subtrees from the treebank. The most probable analysis is estimated on the basis of the occurrence-frequencies of the treebank-subtrees. The model as originally defined imposes no constraints on the size and complexity of the subtrees that may be invoked in parsing new input. Both from a theoretical and from a computational perspective we may therefore wonder whether it is possible to impose constraints on the subtrees that are used, in such a way that the performance of the model does not deteriorate or perhaps even improves. That is the main question addressed in the current paper. Moreover, by imposing different constraints on the subtree set, we can simulate several other stochastic grammars, ranging from stochastic context-free grammars to stochastic lexicalized grammars, thus allowing for a proper performance comparison. Experiments with the ATIS and Wall Street Journal treebanks indicate that very few constraints on the treebank-subtrees are warranted. We conclude with a brief discussion of the consequences of our results.

Keywords: Data-oriented parsing, Corpus-based grammars, Stochastic grammars

1. INTRODUCTION

For quite some time, language processing models dealing with non-trivial aspects of syntactic structure or semantic interpretation were always built around "competence grammars": they assumed a non-redundant, complete

A. Abeillé (ed.), Treebanks: Building and Using Parsed Corpora, 333–349.

and consistent description of the sentence-structures of the language. In Scha (1990, 1992) and Bod (1992, 1995, 1998) it has been argued that human language perception and production processes may very well work with representations of concrete past language experiences, and that language processing models could emulate this behavior if they analyzed new input by combining fragments of representations from an annotated corpus.

This idea was worked out in some detail in Bod (1993a/b, 1998), where we demonstrated how an annotated corpus can in fact be employed directly as a stochastic grammar. The first "data-oriented parsing" system described there maintains a corpus of utterances which are annotated with labeled phrase-structure trees (a "treebank"); it parses new input by combining subtrees from the corpus. The most probable analysis is estimated on the basis of the occurrence-frequencies of the subtrees in the corpus.

Subsequent work (under various labels such as "data-oriented structure processing", "corpus-based interpretation", and "treebank grammar") has shown that this approach can be instantiated in many different ways, by making different assumptions about the corpus annotations, or by employing different disambiguation strategies (cf. van den Berg et al. 1994; Bod 1996, 1998a/b, 2000, 2001; Bod & Kaplan 1998; Bonnema 1996; Bonnema et al. 1997; Carroll & Weir 1997; Charniak 1996, 1997; Coleman & Pierrehumbert 1997; Collins & Duffy 2002; Cormons 1999; Goodman 1996, 1998; Kaplan 1996; Rajman 1995a/b; Scholtes 1992, 1993; Scholtes & Bloembergen 1992a/b; Sekine & Grishman 1995; Sima'an et al. 1994; Sima'an 1995, 1996a/b, 1997; Way 1999).

The model as originally defined imposes no constraints on the size and complexity of the corpus-subtrees that may be invoked in parsing new input. The set of subtrees that is used is thus very large (exponential in the number of corpus-trees) and extremely redundant. From both a theoretical and computational point of view, we may therefore wonder whether it is possible to impose constraints on the subtrees that are used, in such a way that the performance of the model does not deteriorate or perhaps even improves. That is the main question addressed in the current paper. Moreover, by imposing different constraints on the subtree set, we can simulate several other stochastic grammars, ranging from stochastic context-free grammars to stochastic lexicalized grammars, thus allowing for a proper performance comparison.

This paper is organized as follows. We first summarize the general data-oriented parsing (DOP) model. Then we report on a series of experiments carried out with the ATIS and *Wall Street Journal* treebanks to investigate several strategies for restricting the set of corpus subtrees. Finally, we go into some of the consequences of our results.

2. SUMMARY OF DATA-ORIENTED PARSING

To date, the data-oriented parsing model has mainly been applied to corpora of phrase-structure trees (but see Bod & Kaplan 1998, Way 1999 or Neumann, this volume, for DOP models using more sophisticated corpus representations). As an example, consider a very simple corpus consisting of only two trees (we leave out some subcategorizations to keep the example simple):

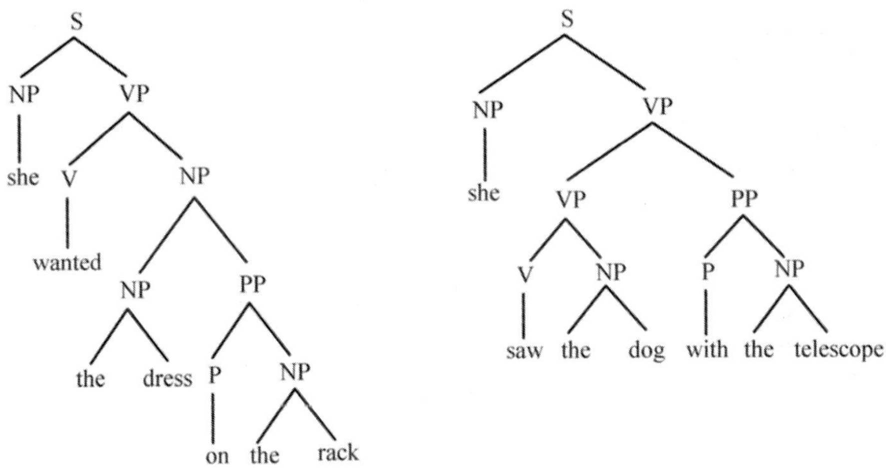

Figure 19.1. A simple example corpus of two trees

New sentences may be parsed by combining subtrees from this corpus, by means of a node-substitution operation indicated as . Node-substitution identifies the leftmost nonterminal frontier node of one tree with the root node of a second tree (i.e., the second tree is substituted on the leftmost nonterminal frontier node of the first tree). A new sentence such as *She saw the dress with the telescope* can thus be parsed as in Figure 19.2.

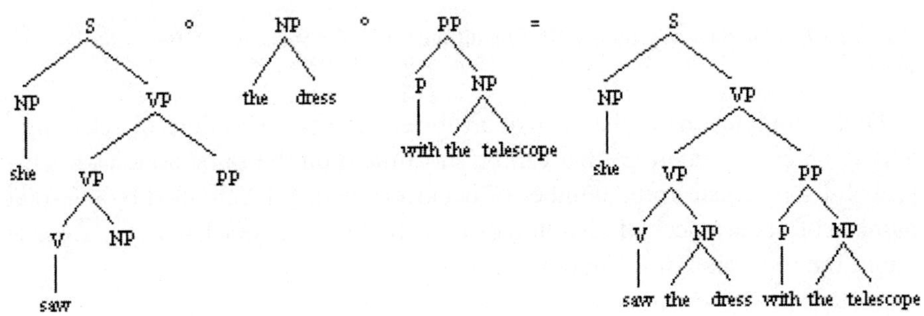

Figure 19.2. A derivation and parse tree for *She saw the dress with the telescope*

Note that other derivations, involving different subtrees, may yield the same parse tree; for instance:

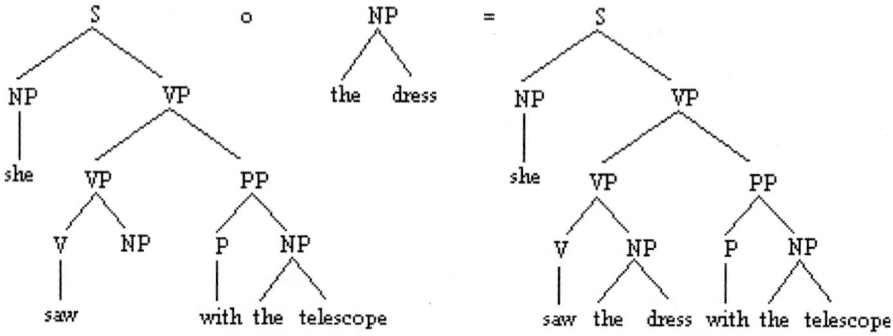

Figure 19.3. Another derivation yielding the same tree as in Figure 19.2

Note also that, given this example corpus, the sentence we considered is ambiguous; by combining other subtrees, a different parse may be derived, which is analogous to the first rather than the second corpus sentence:

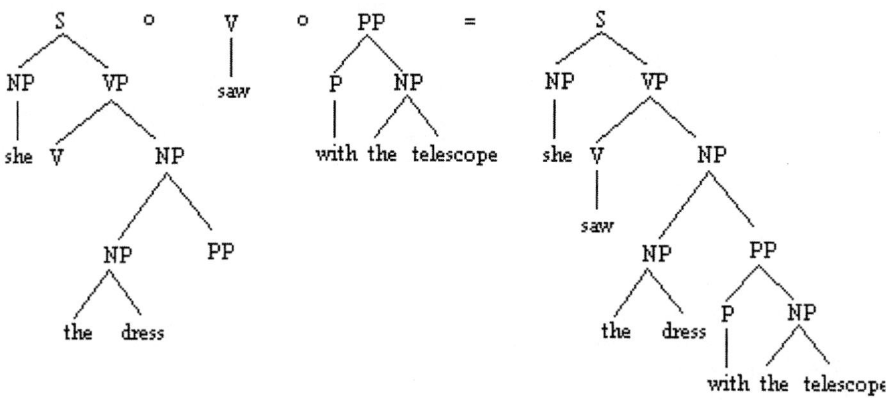

Figure 19.4. Another derivation yielding a different tree for *She saw the dress with the telescope*

DOP computes the probability of a subtree t as the probability of selecting t among all corpus-subtrees that can be substituted on the same node as t. This probability is equal to the number of occurrences of t, $|t|$, divided by the total number of occurrences of all subtrees t' with the same root label as t. Let r(t) return the root label of t. Then we may write:

$$P(t) = \frac{|t|}{\sum_{t':r(t')=r(t)} |t'|}$$

Since each node substitution is independent of previous substitutions, the probability of a derivation $D = t_1 \circ ... \circ t_n$ is computed by the product of the probabilities of its subtrees t_i:

$$P(t_1 \circ ... \circ t_n) = \prod_i P(t_i)$$

The probability of a parse tree is the probability that it is generated by any of its derivations. The probability of a parse tree T is thus computed as the sum of the probabilities of its distinct derivations D:

$$P(T) = \sum_{D \text{ derives } T} P(D)$$

Usually, several different parse trees can be derived for a single sentence, and in that case their probabilities provide a preference ordering. Bod (1992, 1995) showed that DOP can use conventional context-free parsing techniques, by converting subtrees into production rules. That is, every subtree t is converted into a context-free rewrite rule: $root(t) \rightarrow yield(t)$, and every such rule is indexed to maintain the link to its original subtree. The rules obtained in this way are used to construct a chart-like parse forest for the input sentence. Although the exact computation of the most probable parse tree from a parse forest is NP hard (Sima'an 1996b), there exist randomized algorithms to estimate parse probabilities with an error that can be made arbitrarily small (cf. Bod 1995, Chappelier & Rajman 1998). In the current paper, we will employ a Viterbi *n*-best search using a CKY algorithm and estimate the most probable parse from the 1,000 most probable derivations, summing up the probabilities of derivations that generate the same tree. However, in computing the 1,000 most probable derivations by means of Viterbi it is prohibitive to keep track of all subderivations at each edge in the chart. As in most other statistical parsing systems we therefore use the pruning technique described in Collins (1999: 263-4) which assigns a score to each item in the chart equal to the product of the inside probability of the item and its prior probability. Any item with a score less than 10^{-5} times of that of the best item is pruned from the chart.

3. SIMULATING STOCHASTIC GRAMMARS BY CONSTRAINING THE SUBTREE SET

In this section, we go into a number of experiments that were carried out with two different treebanks: the ATIS treebank of 750 trees, and the Wall Street Journal (WSJ) treebank of approx. 50,000 trees. Our main goal is to test whether all, arbitrarily large and complex subtrees are in fact needed for predicting the correct parse trees of new input utterances, or whether we can restrict the subtrees on linguistic or statistical grounds without diminishing the accuracy.

3.1 The base line for the ATIS treebank

A first series of experiments was carried out with the Air Travel Information System (ATIS) corpus (Marcus et al. 1993). We used the blind testing method, dividing the 750 ATIS trees into a 90% training set of 675 trees and a 10% test set of 75 trees. The division was random except for one constraint: that all words in the test set actually occurred in the training set. The 675 training set trees were converted into their subtrees and were enriched with their corpus probabilities. The 75 sentences from the test set served as input sentences that were parsed and disambiguated by means of the subtrees of the training set trees, using the method described in section 2. As a measure for parse accuracy we took the percentage of input sentences for which the most probable parse is identical to the corresponding test set parse. The parse accuracy obtained with the unrestricted subtree collection was 85%. We will use this number as the base line for studying the impact of the various subtree restrictions. (This 85% base line accuracy lies within the range of the standard deviation obtained with 10 different training/test set splits, for which the average parse accuracy was 84.2% with a standard deviation of 2.9%.)

3.2 The impact of overlapping subtrees

The DOP model as defined above chooses as the most appropriate analysis of a sentence the most probable parse of that sentence, rather than the analysis generated by the most probable derivation. The main difference between the most probable parse and the most probable derivation is that by summing up over probabilities of several derivations, the most probable parse takes into account overlapping subtrees, while the most probable derivation does not. Thus the most probable parse includes counts of subtrees of a wide range of sizes: everything from single-level rules to entire trees. In order to test the usefulness of this property, we calculated the accuracies based on the analyses generated by the most probable derivations of the test sentences. The parse accuracy obtained in this way was 69%, which is lower than the 85% accuracy obtained by the most probable parse. We conclude that the most probable parse provides a better estimation for the correct analysis than the most probable derivation, at least for ATIS sentences (in section 3.7 we will test this for WSJ sentences).

3.3 The impact of subtree size

Next, we tested the impact of the size of the subtrees on the parse accuracy. It may be evident that large subtrees can capture more lexico-syntactic dependencies than small ones. We are now interested in the extent to which these dependencies actually lead to better predictions of the appropriate parse.

Therefore we performed experiments with versions of DOP where the subtree collection is restricted to subtrees with a certain maximum depth (where the depth of a tree is defined as the length of the longest path from the root to a leaf). The following table shows the results of these experiments, where the parse accuracy for each maximal depth is given for both the most probable parse and for the parse generated by the most probable derivation (the accuracies are rounded off to the nearest integer).

Table 19.1. Accuracy increases if larger corpus subtrees are used

depth of	parse accuracy	
corpus-subtrees	most probable parse	most probable derivation
1	47%	47%
≤2	68%	56%
≤3	79%	64%
≤4	83%	67%
≤5	84%	67%
≤6	84%	69%
unbounded	85%	69%

The table shows an increase in parse accuracy, for both the most probable parse and the most probable derivation, when increasing the maximum depth of the subtrees. The table confirms that the most probable parse yields better accuracy than the most probable derivation, except for depth 1 where DOP is equivalent to a stochastic context-free grammar (and where every parse is generated by exactly one derivation). The above results clearly show that simple stochastic context-free grammars perform worse than tree-based stochastic grammars.

3.4 The impact of subtree lexicalization

In this section we test the impact of lexicalized subtrees on the parse accuracy. By a lexicalized subtree we mean a subtree whose yield or frontier contains one or more words. The more words a subtree contains, the more lexical dependencies are taken into account. To test the impact of this lexical context on the parse accuracy, we performed experiments with different versions of DOP where the subtree collection is restricted to subtrees whose frontiers contain a certain maximum number of words; the maximal subtree depth was kept constant at 6. These experiments are particularly interesting since we can simulate a number of lexicalized grammars in this way. Lexicalized grammars have become increasingly popular in computational linguistics (e.g. Srinivas & Joshi 1995; Collins 1996, 1999; Charniak 1997, 2000; Chiang 2000). However, all lexicalized grammars that we know of restrict the lexical context that is taken into account. It is an interesting feature of the DOP approach that we can straightforwardly test the impact of the size of the lexical context. The following table shows the results.

Table 19.2. Accuracy increases if more words are in subtree frontiers

number of words in frontiers	parse accuracy most probable parse	most probable derivation
≤1	75%	63%
≤2	80%	65%
≤3	83%	69%
≤4	83%	72%
≤6	83%	72%
≤8	87%	72%
unbounded	84%	69%

Table 19.2 shows an initial increase in parse accuracy, for both the most probable parse and the most probable derivation, when enlarging the lexical context. Note that the parse accuracy deteriorates if the lexicalization exceeds 8 words. Thus, there seems to be an optimal lexical context size for the ATIS corpus. The table confirms that the most probable parse yields better accuracy than the most probable derivation, also for different lexicalization sizes. In the following, we will therefore evaluate our results with respect to the most probable parse only.

3.5 The impact of subtree frequency

We may expect that highly frequent subtrees contribute to a larger extent to the prediction of the appropriate parse than very infrequent subtrees. On the other hand, many infrequent subtrees are larger than the frequent ones. They thus contain more lexical/structural context, and can parse a large piece of an input sentence at once. It is therefore interesting to see what happens if we systematically remove low-frequency subtrees. We performed a set of experiments restricting the subtree collection to subtrees with a certain minimum number of occurrences, without applying any other restrictions. The results of these experiments (table 19.3) indicate that low frequency subtrees contribute significantly to the prediction of the appropriate parse: the parse accuracy seriously deteriorates if low frequency subtrees are discarded.

3.6 The impact of non-headwords

In this section we study what happens if we delete subtrees that are lexicalized only with non-headwords. A non-headword of a subtree is a word which according to Magerman's head scheme (Magerman 1995) is not a headword of the subtree's root nonterminal (although such a nonheadword may of course be a headword of one of the subtree's internal nodes).

Table 19.3. Accuracy decreases if lower bound on subtree frequency increases.

frequency of subtrees	parse accuracy
≥1	85%
≥2	77%
≥3	45%
≥4	28%
≥5	16%
≥6	11%

In our first experiment, we deleted all subtrees whose frontier words were exclusively non-headwords. We did not apply any other restrictions on the subtree collection. The parse accuracy obtained with this subtree collection was 74%. This is a deterioration with respect to the 85% parse accuracy obtained with the complete subtree collection (see table 19.1). Evidently, subtrees with only non-headwords do contain important syntactic relations that are not captured by other subtrees. This goes against common wisdom that only headword dependencies are important. We then considered the number of non-headwords in the subtree frontiers. We may expect that subtrees that are lexicalized with only one non-headword are not important for the prediction of the appropriate parse. After eliminating these subtrees from the subtree collection, but keeping all subtrees with more than one non-headword, we obtained a parse accuracy of 80%, which is worse than the original accuracy of 85%. Again, this shows the difficulty of finding subtree elimination criteria that do not diminish the accuracy: there is already an accuracy decrease if intuitively futile subtrees with just one non-headword are eliminated. However, the following example from the training set shows that such subtrees may not be futile at all, but can in fact describe significant relations:

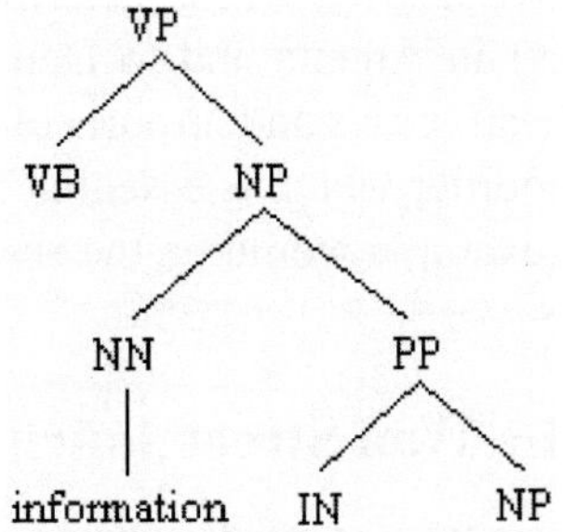

Figure 19.5. A subtree with only one non-head word (with respect to the root label)

This subtree covers many ATIS substrings that are of the form VB *information* IN ... (the tag IN stands for any preposition except to):

find information on ...
get information from ...
give information from/on ...
have information on ...
like information on ...
list information about/on ...
need information on ...
see information from/in ...
show information from/in/on ...

In order to express the tendency that the above substrings occur with a specific structure, regardless the instantiations for VB and IN, we want to have a generalization over the verbs and prepositions but not over the noun information. The fragment above provides exactly this generalization together with the preference for the specific structure. Moreover, the fragment also expresses that information tends to occur in the object position.

An even more interesting example is the subtree in Figure 19.6:

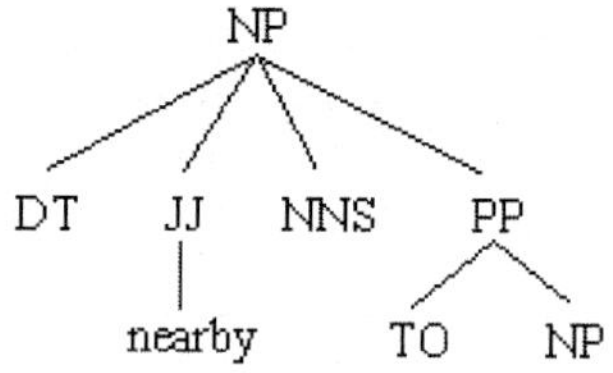

Figure 19.6. A non-head word subtree involving an important dependency

This subtree occurs in sentences such as *What are the nearby cities to Denver airport?* and *What are the nearby airports to Dallas?*. The keyword in these sentences is the adjective nearby, which determines the correct attachment of the PPs to the airport in Atlanta and to Denver. This attachment is independent of the nominal heads cities and airports of which nearby is a modifier. Thus it is a non-head modifier which is essential for the prediction of the appropriate parse. A similar example would be the sentence Show the nearest airport to Dallas.

3.7 Validation on the Wall Street Journal treebank

The above experimental properties were derived on the basis of a very small treebank of only 750 trees. Although such a small treebank allowed us to do a qualitative analysis (i.e. the examples given in section 3.6), it is important to validate the experimentally derived properties on a much larger treebank. We thus performed a series of experiments on the *Wall Street Journal* (WSJ) portion in the Penn Treebank, which consists of approx. 50,000 trees (Marcus et al. 1993). We used the standard division of the WSJ with sections 2 through 21 for training (approx. 40,000 sentences) and section 23 for testing (2416 sentences $\leq$ 100 words). All trees were stripped of their semantic tags, co-reference information and quotation marks. We used all training set subtrees of depth 1 (17,529 subtrees), but due to memory limitations we used a subset of the subtrees larger than depth 1, by taking for each depth a random sample of 400,000 subtrees. These random subtree samples were not selected by first exhaustively computing the complete set of subtrees (this was computationally prohibitive). Instead, for each particular depth >1 we sampled subtrees by randomly selecting a node in a random tree from the training set, after which we selected random expansions from that node until a subtree of the particular depth was obtained. We repeated this procedure 400,000 times for each depth >1 and ≤ 14. Thus no subtrees of depth >14 were used. This resulted in a total set of 5,217,529 subtrees which we will call the base line subtree set. Since our subtrees are allowed to be lexicalized (at their frontiers), we did not use a separate part-of-speech tagger: the test sentences were directly parsed by the training set subtrees. For words that were unknown in our subtree set, we guessed their categories by means of the method described in Weischedel et al. (1993) which uses statistics on word-endings, hyphenation and capitalization. The guessed category for each unknown word was converted into a depth-1 subtree and assigned a probability by means of simple Good-Turing estimation (see Bod 1996). The most probable parse for each test sentence was estimated from the 1,000 most probable derivations of that sentence, as described in section 2.

We used the Labeled Precision and Labeled Recall scores that are commonly employed for the WSJ to compare a proposed parse P (i.e. our estimated most probable parse) with the corresponding correct treebank parse T:

$$\textit{Labeled Precision} = \frac{\#\ \textit{correct constituents in P}}{\#\ \textit{constituents in P}} \qquad \textit{Labeled Recall} = \frac{\#\ \textit{correct constituents in P}}{\#\ \textit{constituents in T}}$$

A constituent in P is "correct" if there exists a constituent in T of the same label that spans the same words.

The Labeled Precision (LP) and Labeled Recall (LR) obtained with the base line subtree set was resp. 89.5% and 89.3%. We used these numbers to study the impact of the various subtree restrictions. The results of these experiments reinforced our results on the ATIS corpus (cf. Bod 2001):

- The impact of overlapping subtrees: computing the best parse tree by the most probable derivation decreased the LP and LR to resp. 84.2%

and 84.5%; this is about 5% lower than the scores obtained by the most probable parse.

- The impact of subtree size: restricting the maximum depth of the subtrees led to a consistent decrease in LP and LR from resp. 89.5% and 89.3% at depth 14 to 76.0% and 71.8% at depth 1.
- The impact of subtree lexicalization: restricting the maximum number of words in the subtree frontiers while keeping the maximum depth constant to 14 also produced a decrease in LP and LR: from resp. 89.5% and 89.3% to 84.4% LP and 84.0% LR if each subtree was lexicalized with only one word. Interestingly, the highest accuracy scores were obtained if the maximum number of words was limited to 12: 90.8% LP and 90.5% LR. Thus, as for the ATIS, there is an optimal lexical context size for the WSJ.
- The impact of non-headwords: the elimination of subtrees with nonheadwords led to a slight decrease in accuracy. The difference between using no and all non-headwords was 1.2% in LP and 1.0% in LR. Although this difference is small, it does indicate that non-headword dependencies are important in the WSJ, for example between more and than in the construction carry more people than cargo where neither more nor than are head words of the NP constituent more people than cargo. Nonheadword dependencies are problematic for head-lexicalized stochastic grammars that focus on headword relations (cf. Collins 1997, 1999; Charniak 1997, 2000). DOP, on the other hand, can easily capture these dependencies since it includes subtrees in which more and than are the only words.

4. DISCUSSION AND CONCLUSION

The experimentally derived properties presented in this paper indicate that almost all restrictions on the subtree set diminish the parse accuracy. We must keep in mind, however, that we have observed this only for one, rather impoverished, representation formalism (phrase structure trees), and for only two treebanks (ATIS, WSJ). Our results nevertheless suggest that the structural units of natural language cannot be defined by a minimal set of rules, as is usually attempted in linguistic theory, but need to be defined in terms of a large set of redundant structures (indeed, a treebank) with virtually no restriction on form, size, lexicalization and non-headwords.

A major difference between the DOP approach and other stochastic parsing approaches is that DOP starts out by taking into account all fragments (i.e. subtrees) seen in a treebank and then investigates restrictions to discover the set of relevant fragments, while other approaches typically limit the statistical dependencies beforehand (for example to headword dependencies) and then try to improve parse accuracy by gradually letting in more dependencies. It is not unlikely that these two opposite directions converge to the same, true set of statistical dependencies for natural language parsing – though we believe this should be tested with richer linguistic representations (cf. Frank et al. 2002).

As it happens, quite a lot of convergence has already taken place. The history of stochastic parsing models shows a consistent increase in the scope of statistical dependencies. Figure 19.7 gives a schematic overview of this increase (see Carroll & Weir 1997, for a more detailed account of a subsumption lattice where SCFG is at the bottom and DOP at the top).

Model	**Scope of Statistical Dependencies**
Charniak (1996)	context-free rules
Collins (1996), Eisner (1996)	context-free rules + headwords
Charniak (1997)	context-free rules + headwords + grandparent nodes
Collins (2000)	context-free rules + headwords + grandparent nodes/rules + bigrams + two-level rules + two-level bigrams + nonhead-words
Collins & Duffy (2002)	all subtrees within parse trees
Bod (1992)	all subtrees within parse trees

Figure 19.7. Overview of the increase of statistical dependencies by stochastic parsers

Thus there seems to be a convergence towards a maximalist model which "takes all fragments [...] and lets the statistics decide" (Bod 1998: 5). While early head-lexicalized grammars restricted the fragments to the locality of headwords (e.g. Collins 1996; Eisner 1996), later models showed the importance of including context from higher nodes in the tree (Charniak 1997; Johnson 1998). The importance of including nonhead-words is now also uncontroversial (e.g. Collins 1997, 1999; Charniak 2000; Bod 2001). Collins (2000) argues for "[...] keeping track of counts of arbitrary fragments within parse trees", which has been carried out in Collins & Duffy (2002) using the same set of subtrees as in Bod (1992).

References

Berg, E. van den, R. Bod, R. Scha (1994). A Corpus-Based Approach to Semantic Interpretation, *Proceedings Ninth Amsterdam Colloquium*, Amsterdam, The Netherlands.

Bod, R. (1992). Data Oriented Parsing (DOP), *Proceedings COLING'92*, Nantes, France.

Bod, R. (1993a). Using an Annotated Language Corpus as a Virtual Stochastic Grammar, *Proceedings AAAI'93*, Morgan Kaufmann, Menlo Park, Ca.

Bod, R. (1993b). Monte Carlo Parsing, *Proceedings Third International Workshop on Parsing Technologies*, Tilburg/Durbuy, The Netherlands/Belgium.

Bod, R. (1995). Enriching Linguistics with Statistics: Performance Models of Natural Language, ILLC Dissertation Series 1995-14, University of Amsterdam.

Bod, R. (1998a). Spoken Dialogue Interpretation with the DOP Model, *Proceedings COLING-ACL'98*, Montreal, Canada.

Bod, R. (1998b). *Beyond Grammar*. Stanford: CSLI Publications.

Bod, R. (2000). Parsing with the Shortest Derivation, *Proceedings COLING'2000*, Saarbrücken, Germany.

Bod, R. (2001). What is the Minimal Set of Fragments which Achieves Maximal Parse Accuracy? *Proceedings ACL'2001*, Toulouse, France.

Bod, R., R. Bonnema, R. Scha (1996). A Data-Oriented Approach to Semantic Interpretation, *Proceedings Workshop on Corpus-Oriented Semantic Analysis*, ECAI-96, Budapest, Hungary.

Bod, R., R. Kaplan (1998). A Probabilistic Corpus-Driven Model for Lexical-Functional Analysis, *Proceedings COLING-ACL'98*, Montreal, Canada.

Bonnema, R., R. Bod, R. Scha, (1997). A DOP Model for Semantic Interpretation, *Proceedings ACL/EACL-97*, Madrid, Spain.

Carroll, J., D. Weir (1997). Encoding Frequency Information in Lexicalized Grammars, *Proceedings 5th International Workshop on Parsing Technologies*, MIT, Cambridge.

Chappelier, J., M. Rajman (1998). Extraction stochastique d'arbres d'analyse pour le modle DOP, *Proceedings TALN 1998*, Paris, France.

Charniak, E. (1996). Tree-bank Grammars, *Proceedings AAAI'96*, Portland, Oregon.

Charniak, E. (1997). Statistical Techniques for Natural Language Parsing, *AI Magazine*, Winter 1997.

Charniak, E. (2000). A Maximum-Entropy-Inspired Parser. *Proceedings ANLPNAACL' 2000*, Seattle, Washington.

Chiang, D. (2000). Statistical parsing with an automatically extracted tree adjoining grammar, *Proceedings ACL'2000*, Hong Kong, China.

Coleman, J., J. Pierrehumbert (1997). Stochastic Phonological Grammars and Acceptability, *Proceedings Computational Phonology*, Third Meeting of the ACL Special Interest Group in Computational Phonology, Madrid, Spain.

Collins, M. (1996). A new statistical parser based on bigram lexical dependencies, *Proceedings ACL'96*, Santa Cruz (Ca.).

Collins, M. (1997). Three generative lexicalised models for statistical parsing, *Proceedings ACL'97*, Madrid, Spain.

Collins, M. (1999). Head-Driven Statistical Models for Natural Language Parsing, PhD-thesis, University of Pennsylvania, PA.

Collins, M. (2000). Discriminative Reranking for Natural Language Parsing, *Proceedings ICML-2000*, Stanford, Ca.

Collins, M., N. Duffy (2002). New Ranking Algorithms for Parsing and Tagging: Kernels over Discrete Structures, and the Voted Perceptron. *Proceedings ACL'2002*, Philadelphia, PA.

Cormons, B. (1999). Analyse et désambiguisation: Une approche purement à base de corpus (Data-Oriented Parsing) pour le formalisme des Grammaires Lexicales Fonctionnelles, PhD thesis, Université de Rennes, France.

Eisner, J. (1996). Three new probabilistic models for dependency parsing: an exploration, *Proceedings COLING-96*, Copenhagen, Denmark.

Eisner, J. (1997). Bilexical Grammars and a Cubic-Time Probabilistic Parser, *Proceedings Fifth International Workshop on Parsing Technologies*, Boston, Mass.

Frank, A., J. van Genabith, L. Sadler, A. Way (2003). From Treebank Resources to LFG F-Structures. This volume.

Goodman, J. (1996). Efficient Algorithms for Parsing the DOP Model, *Proceedings Empirical Methods in Natural Language Processing*, Philadelphia, PA.

Goodman, J. (1998). Parsing Inside-Out, Ph.D. thesis, Harvard University, Mass.

Johnson, M. (1998). PCFG Models of Linguistic Tree Representations, Computational Linguistics 24(4), p. 613–632.

Kaplan, R. (1996). A Probabilistic Approach to Lexical-Functional Analysis, *Proceedings of the 1996 LFG Conference and Workshops*. CSLI Publications, Stanford, CA.

Magerman, D. (1995). Statistical Decision-Tree Models for Parsing, *Proceedings ACL'95*, Cambridge, Mass.

Marcus, M., B. Santorini, M. Marcinkiewicz (1993). Building a Large Annotated Corpus of English: the Penn Treebank, *Computational Linguistics* 19(2).

Neumann, G. (2002). A Uniform Method for Automatically Extracting Stochastic Lexicalized Tree Grammars from Treebanks and HPSG. This volume.

Rajman, M. (1995a). Apports d'une approche à base de corpus aux techniques de traitement automatique du langage naturel, PhD thesis, Ecole Nationale Supérieure des Télécommunications, Paris.

Rajman, M. (1995b). Approche Probabiliste de l'Analyse Syntaxique, *Traitement Automatique des Langues*, vol. 36(1-2).

Scha, R. (1990). Taaltheorie en Taaltechnologie; Competence en Performance, in Q.A.M. de Kort and G.L.J. Leerdam (eds.), *Computertoepassingen in de Neerlandistiek*, Almere: Landelijke Vereniging van Neerlandici (LVVN-jaarboek).

Scha, R. (1992). Virtuele Grammatica's en Creatieve Algoritmen, Gramma/TTT 1(1).

Scholtes, J. (1992). Resolving Linguistic Ambiguities with a Neural Data- Oriented Parsing (DOP) System, in I. Aleksander and J. Taylor (eds.), *Artificial Neural Networks 2*, Vol. 2, Elsevier Science Publishers.

Scholtes, J., S. Bloembergen (1992a). The Design of a Neural Data- Oriented Parsing (DOP) System, *Proceedings of the International Joint Conference on Neural Networks*, (IJCNN), Baltimore, MD.

Scholtes, J., S. Bloembergen (1992b). Corpus Based Parsing with a Self- Organizing Neural Net, *Proceedings of the International Joint Conference on Neural Networks*, (IJCNN), Bejing, China.

Sekine, S., R. Grishman (1995). A Corpus-based Probabilistic Grammar with Only Two Non-terminals, *Proceedings Fourth International Workshop on Parsing Technologies*, Prague, Czech Republic.

Sima'an, K., R. Bod, S. Krauwer, R. Scha (1994). Efficient Disambiguation by means of Stochastic Tree Substitution Grammars, *Proceedings International Conference on New Methods in Language Processing*, UMIST, Manchester, UK.

Sima'an, K. (1995). An optimized algorithm for Data Oriented Parsing, *Proceedings International Conference on Recent Advances in Natural Language Processing*, Tzigov Chark, Bulgaria.

Sima'an, K. (1996a). An optimized algorithm for Data Oriented Parsing, in R. Mitkov and N. Nicolov (eds.), *Recent Advances in Natural Language Processing* 1995, volume 136 of Current Issues in Linguistic Theory. John Benjamins, Amsterdam.

Sima'an, K. (1996b). Computational Complexity of Probabilistic Disambiguation by means of Tree Grammars, *Proceedings COLING-96*, Copenhagen, Denmark.

Sima'an, K. (1997). Explanation-Based Learning of Data-Oriented Parsing, in T. Ellison (ed.) *CoNLL97: Computational Natural Language Learning*, ACL'97, Madrid, Spain.

Srinivas, B., A. Joshi (1995). Some novel applications of explanation-based learning to parsing lexicalized tree-adjoining grammars, *Proceedings ACL'95*, Cambridge (Mass.).

Way, A. (1999). A Hybrid Archtecture for Robust MT using LFG-DOP, *Journal of Experimental and Theoretical Artificial Intelligence* 11(4).

Weischedel, R., M. Meteer, R, Schwarz, L. Ramshaw, J. Palmucci (1993). Coping with Ambiguity and Unknown Words through Probabilistic Models, *Computational Linguistics*, 19(2).

Chapter 20

A UNIFORM METHOD FOR AUTOMATICALLY EXTRACTING STOCHASTIC LEXICALIZED TREE GRAMMARS FROM TREEBANKS AND HPSG

Günter Neumann

DFKI 66123 Saarbrücken, Germany

neumann@dfki.de

Abstract We present a uniform method for the extraction of stochastic lexicalized tree grammars (SLTG) of different complexities from existing treebanks as well as from competence-based grammars , which allows us to analyze the relationship of a grammar automatically induced from a treebank with respect to its size, its complexity, and its predictive power on unseen data. Processing of different SLTG is performed by a stochastic version of the two-step Earley-based parsing strategy introduced in (Schabes and Joshi, 1991).

Keywords: Grammar Extraction, Treebanks, Head-Driven Phrase Structure Grammars, General Learning Method

1. INTRODUCTION

In this paper[1] we present a uniform method for the extraction of stochastic lexicalized tree grammars (SLTG) from existing treebanks as well as from competence-based grammars, especially Head-Driven Phrase Structure grammars (HPSG), (Pollard and Sag, 1994). The use of SLTGs is motivated for two reasons. First, it is assumed that SLTGs capture distributional and hierarchical information better than stochastic CFG (cf. Schabes, 1992; (Schabes and Waters, 1996)), and second, they allow the factorization of different kinds of recursion, viz. extraction of left, right, and wrapping auxiliary trees and possible combinations thereof. Processing of different SLTGs is performed using a stochastic version of the two-phase Earley-based parsing strategy introduced in (Schabes and Joshi, 1991).

A. Abeillé (ed.), Treebanks: Building and Using Parsed Corpora, 351–365.

Existing treebanks are used because they allow corpus-based analysis of grammars of realistic size. HPSG is used in order to extract a domain-independent, phenomena-oriented subgrammar. The ultimate goal then is to merge SLTGs extracted from both sources in order to 1) improve the coverage of treebank grammars on unseen data, and 2) ease adaptation of treebanks to new domains (see also 6).

2. RELATED WORK

Before describing our method in detail, we will first discuss alternative approaches for automatically converting treebanks into tree grammars, namely the Data-oriented Parsing (DOP) framework and approaches based on applying Explanation-based Learning (EBL) to NL parsing.

The general strategy of our approach is similar to DOP (the original DOP model was presented in (Bod, 1993), but see also (Bod, this volume)) with the notable distinction that in our framework all trees must be lexically anchored and that in addition to substitution, we also consider adjunction and restricted versions of it. Furthermore, since DOP tries to compute all possible decompositions of a treebank, the training phase is very complex (actually it is exponential), whereas our approach is polynomial since we consider only a subset of all possible decompositions. A similar approach can be found in (Frank et al., this volume) who derive an LFG grammar from treebanks, and (Xia, 1999; Chen and Vijay-Shanker, 2000; Chiang, 2000) who derive lexicalized tree adjoining grammars from treebanks (based on and partially extending the work presented in (Neumann, 1998) and in this paper).

In the EBL approach to NL parsing, the core idea is to use a competence grammar and a training corpus to construct a treebank. The treebank is then used to obtain a specialized grammar which can be processed much faster than the original one at the price of a small loss in coverage. (Samuelsson, 1994), presents a method in which tree decomposition is completely automatized using the information-theoretical concept of entropy, after the whole treebank has been indexed in an and-or tree. This implies that a new grammar has to be computed if the treebank changes (i.e., reduced incrementality) and that the generality of the induced subtrees depends much more on the size and variation of the treebank than our approach. On the other hand, their approach seems to be more sensitive to the distribution of sequences of lexical anchors than ours, so that we will explore its integration in the future.

In (Srinivas, 1997), the application of EBL to parsing of LTAG is presented. The core idea is to generalize the derivation trees generated by an LTAG and to allow for a finite state transducer representation of the set of generalized parses. The POS sequence of a training instance is used as the index to a generalized parse. Generalization with respect to recursion is achieved by introducing the

Kleene star into the yield of an auxiliary tree that was part of the training example, which allows generalization over the length of the training sentences.

3. GRAMMAR EXTRACTION

Given a set of parse trees, grammar extraction is the process of decomposing each parse tree into smaller units called subtrees. In our approach, the underlying decomposition operation

1 should yield lexically anchored subtrees, and

2 should be guided by linguistic principles.

The motivation behind (1) is the observation that in practice stochastic CFGs perform worse than non-hierarchical approaches, and that lexicalized tree grammars may be able to capture both distributional and hierarchical information, (Schabes and Waters, 1996). Concerning (2) we want to take advantage of the linguistic principles explicitly or implicitly used to define a treebank. This is motivated by the hypothesis that it will better support the development of on-line or incremental learning strategies (the cutting criteria are less dependent on the quantity and quality of the existing treebank than purely statistically based approaches, see also section 2) and that it renders possible the comparison and integration of a grammar which has been extracted from a treebank with a linguistically based competence grammar. Both aspects (but especially the latter one) are of importance because it is also possible to apply the same extraction strategy to a treebank computed by some competence grammar, and to investigate novel methods for combining treebanks and competence grammars (see section 6).

3.1 A common extraction strategy

In the following we introduce a general method for the extraction of stochastic lexicalized tree grammars (SLTG) from treebanks and HPSG, before its specialization to the different data sources at hand is described in the sections 4 and 5.

The extraction method is applied to a set of sentences which have been annotated with their corresponding syntactic tree structure or *parse trees*. For the extraction method, it does not matter what source has been used to determine the parse trees. Thus, the method abstracts away from whether the set of sentences has been decorated manually (a treebank) or whether a parser and a source grammar have been used to compute the parse trees automatically.

The major operation of the extraction method is a recursive tree decomposition operation starting from the root node of a parse tree. As already noted above, the tree decomposition operation should be guided by linguistically oriented decomposition principles. During the traversal of a tree these principles specify which subtrees of a current node should be cut off or not. A major aspect for the definition of meaningful cutting criteria is an assumed classification of the parse tree nodes into head and modifier nodes. We can now define a quite simple *head–driven decomposition principle*: cut off all non-head subtrees. Using HPSG this is (should be) quite a simple task directly making use of the HPSG-principles. In case of treebanks, we assume that a treebank comes with a notion of lexical and phrasal head, i.e., with a kind of *head principle*.

Now we can describe the performance of the extraction method more precisely as follows: Using the head–driven decomposition principle, each tree from the set of parse trees is decomposed from the top downwards into a set of subtrees, such that each non-terminal non-head subtree is cut off, and the cutting point is marked for substitution. The same process is then recursively applied to each extracted subtree. Due to the assumed head notion, each extracted tree will automatically be lexically anchored (and the path from the lexical anchor to the root can be seen as a head-chain). Furthermore, every terminal element which is a sister of a node of the head-chain will also remain in the extracted tree. Thus, the yield of the extracted tree might contain several terminal substrings, which gives interesting patterns of word or POS sequences (see also figure 20.1). For each extracted tree, a frequency counter is used to compute the probability $p(t)$ of a tree t, after the whole treebank has been processed, such that $\sum_{t:root(t)=\alpha} p(t) = 1$, where α denotes the root label of a tree t.

3.2 Lexical anchors

Each extracted subtree will automatically be lexically anchored. The lexical anchors are later used as indices for the retrieval of subtrees during parsing. We have parametrized our extraction method with respect to the exact definition of what counts as a lexical anchor, e.g., a word, stem, part-of-speech (POS) and in case of HPSG the lexical type of a lexical element. This allows us to investigate the trade-off between space (i.e., size of grammar) and time (i.e., more combinatorial power). For example, if we use words as lexical anchors, then each word of an input sentence will be able to identify its individual set of trees. However, the size of the grammar will be quite large. On the contrary, if we use POS as lexical anchors the size of the SLTG will be smaller, but different words will retrieve the same set of trees if they belong to the same POS (see also section 4 paragraph *Experiments*).

3.3 Additional operations

In order to automatically enrich the coverage of the extracted grammar, two additional operations are performed during decomposition. Firstly, each subtree of the head-chain is copied and the copied tree is processed individually by the decomposition operation (e.g., in figure 20.3, the tree $T3$ is copied from the head chain of $T1$.). This means that a phrase which occurs only in a head-position in the training corpus can now also be used in nonhead-positions by the SLTG-parser when parsing new sentences. Secondly, if the SLTG-tree has a modifier phrase attached, then a new tree is created with the modifier "unattached" (applied recursively, if the tree has more than one modifier). Unattachment of a modifier m is simply done by raising the head daughter into the position of m (e.g, in figure 20.3, the tree $T4$ is obtained by replacing the subtree rooted at $HAdj\_I$ of tree $T1$ with the subtree rooted at $HComp$. In a similar way, $T5$ is created from $T2$). The advantage of unattaching modifiers is that we will be able to also recognize sentences with fewer or no modifiers using our extracted grammar. Note that the possible maximum number n of modifier sequences is constrained by the training corpus, i.e., modifiers are implicitly represented as iterations from 0 to n.

3.4 Two-phase parsing of SLTG

The resulting SLTG will be processed by a two-phase stochastic parser along the line of (Schabes and Joshi, 1991). In the first step the input string is used for retrieving the relevant subset of elementary trees. Note that the yield of an elementary tree may consist of a sequence of lexical elements. Thus in order to support efficient access, the deepest leftmost chain of lexical elements is used as index to an elementary tree. Each such index is stored in a decision tree. The first step is then realized by means of a recursive tree traversal which identifies all (longest) matching substrings of the input string (see also section 4 paragraph *Experiments*). Parsing of lexically triggered trees is performed in the second step using an Earley-based strategy. In order to ease implementation of different strategies, the different parsing operations are expressed as inference rules and controlled by a chart-based agenda strategy along the line of (Shieber et al., 1995). So far, we have implemented a version for running SLTIG which is based on Schabes and Waters, 1995. The inference rules can be triggered through boolean parameters, which allows flexible hiding of different kinds of auxiliary trees .

4. SLTG FROM TREEBANKS

We will now decribe how the general method is used for extracting an SLTG. First we will focus on the use of existing treebanks using the Penn treebank (Marcus et al., 1993) and the Negra treebank, a treebank for German, (Skut et al., 1997).

In the Negra treebank, dependency theory has been chosen in order to account for the free word order property of German. The Negra treebank follows an hybrid framework that combines the advantages of phrase-structure and de-

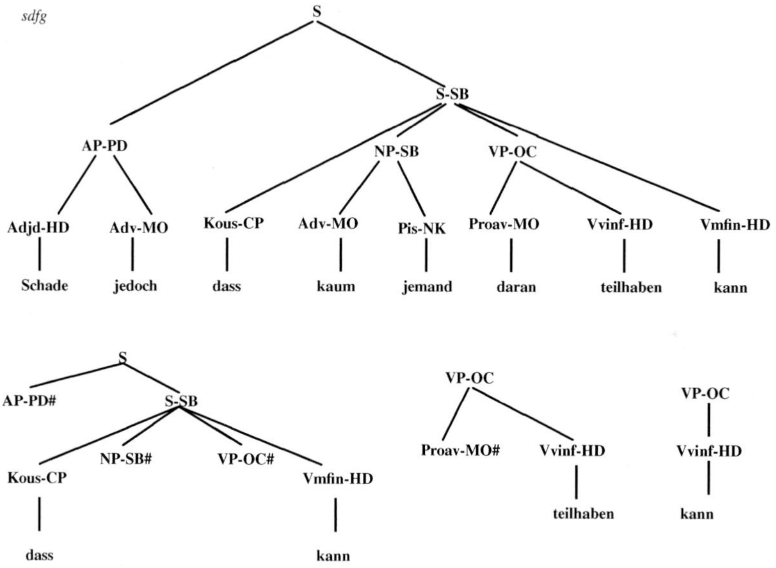

Figure 20.1. The Negra-parse tree of the sentence "Schade jedoch, daß kaum jemand daran teilhaben kann." (**Unfortunate however that almost nobody participate can*) and some of the extracted SLTG-trees. # denotes the substitution marker.

pendency grammars. They do employ phrasal nodes, but try to keep the structure flat such that a phrasal node mostly corresponds to one lexical head (see figure 20.1). The branches of such trees may cross in order to treat non-local dependencies. Negra comes with a tool that transforms the Negra-format to the Penn-format by transforming crossing edges into non-crossing edges and by the introducing of corresponding gap nodes, (Skut et al., 1997; Brants et al., this volume). We are using these transformed Negra trees in our experiments.

We suggested that tree-decomposition should be guided by a head–driven decomposition principle and that we assumed that a treebank comes with a kind of a head principle. In the Negra treebank, head and modifier elements are explicitly tagged. For example, each head is marked by the suffix HD or NK which allows straightforward definitions of the decomposition principles. In case of the Penn treebank (see figure 20.2), the head relation has been determined manually and stored in a head-percolation table.[2] In case it is not possible to uniquely identify one head element, there exists a parameter called DIRECTION which specifies whether the left or rightmost candidate should be selected. Note that by means of this parameter we can also specify whether the resulting grammar should prefer left or right branching.

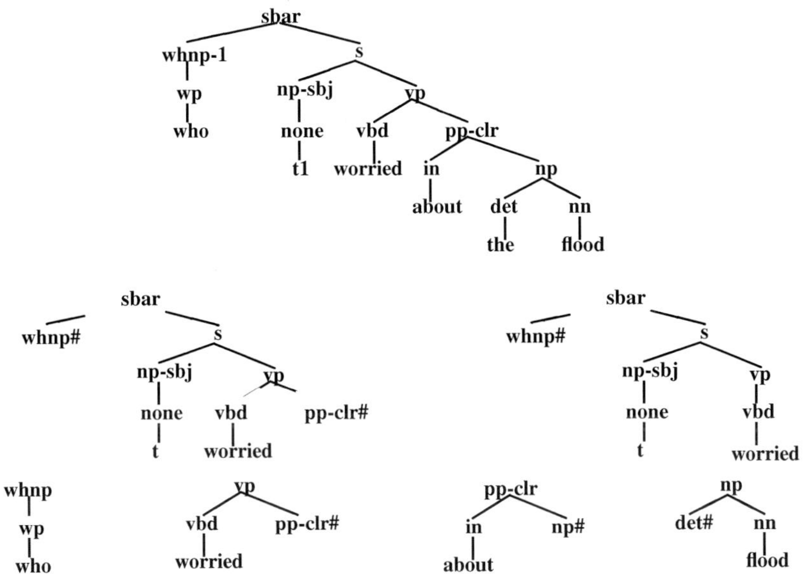

Figure 20.2. The Penn-parse tree of the sentence "who worried about the flood " and some of the extracted SLTG-trees. Here we used the word form as lexical anchor and POS for all other terminal elements. # denotes the substitution marker.

Using the head information, each tree from the treebank is decomposed from the top downwards into a set of subtrees as described in section 3. After a tree has been decomposed completely, we obtain a set of lexicalized elementary trees where each nonterminal of the yield is marked for substitution. In the next step the set of elementary trees is divided into a set of initial and auxiliary trees applying the standard definitions from the TAG literature. The set of auxiliary trees is further subdivided into a set of left, right, and wrapping auxiliary trees following Schabes and Waters, 1995 (using special foot node labels, like :lfoot, :rfoot, and :wfoot). Note that the identification of possible auxiliary trees is strongly corpus-driven. Using special foot node labels allows us to carefully trigger the corresponding inference rules. For example, it might be possible to treat the :wfoot label as the substitution label, which means that we consider the extracted grammar as a SLTIG, or only highly frequent wrapping auxiliary trees will be considered. It is also possible to treat every foot node label as the substitution label, which means that the extracted grammar only allows for substitution. At this point we must stress that we do not factor out modifier recursion explicitly from the Penn treebank. The major reason is that arguments and modifiers for the same head are both sisters of the head. In the

Negra treebank, modifiers are explicitly marked by means of the suffix MO (see figure 20.1). However, since the parse trees are flat, we cannot simply factor out recursion without changing the topological structure of the parse trees. For this reason we "re-do" modifier attachment by iteratively visiting all modifier nodes of an elementary tree *etree*. In each iteration, *etree* is copied and the current modifier is destructively deleted from *etree* (as described in 3).[3]

Experiments. We will briefly report on first results of our method using the Negra treebank (4270 sentences) and the sections 02, 03, 04 from the Penn treebank (the first 4270 sentences). In both cases we extracted three different versions of SLTGs (note that no normalization of the treebanks was performed): (a) lexical anchors are words, (b) lexical anchors are parts of speech, and (c) all terminal elements are substituted by the constant :term, which means that lexical information is ignored. For each grammar we report the number of elementary trees, left, right, and wrapping auxiliary trees obtained for the different sorts of lexical anchors. The following two tables summarize the results:

Table 20.1. Extracted number of trees for the Negra treebank

# trees	anchor=word	anchor=pos	anchor=:term
elem. trees	26553	10384	6515
leftaux trees	184	60	40
rightaux trees	54	35	25
wrapping trees	39	36	29

Table 20.2. Extracted number of trees for the Penn treebank

# trees	anchor=word	anchor=pos	anchor=:term
elem. trees	31944	11979	8132
leftaux trees	701	403	293
rightaux trees	649	246	153
wrapping trees	386	306	249

In a second experiment we evaluated the performance of the implemented SLTIG parser using the extracted Penn treebank with words as lexical anchors. We applied all sentences on the extracted grammar and computed the following average values for the first phase: sentence length: 27.54, number of matching substrings: 15.93, number of elementary trees: 492.77, number of different root labels: 33.16. The average run-time for each sentence (measured on a Sun Ultra 2 (200 mhz): 0.0231 sec. In a next step we tested the run-time behavior of the whole parser on the same input. The average run-time for each sentence (exhaustive mode) is 6.18 sec. This is promising, since the parser has not yet been optimized.

We also tried initial blind tests, but it turned out that the current size of the treebanks considered is too small to get reliable results on unseen data (randomly selecting 10 % of a treebank for testing; 90 % for training). The reason is that if we consider only words as anchors then we rarely get a complete parsing result, very often due to unknown words and different punctuation. If we consider only POS, then the number of elementary trees retrieved through the first phase increases causing the current parser prototype to be slower by factor of about 1/5 (due to the restricted annotation scheme).[4] A better strategy seems to be the use of words for lexical anchors only and POS for all other terminal nodes, or to use only closed-class words as lexical anchors (assuming a head principle based on functional categories).

5. SLTG FROM HPSG

The same approach[5] has been applied to a set of parse trees computed by using an English HPSG-grammar. The grammar used in our study is the English Resource Grammar being developed as part of the LinGO (Linguistic Grammars Online) project at CSLI, (Copestake et al., 2000), Stanford University. The grammar consists of about 7000 types, arranged in a multiple-inheritance hierarchy which defines the properties of lexical entries, lexical rules, and syntactic phrase structure rules. The lexicon includes hand-built entries for about 5000 stems, along with the full set of inflectional lexical rules and 15 derivational rules which are executed at run time. Syntactic coverage of the grammar is relatively broad, with a central focus on providing precise semantic interpretations for each phenomenon that is assigned an analysis, using the Minimal Recursion Semantics framework of (Copestake et al., 1997)[6].

Training of an SLTG starts by first parsing each sentence s_i of the training corpus with the source HPSG system.[7] The resulting feature structure fs_{s_i} of each example also contains the parse tree pt_i, where each non-terminal node contains the label of the HPSG-rule schema (e.g, head-complement rule) that has been applied during the corresponding derivation step as well as a pointer to the feature structure of the corresponding sign. The label of each terminal node consists of the lexical type of the corresponding feature structure. Each parse tree pt_i is now processed by the following interleaved steps (see also figure 20.3).

Each parse tree is decomposed from the top downwards into a set of subtrees such that each non-head subtree is cut off as described above. In case of the HPSG-grammar, testing whether a phrase is a head phrase or not can be done very easily by checking whether the top-level type of a rule's label feature

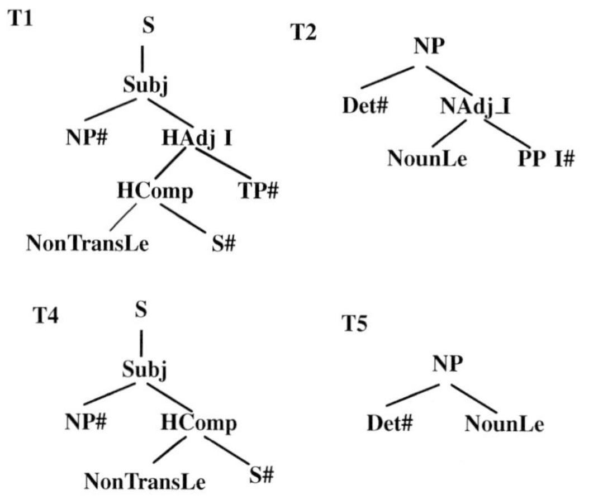

Figure 20.3. Some trees extracted from *I guess we need to figure out a day, within the next two months.* The symbols S, NP, VP, TP, Det, PP_I have been determined by means of specialization (see text). # denotes the substitution marker. Note that the lexical type of a lexical element is used as lexical anchor.

structure is a subtype of a general *headed phrase* which is defined in an HPSG grammar. The same holds for adjunct phrases (see section 3). The root node as well as all substitution nodes of an extracted tree are further processed by replacing the rule label with a corresponding *category label*. The possible set of category labels is defined in the type hierarchy of the HPSG source grammar. They express equivalence classes for different phrasal signs. For example, phrasal signs whose value of the LOCAL.CAT.HEAD feature is of type *noun*, and whose value of the LOCAL.CAT.VAL.SUBJ feature is the empty list, are classified as *NP*s. Now, if the associated feature structure of a rule label $HeadAdjunct$ of the current training sentence is subsumed by the NP type, then $HeadAdjunct$ is replaced by NP. Note that this step actually performs a specialization of the current tree because the same tree might occur in another tree in verbal position. In this case, $HeadAdjunct$ may be replaced by the type VP. The definition of category labels is declarative. Thus it is possible to define more fine-grained labels directly as part of the source grammar leading to more specific SLTG trees. This can be done by the grammar writer without knowing any details of the learning strategy.

After all parse trees of the training set have been decomposed and specialized, we compute a tree's probability as described in section 4.

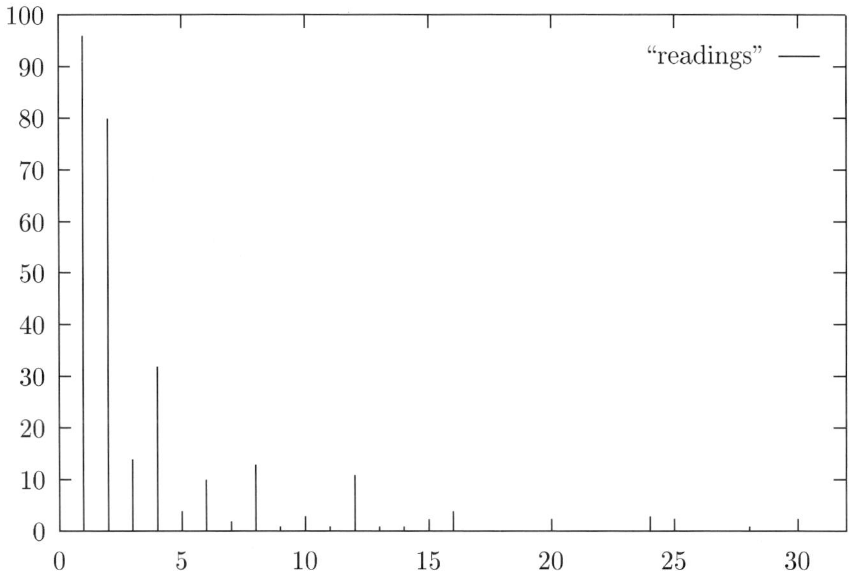

Figure 20.4. In almost all cases the SLTG-parser computes fewer than 16 readings per sentence.

5.1 Experiments

We trained the HPSG-system on a corpus of 2000 English sentences from Verbmobil dialogs (with an average length of 11.5 words per sentence). The size of the extracted SLTG before applying the additional operations (copy of trees of the head-chain and unattachment) is 1922 elementary trees. Copying of trees of the head chain yields 3828 trees, considering only unattachment as additional operation gives 2427 elementary trees. Applying both operations gives an SLTG with a total of 4195 trees.

Using the extracted SLTG-grammar we ran initial performance tests on the training corpus. The average *run-time* of the SLTG-parser (i.e., without off-line expansion, but including morphological and lexical pre-processing) is 170 msec for all readings and 20 msec for the best reading. The overall speed (i.e., including lexical lookup and off-line expansion of the corresponding feature structure of the found SLTG-parse tree by unifying lexical information and the HPSG principles of the source grammar) is improved by a factor of 12 compared to parsing with the original highly tuned HPSG parser at the time of our study. Figure 20.4 shows the number of readings found by the SLTG parser.

From the curve we can see that for most sentences the number of readings lies between 1 and 12 and that only very few sentences have extreme numbers of readings (in one pathological case we had 1024).

6. FUTURE STEPS: TOWARDS MERGING SLTGS

In the near future, we wish to investigate methods for merging SLTGs extracted from treebanks and competence grammars in order to 1) improve the coverage of treebank grammars on unseen data, and 2) ease adaptation of treebanks to new domains. The core idea behind 1) is the extension of an SLTG extracted from a treebank through the domain-independent SLTG extracted from HPSG. It seems that current state-of-the-art treebank grammars can achieve an accuracy of about 87% (see Charniak, 1997). We wish to explore whether integrating knowledge from a competence grammar can improve the accuracy. We believe that SLTGs are well suited since they capture distributional and hierarchical information better than stochastic CFGs. The major obstacle for merging the current grammars is the different nature of syntactic constituent levels. For example, the Penn treebank modifier structure is flat compared to that of an HPSG-based SLTG. Recently, (Xia, 1999; Chen and Vijay-Shanker, 2000), have shown how the Penn treebank can be fully bracketed in order to factor out the recursive structures for elementary trees. This is actually done by inserting additional non-terminal nodes into the treebank trees on the basis of Penn treebank specific head-percolation and argument table lists. Using an HPSG-based SLTG it would be possible to use HPSG-based trees as static tree patterns and to create new trees from similar trees found in the treebank-SLTG such that the HPSG-SLTG serves as a "building plans". (Xia and Palmer, 2000), have presented a method for comparing the hand-crafted lexicalized XTAG English grammar (cf. Doran et al., 1994) with one extracted from the Penn treebank. The core idea is to find out how many trees in one grammar match trees in the other. We will explore its use for our proposed HPSG-based approach.

Another line of future research will be the use of an HPSG-SLTG in order to initialize the induction of a domain-specific SLTG on the basis of a small number of annotated parse trees making use of similar tree matching methods to those described above. Now, it would be possible to adapt an HPSG-SLTG to a new domain following a minimally supervised learning approach by automatically creating new trees using an evolutionary strategy and to measure the fitness of such trees through the application of HPSG principles. Implementation of this method has already started and we hope to be able to report on first results soon.

Acknowledgments

The research carried out for this paper was supported by a research grant from the German Bundesministerium für Bildung, Wissenschaft, Forschung und Technologie (BMBF) to the DFKI project WHITEBOARD ("Multilevel Annotation for Dynamic Free Text Processing"), FKZ 01 IW 002. I would like to thank Thorsten Brants for providing me with the Negra Corpus, as well as Tilman Becker, Ann Copestake, Anoop Sarkar, and Ivan Sag for many helpful comments. Many thanks also to Dan Flickinger for the very fruitful cooperation. I also would like to thank the anonymous reviewers for their valuable comments.

Notes

1. This paper is an extension of a previous version published in the *Proceedings of the 4th workshop on tree-adjoining grammars and related frameworks*, Philadelphia, PA, USA, August, 1998.

2. Of course, we are assuming that the Penn treebank developers made use of a kind of head-principle, e.g., by assuming that the head of an NP is the main noun or that the head of a VP is the main verb, see also Charniak, 1997. Chen and Vijay-Shanker, 2000 describe a sophisticated method carefully considering the determination of a node's status as a complement or adjunct, which I plan to integrate in the near future.

3. I am aware of the fact that this might not be the best strategy. (Johnson, 1999) presents an interesting tree transformation procedure which maps a flat modifier construction of trees in the Penn treebank into Chomsky adjunction representations, and shows that such a representation actually gives better predictive information on unseen data than the original representation. Johnson also remarks that argument PPs are not systematically distinguished from adjunct PPs in the Penn treebank, and states that "... reliably determining whether a particular PP is an argument or an adjunct is extremely difficult, even for trained linguists.", (Johnson, 1999), page 624. It is clear that it is not plausible to check a large enough treebank manually, in order to completely "extract" the implicitly made linguistic assumptions. Thus, only if a treebank comes with an explicit declaration of the general linguistic principles used, will it be possible to predict and interpret the influence of the effect of different tree transformation and extraction methods on the quality of a statistically driven parser.

4. Applying the same test as described above on POS, the average number of elementary trees retrieved is 2292.86, i.e., the number seems to increase by a factor of 5.

5. This part of the work has been carried out together with Dan Flickinger, from CSLI, Stanford. For a more detailed description of the approach see (Neumann and Flickinger, 1999).

6. See Oepen and Flickinger, 1998 for more detailed discussion of the grammar's coverage and of the issues related to such measurement.

7. (Kasper et al., 1995), describe a method for compiling an HPSG source grammar to an LTAG. The basic idea here is to construct elementary trees starting from lexical elements from the bottom-up applying the HPSG-principles. In some sense our approach performs in the opposite direction by decomposing an HPSG-parse tree from the top downwards applying the HPSG principles for guiding the decomposition operation. Furthermore, since our approach is data driven, we are able to capture statistical information into an HPSG framework. Note further that once we have built up an HPSG-SLTG parse tree we are able to reconstruct the whole feature structure by applying the lexical information and all HPSG principles including semantic information of the source grammar. Hence, the resulting feature structure of an input sentence is correct and compatible with respect to the HPSG source grammar.

References

Bod, R. (1993). Using an annotated language corpus as a virtual stochastic grammar. *Proceedings of AAAI'93*, Washington, D.C.

Bod, R. (2003). Extracting stochastic grammars from treebanks. This volume.

Brants, T., Skut, W., H.Uszkoreit (2003). Syntactic annotation of a German newspaper corpus. This volume.

Charniak, E. (1997). Statistical parsing with a context-free grammar and word statistics. *AAAI-97*, Providence, Rhode Island.

Chen, J., Vijay-Shanker, K. (2000). Automated extraction of TAGs from the Penn Treebank. In *6th International Workshop on Parsing Technologies (IWPT'2000)*, Trento, Italy.

Chiang, D. (2000). Statistical parsing with an automatically–extracted tree adjoining grammar. *Proceedings of the 38th ACL*, Honk Kong.

Copestake, A., Flickinger, D., Sag, I. (1997). Minimal recursive semantics: An introduction. Technical report, CSLI, Stanford University.

Copestake, A., Flickinger, D., Sag, I. (2000). Linguistic grammars online (LinGo) project. http://hpsg.stanford.edu/hpsg/lingo.html.

Doran, C., Egedi, D., Hockey, B., Srinivas, B., Zeidel, M. (1994). XTAG system - a wide coverage grammar for English. *Proceedings of the 15th International Conference on Computational Linguistics (COLING)*, Kyoto, Japan.

Johnson, M. (1999). PCFG models of linguistic tree representations. *Journal of Computational Linguistics*, 24(4), p. 613–632.

Kasper, R., Kiefer, B., Netter, K., Vijay-Shanker, K. (1995). Compilation of HPSG into TAG. *Proceedings of the 33rd Annual Meeting of the Association for Computational Linguistics*, Cambridge, MA.

Marcus, M. P., Santorini, B., Marcinkiewicz, M. A. (1993). Building a large annotated corpus of English: The Penn Treebank. *Computational Linguistics*, 19, p. 313–330.

Neumann, G. (1998). Automatic extraction of stochastic lexicalized tree grammars from treebanks. *Proceedings of the 4th workshop on tree-adjoining grammars and related frameworks*, Philadelphia, PA, USA.

Neumann, G. and Flickinger, D. (1999). Learning stochastic lexicalized tree grammars from HPSG. Technical report, DFKI, Saarbrücken.

Oepen, S. and Flickinger, D. (1998). Towards systematic grammar profiling: Test suite technology ten years after. *Journal of Computer Speech and Language*, 12, p. 411–435.

Pollard, C. J. and Sag, I. A. (1994). *Head-Driven Phrase Structure Grammar*. University of Chicago Press, Chicago, London.

Samuelsson, C. (1994). Grammar specialization through entropy thresholds. *Proceedings of the 32nd Annual Meeting of the Association for Computational Linguistics*, p. 188–195.

Schabes, Y. (1992). Stochastic lexicalized tree-adjoining grammars. *Proceedings of the 14th International Conference on Computational Linguistics (COLING)*, p. 426–432, Nantes.

Schabes, Y., Joshi, A. K. (1991). Parsing with lexicalized tree adjoining grammar. In Tomita, M., editor, *Current Issues in Parsing Technology*, p. 25–48. Kluwer, Boston.

Schabes, Y., Waters, R. (1995). Tree insertion grammar: A cubic-time parsable formalism that lexicalizes context-free grammar without changing the trees produced. *Computational Linguistics*, 21, p. 479–513.

Schabes, Y., Waters, R. (1996). Stochastic lexicalized tree-insertion grammar. In Bunt, H. and Tomita, M., editors, *Recent Advances in Parsing Technology*, p. 281–294. Kluwer Academic Press, Dordrecht.

Shieber, S., Schabes, Y., Pereira, F. (1995). Principles and implementation of deductive parsing. *Journal of Logic and Computation*, 24, p. 3–36.

Skut, W., Krenn, B., Brants, T., and Uszkoreit, H. (1997). An annotation scheme for free word order languages. *Proceedings of the 5th International Conference of Applied Natural Language*, Washington, USA.

Srinivas, B. (1997). *Complexity of Lexical Restrictions and Its Relevance to Partial Parsing*. PhD thesis, University of Pennsylvania. IRCS Report 97–10.

Frank, A., Sadler, L., van Genabith, J., and Way, A. (2003). From treebank resources to LFG F-Structures This volume.

Xia, F. (1999). Extracting Tree Adjoining Grammars from bracketed corpora. *Proceedings of the 5th Natural Language Processing Pacific Rim Symposium (NLPRS-99)*, Beijing, China.

Xia, F. and Palmer, M. (2000). Comparing and integrating tree adjoining grammars. *Proceedings of the 5th TAG+ workshop*, Paris, France.

Chapter 21

FROM TREEBANK RESOURCES TO LFG F-STRUCTURES

Automatic F-Structure Annotation of Treebank Trees and CFGs extracted from Treebanks

Anette Frank*
German Research Center for Artificial Intelligence (DFKI), Germany
anette@ims.uni-stuttgart.de

Louisa Sadler
University of Essex
louisa@essex.ac.uk

Josef van Genabith, Andy Way
Dublin City University
{josef;away}@computing.dcu.ie

Abstract We present two companion methods for automatically enriching phrase-structure oriented treebank resources with functional structures. Both methods define systematic patterns of correspondence between partial PS configurations and functional structures. These are applied to PS rules extracted from treebanks, or to flat term representations of treebank trees.

Keywords: Automatic Annotation, Higher-level Syntax, LFG f-structures, Corpus Linguistics, Robustness, SUSANNE Corpus, AP Treebank

*The work presented here was performed while the first author was at Xerox Research Centre (XTCE), Grenoble

A. Abeillé (ed.), Treebanks: Building and Using Parsed Corpora, 367–389.

1. INTRODUCTION

In this contribution we address two important concerns: automatic annotation of treebanks and CFGs extracted from such treebanks with LFG f(eature)-structures (Kaplan and Bresnan 1982; Bresnan 2001; Dalrymple 2001).

Treebanks which encode higher-level functional or basic predicate–argument structure, in addition to pure phrase structure information, are required as training resources for probabilistic unification grammars and data-driven parsing approaches, (e.g. Bod and Kaplan 1998). Manual construction of treebanks with feature structure annotations is very labour and cost intensive. So is the development of new or the scaling-up of existing unification grammars which can be used to analyse large text corpora. What is more, even if a large-coverage unification grammar is available, typically, for each input string it would generate hundreds or thousands of candidate (constituent and feature structure) analyses from which a highly trained expert has to select. Although proposals have been made for filtering and ranking parsing ambiguities (e.g. Charniak 1993; Abney 1997; Frank et al. 2000), to date none is guaranteed to uniquely determine the best analysis. In order not to compromise the quality of the corpus under construction, a linguistic expert is required to find the best among a large number of candidate analyses.

Given this situation, is there a way to automate, or bootstrap, the construction of grammars and treebanks with feature structure annotations reusing existing resources?

In a number of papers van Genabith et al. (1999a,b,c) presented a new corpus based method. Their basic idea is the following: take an existing treebank, read off the CFG following (Charniak 1996), *manually* annotate the extracted CFG rules with f-structure annotations and provide macros for the lexical entries. Then deterministically "rematch" the structure of the original treebank trees (not the strings) with the annotated rules. During this rematching process, the f-structure annotations are resolved, and an f-structure is produced. The entire process is deterministic if the feature structure annotations are, and to a considerable extent, costly manual inspection of candidate analyses is avoided. The method is an improvement but still involves a large labour intensive component, namely *manual* annotation of the extracted grammar rules.

Treebank grammars (CFGs extracted from treebanks) are large and grow with the size of the treebank (Charniak 1996; Krotov et al. 1998). They feature rather flat rules, many of which share and/or repeat significant portions of their right-hand sides (RHS). This causes problems for manual rule annotation approaches such as (van Genabith et al. 1999a,b,c). Manual rule annotation is labour intensive, error prone, repetitive and risks missing generalisations.

In this paper we show how f-structure annotation of both grammar rules and treebank trees can (to a large extent) be *automated*.

The basic idea is simple: functional annotations define systematic correspondences between constituent and higher level feature structure representations. These can be captured in general annotation principles, which are applied either to grammar rules extracted from a treebank or directly to treebank trees.

The observation that constituent and higher-level feature structure representations stand in a systematic relationship informs theoretical work in LFG (Kaplan and Bresnan 1982) and HPSG (Pollard and Sag 1994). In LFG c(onstituent)-structure and f-structure are independent levels of representation which are related in terms of a correspondence function ϕ. The correspondence follows linguistically determined principles which are partly universal, and partly language specific (Bresnan 2001; Dalrymple 2001).

What is new in our approach is that (i) we employ *partial* and *underspecified* annotation principles in a principle-based c- to f-structure interface for the LFG architecture; (ii) we use these to automate functional structure assignment to flat and "noisy" treebank trees and CFGs extracted from them; and (iii) we reuse existing linguistic resources. In contrast to more theoretically informed work in LFG and HPSG, treebanks do not tend to follow highly abstract and general X-bar architectural design principles. The challenge in our approach is to develop grammars and annotation principles for real text.

The potential benefits of automation are considerable: substantial reduction in development effort, hence savings in time and cost for treebank annotation and grammar development; the ability to tackle larger fragments in a shorter time, a considerable amount of flexibility for switching between different treebank annotation schemes, and a natural approach to robustness. Our methods can also be viewed as a new corpus- and data-driven approach to grammar development, an approach that as much as possible recycles existing resources.

In our work to date we have developed two related but interestingly different methods. Both methods define annotation principles as correspondences between *partial* and *underspecified* c- and f-structure configurations. In one approach (Sadler et al. 2000) we read off a CFG treebank grammar following the method of Charniak (1996) and then compile regular expression based annotation principles over the extracted grammar. In the companion approach (Frank 2000) we operate on treebank trees encoded as flat term representations and annotate them with f-structures.

Both methods are partial and robust in the following further sense: they yield partial, unconnected f-structures in the case of missing annotation principles. In the case of conflicting feature assignments (Frank 2000) admits partially unresolved f-structures to achieve further robustness.

We describe two experiments, one for each method. For the first experiment we developed a regular expression based annotation principle interpreter which operates on grammar rules with *order independent* and monotonic interpretation of annotation principles. For the second experiment we employed an existing term rewriting system (Kay 1999; Frank 1999), which we use to apply annotation principles to flat, term-based representations of treebank trees. The term rewriting system allows us to exploit both *order dependent*, cascaded and *order independent* formulations of annotation principles. In our first experiment we used the first 100 trees of the AP treebank (Leech and Garside 1991), in the second, 166 trees of the Susanne treebank (Sampson 1993).

The paper is structured as follows: in Section 2 we motivate and describe our annotation methods in more detail. In Section 3 we report on our two experiments. For each experiment we explain the design, describe the data and evaluate the results. In Section 4 we compare the two methods and outline ongoing research. Section 5 concludes.

2. METHODS FOR AUTOMATIC F-STRUCTURE ANNOTATION

In LFG the correspondence between c- (constituent) and f- (functional) structure is defined in terms of functional annotations of the RHS categories in CFG rules and lexical information.

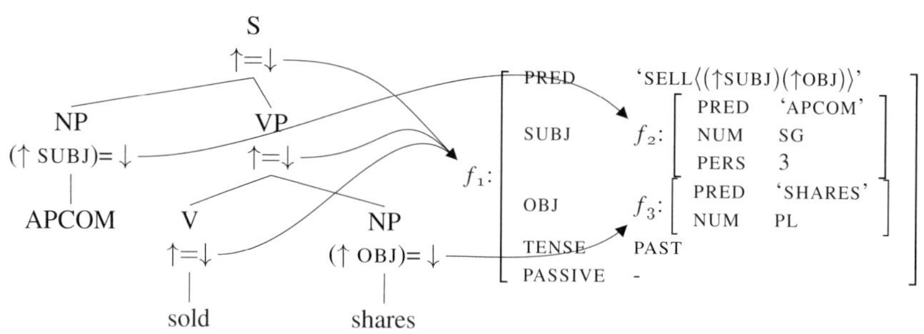

PS rules define f–structure via functional descriptions

$$S \rightarrow \begin{array}{cc} NP & VP \\ (\uparrow \text{SUBJ}) = \downarrow & \uparrow = \downarrow \end{array} \qquad VP \rightarrow \begin{array}{cc} V & NP \\ \uparrow = \downarrow & (\uparrow \text{OBJ}) = \downarrow \end{array}$$

APCOM: N	(↑ PRED) = 'APCOM'	sold: V	(↑ PRED) = 'SELL⟨(↑SUBJ)(↑OBJ)⟩'
	(↑ NUM) = SG		(↑ TENSE) = PAST
	(↑ PERS) = 3		(↑ PASSIVE) = -

The c-structure/f-structure correspondence follows universal and language specific principles. In our work, we define annotation principles as involving *partial* and *underspecified* phrase structure configurations and apply them to CFG rules or tree fragments that meet the relevant *partial* configuration. To illustrate the idea: a head principle assigns ↑ = ↓ to the X daughter in all XP → ...X... configurations, irrespective of the surrounding categorial context. For the example at hand, the challenge in our approach is to provide annotation principles that identify heads in the flat treebank tree and rule configurations which deviate significantly from X-bar design principles. Annotation principles capture generalisations and can be used to *automatically* annotate PS configurations with functional structures in a highly general and economical way. Both our annotation methods are built on this insight: in the first, annotation principles are applied to CFG rules extracted from treebanks while in the second annotation principles are applied directly to flat term representations of treebank trees and tree fragments.

2.1 Regular expression based f-structure annotation of extracted CFGs

In this method, described in (Sadler et al. 2000), we extract a CFG from the treebank following (Charniak 1996) and develop a set of regular expression based annotation principles. The principles are applied to the extracted CFG to produce an annotated CFG. Annotated rules are then rematched against the original treebank trees and f-structures are produced from the annotations.

Annotation Principle Interpreter. Our CFG rule annotation principles are of the form `L>R@A`. `A` is a set of attribute-value structure annotations (rule decorations). `L` and `R` are regular expressions (under)specifying LHSs and RHSs of CFG rules in terms of categorial and configurational constraints. The regular expressions provided include Kleene and positive Kleene "`*`, `+`", optionality "`( )`", disjunction "`|`" and a limited form of complement "`~`". Operators are prefix and "{ }" is used to indicate grouping. "`*`" without argument denotes any string.

Given a grammar rule of the form `M->Ds` (expanding a mother category `M` into a sequence of daughter categories `Ds`) and a regular expression based annotation principle `L>R@A`, if the LHS `L` of the principle matches `M` and the RHS `R` matches `Ds`, then `M->Ds` is annotated with `A`. A single grammar rule can match multiple principles and a single principle may match a given grammar rule in more than one way. The annotations resulting from all possible matches are collected and the grammar rule is annotated accordingly.

More formally, let the denotation $[\![\texttt{E}]\!]$ of a regular expression `E` be the set of strings denoted by `E`. Given a CFG rule `M->Ds` and a set of annotation principles `AP` of the form `L>R@A`, `M->Ds` is annotated with the set of feature structure annotations `F`:

$$\texttt{M->Ds@F} \ \text{iff} \ \texttt{F} = \{\texttt{A} | \exists \texttt{P} \in \texttt{AP} \text{ with } \texttt{P} \equiv \texttt{L>R@A} \text{ and } \texttt{M} \in [\![\texttt{L}]\!] \text{ and } \texttt{Ds} \in [\![\texttt{R}]\!]\}$$

Annotation is monotonic and order independent.

Partial and Underspecified Annotation Principles. In our Prolog implementation, CFG grammar rules extracted from the treebank are represented as

```
C:F -> C1:F1, ... , Cn:Fn.
```

where syntactic categories C and (optional) logical variables F representing feature-structure information are paired C:F. Regular expression based annotation principles can underspecify the LHS and RHS of grammar rules. To give a simple example, the following annotation principle[1] states that infinitival phrases infp following the final v0 in vp rules are open complements (xcomp) controlled by the subject of the final v0:

```
vp > *  v0:V0  *{~v0}  infp:I  *
   @ [ V0:xcomp = I, V0:subj = I:subj ].
```

The next principle states that in non-conjunctive contexts[2] v0 sequences, possibly separated by adverbials adv, form open complement sequences where the subject of the preceding v0 controls that of the following:

```
vp > *{~conj}  v0:V1  (adv)  v0:V2  *{~conj}
   @ [ V1:xcomp = V2, V1:subj = V2:subj ].
```

Note that the principle applies twice to a ...v0:V1, v0:V2, v0:V3 ... RHS rule configuration with [V1:xcomp = V2, V1:subj = V2:subj, V2:xcomp = V3, V2:subj = V3:subj] as the resulting annotation. Finally observe that the formalism supports the statement of generalisations over LHSs of CFG rules:

```
{fn:X|infp:X|tgp:X|si:X|vp:X}
   > *{~{v0|conj}}  v0:V0  *{~conj}
   @ [ X = V0 ].
```

This principle states that for a variety of constructions including verbal (vp) and infinitival (infp) phrases in non-conjunctive contexts the initial v0 is the head of the clause.

Example output (automatically annotated grammar rules from the AP fragment) is shown below:[3]

```
vp:A -> v0:B,v0:C,v0:D,np:E,fa:F
     @ [A=B,D:obj=E,C:xcomp=D,C:subj=D:subj,
        B:xcomp=C,B:subj=C:subj,A:vp_adjunct:1=F].

vp:A -> v0:B,v0:C,v0:D,rp:E,pp:F
     @ [(D:obl=F;D:vp_adjunct:1=F),A=B,D:part=E,
        C:xcomp=D,C:subj=D:subj,B:xcomp=C,
        B:subj=C:subj].

vp:A -> vp:B,pnct:_,vp:C,pnct:_,conj:D,vp:E
     @ [A:conj:3=C,A=D,A:conj:2=B,A:conj:1=E]).

vp:A -> vp:B,conj:C,vp:D,pp:E,fa:F
```

```
@ [(D:obl=E;D:vp_adjunct:1=E),A=C,A:conj:2=B,
   A:conj:1=D,A:vp_adjunct:1=F]).
```

In the first and in the second rule the leftmost v0 is identified as the head of the construction. In v0,v0 sequences the second v0 provides an open complement xcomp to the first with the subject of the second controlled by the subject of the first. The np in the first rule is analysed as the object of the rightmost v0, while the pp in the second rule is either an adjunct or an oblique argument to the vp. The last two example rules show coordinate structures. Note that in the final rule the pp is analysed as oblique or as an adjunct to the rightmost vp. Here our current annotation principles miss a possible attachment of the pp to the mother vp.

Automatic annotation is completed with macros for the preterminal tags contributing lexical information, e.g.:

```
nn1(Word):A @ [A:pred=Word, A:num=sg, A:pers=3rd].
```

The annotation principles together with the lexical macros constitute a principle-based c-structure/f-structure interface architecture for LFG.

2.2 F-structure annotation of treebank trees using flat tree descriptions

This method, described in (Frank 2000), builds on a pure correspondence view of the LFG architecture, where the mapping from c- to f-structure is encoded by the projection function ϕ. Annotation principles define ϕ-projection constraints which associate partial c-structures with their corresponding partial f-structures. Application of annotation principles to flat set-based encodings of treebank trees directly induces the f-structure, allowing us to skip the (re)matching process for f-structure composition. What is more, the principles can apply to non-local tree fragments, as opposed to local CFG rules.

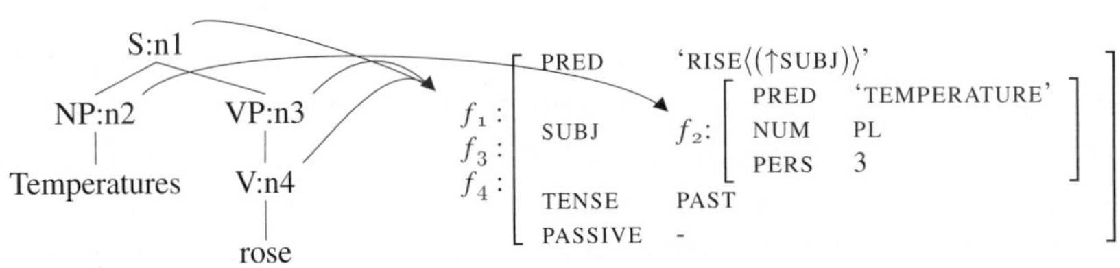

ϕ–correspondence:
$\phi(\text{n1}) = f_1 \quad \phi(\text{n2}) = f_2$
$\phi(\text{n3}) = f_3 \quad \phi(\text{n4}) = f_4 \quad \phi(\text{n1}) = \phi(\text{n3}) = \phi(\text{n4})$

f–structure:
$(f_1$ SUBJ$)= f_2$, $(f_2$ PRED$)=$ 'temperature'
$(f_4$ PRED$=$ 'rise' ...

Modular projection principles for f-structure annotation of tree fragments. To illustrate the key idea of partial f-structure annotation principles, below we display the representation of a complex NP. This complex configuration can be broken down into modular, piece-wise correspondences of *partial* c- and f-structures, abstracting away from irrelevant material in the surrounding context.

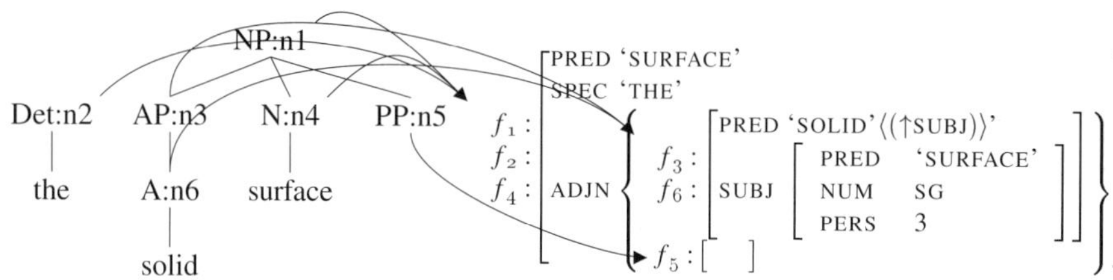

The functional contribution of the prenominal determiner *the* is independent of the presence of AP or PP, and is captured by the partial correspondence constraints stated on the right hand side.

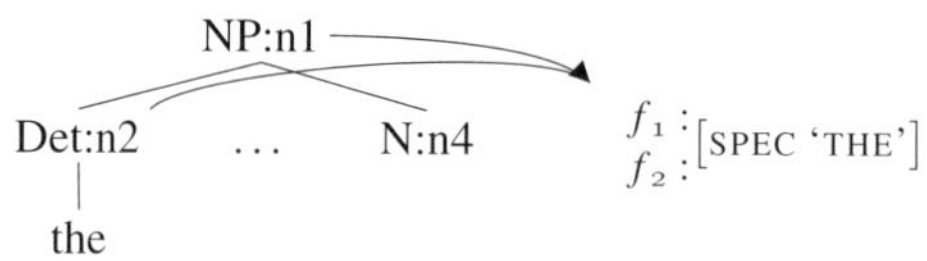

$\phi(\text{n1}) = f_1$ $\quad \phi(\text{n1}) = \phi(\text{n2})$
$\phi(\text{n2}) = f_2$ $\quad \text{spec}(f_1, \text{the})$

An AP daughter of NP is analysed as an ADJUNCT of the nominal head, unless the N head is omitted. This generalisation is captured below.

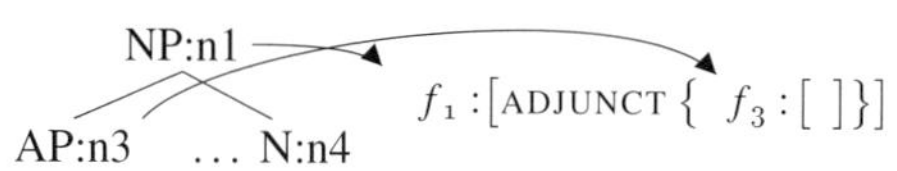

$\phi(\text{n1}) = f_1$ $\quad \text{adjunct\_x}(f_1, f_3)$
$\phi(\text{n3}) = f_3$

Projection principles for head categories and lexical nodes (here for nominal categories) are straightforward:

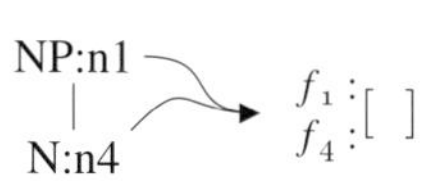

$\phi(\text{n1}) = f_1$
$\phi(\text{n4}) = f_4$
$\phi(\text{n1}) = \phi(\text{n4})$

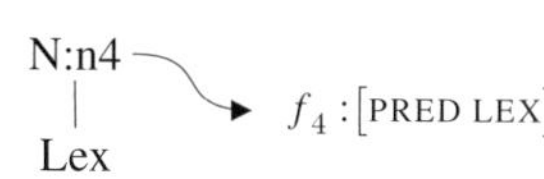

$\phi(\text{n4}) = f_4$
$\text{pred}(f_4, \text{LEX})$

Similar correspondences are defined for the remaining c-structure fragments. These correspondences all apply to the complex NP structure above, conspiring to define the ϕ-projection and f-structure in a modular, declarative way. By abstracting away from immaterial c-structure context, the principles generalise over specific tree configurations, and therefore apply to fragments of unseen trees.

In the correspondence-based approach annotation principles can apply to *non-local* tree fragments. This allows us to associate partial f-structures with complex c-structure fragments. For example, by specifying non-local c-structure fragments in binary branching VPs, we capture tense and active/passive distinctions of the verbal complex in a natural way. This is illustrated for the characteristic construction indicative of present perfect tense.

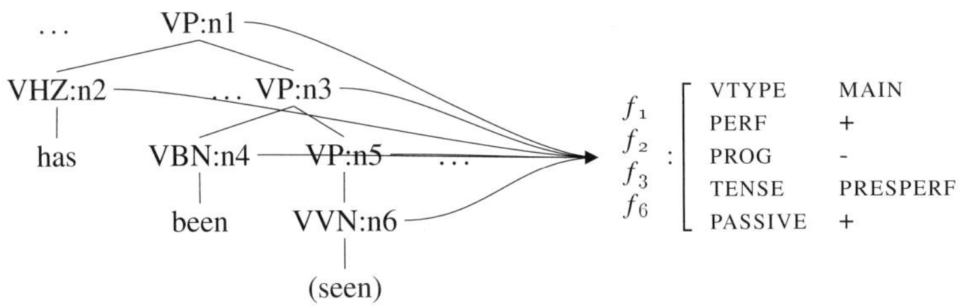

The idea of modular annotation principles is much in the spirit of projection principles as proposed by (Dalrymple 2001) and (Bresnan 2001), and provides a principle-based c- to f-structure interface in the LFG architecture.[4]

A term rewriting system for f-structure annotation. To define and process annotation principles we make use of an existing term rewriting system, originally designed for transfer-based Machine Translation (Kay 1999; Frank 1999).

The system takes as input an unordered set of n-ary terms `p,q, r` ..., and an ordered set of rewrite rules $\mathtt{p}_i \ldots \mathtt{p}_j \Rightarrow \mathtt{q}_k \ldots \mathtt{q}_l$.[5] If the LHS terms $\mathtt{p}_i \ldots \mathtt{p}_j$ match the input, the matching terms are eliminated from the input set, and the terms $\mathtt{q}_k \ldots \mathtt{q}_l$ are added to the output set. A rule applies to *each instantiation* of the LHS terms in the input. Besides terms `p` that are to be eliminated from the input, the LHS may state positive `+p` and negative `-p` terms. A rule with positive term `+p` only applies if `p` matches some term in the input but positive terms are not eliminated from the input set. A rule with negative term `-p` only applies if `p` does not match any term in the input. The order in which the rules are stated is crucial: Each rule applies to the *current* input set, and yields an output set. The output set of a rule constitutes the input set for the next rule.

A flat, term-based representation of the LFG architecture We encode the LFG projection architecture in a term representation language as follows:

immediate dominance:	`arc(MNode, MLabel, DNode, DLabel)`
immediate precedence:	`prec(CsNode_x, CsNode_y)`
lexical insertion:	`lex(TerminalNode, Lex)`
ϕ-correspondence:	`phi(CsNode, FsNode), equal(FsNode_x, FsNode_y)`
f-structure attributes:	`attr(FsNode_x, FsNode_y), attr(FsNode, Value)`

With this, the traditional representation

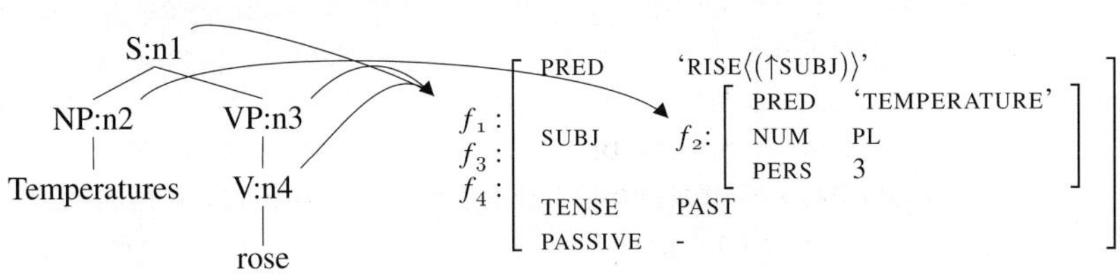

is translated into the following set of terms:

```
arc(n1,s,n2,np), arc(n1,s,n3,vp), arc(n3,vp,n4,v), prec(n2,n3),
lex(n2,Temperatures), lex(n4,rose),
phi(n1,f1), phi(n2,f2), phi(n3,f3), phi(n4,f4),
equal(f1,f3), equal(f3,f4),
pred(f1,rise), subj(f1,f2), pred(f2,temp.), num(f2,pl), tense(f1,past),..
```

Automatic annotation of flat tree descriptions with f-structures.

Initialisation Starting from the c-structure term representation, we induce a 1-1 ϕ-correspondence from c-structure nodes to empty f-structure nodes.[6]

```
+arc(n1,_,_,_) ==> phi(n1,f1).
+arc(_,_,CsNode,_) ==> phi(CsNode,FsNode).
```

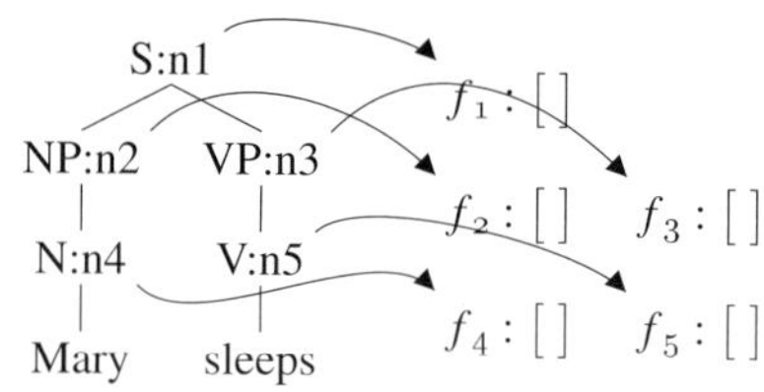

Partial and underspecified annotation principles associate partial c-structure configurations with their corresponding partial f-structures, and further restrict the trivial 1-1 ϕ-correspondence via the predicate `equal(Fx,Fy)`. The rule below defines the VP-external NP as the SUBJ of f_1, the f-structure projected from the S node. The predicate `prec_x(B,C)` is defined (by use of macros) as a finitely constrained transitive closure over the precedence relation `prec`. It can be used to underspecify precedence constraints holding between nodes n_x and n_y, allowing for an arbitrary or else a restricted sequence of intervening categories.

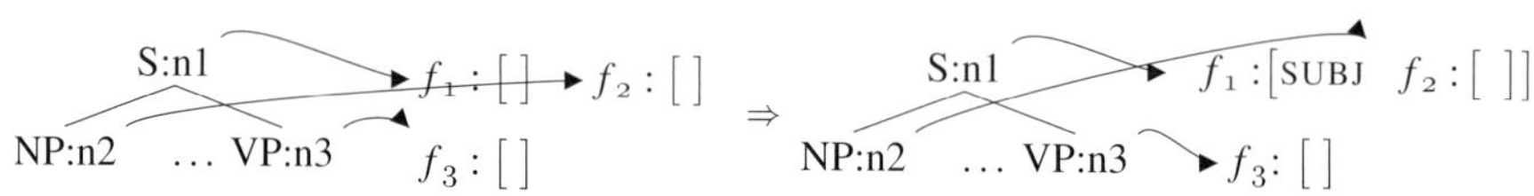


```
+arc(A,s,B,np), +phi(A,FA), +phi(B,FB),
+arc(A,s,C,vp), +prec_x(B,C) ==> subj(FA,FB).
```

The following rule applies to the output resulting from the previous rule application. The predicate `equal(Fx,Fy)` restricts the ϕ-function to map the VP and S nodes to identical nodes in f-structure.

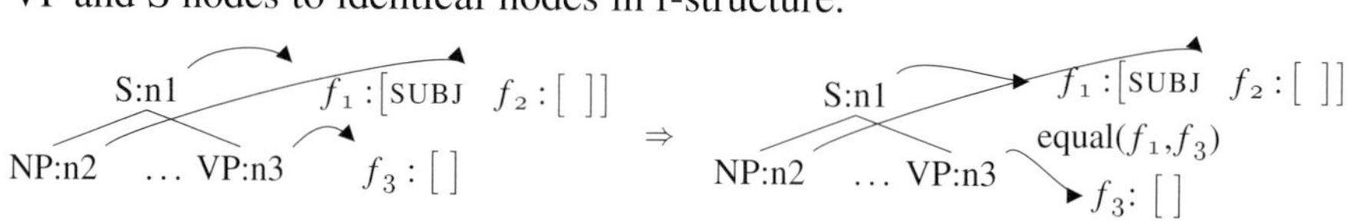


```
+arc(A,s,C,vp), +phi(A,FA), +phi(C,FC) ==> equal(FA,FC).
```

Formal restrictions Apart from initialisation we restrict `phi` predicates to only occur in LHSs of rules as *positive constraints*. Given the input specification of a 1-1 ϕ-projection, this guarantees that the functional property of the ϕ-correspondence is preserved. `equal` predicates only *restrict* the ϕ-correspondence, while preserving its functional property.

Order independence in a cascaded rewrite system Although annotation rules operate in a cascaded, order dependent way, order independence can be obtained by requiring that no annotation rule refers to f-structure information introduced by other rules, and no rule consumes (or adds) any c-structure information referred to by other rules. These constraints ensure that annotation rules have access to the full initial input structure, and no more than this, and thereby guarantee order independence of annotation, irrespective of the order in which the rules are stated and applied. The effect of order independence can be observed by inverting the application order of the subject and head-projection rules above: while the intermediate term set will be different, the final output set will be identical.

There is a trade-off between order dependence and independence. Constraining rules to c-structure information only can require complex rule constraints to prevent application of conflicting annotation rules to the same tree fragment, thereby avoiding inconsistencies. Moreover, reference to f-structure information can be used to generalise annotation rules. If several PS configurations are indicative of e.g. a subject function, or passive voice, such diverse configurations can be captured by referring to the more abstract f-structure information to further guide f-structure construction. The order of annotation rules must then ensure that the required f-structure information is introduced by previous annotation rules.

An annotation grammar consists, just like an ordinary LFG grammar, of different types of annotation rules: lexical, morphosyntactic, and phrasal.

Lexical and morphosyntactic rules Morphosyntactic rules introduce morphological (and some semantic) information encoded in lexical category labels into the f-structure space. The example given below illustrates how highly specific category distinctions in treebank encodings can be neutralised: once NUMber is encoded in f-structure, based on the `nn1` vs. `nn2` distinction, this categorial distinction can be neutralised by mapping both lexical category labels to the generalised label `nn` (see van Genabith et al. 1999b for a similar approach). Such generalisations are essential for compact definition of annotation principles. For example, below the instantiation of the PRED-value of nouns is captured in a single lexical rule which applies to all "generalised" `nn`-daughters.

```
arc(A,ML,B,nn1) ==> num(B,sg), ntype(B,common), arc(A,ML,B,nn).
arc(A,ML,B,nn2) ==> num(B,pl), ntype(B,common), arc(A,ML,B,nn).

+arc(A,n,B,nn), +lex(B,Lex) ==> equal(A,B), pred(B,Lex), pers(B,'3').
```

Tense information as well as the active/passive distinction can be captured by stating constraints on the partial c-structure context of verbs, as illustrated below for present perfect tense in a flat VP, as it is assigned in the Susanne corpus. For binary branching VPs (as assigned in the Penn-II Treebank, cf. Marcus et al 1994), we can define complex tense information in similar ways, by extending annotation rules to *non-local* tree fragments (see above and Frank 2000).

```
+arc(A,vp,B,vhz)    % have-aux
-arc(A,vp,D,vbn)    % no been-aux !
+arc(A,vp,C,vvn)    % main verb participle
==> perf(A,+), prog(A,-),
    tense(A,presperf), passive(A,-).
```

```
+arc(A,vp,B,vhz),   % have-aux
+arc(A,vp,C,vbn),   % been-aux
+arc(A,vp,D,vvn),   % main verb part.
==> perf(A,+), prog(A,-),
    tense(A,presperf), passive(A,+).
```

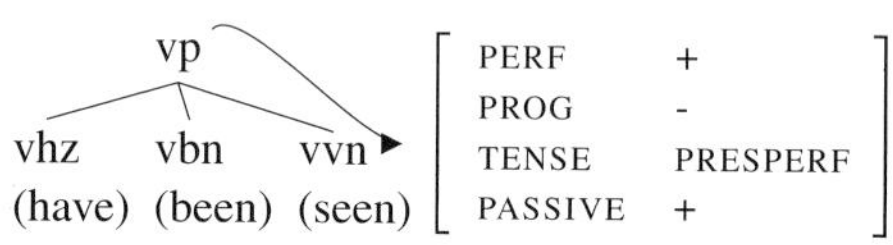

Partial phrasal rules and underspecification Annotation principles are designed to apply to modular, partial c-structure configurations, to define their corresponding functional projections. Even though treebanks do not tend to follow classical X-bar syntax, specific types of tree branches correspond to functional dependencies in f-structure. Annotation principles apply, in the general case, to single tree branches, with some contextual constraints, and generalise to unseen tree configurations. Below, *that*-clauses (category `f`) are associated with a function COMP in f-structure by referring to a single branch (`arc`) in c-structure, abstracting away from irrelevant co-occurrences in the c-structure context.

The example also illustrates the effect of underspecification. *That*-clauses can appear in different syntactic contexts. By referring to an *underspecified* (variable) mother node label `ML`, we generalise over various possible mother labels (e.g. (in)finite, modal, nominal or adjective phrases).

```
+arc(A,ML,B,f), +comp_form(B,that) ⇒ comp(A,B).
```

Finer categorial restrictions can be captured by defining classes of category labels in disjunctive templates.[7] Below, the disjunctive template `np_cat(XL)` defines a class of category labels (`n`, `d`, `m`). The template is called (by logical "and" &&) in the annotation rule for PPs (p) to define this restricted class of alternative NP-types as complements (i.e., OBJ) of prepositions.

```
template definition:  np_cat(XL) :: { XL == n } ==> 0;   % n: nominal phrase
                                     { XL == d } ==> 0;   % d: determiner phrase
                                     { XL == m } ==> 0.   % m: number phrase

annotation rule:      +arc(A,p,B,NPL) ==> obj(A,B) && np_cat(NPL).
```

Grammatical function assignment In languages like English, grammatical function assignment relies heavily on c-structure configurations, while still not being fully deterministic. In case marking languages, morphological marking will be used to constrain grammatical function assignment. Below we give an example for the assignment of OBJ vs. OBJ2 functions for transitive and ditransitive verbs in English, which is determined by surface order. Long-distance phenomena are captured by path expressions (see Frank 2000 for further details).

```
+arc(A,vp,C,np), +arc(A,vp,D,np), +prec_x(C,D) ==> obj2(A,D).% OBJ2 ditrans
+arc(A,vp,C,np), +arc(A,vp,D,np), +prec_x(C,D) ==> obj(A,C). % OBJ ditrans
+arc(A,vp,C,np), -arc(A,vp,D,np), {D \== C} ==> obj(A,C).8   % OBJ trans
```

Subcategorisation assignment We induce subcategorisation frames (the semantic forms) by collecting grammatical functions assigned by annotation rules into the predicate's semantic form, following the method of (van Genabith et al. 1999a).

Obviously, pure c-structure information does not allow us to distinguish between NP, PP, and infinitival arguments vs. adjuncts. Similarly, lacking lexical information, raising and control constructions can only be represented as involving anaphoric control. In (Frank 2000) we show how to extend this model by integration of lexical subcategorisation information, combined with strategies for OT-based ambiguity ranking and filtering (cf. Frank et al. (2000)).

Partial annotation and robustness Our f-structure annotation method embodies an important aspect of robustness. In the case of missing annotation principles the system does not fail, but partial trees are left without f-structure annotation. We obtain (typically large) partial, unconnected f-structures.

Moving treebanks Our framework can also be used to adjust particular treebank encodings, by "moving" treebanks to a different structural encoding, thereby facilitating principle-based f-structure induction. In our treatment of the Susanne corpus, we defined a set of c-structure rewriting rules to transform the encoding of coordination and flat modal VP structures into more standard PS analyses, which lend themselves to principle-driven f-structure annotation.

3. TWO EXPERIMENTS

3.1 Experiment I

Experiment Design. Our first experiment involves the first 100 trees of the AP treebank (Leech and Garside 1991). We refer to this subsection as AP01. We preprocess the treebank using the structure preserving grammar compaction method reported in (van Genabith et al. 1999b) preserving as much categorial fine-grainedness as is required to guide annotation. From this we extract a treebank grammar following (Charniak 1996). We develop a set of feature structure annotation principles. The regular expression based interpreter described in Section 2.1 compiles the principles over the rules extracted from the AP01 treebank fragment. The results obtained are compared against a manually annotated "gold standard" reference grammar and precision and recall measures are reported.[9]

Data. The AP treebank annotation schema employs 183 lexical tag types and 53 phrasal category types, with tree structure encoded in terms of labelled bracketing. The corpus is "skeletally parsed", that is, it contains some unlabelled brackets. We remove these in an automatic pre-editing step. The sentences in the AP01 fragment range from 4 to 50 leaf tokens (including punctuation symbols). The AP01 section of the corpus attests 94 of the 183 lexical tag types and 25 of the 53 phrasal tag types. The large number of highly discriminating lexical and phrasal categories results in a large number of flat and often very specific rules. To facilitate annotation we use the structure preserving grammar compaction method presented in (van Genabith et al. 1999b) to compact the grammar into a more general one that still preserves important categorial information to drive automatic annotation. Compaction works by generalising tags, i.e. collapsing tags (and categories) into supertags. This reduces the number of CFG rule types in the fragment from 511 to 330. AP01 and the compacted AP01^{C} are summarised in **Table 1** below:

T1	sentences	average length	phrasal types	lexical types	CFG rule types
AP01	100	20	25	94	511
AP01^{C}	100	20	12	28	330

Manually Annotated Reference Grammar. In order to evaluate Experiment I, we manually constructed a "gold standard" reference grammar following (van Genabith et al.1999a,b,c). The grammar features 1143 annotations, on average 3.46 annotations per rule.

Automatic Annotation and Evaluation. For the experiment we constructed 119 annotation principles, this against 330 CFG rules resulting in a template/rule ratio of 0.36. We expect the ratio to skew substantially in favour of templates as we proceed to larger fragments (see Section 4). Automatic annotation generates 1029 annotations, on average 3.12 annotations per rule. Experiment I is evaluated in terms of *precision* and *recall* measures:

$$\text{precision} = \frac{\text{\# generated annotations also in reference}}{\text{\# generated annotations}}$$

$$\text{recall} = \frac{\text{\# reference annotations also generated}}{\text{\# reference annotations}}$$

The results are summarised in **Table 2**:

T2	Experiment I
precision	93.38
recall	91.58

The numbers are conservative: *precision* and *recall* are computed automatically for a first pass encoding of annotation principles as regular expressions. The results are encouraging and indicate that automatic annotation is more often partial than incorrect.

3.2 Experiment II

Our method for f-structure annotation of trees in Section 2.2 is evaluated in Experiment II, this time based on the Susanne corpus (Sampson 1993).

Data The Susanne treebank encodes labelled bracketed structures with surface form and lemmatised lexical entries. Functional category labels (subj, obj) and traces indicating control or long-distance dependencies are eliminated in preprocessing, to guarantee a non-biased evaluation with conventional PS trees as input. In preprocessing we also collapse overspecific phrasal categories.

Some decisions on PS assignment in the Susanne corpus are debatable. We defined a set of c-structure rewriting rules that transform the encoding of coordination and flat modal VP structures to more standard PS analyses.

Experiment Design We chose two sections of the Susanne corpus, J01 and J02 (text type J: learned writing). On these, we ran an experiment in 3 steps:

First, we develop f-structure annotation principles for the first 66 sentences of J01. These generate fully connected f-structures for 50 out of the 66 sentences. In step 2 we apply the resulting annotation grammar AG1 to the first 50 (unseen) sentences of J02 (J02-1), and measure the annotation results. Grammar AG1 is then upgraded to AG2, to fully cover these additional 50 sentences. We record the number of principles added or modified. In step 3, the annotation grammar AG2 is applied to the remaining 46 (unseen) sentences of the second part of J02 (J02-2). Again, we measure the results. In this experiment we applied an order dependent annotation scheme that consumes c-structure terms while building up the f-structure (cf. Frank 2000). We established a natural order for the different types of annotation principles discussed in Section 2.2.

Evaluation and Results Table 3 provides basic data of the treebank subsections: the number of sentences and average sentence length; the number of phrasal and lexical categories and the number of distinct PS rules and PS branches encoded by the corpus trees. Note that the percentage of new (unseen) PS rules in J02-1 and J02-2 is considerably higher than for new (unseen) tree branches. This is not surprising, and supports our annotation scheme, where annotation involves underspecified, partial trees (often single branches; cf. discussion in Section 4).

Table 3	sent.	av. length	phrasal cat	lexical cat	PS rules	tree branches
J01	66	34.27	32	73	430	281
J02-1	50	21.68	25 (3 new)	64 (8 new)	249 (60.34% new)	172 (20.93% new)
J02-2	46	24.8	24 (4 new)	57 (3 new)	212 (45.28% new)	163 (15.95% new)

The results of automatic f-structure annotation are summarised in Table 4. We measured correctness of f-structure assignment modulo the argument/adjunct distinction for PPs and infinitival VPs, and the missing assignment of control/raising equations. Also, attachment or labelling mistakes in the treebank are not counted as annotation mistakes if the resulting f-structure is predicted from the given tree.

AG1 features 118 non-lexical (phrasal) annotation principles and assigns correct f-structures to 48% of the unseen section J02-1. As expected, the upgrade from AG1 to AG2 required little effort: it involves 28 new and 5 modified rules and required approximately one person-day of work. AG2 applied to the unseen section J02-2 yields 76.09% of correct f-structures.

Table 4	correct fs		partial fs		tag rules	lexical rules	phrasal rules	all rules
	#	%	#	%				
J01 w/ AG1	50	75.76	16	24.24	41	132	118	291
J02-1 w/ AG1	24	**48**	26	**52**	41	132	118	291
J02-1 w/ AG2	49	98	1	2%	41+4	132+4 (2 mod)	118+20 (3 mod)	291+28
J02-2 w/ AG2	35	**76.09**	11	**23.91**	45	136	138	319

Although small scale, we consider these results promising. Our experiment yields 76% correctly assigned complete and fully connected f-structures when applied to unseen trees, on the basis of a stepwise extended annotation grammar, developed for about 100 sentences. The increase of coverage when moving from AG1 to AG2 is considerable. Upgrading to larger fragments takes little effort due to the generalisation capacity of partial annotation principles.

The latter is confirmed by the increasing percentage of correct f-structure assignments to unseen trees, and the fact that partial f-structure assignments generally consist of large pieces of partial f-structures.

4. DISCUSSION AND CURRENT RESEARCH

We have presented two companion automatic f-structure annotation methods (Sadler et al. 2000; Frank 2000) for treebanks and grammars. Both methods and the experiments show considerable overlap and several interesting differences.

Annotation principles can apply to extracted PS rules or to PS tree fragments encoded as flat term representations. Our second method can be specialised to PS rules by restricting trees to depth one. The first method generates an annotated grammar, which can be used to rematch treebank trees to induce f-structures or serve as a basis for developing a stand-alone LFG resource. In the second approach an f-structure is built during the annotation process. In order to parse free text, this method can be applied to the output of (P)CFG parsing. The same architecture can be implemented using the principles designed in the first approach. Our second approach can be modified to annotate (non-local) tree fragments with f-descriptions for the rematching scenario applied in the first method. Both methods use compaction techniques for generalising over-specific categorisation. In the first experiment the structure of treebank entries remains unchanged, while in the second certain structures are transformed to conventional PS analyses to support principle-based annotation. For our first method, we implemented an order independent and monotonic annotation principle interpreter. For the second, a more general term rewriting system was used. The term rewriting system allows us to define order dependent, cascaded processing of annotation principles. Alternatively, the term rewriting system can implement order independent annotation. Order independence can sometimes ease maintenance of annotation principles, but requires more complex and verbose constraints in order to avoid inconsistent annotations. By contrast, order dependent cascaded rewriting allows for a compact representation of annotation principles. The extra power of an order dependent system can be useful in category generalisation and subcategorisation induction during the annotation process. Experiment I uses a manually constructed "gold standard" reference grammar for evaluation, experiment II is evaluated with respect to how it performs on unseen, extended treebank fragments.

Robustness is an inherent property of the approaches presented here. It resides in a number of levels: First, our principles are partial and underspecified and will match new, as yet unseen configurations. Second, the principles are conditional. If a certain context (a regular expression or a constraint set) is met, a principle applies. Even if only few principles apply, the system will not fail but deliver partial annotations. Third, the constraint solver employed in our second method can cope with conflicting information. A constraint solver of this type can also be imported into the processing of rules annotated by our first method.

Both approaches factor out information spread over many CFG grammar rules into a smaller number of modular and general principles. To a first approximation, the reason why our principles allow a compact representation of grammatical knowledge is the following: by and large the annotation principles capture statements about single mother-daughter relationships in CFG rules or local trees of depth one. This means that the principles are essentially about single branches in local configurations. Given a treebank (grammar) with n distinct categories the worst case number of distinct branches is n^2. Contrast this with the worst case number of possible grammar rules:

$$\begin{array}{lll} \#(x \rightarrow y_1) & \hat{=} & n^2 \\ \#(x \rightarrow y_1 y_2) & \hat{=} & n^3 \\ \ldots & \ldots & \ldots \\ \#(x \rightarrow y_1 \ldots y_m) & \hat{=} & n^{m+1} \end{array}$$

Clearly, given a grammar with n categories and a RHS rule length of at most m, the worst case number of different grammar rules

$$\sum_{i=1}^{m} n^{i+1} \gg n^2$$

for $m > 2$ is much higher than the worst case number n^2 of distinct branches.

In recent research we have scaled an automatic f-structure annotation approach evolved from the methods presented here to the complete Penn-II treebank resource (Cahill et al. 2002a, 2002b) to generate f-structures for 49,000 trees and 1 million words.

In order to develop stand-alone LFG grammars we need semantic forms (subcategorisation lists) to enforce subcategorisation requirements. We are currently exploring a number of ways of semi-automatically compiling these from machine readable dictionaries and the f-structure annotated corpus resources produced.

We expect that our approach can also feed into grammar development efforts. To be sure, because treebank grammars are large and flat, automatically annotated treebank grammars are less maintainable than the more compact, linguistically designed grammars which follow X-bar design principles. However, as pointed out above, our approaches allow for a novel grammar design and processing architecture: given a treebank, a probabilistic context-free grammar compiled from the treebank parses new text. For each input string, the (possibly *n*-) best parse trees are passed on to the annotation interpreters which annotate or rewrite the parse trees and induce f-structures. This and other probabilistic parsing architectures are developed in (Cahill et al. 2002b) and applied to parse the WSJ section of the Penn-II treebank into proto-f-structures. We consider this a promising new approach to partially automate large-coverage, corpus-based unification grammar development.

Current research also investigates further applications of flat, term-based tree structure conversion to induce grammars for alternative formalisms from existing treebanks. (Frank 2001) describes a treebank conversion method, applied to the German NEGRA corpus (Brants et al. 1997) to extract an LTAG grammar of German. The same method and corpus was used in (Becker and Frank 2002) to extract a stochastic topological grammar of German, to be used for integrated shallow and deep parsing.[10] (Liakata and Pulman 2002) present a method on flat, term-based tree representations that closely resembles the original approach in (Frank 2000), in order to annotate the Penn-II treebank trees with Quasi-Logical Forms information while (Cahill et al. 2003) show how Quasi-Logical Forms can be generated from f-structures produced for the Penn-II trees in (Cahill et al. 2002a, 2002b).

5. SUMMARY

We have presented two companion automatic f-structure annotation methods (Sadler et al. 2000; Frank 2000) for treebanks and grammars. The approaches make use of a corpus-based strategy that takes disambiguated tree structures as input, and annotate using (linguistically motivated) annotation principles. The principles are used to automatically enrich treebanks or extracted treebank grammars with higher-level functional information not present in the original corpora. Automatic annotation holds considerable potential in curtailing f-structure bank development costs and opens up the possibility of tackling large fragments. The work reported here is proof of concept. (Cahill et al. 2002a, 2002b) have further developed automatic f-structure annotation technology based on the methods described here and successfully scaled it to the Penn-II treebank resource. Here, we have presented a grammar development and treebank annotation methodology which is data-driven, semi-automatic, reuses existing resources and covers real text. We found the LFG framework very conducive to our experiments. We do believe, however, that the methods can be generalised, and we intend to apply them in an HPSG scenario and we and other researchers have applied similar technology to automatic semantic representation based annotation (Liakata and Pulman 2002; Cahill et al. 2003).

Our approach encourages work in the best linguistic tradition as (i) it is concerned with real language and (ii) enforces generalisations in the form of annotation principles. Our methods factor out information spread over many

CFG rules into a small number of modular and general principles. What is new in our approach is that (i) the principles state partial and underspecified correspondences between c- and f-structure configurations and (ii) they are applied to flat and noisy treebank representations that do not follow general X-bar design principles. Our experiments show how theoretical work and ideas on principles can translate into grammar development for real texts. In this sense our approach may contribute to bridge the often-perceived gap between theoretically motivated views of grammar as a set of principles vs. grammars for "real" text.

Acknowledgements

The authors wish to thank Tracy H. King, the members of the Pargram group, in particular Ron Kaplan, Mary Dalrymple and John Maxwell as well as Joan Bresnan, for helpful discussions and feedback.

Notes

1. For expository purposes, these are slightly simplified principles from our annotation grammar.

2. The annotation principles have to take into consideration that, in many cases, the representation of coordination in treebank rules is overly flat.

3. The annotation process itself is fast: in our experiments the interpreter annotates about 40 treebank CFG rules per second (Sparc 400Mhz).

4. It is also closely related to the principle-based grammar architecture of HPSG, cf. related work by (Neumann and Flickinger 1999) and (Neumann, this volume).

5. There are obligatory ($\Rightarrow$) and optional ($?\Rightarrow$) rewrite rules.

6. $\texttt{n}_1$ refers to the tree's root node.

7. Disjunctive templates encode alternative rewrite rules, and can be unioned (by logical "and" `&&`) with annotation rules. While this does still involve disjunctive processing, the rules can be stated in a generalised, compact way.

8. We require B and C to be distinct variables through inequality constraints (in curly brackets).

9. Templates, grammars and f-structures generated are available at: `http://www.compapp.dcu.ie/~away/Treebank/treebank.html`.

10. In this work, we developed a simple rewriting system modeled after the term rewriting system of Kay(1999).

References

S. Abney. (1997). Stochastic Attribute-Value Grammars. In: *Computational Linguistics*, 23(4), p. 597–618.

M. Becker, A. Frank. (2002). A Stochastic Topological Parser of German. *Proceedings of COLING 2002*, Taipei, Taiwan.

R. Bod, R. Kaplan. (1998). A Probabilistic Corpus-driven Model for Lexical-Functional Analysis. *Proceedings of COLING/ACL'98*, p. 145–151.

T. Brants, W. Skut, B. Krenn. (1997). Tagging Grammatical Functions. *Proceedings of EMNLP*, Providence, RI, USA.

J. Bresnan. (2001). *Lexical-Functional Syntax*. Blackwells Publishers, Oxford.

A. Cahill, M. McCarthy, J. van Genabith, A. Way. (2002a). Automatic Annotation of the Penn-Treebank with LFG F-Structure Information. A. Lenci, S. Montemagni and V. Pirelli, editors, In: *LREC 2002 Workshop on Linguistic Knowledge Acquisition and Representation - Bootstrapping Annotated Language Data*, LREC 2002, Third International Conference on Language Resources and Evaluation, p. 8-15.

A. Cahill, M. McCarthy, J. van Genabith, A. Way. (2002b). Parsing with PCFGs and Automatic F-Structure Annotation. In: M. Butt and T.-H. King, editors: *Proceedings of the LFG 2002 Conference*, Technical University Athens, Greece.

A. Cahill, M. McCarthy, J. van Genabith, A. Way. (2003). Quasi-Logical Forms from F-Structures for the Penn Treebank. Fifth International Workshop on Computational Semantics (IWCS-5). *Proceedings of the Workshop*, Tilburg, The Netherlands.

E. Charniak. (1993). *Statistical Language Learning*. MIT Press, Cambridge MA.

E. Charniak. (1996). Tree-bank Grammars. *AAAI-96. Proceedings of the Thirteenth National Conference on Artificial Intelligence*, p. 1031–1036. MIT Press.

M. Dalrymple, R.M Kaplan, J.T. Maxwell III, and A. Zaenen, editors. (1995). *Formal Issues in Lexical-Functional Grammar*. CSLI Lecture Notes, No. 47. CSLI Publications.

M. Dalrymple. (2001). *Lexical-Functional Grammar*. Syntax and Semantics 34, Academic Press.

A. Frank. (1999). From Parallel Grammar Development towards Machine Translation. A Project Overview. *Proceedings of Machine Translation Summit VII "MT in the Great Translation Era"*, p. 134–142.

A. Frank. (2000). Automatic F-Structure Annotation of Treebank Trees. In: M. Butt and T.H. King editors, *Proceedings of the LFG00 Conference*, University of California at Berkeley, CSLI Online Publications, Stanford, CA, `http://www-csli.stanford.edu/ publications/`.

A. Frank, T. King, J. Kuhn, J. Maxwell. (2000). Optimality Theory Style Constraint Ranking in Large-scale LFG Grammars. In: Sells, P., editor, *Optimality Theoretic Syntax*. CSLI Publications, Stanford, CA.

A. Frank. (2001). Treebank Conversion. Converting the NEGRA Treebank to an LTAG Grammar. *Proceedings of the Workshop on Multi-layer Corpus-based Analysis*, Workshop of the EUROLAN 2001 Summer Institute on Creation and Exploitation of Annotated Language Resources, Iasi, Romania.

R.M. Kaplan, J. Bresnan. (1982). *Lexical Functional Grammar*, p. 173–281. MIT Press, Cambridge, Mass.

M. Kay. (1999). Chart Translation. *Proceedings of Machine Translation Summit VII "MT in the Great Translation Era"*, p. 9–14.

A. Krotov, M. Hepple, R. Gaizauskas, Y. Wilks. (1998). Compacting the Penn Treebank Grammar. *Proceedings of COLING/ACL'98*, p. 699–703.

G. Leech, R. Garside, (1991). *Running a Grammar Factory: On the Compilation of Parsed Corpora, or 'Treebanks'* in *S. Johansson et al (eds) English Computer Corpora: selected papers*, p. 15–32. Mouton de Gruyter, Berlin.

M. Liakata, S. Pulman. (2002). From Trees to Predicate-Argument Structures. *Proceedings of COLING 2002*, Taipei, Taiwan.

M. Marcus, G. Kim, M. Marcinkiewicz, R. MacIntyre, A. Bies, M. Ferguson, K. Katz, B. Schasberger. (1994). The Penn treebank: Annotating predicate argument structure. In: *ARPA Human Language Technology Workshop*.

G. Neumann, D. Flickinger. (1999). HPSG-DOP: Data-oriented Parsing with HPSG. Learning Stochastic Lexicalized Tree Grammars from HPSG. DFKI Technical Report, Saarbrücken, 1999.

G. Neumann. (2003). A Uniform Method for Automatically Extracting Stochastic Lexicalized Tree Grammars from Treebanks and HPSG. In this volume.

C. Pollard, I. Sag. (1994). *Head-Driven Phrase Structure Grammar*. The University of Chicago Press, Chicago, Illinois.

L. Sadler, J. van Genabith, A. Way. (2000). Automatic F-Structure Annotation from the AP Treebank *Proceedings of the LFG 2000 Conference*, The University of California at Berkeley, CSLI Publications, Stanford, CA, `http://www-csli.stanford.edu/ publications/`

G. Sampson, (1993). *The Susanne Corpus*. Release 2.

J. van Genabith, L. Sadler, A. Way. (1999a). Data-driven Compilation of LFG Semantic Forms. In: *EACL'99 Workshop on Linguistically Interpreted Corpora (LINC-99), Bergen, Norway, June 12th*, p. 69–76.

J. van Genabith, L. Sadler, A. Way. (1999b). Structure Preserving CF-PSG Compaction, LFG and Treebanks. *Proceedings ATALA Workshop - Treebanks*, Journées ATALA, Université Paris 7 p. 107–114.

J. van Genabith, A. Way, L. Sadler. (1999c). Semi-Automatic Generation of f-Structures from Tree Banks. In: M. Butt and T.H. King, editors, *Proceedings of the LFG99 Conference*, Manchester University, CSLI Online Publications, Stanford, CA. `http://www-csli.stanford.edu/publications/`.

Appendix: Example of an Automatically Generated F-Structure (Susanne Corpus)

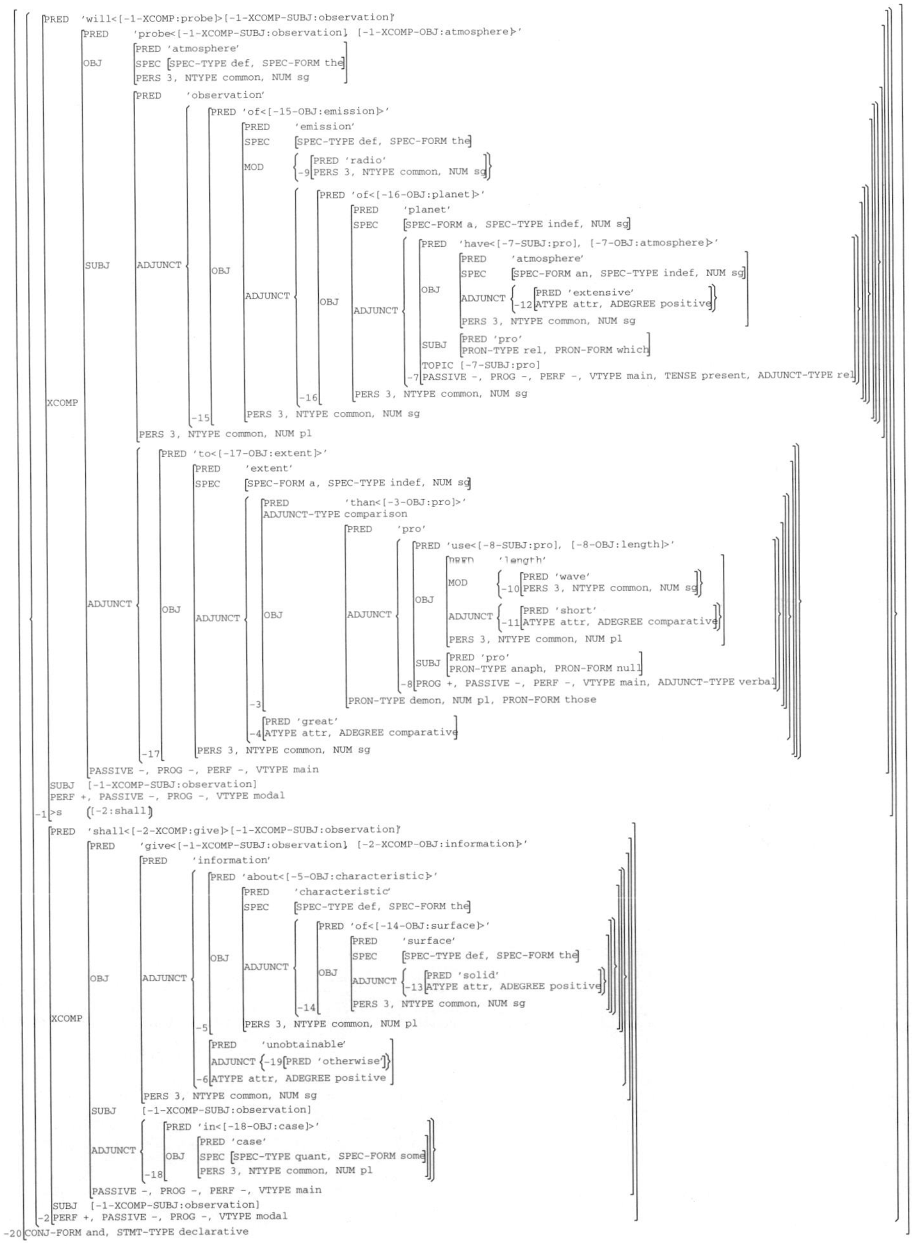

Figure 21.A.1. F–structure for: "Observations of the radio emission of a planet which has an extensive atmosphere will probe the atmosphere to a greater extent than those using shorter wave lengths and should in some cases give otherwise unobtainable information about the characteristics of the solid surface."

Contributing Authors

Anne Abeillé *abeille@linguist.jussieu.fr*	Laboratoire LLF 2, place Jussieu 75251 PARIS CEDEX 05 FRANCE
Mário Amado Alves	CENTRIA Departamento de Informática Faculdade de Ciêcias e Tecnologia Universidade Nova de Lisboa PORTUGAL
Francesco Barsotti *simonetta.montemagni@ilc.cnr.it*	Instituto di Linguistica Computazionale Area della Ricerca di Pisa Via Moruzzi 56124 Pisa ITALY
Roberto Basili *basili@info.uniroma2.it*	Università degli Studi di Roma "Tor Vergata" Via Orazio Raimondo, 18 00173 Roma ITALY
Marco Battista *marcor.battista@ilc.cnr.it*	Instituto di Linguistica Computazionale Area della Ricerca di Pisa Via Moruzzi 56124 Pisa ITALY
Markus Becker *markus.becker@dfki.de*	DFKI GmbH Language Technology Stuhlsatzenhausweg 3 D-66123 Saarbrücken GERMANY
Rens Bod *rens@science.uva.nl*	Institute for Logic Language and Computation University of Amsterdam THE NETHERLANDS
Alena Böhmová *bohmova@ufal.mff.cuni.cz*	Institute of Formal and Applied Linguistics Faculty of Mathematics and Physics Charles University Malostranské nám. 25 CZ-11800 Prague 1 CZECHOSLOVAKIA

Thorsten Brants *brants@parc.xerox.com*	Xerox Parc Palo Alto California USA
Andrew Bredenkamp *andrew.bredenkamp@dfki.de*	DFKI GmbH Language Technology Stuhlsatzenhausweg 3 D-66123 Saarbrücken GERMANY
Ted Briscoe *ejb@cl.cam.ac.uk*	Computer Labotory University of Cambridge Pembroke Street Cambridge CB2 3QG UK
Nicoletta Calzolari *glottolo@ilc.cnr.it*	Instituto di Linguistica Computazionale Area della Ricerca di Pisa Via Moruzzi 56124 Pisa ITALY
John Carroll *johnca@cogs.susx.ac.uk*	Cognitive and Computing Sciences University of Sussex Brighton BN1 9QH UK
Ming-Chung Chang *mjchung@iis.sinica.edu.tw*	Institute of Information Science Academia Sinica TAIWAN
Chao-Jan Chen *richard@iis.sinica.edu.tw*	Institute of Information Science Academia Sinica TAIWAN
Feng-Yi Chen *apple@iis.sinica.edu.tw*	Institute of Information Science Academia Sinica TAIWAN
Keh-Jiann Chen *kchen@iis.sinica.edu.tw*	Institute of Information Science Academia Sinica TAIWAN
Lionel Clément *lionel.clement@inria.fr*	Attol INRIA Roquencourt FRANCE
Ornella Corazzari *ornella.corazzari@ilc.cnr.it*	Instituto di Linguistica Computazionale Area della Ricerca di Pisa Via Moruzzi 56124 Pisa ITALY
Berthold Crysmann *crysmann@dfki.de*	DFKI GmbH Language Technology Stuhlsatzenhausweg 3 D-66123 Saarbrücken GERMANY

Rodolfo Delmonte *delmont@unive.it*	Università Ca'Foscari Ca' Garzoni-Moro San Marco 3417 30124 Venezia ITALY
Francesca Fanciulli *fanciulli@synthema.it*	Synthema SRL Lungarno Mediceo 40 56127 Pisa ITALY
Anette Frank *anette@ims.uni – stuttgart.de*	IMS Stuttgart University GERMANY
Zhao-Ming Gao *zmgao@xxms.ntu.edu.tw*	National Taiwan University TAIWAN
Josef van Genabith *josef@computing.dcu.ie*	Dublin City University IRELAND
Ralph Grishman *grishman@cs.nyu.edu*	New York University USA
Jan Hajič *hajic@ufal.mff.cuni.cz*	Institute of Formal and Applied Linguistics Faculty of Mathematics and Physics Charles University Malostranské nám. 25 CZ-11800 Prague 1 CZECHOSLOVAKIA
Eva Hajičová *hajicova@ufal.mff.cuni.cz*	Institute of Formal and Applied Linguistics Faculty of Mathematics and Physics Charles University Malostranské nám. 25 CZ-11800 Prague 1 CZECHOSLOVAKIA
Dilek Zeynep Hakkani-Tür *hakkani@research.att.com*	AT&T Labs-Research 180 PArk Avenue Florham Park NJ 07928 USA
Barbora Hladká *hladka@ufal.mff.cuni.cz*	Institute of Formal and Applied Linguistics Faculty of Mathematics and Physics Charles University Malostranské nám. 25 CZ-11800 Prague 1 CZECHOSLOVAKIA
Chu-Ren Huang *hschuren@ccvax.sinica.edu.tw*	Institute of Linguistics Academia Sinica TAIWAN
Nancy Ide *ide@cs.vassar.edu*	Department of Computer Science Vassar College Poughkeepsie New York 12604-0520 USA

Timo Järvinen *timo.jarvinen@conexor.fi*	Conexor oy Helsinki Science Park Koetilantie 3 00710 Helsinki FINLAND
Judith Klein	DFKI GmbH Saarbrücken GERMANY
Anna Kupść *aniak@ipipan.waw.pl*	Institute of Computer Science Polish Academy of Sciences POLAND
Sadao Kurohashi *kuro@kc.t.u-tokyo.ac.jp*	Graduate School of Information Science and Technology University of Tokyo JAPAN
Alessandro Lenci *alessandro.lenci@ilc.cnr.it*	Instituto di Linguistica Computazionale Area della Ricerca di Pisa Via Moruzzi 56124 Pisa ITALY
Dekang Lin *lindek@cs.ualberta.ca*	Department of Computing Science University of Alberta Edmonton Alberta CANADA T6G 2H1
J. Gabriel Lopes	CENTRIA Departamento de Informática Faculdade de Ciêcas e Tecnologia Universidade Nova de Lisboa PORTUGAL
Susana López *susana@maria.lllf.uam.es*	Universidad Autónoma de Madrid SPAIN
Chi-Ching Luo *airport@iis.sinica.edu.tw*	Institute of Information Science Academia Sinica TAIWAN
Nadia Mana *mana@irst.itc.it*	ITC-irst Via Sommarive 18 Povo 38050 Trento ITALY
Małgorzata Marciniak *mm@ipipan.waw.pl*	Institute of Computer Science Polish Academy of Sciences POLAND
Mitchell Marcus *mitch@linc.cis.upenn.edu*	University of Pennsylvania Philadelphia PA USA
Maria Massetani *massetani@synthema.it*	Synthema SRL Lungarno Mediceo 40 56127 Pisa ITALY

Guido Minnen *guido.minnen@motorola.com*	Motorola Human Interface Laboratory Schaumburg IL 60196 USA
Simonetta Montemagni *simonetta.montemagni@ilc.cnr.it*	Instituto di Linguistica Computazionale Area della Ricerca di Pisa Via Moruzzi 56124 Pisa ITALY
Antonio Moreno *sandoval@maria.lllf.uam.es*	Universidad Auónoma de Madrid SPAIN
Agnieszka Mykowiecka *agn@ipipan.waw.pl*	Institute of Computer Science Polish Academy of Sciences POLAND
Makoto Nagao *nagao@kuee.kyoto − u.ac.jp*	Kyoto University JAPAN
Günter Neumann *neumann@dfki.de*	DFKI GmbH 66123 Saarbrücken GERMANY
Kemal Oflazer *oflazer@sabanciuniv.edu*	Faculty of Engineering and Natural Sciences Sabanci University Istanbul TURKEY
Maria Teresa Pazienza *pazienza@info.uniroma2.it*	Università degli Studi di Roma "Tor Vergata" Via Orazio Raimondo, 18 00173 Roma ITALY
Fabio Pianesi *pianesi@irst.itc.it*	ITC-irst Via Sommarive 18 Povo 38050 Trento ITALY
Adam Przepiórkowski *adamp@ipipan.waw.pl*	Institute of Computer Science Polish Academy of Sciences POLAND
Remo Raffaelli *raffaelli@synthema.it*	Synthema SRL Lungarno Mediceo 40 56127 Pisa ITALY
Vitor Rocio *vjr@di.fct.unl.pt*	CENTRIA Departamento de Informática Faculdade de Ciêncas e Tecnologia Universidade Nova de Lisboa PORTUGAL
Laurent Romary *romary@loria.fr*	LORIA/CNRS Campus Scientifique BP 239 54506 Vandoeuvre-les-Nancy FRANCE

Louisa Sadler *louisa@essex.ac.uk*	University of Essex UK
Geoffrey Sampson *geoffs@cogs.susx.ac.uk*	School of Cognitive & Computing Sciences University of Sussex Falmer BRIGHTON BN1 9QH UK
Fernando Sánchez *fernando@maria.lllf.uam.es*	Universidad Autónoma de Madrid SPAIN
Beatrice Santorini *beatrice@linc.cis.upenn.edu*	University of Pennsylvania Philadelphia PA USA
Dario Saracino *d.saracino@knowledgestones.com*	Università degli Studi di Roma "Tor Vergata" Via Orazio Raimondo, 18 00173 Roma ITALY
Bilge Say *bsay@ii.metu.edu.tr*	Informatics Institute Middle East Technical University Ankara TURKEY
Wojciech Skut *skut@coli.uni – sb.de*	Saarland University FR 8.7 computational linguistics P.O. Box 171150 D-66041 Saarbrücken GERMANY
Ann Taylor *at9@york.ac.uk*	University of York Heslington York UK
François Toussenel *ftoussen@linguist.jussieu.fr*	Laboratoire Lattice/TALaNa Université Paris 7 75251 PARIS CEDEX 05 FRANCE
Gökhan Tür *tur@research.att.com*	AT&T Labs-Research 180 Park Avenue Florham Park NJ 07928 USA
Hans Uszkoreit *uszkoreit@coli.uni – sb.de*	Saarland University FR 8.7 computational linguistics P.O. Box 171150 D-66041 Saarbrücken GERMANY
Gracia Vicente	Faculdade de Ciêncas Sociais e Humanas Universidade Nova de Lisboa PORTUGAL
Sean Wallis *s.wallis@ucl.ac.uk*	University College London UK
Andy Way *away@computing.dcu.ie*	Dublin City University IRELAND

Antonio Zampolli *antonio.zampolli@ilc.cnr.it*	Instituto di Linguistica Computazionale Area della Ricerca di Pisa Via Moruzzi 56124 Pisa ITALY
Fabio Zanzotto *zanzotto@info.uniroma2.it*	Università degli Studi di Roma "Tor Vergata" Via Orazio Raimondo, 18 00173 Roma ITALY
Maria Francisca Xavier *mf.xavier@fsch.unl.pt*	Faculdade de Ciêcas Sociais e Humanas Universidade Nova de Lisboa PORTUGAL

Index

Accuracy, 34, 35, 53, 63, 64, 69, 77–82, 224, 250, 255, 259, 299, 300, 308, 309, 312, 337–341, 344, 345, 362
Acquisition, 39
Address, 149, 151, 281, 282, 368
Adjective, 8, 9, 25, 46, 69, 135, 167, 172, 221, 257, 263, 266, 276, 342, 378
Adjunct, xx, 12, 28, 116, 235, 238, 243, 268, 270, 360, 363, 373
Adverb, 8, 9, 13, 25, 46, 87, 167, 170, 172, 175, 182, 256
  adverbial locution, 192
Agreement, xviii, 64, 77, 82, 95 99, 131, 133–136, 153, 154, 161, 167, 223, 224, 263, 272, 276, 277, 308
  error, 92
Algorithm, 17, 130, 254, 257, 320, 321, 337
  parsing, xiv
Amalgam, 151
Ambiguity, xiii, xix, xx, 13, 46, 52–54, 57, 123, 171, 172, 224, 240, 274, 304, 311, 379
  lexical, 310
  rate, 47, 52
  remaining, 47, 258
  spurious, 52
  syntactic, xix, 53, 256, 257
Analyser, 43, 44, 47–49, 204, 211, 212, 215, 217, 218, 220, 223
  morphological, 43–45, 310
  syntactic, 220
Analytical Tree Structure, 107, 118–120
Anchor, 354, 357, 360
Annotation, xiv–xx, xxiii, xxiv, 8–10, 13, 15, 20, 24, 26, 43, 44, 47–52, 56, 64, 69, 73–84, 90–96, 104, 106–109, 111, 112, 114, 116, 121–123, 137, 149, 150, 153–157, 159–161, 165–167, 170, 174, 180, 189–206, 211, 212, 238, 241, 244, 270, 271, 281–291, 304, 307, 308, 359, 363, 368–383, 386
  automatic, xviii, 16, 61, 89, 166, 172, 273, 367, 373, 380, 381, 385
  error, 300
  guidelines, 27, 35, 83, 92, 160, 165, 166, 231, 232, 235, 240, 261, 273
  interactive, 74, 77, 81, 84
  manual, xviii, 47, 91, 95, 109, 119, 121, 123, 301
  scheme, xv, xvi, 5, 6, 27, 35, 37, 39, 50, 63, 74, 75, 80, 81, 83, 84, 93, 99, 103, 106, 130, 149, 150, 153–155, 159, 160, 173, 193, 195, 196, 206, 282, 284–288, 291, 293, 294, 299, 302, 313, 382
  speed, 20, 79
  tool, xv, xviii–xx, 61, 73, 75, 92, 93, 157, 166, 170, 200, 261, 270, 271, 273
Annotator, xiv, 7, 20, 68, 69, 74, 77–82, 84, 92, 96, 106, 111, 113, 116, 159, 173, 179, 197, 199, 200, 253, 270, 273, 274, 281, 282
Answer, 254, 319, 320, 323, 324, 326, 327
Argument, 9, 12, 13, 21, 64, 156, 221, 224, 233, 235–238, 242, 256, 285, 286, 303, 304, 310, 312, 362, 363, 371, 373
ASCII, 48, 49, 142
Aspect, 67, 116, 132, 133, 191, 205, 263, 354, 379
ATS, *see* Analytical Tree Structure
Attachment, xvii, 19, 47, 76, 77, 108, 178, 194, 223, 224, 300, 317, 322–324, 342, 358, 382
  PP, 179, 324
  pseudo, 13
Automata
  finite state, 221, 266, 352
Auxiliary, 87, 107, 118, 137
  tree, 351, 353, 355, 357, 358
  verb, 126, 133, 159, 251, 311

Bank of English, xvi, xxi, 43, 47–49, 51, 54, 56
Boundary, 25, 97, 177, 179, 300, 320, 326
  sentence, 77, 114, 157
Branch, 30, 378
  crossing, 73, 75, 77, 81, 83, 286, 290
Brown corpus, 6, 7, 17, 300, 309, 321

Bulgarian, xxiv
Bunsetsu, xvii, 251–253, 255–259

C-structure, 374, 376–379, 381
Case, xviii, 63, 66, 67, 92, 97–99, 104, 111, 123, 126, 134, 135, 138, 173, 233, 252, 254–256, 258, 263, 268, 276, 389
Category, xiv, xxiii, 9, 10, 26, 32, 35, 70, 74, 104, 133, 153, 154, 156, 158, 174, 176, 182, 223, 232, 233, 235–238, 276, 284, 286–289, 291, 293, 294, 319, 321–323, 343, 360, 371, 378, 380, 381, 383
  lexical, 237, 318, 377
Causative, 263, 277
CES, *see* Corpus Encoding Standard
Chinese, xvii, xix, 190, 231–234, 240–245
Christine corpus, 23, 26, 38
Chunk, 19, 223, 250
Chunker, 157
Clitic, 167, 173, 175, 177, 191, 202, 217, 221
Coindexation, 194
Collocation, 266, 270, 274
Comma, 8, 126, 224
Competence, 91, 92, 99, 352, 353, 362
Complement, xvii, 13, 30, 37, 52, 54, 69, 118, 134, 175, 210, 221, 305, 309, 324, 325, 363, 371–373
  missing, 119
  predicative, 118
Complementation, 50, 133, 135, 311
Complementizer, 98
Complexity, xvii, xix, 25, 27, 33, 38, 39, 63, 69, 104, 130, 131, 150, 157, 231–233, 238, 239, 291, 333, 334, 351
Compound, xiii, 108, 126, 152, 155, 167, 170–172, 182, 198, 203, 205, 221, 266
Conjunction, 76, 116, 118, 126, 134, 167, 175, 177, 203, 224, 235, 257, 272, 273, 324, 325
  coordinating, 15, 46, 210, 272
  subordinating, 46, 118, 167
Consistency, xvii, 8, 21, 34, 47, 50, 53, 61, 63, 65, 68, 74, 76, 144, 171, 232, 240, 291, 293, 294, 321
Constraint Grammar, 43, 44, 52, 53, 56
Control, 153, 156, 196, 200, 305, 306, 379, 381
Convergence, xiv, 345
Coordination, xviii, 62, 92, 109, 110, 116, 126, 134, 135, 175, 179, 195, 224, 225, 236, 252, 260, 273, 379, 381
Corpus, xiv–xix, xxi, xxii, xxiv, 5–8, 14, 17, 20, 24, 25, 29, 34, 35, 40, 43, 47–50, 73–75, 77–79, 81–83, 89–93, 96, 98, 103, 104, 106, 114, 123, 129, 149, 160, 165–168, 170–173, 182, 189–191, 197–200, 204–206, 211–213, 218, 220, 222, 224, 231, 232, 240, 249–253, 257, 262, 265, 281–284, 291, 299, 300, 302, 308–311, 313, 321–323, 333–336, 338–340, 343, 352, 355, 359, 361, 368, 380, 382, 384, 385
  annotation, xv, xviii, 44, 61, 73, 74, 78, 82, 89, 93, 99, 150, 157, 194, 199, 211, 249, 281, 299, 300, 311
  balanced, 244
  newspaper, 73, 165, 249
  parsed, 21, 61, 63, 174, 178, 180, 212, 214, 249–251, 255, 259
  spoken, 35
  tagged, xxiii, 168, 171, 177, 180, 181, 213, 215, 225
Corpus Encoding Standard, 167
Czech, xv, xxiii, 29, 103–105, 108, 112, 114, 122, 123, 143

Data Type Description, 160, 290
Data-oriented Parsing, 335–339, 344, 345, 352
Date, 39, 62, 67, 273, 307, 335, 368, 369
DCG, *see* Definite Clause Grammar
Default, 12, 56, 236–238, 263
Definite Clause Grammar, 220, 221
Dependency, xv–xviii, xxiii, 43, 44, 47, 54, 56, 57, 74–76, 78, 83, 84, 93, 103, 106, 107, 109, 111, 113, 114, 118, 120, 123, 130, 143, 181, 190, 191, 195, 210, 233, 234, 249–253, 255–262, 266, 267, 272–274, 285, 290, 291, 293, 301, 302, 306, 312, 317–320, 322–328, 355, 356
  relation, xvii, 93, 107, 118, 120, 191, 195, 210, 234, 259, 261, 262, 301, 317–320, 322–324, 326, 327
  structure, 57, 106, 109, 181, 249, 250, 253, 257, 266, 285, 301, 318, 326
Derivation, xxii, 91, 261, 265, 266, 276, 335–340, 343, 352, 359
Determiner, xiv, 8, 46, 166, 167, 171, 172, 177, 193, 374, 379
Dialect, 288, 291
Dictionary, xvi, xxi, 44, 50, 99, 123, 137, 140, 204, 205, 215, 225, 254, 255, 258, 268
DiET, 89, 93–96, 98
Discontinuity, 194
Discourse, 15, 37, 64, 150, 206, 263, 284
Disfluency, 15, 16, 20
Disjunction, 116, 197, 371
DOP, *see* Data-oriented Parsing
DTD, *see* Data Type Description
Dummy, 170, 235, 236, 238, 272
DyALog, 221

EAGLES, 165, 191, 283, 286

Ellipsis, 112, 126, 153, 194, 202, 272
Emacs, 16, 17
Email, 89, 90, 92, 93, 95
ENGCG, 44–48, 50–54, 56, 57
English, xiv, xv, xix, xxi, xxiii, 5, 21, 23, 24, 29, 30, 33, 36–40, 43, 44, 48–50, 53, 54, 61, 62, 74–76, 103, 132, 170, 205, 225, 251, 258, 263, 268, 276, 300, 302, 304–306, 308, 313, 317, 320, 321, 359, 361, 362, 379
ENGTWOL, 45, 49, 50
Error, xvi, 29, 68, 80, 89–99, 113, 159, 171, 241, 273, 317, 337, 368
  annotation, xvi, 89, 93, 95
  rate, 17, 47, 54, 64, 65, 69, 171, 322
Evaluation, xvi, xxii, 45, 54, 80, 89, 99, 123, 130, 131, 143, 158–161, 178, 189, 190, 195, 203, 205, 206, 225, 249, 259, 281, 282, 293, 299–302, 307, 311–313, 319–321, 323, 324, 326–328, 381, 383
  checker, xx
  parser, xvi, xx, xxiii, 181, 299, 302, 308, 317, 321, 326
Extraction, xv, xx, xxi, 211, 215, 244, 284, 288, 291, 311, 313, 351, 353, 354, 363
Extraposition, 13, 83, 325

F-structure, 367–369, 371, 373–379, 381–386
FDG, *see* Functional Dependency Grammar
Feature, 35, 46, 70, 130, 152, 153, 155, 156, 158–161, 198, 199, 202, 203, 218, 221, 242, 257, 259, 263, 264, 273, 289, 339, 359–361, 363, 368, 369, 380
  morphological, 52, 263, 264, 274, 276
  semantic, 153
  structure, 130, 160, 202, 203, 359–361, 363, 368, 369, 380
  syntactic, 234
Fidditch, 17–19, 74, 250
Finnish, 54, 57
Formalism, xxiii, 54, 75, 157, 171, 200, 204, 251, 255–257, 259, 344, 372
French, xiii, xv, xviii–xx, 132, 165–167, 170, 173, 175, 180, 181, 263, 264, 267, 302, 306
FTAG, 181
Function, 7, 10, 11, 37, 107, 110, 111, 114, 118–120, 126, 172, 174, 175, 177, 180, 182, 196, 235, 236, 241, 242, 256, 265, 285, 286, 307, 373, 377–379
  grammatical, xiv, xvii, xxii, xxiii, 11, 74, 76, 77, 81, 82, 87, 181, 182, 379
Functional Dependency Grammar, xxiii, 54–57

GB, *see* Government and Binding
Gender, 104, 131, 153, 167, 173, 191, 222–224, 288
Generation, 290
Genotype, 182
German, xv, xviii, xxi, 28, 57, 73–76, 78, 83, 89, 91, 99, 132, 259, 306, 355, 363, 385
Gerund, 153, 160
Government and Binding, 232
GPSG, 234
Grammar, xiv–xvi, xx, xxi, 27, 29, 38, 43, 44, 48, 50, 52–54, 57, 62–64, 70, 75, 76, 89, 97–99, 131, 157, 159, 160, 170, 178, 182, 192, 220, 221, 224, 233, 235, 237, 241, 250, 251, 255–257, 259, 272, 300–302, 310, 311, 320–322, 351–360, 362, 363, 377, 380–386
  attribute-value, 130
  book, xiv, xxi, 91, 109, 178, 182, 253
  coverage, 205, 212
  generative, 301
  hand-crafted, xxiii
  lexicalized, 333, 334, 339
  rule, xxiii, 205, 290, 311, 368, 369, 371, 372, 384
  stochastic, 333, 334, 339, 344
Grammateme, 116
Grammatical relation, xvi, 285, 299, 302, 303, 307, 309, 328

Head, xvii, 7, 23, 35, 52, 56, 111, 159, 161, 174–176, 193–196, 214, 234–239, 242, 243, 256, 268, 273, 274, 285, 290, 302–306, 311, 312, 318, 319, 324–326, 340, 344, 354–357, 359, 361, 363, 370, 372–374
  semantic, 236, 237
  syntactic, 75, 76, 236
Head-driven Phrase Structure Grammar, xv, xxi, 129, 130, 137, 142–144, 233, 234, 238, 259, 352–354, 359–363, 369, 385, 386
Hebrew, xxiv
HMM, 310
HPSG, *see* Head-driven Phrase Structure Grammar

ICE, *see* International Coprus of English
Idiom, 198, 311
Imperative, 9, 25, 37, 132, 134, 167
Impersonal, 155, 156
Infinitive, 9, 12, 46, 107, 153, 154, 156, 219, 268
Inflection, xvii, 165, 166, 171, 266, 269, 276, 304
Inflectional group, 261, 262, 266, 267, 269
Inheritance, 130, 136, 137, 235–237

Interface, 17, 19, 64, 77, 81, 82, 93, 140, 141, 180, 189, 190, 243, 244, 252, 253, 270, 271, 299, 369, 373, 375
  graphical, 111, 140, 202
International Corpus of English, 61, 64, 69
ISST, 190–198, 200, 204–206
Italian, xv, xviii, 175, 189, 190, 192–194, 204–206, 304, 306

Japanese, xv, xvii, xix, 84, 249–251, 253–256, 258–260
Java, 94, 177
JUMAN, 250, 252–256, 258, 259

Kana, 254
Kanji, 254
Key, 302, 319, 320, 323–327, 373
Kleene, 310, 353

Language,
  meta, 195
  natural, xiii, xxii, 20, 23, 24, 29, 31–34, 40, 44, 75, 122, 190, 206, 262, 283, 299, 344
  programming, 29, 117, 286
Learning, xxi, xxii, 20, 39, 64, 65, 212, 351–353, 360
  supervised, 73, 259, 362
  unsupervised, 259
Lemma, 104, 116, 123, 157, 166, 167, 173, 177, 191, 199, 268
Lemmatization, 168
Lemmatizer, xiv, 181
Lexical Functional Grammar, 130, 302, 352, 367–370, 373, 375, 377, 383–385
Lexicalized Tree-adjoining Grammar, 352, 363, 385
Lexicon, xx, xxiii, 45, 49, 50, 52, 142, 155, 157, 170–172, 181, 182, 197, 199, 200, 211, 212, 215, 220, 221, 223, 224, 233, 235, 239, 254, 321, 359
LFG, *see* Lexical Functional Grammar
LinGO, 359
Linguistics, xiii, xvi, xviii, 30, 34, 40, 106, 122, 130, 157, 158, 211, 213, 240, 253, 308, 313, 322, 367
  computational, xiv, xx, xxiv, 21, 23, 24, 27, 33, 43, 73, 103, 161, 190, 211, 215, 245, 339
  generative, xix
Linux, 106
LISP, 16, 17
LTAG, *see* Lexicalized Tree-adjoining Grammar
LUCY, 24, 39

Markov Model, 78–82
MINIPAR, 317, 318, 320–326, 328
Mittelfeld, 83
Modality, 116
Modifier, 28, 87, 114, 133, 135, 243, 262, 263, 265, 268, 269, 274, 301, 313, 318, 319, 324, 342, 354–358, 362, 363
Mood, 167
Morpheme, 262–264, 268, 269
Morphology, 52, 97, 98, 103, 122, 123, 157, 167, 170, 171, 223, 225
MULTEXT, 170, 172
Multi-word expression, 192, 197, 199, 202, 205

Name, 26, 131, 133, 136, 142–144, 213, 242, 277
Natural Language processing, xv, xxi, 73, 89, 190, 206, 232, 249, 250, 299, 300
Negation, 134, 135, 171, 175, 177, 193, 301
NEGRA corpus, xvii, 78, 84, 286, 290, 363
NLP, *see* Natural Language processing
Node, 13, 19, 70, 76, 80, 107–109, 111, 114, 116–120, 126, 159, 182, 193, 201, 285, 288–291, 318, 321, 326, 335–337, 343, 359, 376
  foot, 357
  label, 123, 302, 357, 378
  modifier, 354, 358
  phrasal, 76, 356
  root, 107, 126, 353, 360, 386
Noun, xiv, xix, xx, 7–9, 25, 26, 30, 32, 37, 46, 52, 69, 87, 105, 111, 114, 118, 134, 135, 143, 154, 171, 172, 174, 175, 177, 193, 203, 213, 221, 222, 224, 235, 238, 248, 251, 263, 264, 266, 268, 274, 276, 284, 303, 311, 327, 363
  common, 7, 87, 166, 172, 191, 221-224
  proper, 8, 87, 170, 177, 197–199
Number, xxi, xxii, 6, 8, 11, 13, 26, 27, 29, 30, 32, 38, 45, 50, 52, 53, 55, 56, 62, 63, 67, 68, 80, 83, 90, 92, 93, 95, 96, 99, 107, 114, 116–118, 123, 127, 129, 131–134, 140, 150, 153, 155, 157–159, 167, 168, 173, 180, 191, 193, 194, 201, 205, 217, 222–224, 240, 252, 262, 264, 265, 268, 269, 274, 277, 300, 301, 304, 308, 309, 320, 322, 323, 326, 334, 336–341, 344, 355, 358, 359, 361–363, 368, 379–384, 386
Numeral, 46, 118, 133, 134, 167

Paragraph, xiii, 213
Parenthetical, 209
PAROLE, 192
Parse forest, 337
Parser, xiv, xvi, xix, xx, xxii, xxiii, 17, 19, 43, 44, 54, 56, 57, 69, 74, 77, 80, 81, 84, 112–114, 123, 130, 131, 153,

159–161, 181, 212, 213, 215, 220, 221, 224, 232, 235, 236, 239, 240, 249, 250, 257, 282, 299–302, 304, 307–313, 317, 320–326, 328, 353, 355, 358, 359, 361–363
rule-based, xxiii, 63, 177
shallow, xxii, 43, 165, 177, 178, 181, 194, 307
PARSEVAL, xxiii, 282
Parsing, xiv, xvi, xviii, xix, xxii, xxiii, 5, 10, 21, 23, 43, 44, 48–50, 52, 54, 61–64, 69, 80, 112, 113, 121, 123, 165, 166, 173, 176, 177, 180, 195, 206, 211, 212, 221–223, 239–242, 249, 251, 257–259, 274, 301, 302, 310–313, 321, 323, 333–335, 337, 344, 345, 351, 352, 354, 355, 359, 361, 368, 383, 385
Part of speech, 5–8, 16, 17, 19, 20, 53, 160, 166, 170–172, 177, 182, 191, 212, 213, 215, 218, 220, 222–225, 251, 252, 255–257, 259, 264, 268, 276, 310, 352, 354, 357, 359, 363
Particle, 8, 46, 126, 151, 160
Passive, 9, 87, 133, 290, 302, 304, 307, 328, 377
PDT, *see* Prague dependency treebank
Penn treebank, 285, 289–293
Performance, xx, xxii, 20, 28, 32, 45, 55, 64, 90, 91, 97, 99, 106, 159, 160, 224, 250, 254, 259, 317, 322–324, 328, 333, 334, 354, 358, 361
PERL, 19, 157, 158, 160
Person, 33, 92, 123, 155, 167, 191, 217, 277, 304
Phrase, xvii, 7, 9, 18, 23, 25–27, 30, 32, 35, 37, 52, 69, 78–82, 84, 87, 131, 133, 151, 174–177, 179, 181, 209, 214, 222, 224, 234–236, 251, 266, 284–286, 300–302, 317, 320, 322, 325–328, 355
adverbial, 221
nominal, 135, 235, 379
structure, xxiii, 108, 112, 130, 137, 139, 158, 159, 234, 235, 301, 302, 310, 318, 351, 359, 368
verbal, 133, 175, 193
Polish, xv, xxiii, 129–134, 137, 143
Portuguese, xv, xviii, xix, 57, 212, 213, 215, 217, 225
contemporary, 211, 212, 217
medieval, xix, 211–214
POS, *see* Part of speech
Postposition, 256
Prague dependency treebank, 8, 104, 108, 114, 121, 122
Precision, xxiii, 31, 46, 54, 96, 97, 99, 157, 160, 178, 232, 300, 301, 311–313, 317, 319–322, 324, 325, 327, 328, 343, 380, 381
Preference, 172, 234, 240, 258, 311, 337, 342
syntactic, 181
Prefix, 105, 136, 371
Preposition, 8, 46, 69, 126, 167, 170, 172, 196, 213, 224, 235, 238, 305, 306, 325, 342
complex, 45, 118
PRO-drop, 119, 153, 192, 194, 196, 263, 272, 304, 307
Probabilities, xiii, xxii, 74, 78–80, 84, 310, 337, 338
Productivity, xxi
Projection, 373–375
maximal, 310
Projectivity, 115, 260, 274
Pronoun, xiv, 8, 46, 56, 87, 155, 156, 167, 172, 175
clitic, 167, 173, 191
reflexive, 29
relative, 87, 98, 114, 170, 172
Psycholinguistics, 181, 182
PTB, *see* Penn treebank
Punctuation, 7, 8, 27, 36, 45, 76, 77, 97, 98, 104, 105, 107, 120, 126, 177, 180, 213, 224, 301, 310, 359, 380

Query, xix, xxi, 67, 142, 143
language, xxi
Quotation, 36, 37, 325

Raising, xv, 13, 355, 379
Recall, 46, 54, 96, 97, 157, 160, 178, 300, 301, 311–313, 319, 320, 322–325, 327, 328, 343, 381
Relative clause, xix, xx, 35, 76, 80, 83, 87, 114, 132, 134, 174, 177, 179, 214, 221, 324, 327
Romance, 225
Rule, xxi, 29, 50, 52, 54, 110, 135, 158–160, 171, 177, 178, 219, 220, 223, 258, 310, 337, 360, 368, 371–373, 375–377, 379–381, 384
context free, xxi
lexical, 170, 359, 377
rewrite, 337, 375, 386

Semantic, xx, 9–11, 97, 98, 126, 137, 153, 155, 156, 172, 179, 202, 203, 205, 206, 231–241, 262, 269, 290, 304, 307, 310, 324, 327, 333, 343, 359, 363, 379, 384
annotation, xxiv, 189–191, 283
lexical, 233, 268
type, 191, 197, 198
Sentence, xiii, xvi, xx, 9, 17, 18, 25, 27–30, 44, 45, 49, 54–57, 63, 66, 67, 69,

75–77, 79–83, 87, 92, 96, 105, 106, 108–115, 120, 121, 123, 126, 129, 140, 141, 143, 157, 159, 170, 180, 182, 191–193, 196, 200, 203, 205, 209, 214, 221, 237, 240, 242, 251–253, 256, 257, 259, 267–270, 273, 276, 285, 290, 294, 300, 302, 306, 307, 309, 313, 318, 320–323, 325, 327, 335–338, 340, 342, 343, 354, 356–361, 363
correct, 131, 134, 135, 137
incorrect, 131, 134, 135
length, 81, 150, 201, 323, 358, 382
number, 95
well-formed, 240, 242
SGML, 62, 104–106, 108, 109, 114, 181, 283
Sinica treebank, 232, 233, 235, 236, 243, 244
SPANISH, 149
Spanish, xv, xviii, 54, 149–153, 155, 159–161
SPARKLE, 206
Speech, xiii, xiv, xvi, xviii–xx, xxii, xxiii, 5, 7, 15, 24–26, 36–39, 46, 52, 61, 165–167, 173, 191, 215, 263, 284, 321, 358
direct, 120, 126, 182
indirect, 36, 37
Spelling, 34, 62, 77, 212
Stochastic Lexicalized Tree Grammar, 351, 354, 355, 359–362
Subcategorisation, 97, 98, 191, 221, 222, 224, 225, 310, 313, 379, 383
Subcategory, 172, 174, 182
Subject, xiii, 6, 9, 12, 25, 37, 52, 56, 69, 70, 87, 119, 126, 131, 133–135, 155, 156, 168, 175, 192, 193, 195, 202, 214, 224, 235, 243, 263, 267–269, 272, 274, 290, 302, 304, 305, 307, 312, 313, 324, 372, 373, 377
empty, xvii, 153
logical, 8, 10, 11, 26, 322
Subjunctive, 167
Substitution, 116, 337, 352, 354, 356, 357, 360
Subtree, 117, 119, 333, 334, 336–344, 354, 355, 359
Suffix, 78, 110, 217, 356, 358
Susanne Corpus, xvii, xviii, xxiii, 23, 75, 81, 317, 321, 322, 324, 367, 378, 379, 381
Swedish, 40, 54, 57
Switchboard corpus, xvi, 6, 15, 21

Tagger, xiv, xxiii, 57, 77, 78, 81, 84, 123, 165, 168, 170–173, 177, 181, 182, 192, 211–213, 215, 310, 321
Tagging, xviii, xix, 5–7, 16–20, 43, 78, 79, 81, 104, 123, 165, 166, 168–173, 180, 190, 196, 197, 213, 215, 220, 222–225, 232, 255, 281, 282, 310
Tagset, xviii, xxi, xxii, 6, 7, 17, 57, 78, 165, 168, 170–173, 177, 181, 191, 259, 262–264, 286
syntactic, 7, 9, 174
Teaching, 24, 62
Tectogrammatical Tree Structure, 115–121, 127
TEI, 180
Template, 378, 379
Tense, 8, 46, 116, 119, 123, 132, 133, 153, 209, 223, 277, 374, 378
Terminology, xx, 283
Test suite, 90, 96, 302
Thematic role, 231, 232, 234–236, 238, 240, 241
TIGER, 74, 83
Title, 197, 198, 203, 249, 259
Token, xiv, 40, 45, 52, 55, 77, 104, 109, 111, 193, 218, 265, 270, 274, 311, 320
Tokenization, 96, 320
Tokenizer, 92, 170, 181
Topicalization, 11, 242
Training, xvi, xxi, xxii, 20, 63, 73, 78, 79, 81, 83, 121, 123, 161, 181, 190, 212, 215, 268, 313, 321, 338, 341, 343, 352, 353, 355, 359–361, 368
unsupervised, 103
Transcription, xvi
Translation, 110, 112, 190, 204, 205, 268, 294, 326
Tree, xvii, 19, 26, 31, 36, 37, 57, 61–64, 66, 67, 70, 74–76, 81, 82, 93–95, 109, 111–114, 116–119, 126, 137, 139, 144, 157–160, 170, 179, 193, 200, 201, 223, 233–235, 240, 241, 250, 285, 286, 289, 290, 318, 325, 339, 351–363, 370, 371, 374, 377, 378, 380, 382, 383
dependency, xvii, xviii, xxiii, 47, 74, 103, 107, 190, 191, 233, 262, 267, 306, 317–320, 325, 326, 328
description, 373, 376
flat, 370, 373, 376
parse, 6, 23, 27, 30, 53, 112, 140, 302, 311, 313, 321, 326–328, 335–337, 343, 345, 353, 354, 358–360, 362, 363, 385
Tree-adjoining Grammar, 7, 10, 13, 14, 17, 21, 53, 68, 78, 104, 106, 107, 143, 153, 166, 170, 171, 173, 174, 177, 179, 198, 220, 221, 224, 264, 288, 289, 307, 310, 342, 357, 380, 382
Treebank, xiv–xvi, xviii, xix, xxi–xxiv, 5–10, 15–17, 20, 21, 23, 24, 27–32, 34, 35, 38–40, 43, 44, 47, 52, 63, 64, 69, 74–76, 81, 84, 103, 104, 113, 122, 129, 130, 143, 150–153, 158–160, 165, 166, 168, 173, 177, 181,

190, 194, 214, 225, 231–233, 235, 238, 243, 244, 250, 259, 261–264, 268–271, 273, 281, 284, 285, 290, 300–302, 307, 308, 322, 333, 337, 342–344, 351–359, 363, 367–371, 373, 377–386
grammar, xxiv, 352, 362, 368, 369, 380, 384, 385
reuse, xix
TSNLP, 129, 302
Turkish, xvii–xix, 261–270, 272–274, 276
Type, xxi, 16, 26, 30, 32, 33, 47, 48, 75, 78, 91, 93, 95–97, 106, 109, 111, 126, 130, 133, 134, 136, 137, 140, 142, 143, 155, 160, 189, 197, 198, 200, 203, 251, 252, 258, 259, 270, 285, 286, 289, 290, 301, 307, 309, 311, 312, 324, 354, 359, 360, 381, 384

Unification, 259, 310, 368, 385

Valence, xxiii, 167, 177, 181, 182
Variation, 49, 50, 192, 193, 199, 215, 263, 293, 352
Verb, xiv, xix, xx, xxiii, 8–10, 12, 13, 25, 26, 30, 46, 47, 52, 56, 69, 70, 75, 99, 107, 108, 111, 118–120, 131–135, 151–153, 155, 159, 167, 193, 194, 202, 214, 217, 218, 221–224, 234, 238, 240, 242, 248, 251, 256, 257, 263, 266, 268–270, 272, 274, 277, 285, 304, 327, 363, 378
final, 267
missing, 119
modal, 87, 116, 118
support, 196, 198, 199
Vocabulary, 32, 220

Web, xx, 27, 160, 283
Word, xiv, xvii–xx, xxii, xxiv, 10, 12, 17, 18, 25, 30, 35, 37, 38, 43, 45, 47–49, 54, 56, 61, 70, 76, 97–99, 104, 105, 107, 109, 117, 120, 123, 132, 137, 141–143, 151, 167, 170–172, 179–182, 190, 191, 193, 197–199, 204, 239, 248, 251, 252, 254–257, 261–265, 267–270, 274, 290, 303, 304, 310, 318–321, 324, 327, 340–342, 344, 354, 357
class, 26, 268
compound, xiii, 155, 205
content, 197, 202, 206, 251, 257, 328
foreign, 8, 49, 157, 166, 192
function, 114, 119, 120, 172, 177, 180, 182, 265
grammatical, 171, 173, 195, 202, 217
portmanteau, 152
unknown, 78, 170, 172, 180, 215, 343, 359
Word order, xix, 12, 75, 83, 92, 95, 97, 98, 109, 122, 134, 135, 193, 212, 214, 221, 224, 355

X-bar, 18, 232, 302, 310, 369, 371, 378, 386
XCES, xxi, 180, 281–283, 286, 287, 290, 291, 293, 294
XML, 83, 160, 173, 180, 203, 204, 206, 281–284, 286, 288–294
XSLT, 284, 288, 291
XTAG, 362

Text, Speech and Language Technology

1. H. Bunt and M. Tomita (eds.): *Recent Advances in Parsing Technology.* 1996 ISBN 0-7923-4152-X
2. S. Young and G. Bloothooft (eds.): *Corpus-Based Methods in Language and Speech Processing.* 1997 ISBN 0-7923-4463-4
3. T. Dutoit: *An Introduction to Text-to-Speech Synthesis.* 1997 ISBN 0-7923-4498-7
4. L. Lebart, A. Salem and L. Berry: *Exploring Textual Data.* 1998 ISBN 0-7923-4840-0
5. J. Carson-Berndsen, *Time Map Phonology.* 1998 ISBN 0-7923-4883-4
6. P. Saint-Dizier (ed.): *Predicative Forms in Natural Language and in Lexical Knowledge Bases.* 1999 ISBN 0-7923-5499-0
7. T. Strzalkowski (ed.): *Natural Language Information Retrieval.* 1999 ISBN 0-7923-5685-3
8. J. Harrington and S. Cassiday: *Techniques in Speech Acoustics.* 1999 ISBN 0-7923-5731-0
9. H. van Halteren (ed.): *Syntactic Wordclass Tagging.* 1999 ISBN 0-7923-5896-1
10. E. Viegas (ed.): *Breadth and Depth of Semantic Lexicons.* 1999 ISBN 0-7923-6039-7
11. S. Armstrong, K. Church, P. Isabelle, S. Nanzi, E. Tzoukermann and D. Yarowsky (eds.): *Natural Language Processing Using Very Large Corpora.* 1999 ISBN 0-7923-6055-9
12. F. Van Eynde and D. Gibbon (eds.): *Lexicon Development for Speech and Language Processing.* 2000 ISBN 0-7923-6368-X; Pb: 07923-6369-8
13. J. Véronis (ed.): *Parallel Text Processing.* Alignment and Use of Translation Corpora. 2000 ISBN 0-7923-6546-1
14. M. Horne (ed.): *Prosody: Theory and Experiment.* Studies Presented to Gösta Bruce. 2000 ISBN 0-7923-6579-8
15. A. Botinis (ed.): *Intonation.* Analysis, Modelling and Technology. 2000 ISBN 0-7923-6605-0
16. H. Bunt and A. Nijholt (eds.): *Advances in Probabilistic and Other Parsing Technologies.* 2000 ISBN 0-7923-6616-6
17. J.-C. Junqua and G. van Noord (eds.): *Robustness in Languages and Speech Technology.* 2001 ISBN 0-7923-6790-1
18. R.H. Baayen: *Word Frequency Distributions.* 2001 ISBN 0-7923-7017-1
19. B. Granström, D. House and. I. Karlsson (eds.): *Multimodality in Language and Speech Systems.* 2002 ISBN 1-4020-0635-7
20. M. Carl and A. Way (eds.): *Recent Advances in Example-Based Machine Translation.* 2003 ISBN 1-4020-1400-7; Pb 1-4020-1401-5
21. A. Abeillé: *Treebanks.* Building and Using Parsed Corpora. 2003 ISBN 1-4020-1334-5; pb 1-4020-1335-3

KLUWER ACADEMIC PUBLISHERS – DORDRECHT / BOSTON / LONDON